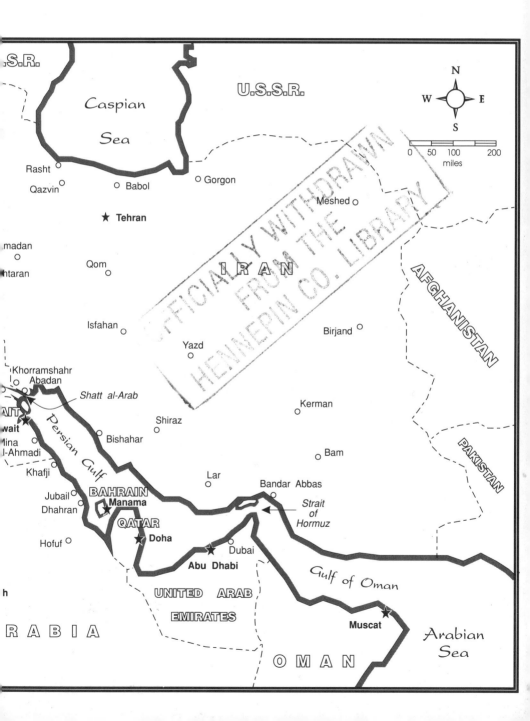

U.S.R.

U.S.S.R.

N
W ← → E
S

0   50   100   200
miles

Caspian

Sea

Rasht ○
Qazvin ○   ○ Babol   ○ Gorgon

★ Tehran

Meshed ○

madan
○
ntaran   Qom ○

IRAN

AFGHANISTAN

Isfahan ○   Birjand ○

Yazd ○

Khorramshahr ○
Abadan ○   Shatt al-Arab

AIT ★
wait   Kerman ○
Mina ○   Bishahar ○
l-Ahmadi ○   Shiraz ○

Khafji ○   Bam ○

Lar ○

Jubail ○   BAHRAIN   Bandar Abbas
Dhahran ○   ● Manama   Strait
                        of
            QATAR   Hormuz

Hofuf ○   ● Doha
                Dubai
        ★ Abu Dhabi

h   Gulf of Oman

        UNITED ARAB
        EMIRATES   Muscat ★   Arabian

RABIA   Sea

        OMAN

Persian Gulf

Payback

Other Books by John K. Cooley

Libyan Sandstorm: The Complete Account of Qaddafi's Revolution (1981)

Green March, Black September: The Story of the Palestinian Arabs (1973)

East Wind over Africa: Red China's African Offensive (1966)

Baal, Christ and Mohammad: Religion and Revolution in North Africa
  (1965)

JOHN K. COOLEY

Payback
America's Long War in the Middle East

Foreword by Pierre Salinger

BRASSEY'S (US), Inc.
A Division of Maxwell Macmillan, Inc.

Washington • New York • London • Oxford
Beijing • Frankfurt • São Paulo • Sydney • Tokyo • Toronto

Brassey's (US), Inc.

Editorial Offices	*Order Department*
Brassey's (US), Inc.	Macmillan Publishing Co.
8000 Westpark Drive, 1st Floor	Front and Brown Streets
McLean, VA 22102	Riverside, NJ 08075

Brassey's (US), Inc., books are available at special discounts for bulk purchases for sales promotions, premiums, fund-raising, or educational use through the Special Sales Director, Macmillan Publishing Company, 866 Third Avenue, New York, New York 10022.

LIBRARY OF CONGRESS CATALOGING-IN-PUBLICATION DATA

Cooley, John K., 1927–
　　Payback : America's long war in the Middle East / John K. Cooley.
　　　p.　cm.
　　Includes index.
　　ISBN 0-08-040564-9
　　1. Middle East—Foreign relations—United States.　2. United States—Foreign relations—Middle East.　3. Iran—Foreign relations—United States.　4. United States—Foreign relations—Iran.
5. United States—Foreign relations—1945–　6. Middle East—Politics and government—1945–　I. Title.
DS63.2.C67　1991
327.73056—dc20

　　　　　　　　　　　　　　　　　　　　　　　　　　90-19254
　　　　　　　　　　　　　　　　　　　　　　　　　　CIP

British Library Cataloguing in Publication Data
Cooley, John K.
　　Payback : America's long war in the Middle East.
　　1. Iran. Foreign relations with United States
　　I. Title
　　327.55073

　　ISBN 0-08-040564-9

10　9　8　7　6　5　4　3　2　1

PRINTED IN THE UNITED STATES OF AMERICA

For Alexander Anthony Cooley

Contents

Foreword

As the year 1989 was coming to a close, the world was focused with excitement on the events going on in the Eastern European nations and the Soviet Union. The collapse of communism, the fall of the Berlin Wall, and the overthrow of the Romanian dictator, Nicolae Ceauşescu, had riveted the Western media to the point where few people were looking at other areas of the world where powerful events were also on course. I remember toward the end of the year when John Cooley came into my office. "We can't overlook what is happening in the Middle East," he told me. "What is happening in the Eastern bloc is important, but we are moving closer and closer to confrontation in the Middle East, and it is something we cannot ignore." It was something I agreed with totally, but it was difficult to implement. The year 1990 has dramatically proved that John Cooley was right.

Since the early 1970s, the Middle East has moved toward chaos. The civil war in Lebanon, the arrival of the Ayatollah Khomeini in power in Iran, the rise of Islamic Fundamentalism, the killing of Egyptian President Anwar Sadat, the launching of the *intifada* in the occupied territories of Israel, the brutal increase in terrorism, and the kidnapping of Western hostages have all contributed to this chaos. And the Gulf crisis, which broke out on August 2, 1990, and which was not ended when this book was written, is certain to add to that chaos. One of the critical problems of the Middle East is the basic lack of understanding in the West of the region's religious and political mind-sets and of their long-term objectives. Nation after nation in the West, led by the United States, have made dramatic mistakes in that region. The Americans never understood that the Egyptian leader Anwar al-Sadat, admired in the Western world, was hated in his own country and always a target for assassination. When we intervened in Lebanon during the Reagan administration, the death of several hundred Americans in terrorist attacks showed how little we knew of the situation in that country. And as Saddam Hussein worked his way forward toward the invasion of Kuwait, the United States did almost nothing but send him green lights that convinced him that the United States would not react strongly if he took over his neighboring country.

In my career as a journalist, I have never met anyone in our business who understands the Middle East better than John Cooley. *Payback* is essential to break down the lack of understanding in the Western world. It is well known that one cannot look at the future of history without understanding the past. The future of the Middle East is sure to be complicated and even dangerous. But by reading this book, you will have made a contribution to your knowledge of the area that will give you a better chance to assess the future. I am proud to be associated with John Cooley. This association has done remarkable things for my own understanding of the Middle East. The only thing I don't understand is how a man who works eighteen hours a day covering that part of the world has time to write books as well. But John Cooley always finds time to do important things, and this is an important book.

PIERRE SALINGER

Preface

One of my dearest friends and colleagues, correspondent Joe Alex Morris of the *Los Angeles Times*, understood the Middle East better than anyone I have ever known. I last spoke with Joe in 1978, a few months before he was killed by a bullet in the chest while covering the Iranian Revolution in Tehran. He said to me, "Never consider yourself an expert on the Middle East. If you do, you're already in deep trouble."

Joe was right about that. The United States has replaced the old colonial powers, Britain and France, as the preeminent Western influence in the area. The other superpower, the Soviet Union, is too preoccupied with survival at home to be a major factor in the Middle East. As America's power in the region has grown, so has its responsibility. Unfortunately, right through the Iraqi invasion of Kuwait and the resulting allied counterattack to free that state, the degree of American understanding of the Middle East has rarely seemed to match America's ability to plan and carry out military operations.

I began to cover North Africa and the Middle East as a newsman in the late 1950s and in 1965 became Mideast correspondent for the *Christian Science Monitor*, based mainly in Beirut. In 1981 I joined the staff of ABC News; London has since been my base for reporting and trying to understand the peoples, religions, and conflicts of the Middle East, that fascinating part of the world where civilized history began.

During the critical years from 1979 to 1991, the focus of this book, the United States was repeatedly paid back for poor judgment and often disastrous policy errors. Not only did there seem to be few experts in charge of U.S. Mideast policy, but the few specialists there—such as CIA analysts who tried to warn the White House in 1990 that Saddam Hussein might invade Kuwait—seemed to operate outside the corridors of power.

American misunderstanding of the Middle East and its ethnic, religious, and political conflicts sometimes, as in Lebanon, showed up when the government took sides in parochial quarrels. Sometimes, too, there was terrible confusion because various U.S. agencies and individuals backed opposing sides in a conflict. The Iranian-American arms-for-hostages affair is a case in point: it can ultimately be attributed to conflicting loyalties during the Iran-Iraq War. Inconsistent and ignorant policies ensured that Mideast adversaries would pay America back. When it moved into the void created by the retreat of colonial powers, the United States stumbled into a long and secret war.

As a journalist, I try to treat the news as unfolding history rather than the ephemeral flash of a day's events. It has always seemed obvious to me that unless we try to understand present events and past errors we are condemned to repeat those errors, especially in a troubled region like the Middle East. This book concentrates on one packed decade in which errors appear and reappear like so many points of darkness.

After thirty years of observing U.S. involvement in the Middle East, I still do not profess any special expertise. I do hope, however, that in illuminating those points of darkness this book might encourage more enlightened policies in the future. It is time for America's long war in the Middle East to come to an end. It is time for the paybacks to stop.

Acknowledgments

During the years from 1978 to 1991, I worked for three employers: *The Christian Science Monitor* (as Mideast and, later, Pentagon correspondent until 1980); the Carnegie Endowment for International Peace (as senior associate, 1980–81); and finally, from 1981 on, as a correspondent based in London for ABC News. I owe much to several people at all three institutions.

One is the late Geoffrey Godsell, the *Monitor's* wise and generous overseas news editor, who gave me so much guidance during my time in North Africa and the Middle East in the 1960s and 1970s. Geoffrey's successor, David Anable, is as thoughtful and sensitive an editor as anyone could want. And then there is Dr. William Polk, historian and Mideast adviser to Presidents Kennedy and Johnson, whose knowledge and experience have proved invaluable in the making of this book.

Carnegie Endowment President Tom Hughes, Larry Fabian, and *Foreign Policy* editor William Charles Maynes gave much aid and encouragement.

Peter Jennings of ABC News, whom I first met in Beirut, and ABC's chief foreign correspondent Pierre Salinger are two of the senior colleagues who provided help or inspiration for this book. ABC News Vice President Walter Porges carefully read the manuscript and offered useful suggestions. Carol Marquis of ABC News London gave unstintingly of her time to painstakingly decipher and type the first draft. Photographer Claude Salhani, through his recollections of some dramatic times we experienced together in Beirut, was extremely helpful. Christine Powell shared with me her personal reminiscences of the U.S. Embassy takeover in Tehran in 1979.

I owe a special debt of gratitude to free-lance journalist Linda Mack. She performed untiring research on the investigation of one of the biggest Mideast paybacks to the United States during this period: the 1988 bombing of Pan Am Flight 103 over Lockerbie, Scotland. Much of the account in chapter 13 is hers. Linda Albin, ABC News Radio's London bureau chief and an outstanding friend and colleague during my time with ABC's London bureau, suggested the title.

It was Mrs. Nancy Troxler's basic research and careful typing of the manuscript that made it possible to finish the book during the heat of the Gulf crisis of 1990–91. Bob Donahue, editor of the op-ed page of the *International Herald Tribune* in Paris, and several other staff members encouraged me to write columns for that newspaper in the late 1980s and early 1990s. With the kind permission of the *Tribune*, some of that material, dealing mainly with the Iran-Iraq war, has been included in this book. Frank Margiotta and Don McKeon of Brassey's (US), through patience and perseverance, and the copy editor, Connie Buchanan Leyden, who worked with sensitivity and thoroughness, were enormously helpful. Vicki Chamlee, Brassey's production manager, was both patient and inspired.

It would be foolish of me, because possibly dangerous for them, to mention many more people in the United States, Europe, and the Middle East who helped. They include Americans, Europeans, Arabs, Israelis, and Iranians, among others. They know who they are, and they should be aware of my debt to them. I am, of course, responsible for errors, not they.

Finally my wife, Eugenia Katelani, an artist, novelist, and poet since giving up her career with the Greek diplomatic service to throw in her lot with me, and my son, Alexander, to whom my book is dedicated—both provided major support in this enterprise. May the three of us have more time together for new projects in the future.

1

King of Kings, Light of the Aryans

An Interview with the Shah

Tehran, September 20, 1978. A rumble, as though of distant drums, breaks the dead stillness as I enter the palace grounds. Only a few sleepy guards seem to be standing watch. The silent chauffeur who piloted me to the palace in the black limousine looked like some dark-clad messenger from the netherworld in a surrealist film.

With a gesture the chauffeur hands me over to a palace flunky and a lean, muscular protocol man—possibly an armed member of SAVAK, the dreaded secret police, or possibly one of the Immortals, the hand-picked imperial guardsmen—wearing civilian clothes. Flanked by my escorts, I crunch underfoot the last pebbles of the driveway. Next are flagstones flanked by rosebushes. As we mount marble steps, the same remote, stuttering thunder troubles the hush again.

For an instant, I wonder about the sound. Is it the mob in south Tehran again? Shouting, milling, and churning in its rage, carried all this distance northward on an ill wind that was blowing no good for the ruler? That rage ripening in the collective memory of the crowd, remembering the hundreds killed in the massacre of rioters in Jaleh Square a few days earlier. . . . And why are there no visible defenses, soldiers, or palace sentries?

Suddenly the two escorts are gone, and with them, thoughts of the mobs down in the city.

The man standing before me, alone in the audience rooms during all of the previous interviews since they began twelve years earlier, is Muhammad Reza Shah Pahlavi. To his sycophants and propagandists, he is *Shan-en-Shah, Aryamehr*— King of Kings, Light of the Aryans.

But can he really be the same man? The Shah with whom I spoke a dozen times or so over the past decade was proud and stiff, consciously regal, fixing you with a cold stare, condescending, willing to concede a faint smile of greeting or to flicker a smug, sometimes ironic grin after pointing out the decadence of Western societies, for example, or mocking the notion of human rights in the United States, Britain, or France, whose governments faithfully supported him until now.

The man before me now is different, shockingly different. He still has the silver-gray hair, matching his double-breasted silver-gray suit, and large, though not owlish, reading glasses easily slipped on. These are all outward traits of the same imperial self. What has changed is the frame inside the silver-gray suit; it is wasted, emaciated by illness. Somehow, like nearly all those in brief contact with the Shah, I didn't see the illness. The face is pallid, waxen almost. His welcoming stare is cold and fixed, barely polite.

Knowing nothing of what is to come, I try to steer the interview toward what I think my editors and readers want to know. Is this man whom President Jimmy Carter recently called a "pillar of stability"—and therefore a pillar of U.S. foreign policy—going to survive? Behind my questions lies another, unstated one: What will become of the unwritten but often spoken American doctrine of depending totally on the Shah for crucial help in the Middle East, from supplying Israel with oil to acting as policeman of the Persian, or as the Arab states prefer to call it, the Arab Gulf?

Then I remember there is one question that could make or break this interview. Had I asked it a few years, or perhaps only a few months ago, the Shah probably would have gotten to his feet and ended the interview then and there. There would have been a parting scolding for me, or any other visitor who asked such questions for publication.

I take a long breath. There is odd encouragement in the almost meek demeanor of the man facing me.

"What do you say"—remembering this years later, I am certain I omitted the customary "Your Majesty"—"to these mullahs and clerics who accuse you of violating the tenets of the Muslim religion?

Instead of exploding with rage, or stiffening with anger, the Shah seems to stare over and beyond my shoulder, fixing on a point somewhere in space. He is silent five, nearly ten seconds. For a brief instant, I wonder whether he has pressed some hidden button and whether escorts will suddenly reappear to show me out. Instead, he glances at me. "Well," he says mildly, "I don't think I've violated anything in the Muslim religion. *But if they think so, I'm willing to discuss it with them.*"

My thoughts revert to editors and readers. The Shah has never said anything like this before, at least not since the political and religious troubles of the early 1960s, when the Ayatollah Khomeini was exiled and when many people, even Iran specialists, heard his name for the first time. Muhammad Reza Pahlavi, who took the throne in 1947 and regained it with the help of the CIA after his flight in 1953, has always at best downgraded organized religion and, at worst, ignored it. He feels mullahs and their betters, all the way up to the rank of grand ayatollah, are people to watch and occasionally to punish, exile, or propitiate, but never to negotiate with—neither about theology nor theocracy, nor about recasting the entire Iranian state along modern, secular lines. Back in the 1960s, the Shah took the Shi'a clergy's lands and properties in the reforms he called his "White Revolution."

I ask a few more questions now about devolution of power and the Shah's hopes for his son, Crown Prince Reza. Will he inherit a kingdom that, by the time he is ready to rule (he is now in the United States, training as a U.S. Air Force pilot) will be a constitutional monarchy? This is something I have been hearing from the "loyal" opponents of the Shah, like the National Front's Karim Sanjabi.

The Shah makes brief, vague answers. The formal portion of the interview is over. I turn off my small tape recorder. It is time to talk off the record. For the first time, the Shah seems to relish this. Eagerly he leans forward. The dead eyes suddenly come to life. He raises his arm and extends his forefinger.

"Do you know," he exclaims, wagging the finger, "do you know what my *people* are telling me?" He means his courtiers, advisers, and cabinet ministers, not the people who have been demonstrating in the streets.

"No, I don't."

"My people are telling me that it is not only the Soviets and the Eastern bloc behind these troubles and riots. They say that Western people are behind them too. Americans, British too, probably."

"Surely that can't be," I say. "You're not saying that the CIA is cutting off its nose to spite its face by working against you?"

Impatiently, the Shah leans back and waves his hand from side to side. "No, my people are saying that certain oil companies—British and American ones—are involved in all this." And then, suddenly, as though snapping out of a trance, he resumes his stiff, formal posture.

Our meeting is over. The escorts appear. Within minutes, I am back in the silent black limousine, heading for my own safe haven, the Hilton Hotel. A hundred topics I should have raised with the Shah and didn't now race to mind.

Why didn't I keep my promise to the hostess of last night's nostalgic party in north Tehran? She is a Baha'i, a member of a sophisticated faith persecuted sporadically over the past century in its ancestral home of Persia and in the Arab and outer Muslim worlds as well. Despite this, it is now firmly established in the United States and other parts of the West. When she heard of the audience I had scheduled for today, my hostess wanted me to "ask that man what he is going to do to protect *us* after all the loyalty we've shown him?" And what about Iran's Jews, many of whom have prospered under the regime of Muhammad Reza Pahlavi? He is a highly important, if secret, ally of Israel. I should have pushed for some concrete discussion of the oil situation, too. That would have drawn the Shah out. Why does he think the oil companies want to undermine him? But he cut that particular discussion short. Somehow, I know that the uneasy relationship established at our first meeting in 1966 is over.

Revolution and Counterrevolution

At the start, the Shah expressed a wish for a better relationship with my newspaper, the *Christian Science Monitor*. A free-lance contributor of the early 1960s ("he was," the Shah said, "a black man, I believe") had offended or least annoyed him with articles "very unfair to my country." He didn't say "unfair to me."

Those were the days when the United States relied on the Shah's Arab neighbor and rival, King Faisal of Saudi Arabia, to act as the keystone in the fragile arch of affinities and alliances then spanning the Middle East. The Shah did not yet vie seriously with the Saudi king for the affections of the Americans. He was still a tentative partner, although he was becoming the region's best customer for the technology and arsenals offered by the great arms bazaars of the West, especially of America.

My interview, on September 20, 1978, was one of the last he gave to American and European newsmen before illness and the revolution engulfed him and before he departed for his final exile in early 1979. His fate was to languish, dying, in Morocco, Panama, the United States, and Egypt, rejected by the world, thus paving the way for the return and rule of the old, angry Ayatollah Khomeini he himself had exiled a decade and a half earlier.

Back in 1953 the Shah himself had been forced out of his country for a few days by the fervor of a people devoted to his nationalistic rival, Prime Minister Muhammad Mussadeq. Mussadeq had defied the Shah, the Americans, and the British. CIA officers Kermit Roosevelt and Miles Copeland, among others, paid counterrevolutionary crowds to shout and break heads in support of the absent Shah. "Royalist" mob leaders confronted and beat up supporters of the nationalistic prime minister.

Mussadeq had also defied the Anglo-Iranian Oil Company by daring to proclaim that Iran's oil belonged to the Iranians and should be purchased from them in normal ways and at fair prices, instead of being controlled by a foreign monopoly profiting from low wages and cheap production costs. British and American power were brought to bear. Soon the Shah and his queen returned in triumph from their comfortable hotel in Rome. Mussadeq ended his days in tearful retirement, the dying symbol, to a whole generation of Iranians who are now mostly old men and women, of nationalistic aspirations.

A decade later came the 1963 revolt. One of its central figures was Khomeini, and religion was at its heart. It was far more serious, in its portents for the coming revolution of 1978–79, than the Mussadeq movement or the counter-coup that restored the Shah in 1953. And, as so often in American dealings with Iran, few of the U.S. experts noticed its importance at the time.

The Opposition Stiffens

The day after my final interview with the Shah, I set out with a Turkish colleague. We drove through the back streets and shantytowns of south Tehran in the early morning and down across the bleak desert to the gates of the holy city of Qom. There we hoped to find out if the Shah's offer to negotiate with the Muslim clergy had any appeal at all for them.

We moved slowly through the baking heat of late morning and found ourselves in the mud and brick alleys of a dour, austere city. Little did we realize then how much this drab setting, with its black-clad women gliding silently around in their *chadors* and its turbaned theological students, mirrored the Iran that Khomeini was to recreate in the more modern secular cities.

We found the home of tiny, wizened Ayatollah Kassem Shariat-Madary, whose main base was Tabriz, in Azerbaijan. In the cool inner courtyard, there was re-freshing tea and an assemblage of some of the Shah's most distinguished opponents. One of these was Mehdi Bazargan, a tough, honest, French-educated engineer with a long history of being embroiled in political struggles. He had just gotten out of jail. Bazargan was seventy-two but hardly showed his age.

He arrived later than the others. Here in the sanctuary of Shariat-Madary's Qom residence, he and the others assumed the police would not follow or molest them, though very probably SAVAK was monitoring the meeting by one means or an-other. After exchanging greetings with his countrymen, Bazargan settled down to chat with us for a few minutes.

Later, in 1979, Bazargan would head the revolutionary government. Then Khomeini would use the pretext of the U.S. Embassy hostage crisis in Tehran to fire him. Bazargan had served in the Mussadeq government in the early 1950s. Thus he was a link between the revolutionary mullahs and the secular politicians of the past. He had stayed in opposition politics, which cost him four prison terms. In 1977, sensing, as he told me, the coming storm, he helped form the Iranian Committee for the Defense of Liberty and Human Rights.[1]

Like the Soviet revolution, the Iranian revolution was imbued with a sense of its own ideological superiority. Its leaders believed their mission was to sweep across the world, at least across the Muslim world, and win absolute power. Seek-ing recognition as Islamic revolutionaries, they began to proselytize, especially in lands like Lebanon, Afghanistan, and Pakistan, where Shi'a Muslims lived. And it sought allies such as Syria whose rulers were members or associates of the Shi'a movement.

The Iranian revolution was to bring about warfare between its advocates and the United States. All the hostility toward Western civilization, hostility pent up during the Shah's iron rule, emerged. In its response to the U.S. military's open tilt toward Iraq in the latter stages of the 1980–88 Iran-Iraq War, Tehran used the weapons of subversion, terrorism (acts often committed by allies and sympathizers such as Lebanon), and open warfare.

Amid the circle of men, many of whom, like Bazargan, had just been let out of the Shah's prisons, the little Ayatollah Shariat-Madary presided.[2] He squatted like a tailor in a Persian or Arab bazaar, with tiny, steel-rimmed glasses twinkling on his nose.

A hush fell over the room. My friend had just translated for the Turkish-speaking Shariat-Madary the Shah's comment of the day before, that he was willing to discuss with the opposition his alleged transgressions against Islam. Now everyone in the courtyard was listening for the ayatollah's hesitant, muttered response.

He shook his head slowly, almost sadly. "He should have thought of that much earlier. It's far too late for any talking with him now."

The American Dilemma

We drove back to Tehran in silence. Both of us realized that irrevocable change was coming. But neither of us had any idea of its nature or true magnitude.

It was autumn of 1978. Events in Iran and the Middle East as a whole, from the fall of the Shah in 1979 to the 1990s, would dog U.S. presidents and their planners. For them, the Iranian revolution would prove more formidably troublesome than anything that had happened since the Bolsheviks fired their first shots against the palace of Czar Nicholas II.

American responses to the multiform challenges spawned by the Iranian revolution would often be shortsighted, even purely reactive, badly planned, and in some cases, like the Iranian hostage rescue mission of 1980, poorly executed. American statesmen, bureaucrats, soldiers, and spies would find themselves caught up in a cycle of paybacks—reprisal and revenge. It included, most notably, kidnappings of Americans in Lebanon, triggered partly by kidnappings of Iranians there, and the mid-air destruction of Pan American World Airways Flight 103 over Scotland in response to the accidental shooting down of an Iran Air civilian airliner over the Persian Gulf during the final days of the Iran-Iraq War.

Other paybacks for America, because of its overreliance on strong rulers not popular with their own people, succeeded one another. In Egypt, the best-disposed friend the West had ever had in recent times, President Anwar al-Sadat, was murdered by religious zealots inside and outside the army because he had made a separate peace with Israel. To them, Sadat had seemed to prefer the West to his own people. In Lebanon, where the United States tried to help people who said they were friends, first Israel and then the U.S. Marines seemed to find only deadly foes.

The biggest payback of all, in 1990–91, came this time not from bitter and homeless Palestinians, Iranians possessed by religious zeal, or other individuals turned terrorists. It came from Saddam Hussein, the would-be godfather of the Gulf. The U.S. government had coddled and aided Saddam with more than a nod and a wink, when he posed as the defender of secular Western values against his enemy, fundamentalist Iran. America and its friends in Europe made a lot of money supplying technology for Saddam Hussein's war industries, including his chemical, biological, and nascent nuclear capabilities. Saddam paid the West back by conquering Kuwait, one of the most important oil suppliers, banking centers, and markets. His troops sabotaged Kuwait's oil industry, setting wells and installations ablaze and perhaps ending for good not its production of oil but its production of cheap oil. He plundered all of its wealth that he could put his hands on; tortured and murdered thousands of Kuwait's people; and, after the failure of American, Arab, and European diplomacy to solve the problem by peaceful means, put the country to the torch as the stunned and bomb-shocked remnants of his army retreated to a homeland devastated by American and allied bombing.

The paybacks of 1979–91 were partly, at least, the consequences of American dependence, at the end of the 1970s, on the three main pillars of its Mideast policies. The first pillar was the Shah of Iran and the might of his U.S.-supplied armed forces—a might financed by Iranian oil. The second was Israel, sustained, to use the words of the late President Sadat of Egypt, by American financial aid in everything "from butter to cannons." The third was Saudi Arabia. Ever since the administration of President Franklin D. Roosevelt, defense of Saudi oil and of the rulers who controlled that oil has been the less-publicized but perhaps in some ways the most important pillar of American Mideast policy.

In once-neutral Lebanon, where many people lived what was for the Middle East a relatively good life amid mutual tolerance by diverse religions and some of the trappings of parliamentary democracy, the fall of the U.S.-backed Shah of Iran made things worse. With Syria's help, Iranian revolutionaries infiltrated Lebanon. The United States sought to cure Lebanon's growing illness and end its civil strife with the balm of American reassurances, then with the steel of the U.S. Marines. Neither was to any avail. Goaded by neighbors and foreign occupiers, the Lebanese increased their slaughter of one another. They scarcely paused to watch the forced retreat of U.S. servicemen, diplomats, and educators from their once-enlightened land.

In 1990–91, Desert Storm and its traumatic aftermath were to be the climax of this drama of America's involvement in the Middle East—the final payback for years of miscalculation and errors. After it ended, the region faced a monumental problem of displaced people. The Kurdish refugee exodus of 1991 was to become one of the largest and most tragic population movements since the Armenian exodus from Turkey during and after World War I. The first act, however, was destined to be played out in revolutionary Iran.

2

Eyes on the Ground, Spies in the Sky

Aftermath

On a snowy day in early February 1979, President Carter's defense secretary, Harold Brown, flew out of Andrews Air Force Base on a trip best described in Washington parlance as a "hand-holding" mission. Some correspondents, including myself, flew with him. Brown's immediate purpose was to consult with America's leading Arab allies, the Saudis, as well as the Israelis about the shock waves that the Shah's January 16 departure from Tehran was already sending throughout the Middle East.

We flew first toward Riyadh, the Saudi capital, where Brown would meet King Fahd and his top defense officials. One of Brown's briefs was to try to reassure the Saudis that even though the United States was being accused of "letting down" the Shah, this would not be allowed to happen in Saudi Arabia or elsewhere.

As we flew, the bad news from Iran kept crackling through the radio. The provisional government of Shahpour Bakhtiar, the last to be installed by the Shah, had fallen February 11, following two days of pitched battles in Tehran between loyal troops of mostly the Shah's guards and Khomeini supporters. The latter were aided by the *homofars*, a new factor in the revolutionary scene. The *homofars* were air force technicians, already trained or still in training, who had obtained arms from several major air bases and who joined the insurgents.

The worst news for me and several other Mideast correspondents aboard the plane was that an old and close friend, Joe Alex Morris of the *Los Angeles Times*, had been killed in the fighting between the *homofars* and government troops at Doshan Tappeh Air Base, on the outskirts of Tehran. The battle had broken out February 9 when a unit of the Immortals, the imperial guards, had in a last hopeless fight for king and country attacked pro-Khomeini demonstrators. The latter had practically taken over the base after Khomeini's triumphal return to Tehran from France on February 1.

Joe and several other newsmen were watching from a nearby window. When Joe stood up to get a better view, a bullet struck him in the chest, killing him almost at once. His wife and children were in Athens, Joe's home base. The *Los Angeles Times* asked Bill Touhy, another of its correspondents, to fly to Tehran and bring Joe's body home. The day Joe was killed, several American CH-47 helicopters were able to move seventy more fortunate Americans—U.S. Air Force and contractor personnel mostly—out of Doshan Tappeh to safety.

We arrived in Riyadh under a baking sun to a ceremonial reception by Saudi royal guards. My sense of personal loss was far keener than my sense of the deteriorating American position in Iran. The Saudis made haste to brief us about that position. Antigovernment forces were seizing control of Iranian military garrisons from the Soviet border to the Persian Gulf. The fearful Saudis, orthodox Sunni Muslims, dreaded a takeover of Iran by Khomeini's fundamentalist Shi'a clergy almost as much as they dreaded a communist invasion or takeover. They were looking to their own defenses and to those of small Gulf allies like Bahrain, the main U.S. naval port in the area. All concerned felt exposed to the possible onslaught of what the Saudis freely described as Khomeini's hordes.

On February 11, all semblance of power passed from the hands of the disintegrating Bakhtiar government to Ayatollah Khomeini's supporters. Prince Turki, the chief of Saudi military intelligence, told us in Riyadh that the Saudis had intercepted Iranian broadcasts ordering all soldiers to return to their barracks. We monitored reports from the CIA's Foreign Broadcast Information Service (FBIS) station near Dhahran, center of the giant Arabian-American Oil Company (ARAMCO) complex. They told us that the Iranian army commander, General Qarabaghi, had assured Mehdi Bazargan, Khomeini's choice as prime minister, of his backing.

Bakhtiar resigned that evening and disappeared, turning up weeks later in Paris to begin a permanent exile. Later, we learned that he had been sheltered for many days in Bazargan's own home before secretly leaving Tehran.

At the reception for Secretary Brown that evening in Riyadh, we heard that clashes had broken out in Iran between rival guerrilla groups, Mujaheddin-e Khalq and the far leftist Cherik Fedayeen-e Khalq. Armed groups were molesting foreigners. The U.S. Embassy in Tehran was occupied by a mob, including 150 guerrillas, wearing Iranian army and air force uniforms. As an official U.S. government memo later reported, they were "armed with military-issue rifles. An unarmed Iranian employee of the embassy had been shot and killed, a marine had been kidnapped and embassy personnel including Ambassador William H. Sullivan, had been taken hostage. Only skillful negotiating" by Bazargan and American-educated Ibrahim

Yazdi, who held a U.S. passport, had resolved the issue without further bloodshed.

The one-day takeover of the U.S. Embassy proved to be a rehearsal for the main event. This was the seizure of the embassy and over fifty U.S. diplomats on November 4, 1979, which touched off an international crisis lasting 444 days, until the inauguration of Ronald Reagan as president on January 21, 1981. Others, including the hostages, have described what happened with a wealth of detail; there is no point in repeating it here. Senior embassy officials repeatedly warned Washington what would happen if the ailing Shah were admitted to the United States for medical treatment; Khomeini's supporters viewed admittance simply as a pretext to give the Shah a base for a comeback. The embassy was poorly protected and unprepared. "The inaction and blundering of the Carter administration," Pierre Salinger wrote, "assured the succession of a revolutionary government profoundly hostile to the United States."[1]

There was a highly serious question raised by the November 1979 embassy takeover in Tehran, one that has scarcely been examined in public up to now. Were secret communications, including codes and coding equipment, compromised in that takeover? If so, to what extent?

Anyone who has seen the more than sixty volumes of material dating from the 1960s and published later by the Iranian militants under the title "Documents from the Den of Spies" knows how shredded documents from the embassy's political section and CIA station were painstakingly reconstituted and pasted together for photoreproduction. The shredder, a cheap one that only shredded papers in strips of a single direction, was no match for the nimble fingers of Iranian girls and women used to weaving carpets; they were the ones who pieced the thin strips together.

The documents were a mixed but rich harvest for the militants and for the eager publishers of the stolen horde. The U.S. writer Edward Jay Epstein, in a study of how deception tactics have won wars and hoodwinked nations into compromising their interests, reprints one five-page secret dispatch sent by CIA main headquarters to stations around the world. The dispatch permits CIA stations to recruit walk-in defectors from the Soviet bloc without thoroughly checking their backgrounds or bona fides. This reversed previous policy.[2] Possession of such a dispatch must have been of great value to the Iranians, not too mention the Soviets and others.

Access to embassy archives also gave Iranian militants potent means to blackmail and destroy moderates in the Bazargan government, which fell shortly after the hostage crisis began. Many memorandums and reports showed the moderates and others to have had close links with the Americans. One series of memos, for example, chronicled the CIA's attempt to recruit Abol Hassan Bani-Sadr, soon to become revolutionary Iran's first president and later a bitter exile.

During the summer of 1979, a veteran CIA agent named Vernon Cassin cultivated Bani-Sadr. Cassin, who had served in Amman and Damascus, had taken the cover name Guy Rutherford and claimed to work for a Pennsylvania company named Carver Associates. Cassin worked with the CIA station chief, Thomas Aherne, on Bani-Sadr's case. They assigned Bani-Sadr the codename SDLure/1.

Bani-Sadr claims he told Cassin, who "offered him $5,000 a month," to "go away,"[3] The contacts, catalogued in the compromised documents, certainly contributed to Bani-Sadr's eventual downfall; he had to flee Iran for his life in 1982. Other embassy memorandums published by the militants disclosed that not only Aherne but also William Daugherty and Malcolm Kalp were CIA officers. As a result, these three Americans were treated more harshly than the other hostages. Kalp, in fact, was beaten up and kept in solitary confinement for 374 days.[4] Many Iranians recorded as having met with U.S. officials, socially or otherwise, were arrested, questioned by the vigilantes of the neighborhood komitehs (committees) formed after Khomeini's return, and sometimes killed.

There may have been an even more damaging compromise: that of secret communications and cryptographic material. Most of the U.S. officials concerned, when willing to discuss the subject at all, have insisted that incendiary bombs were used to destroy code machines, related computers, and their keying documents in the embassy code room. A few weeks after the November 1979 takeover, however, militants were seen in streets near the embassy hawking copies of pictures of the communications room, including some pieces of equipment that may have been cryptographic. Herman Kahn, author of the classic history of cryptography, The Codebreakers, told me in a phone interview in January 1980 that "if they (the Iranians) got some of the equipment, it might not be too serious. Of course, if they got also the cipher key computer cards which determined the code machine settings, that could be very serious indeed."

When I reported the possibility of such an intelligence disaster in the Christian Science Monitor on January 8, 1980, I was called to the Pentagon. A polite and somewhat embarrassed army colonel gave me to understand that the National Security Agency (NSA) in Fort Meade, Maryland, responsible for secret signal and communication matters, had ordered that I should be given a talking to. The Pentagon was concerned about the grave nature of the Monitor's reports from Tehran and about my background story, written while I was Pentagon correspondent.[5] The colonel's instructions apparently included an admonition to neither confirm nor deny my story. The uncertainty lingers today.

An equally serious disaster took place during the aborted mission to rescue the embassy hostages in April 1980. Sensitive material in one of the downed U.S. helicopters was abandoned, and perhaps additional material in a damaged C-130 was abandoned. The C-130 had been set afire by a collision as the mission was aborted. According to Col. "Chargin' Charlie" Beckwith, the veteran Delta Force mission commander, his unit "left without their equipment, which had been stored in the aircraft." Beckwith and his superiors, including the overall mission commander, Gen. James Vaught, requested an air strike to destroy the sensitive gear and papers in the choppers and the C-130; this was vetoed by the White House. President Carter apparently feared that it would endanger the lives of passengers in a passing Iranian bus, briefly held prisoner to prevent them from giving away the operation.[6]

Following this, there were urgent efforts to get U.S. agents out of Iran. "We were really scrambling for awhile," said one U.S. official. Documents left behind in the

desert showed secret escape routes as well as identification of agents who were to
have helped with the operation, and procedures and codes for making contact with
them. All the codes and operational plans were quickly changed.[7]

The Shah's fall and its aftermath had inflicted yet one more scar on the collective
psyche of America. Other scars, more serious in their effects, were to follow in rapid
succession.

The Fate of U.S. Intelligence Facilities

In addition to lives lost and tactical intelligence and military reputations compromised by American blunders and defeats in Iran, the Shah's demise brought with
it something far more serious for defense planners in Washington: the "blinding"
and loss of U.S. facilities collecting intelligence on the Soviet Union. Ever since
the U.S. military partnership with the Shah of Iran began in the 1950s, American
spy satellites had been providing detailed photographs of Soviet missile-testing and
launching operations.[8] The U.S. Embassy in Tehran was an important part of a
network of U.S. foreign service posts and CIA stations gathering intelligence on the
Soviet Union, supplementing what was gathered by the robot spies in space. After
the much publicized affair involving Francis Gary Powers (pilot of the American
U-2 reconnaissance plane shot down over the USSR in 1960 after takeoff from a
base near Peshawar, northern Pakistan), surveillance flights were reduced, and spy
satellites began to take on more importance as their technology developed further.

This technology was largely that of the original Discoverer space program. It
became clear that an effective reconnaissance system would need satellites that
could pick up and transmit by radio wide-area photos, especially of the Soviet
Union and China. There also had to be facilities on land and at sea for retrieving
the close-up pictures dropped to earth.

The U.S. Air Force and the CIA began to share this work beginning in the 1960s,
even before the Apollo moon mission. The photographic spy satellites were codenamed Keyhole (KH). Successive generations were assigned KH numbers, still in
use in 1989–90. By the late 1980s, imaging systems that transmitted pictures in real
time to earth were efficient enough to eliminate the need for dropping off film.
Satellite pictures were being used for a host of open, peacetime jobs, from surveying
the earth's water, land, and mineral resources to studying the atmosphere and the
troposphere. Secrets were harder and harder to guard. Satellite deception was growing into an art.

By 1986, France had launched its first commercial Spot satellite on an Ariane
rocket from French Guyana. France's Spot Image and Eosat, which sells the
imagery from America's own commercial satellite, Landsat, were soon offering
whatever pictures they could get—such as photos of the Iran-Iraq War front and the
Persian Gulf during that war—to anyone willing to pay the price, often well over
$10,000 for a single set of computer-enhanced pictures. In 1983, for example, three
U.S. TV networks were offered a photo purporting to show that Israel was diverting

the waters of southern Lebanon's Litani River into northern Israel, something many of Israel's founders had urged since 1919. It didn't take much investigation to prove that this was a hoax: all the photo showed was flooding and runoff from the Litani after heavy winter rains.[9]

Back in the 1960s and 1970s, however, when the United States and the Shah were carrying out mainly verbal agreements to exchange intelligence and provide the United States with support in its surveillance of the Soviet Union, things were different. Satellite imagery was one of the most closely held government secrets. From 1960, the year of Francis Gary Powers's disaster, until 1973, area-intelligence photographic surveys were carried out by U.S. Close Look satellites and, until 1973, by SAMOS (satellite and missile observation system), which became the KH series. It was a versatile system. When, for example, a launch apparently intended to observe India's first nuclear tests in the Rajestan Desert in 1974 failed, another launch the next day was successful. The United States got its pictures of the tests.[10]

SAMOS paid off almost from the beginning. SAMOS 2, launched on January 31, 1961, carried 150 kilograms of instruments that transmitted its pictures of the Soviet Union over U.S. territory. From this, President John F. Kennedy's administration learned that the United States had greatly overestimated the number of Soviet intercontinental ballistic missiles (ICBMs) and the size of the so-called missile gap, according to which the Soviet Union had vast superiority over the United States.[11]

By now, it was clear to America's intelligence planners that a new generation of "eyes and ears" was needed on the ground as well as in space to monitor Soviet missile developments. Many if not most of these developments took place at what the Soviets call the Baikonour Cosmodrome, northeast of the Aral Sea in Soviet Kazakhstan at a place called Tyuratam.

During a generation of Soviet space flight and missile developments, Tyuratam has been the USSR's main space launch and missile test center. It is the main test site for ICBMs as well as for medium- and short-range ballistic missiles (MRBMs and SRBMs). The impact points for the missiles launched from Tyuratam are at Kamchatka, in far eastern Siberia, and in the Pacific Ocean, six hundred miles northeast of Midway and six hundred miles southeast of Wake Island. The Soviets conduct what used to be highly secret missile-crew training and operational testing at Tyuratam. They also do new ICBM research, development, and operational testing for liquid-fuel missiles. In 1985, at least eighteen launchers for Soviet SS-18 missiles spotted there were thought to have the ability to launch missiles with armed warheads in a war contingency.[12]

By the early 1960s, the United States had already found the ideal *ground* location to monitor the Tyuratam complex—northern Iran. With the Shah's verbal permission, the United States set up two highly sophisticated listening posts. One was installed at Bishahr, on the Caspian Sea, facing the Soviet coastline. It was probably of tremendous value in monitoring Soviet communications, air movements, and such activities as oil operations in the Baku area of Soviet Azerbaijan. This was to be the scene of turbulent conflict and separatist political activity during Soviet

President Mikhail Gorbachev's era of *glasnost* and *perestroika* in the late 1980s. As the heart of Soviet-directed separatist activity and the launching pad for Soviet invasions of Iranian Azerbaijan in 1921 and 1946, Baku was especially sensitive for Iranian regimes, royal, revolutionary, or otherwise. The Bishahr site was designated "Tracksman 1" by the U.S. government.

Even more valuable was "Tracksman 2." This was an intercept station set up at Kapkan, forty miles east of the Iranian holy city of Mashhad. A senior U.S. defense official told me that Tracksman 2 was "irreplaceable." It was able, among other things, to monitor and record all details of the liftoff and early flight of missiles from the Baikonour Cosmodrome at Tyuratam, seven hundred miles across a clear line of sight to the north. This meant that there was clear passage for electronic signals in between.

Technicians of the U.S. armed forces and the NSA were able at Tracksman 2 to record details of the liftoff and early trajectory of missiles on their way out. They could also notify satellites to switch on their cameras and recording equipment to monitor the electronic emissions, or telemetry, of the Soviet missiles.

Air crews flying electronic reconnaissance missions out of U.S. bases in such places as Okinawa or Alaska were alerted by Tracksman messages to watch for Soviet missiles.[13] The only intelligence asset the United States then possessed that came anywhere near rivaling Tracksman was Rhyolite, a satellite able to monitor high- and very-high-frequency (VHF) transmissions and therefore valuable for analyzing Soviet missile telemetry. The Soviets had not bothered to encrypt this telemetry. They believed wrongly that it could be received only near the launch site. Rhyolite was able to watch *all* Soviet missile and rocket activities at Tyuratam and elsewhere.[14] One problem with Rhyolite, however, was its orbital position—22,300 miles away from Tyuratam. Telemetry signals reaching it were only one-thousandth the magnitude of those scooped up by Tracksman 2 on the ground.[15] Rhyolite had been operating since 1973, when it replaced an earlier spysat system called Big Bird.

Then, in 1974–75, Christopher John Boyce and Andrew Dalton Lee handed Soviet agents in Mexico Rhyolite plans, computer cipher key cards, and clear-text messages from the TRW Corporation in Redondo Beach, California, which made Rhyolite. This enabled Soviet cryptanalysts to solve the ciphers. Boyce and Lee also gave the Soviets a supersecret plan, codenamed Pyramider, for a worldwide, miniature instant CIA communications system that also used satellites.

No sooner was the newest KH-11 satellite in orbit than former CIA employee William Kampiles, in 1978, sold the KH-11 operating manual to the Soviets in Athens. All this helped the Soviets to cover up ground activities they did not want seen or monitored and, in some cases, to feed electronic or visual disinformation to various cameras, receivers, and sensors spying on them from the sky.

Texas Governor William Clements, Jr., deputy secretary of defense while Boyce and Lee were selling material to the Russians and a staunch supporter of U.S. intelligence sites in Iran, summed up the TRW case: "Our intelligence community is in disarray. A major satellite intelligence system, developed and deployed at a cost of billions of dollars over the past decade, has been compromised by intelligence procedures as porous as Swiss cheese."[16]

Shortly after the TRW and Kampiles cases, the Soviets began encrypting their missile telemetry. This made it doubly important for the CIA and the National Reconnaissance Office (NRO) to capture those encrypted emissions and other data at the Tracksman sites in northern Iran. When the Iranian revolution erupted in the autumn of 1978, there was a quiet panic, carefully kept from the media, throughout the U.S. intelligence community over the fate and future of the two Tracksmen.

By late 1978, demonstrations and strikes, many with a strong anti-American and anti-Western flavor, had crippled the country's economy. Iranian Navy personnel, as Ambassador Ardeshir Zahedi, the Shah's former son-in-law, explained to me in Washington, had tried to run to oil installations, but to no avail. Over a million civil servants were on strike too. The Shah installed the army chief of staff, Gen. Gholan Reza Azhari, as chief of a military government. On December 10 and 11, when the Shah, in one of his periodic pendulum swings, again tried to offer the carrot of concession, two anti-Shah rallies involving over a million people each erupted in the heart of Tehran.

It was then that the Carter administration, finally facing facts, reluctantly decided to begin slowing down U.S. intelligence activity in Iran.

Before Christmas 1978, the Bishahr site on the Caspian, Tracksman 1, was closed down, and personnel were quietly removed. (Accounts differ about what material was left there and what finally became of it.) On January 4, 1979, President Carter and his military chiefs moved to bolster the authority and the reporting capability of Ambassador William H. Sullivan by sending Gen. Robert E. ("Dutch") Huyser to Tehran. His official task was to hold together the Iranian military and encourage it to support what was left of the Shah's regime. If the Shah left, a military takeover might be supported to save Iran from either communism or Khomeini, or both.

Huyser received additional orders in a phone call from Gen. David Jones, chairman of the Joint Chiefs of Staff (JCS). I had met Jones in Washington in November at Ambassador Zahedi's gala birthday party, which had more than a touch of pathos, for Crown Prince Reza Pahlavi, already ironically nicknamed the Baby Shah. Reza had just completed his U.S. Air Force pilot training in Colorado. Even that early, Jones spoke of his preoccupation about the fate of huge amounts of sensitive U.S. military gear still reaching Iran.

In January 1979, Jones ordered Huyser to "take extra measures to protect the newest and most sensitive equipment shipped to Iran—particularly the F-14s and their weapons."[17] By this time, the Shah had played his last political card. On December 28, 1978, he turned the government over to Shahpour Bakhtiar, a veteran member of the main secular opposition movement, the National Front. His cabinet immediately declared a program of appeasement. This included the release of political prisoners, the punishment of human rights violators and corrupt officials, an end to oil exports to Israel and South Africa, and support for the Palestinians. All these were among the demands of the Ayatollah Khomeini, exiled in France since moving from the holy city of An-Najaf, Iraq, in October.

The day before General Huyser arrived in Tehran, January 3, Bakhtiar promised that the Shah would leave Iran for "a period of rest and holiday" after the new government was installed. A regency council would be set up to rule in his absence. From France, Khomeini warned on January 6 that obeying the new government would be "obeying Satan." This was a typically ambiguous remark, implying both the Satan of the Muslim religion and the other demonic power, the Great Satan, Khomeini's description of the United States. Huyser talked with Gen. Amir Rabii, the current Iranian air force commander, and Adm. Kamal Habiballahi, chief of the navy. Both agreed to take special precautions to protect sensitive U.S. military equipment, especially F-14 fighters and their weapons, including Phoenix air-to-air missiles recently shipped to Iran. In return, Huyser arranged to ship cold-weather equipment to the Iranian armed forces.

All this time, with no publicity given to the closedown of Tracksman 1, Tracksman 2 was still ticking away in the northeast and gathering its harvest of priceless intelligence (or so the United States thought—intelligence experts later came to believe that the Soviets were "cooking" the telemetry broadcast from Tyuratam to deceive the Americans).

A threat remained to U.S. personnel in Iran, reduced from fifty-eight thousand in October, when Israeli intelligence began to warn the United States that the Shah could not survive, to a more manageable twenty thousand or so.[18] The radical *homofars* had by now begun moving into two key air bases, Khatami Air Base near Isfahan and Shiraz Air Base. Both had stockpiles of F-14 spares, the planes themselves, and sensitive electronic gear as well as the Phoenix missiles. Senior officials ordered supposedly loyal Iranian special forces onto the bases to protect the planes and hardware. When Huyser advised Washington that he planned to move the equipment to better-protected bases in the south near Bandar Abbas on the Persian Gulf and Shahbehar on the Indian Ocean, the Iranians intercepted the message on their computer net. During trials on June 2, 1980, it was later played back as evidence of "U.S. intervention in Iran."[19] (The planes and most of the equipment remained in Iran, and some came into combat with Saudi forces, America's ally, in the Iran-Iraq War. The U.S.-supplied air force and many Iranian navy ships of American origin, as well as much ground equipment bolstered by new arms purchases, were the mainstay of Iran's forces during that war.)

All this time, January–February 1979, the Soviet media were publishing reports about the movements and activities of Huyser that were more accurate than those published by the Western or Iranian media. Later, Huyser and others discovered that there was a Soviet "mole" already at work. He was Maj. Gen. Hussein Fardust, working on the supreme commander's general staff. He was tipping off the Soviets and would later be rewarded by Khomeini with an appointment as chief of SAVAMA (Sazemane Amniyat va Ettelaate Mellate Iran), the revolution's successor to SAVAK, the Shah's secret police. In December 1985, however, he was arrested for being a Soviet informer and disappeared, apparently forever, only one of many of the revolution's own whom it devoured.[20]

The problem of Tracksman 2, the Kapkan intercept station, remained. On February 24, the first Iranian hostage crisis erupted. It was one of the earliest collisions between Iranian militants and Americans in Iran.

On February 21, Iranian Chief of Staff Gen. Wali Qaraneh had broadcast on Tehran radio a statement that no American spying installations were to be allowed on Iranian soil. His message got through loud and clear to local Iranian employees at Kapkan. Owed several months' back pay—no one had been able to get money or supplies from Tehran to the site during the recent violence—they mutinied and took twenty-two U.S. technicians hostage.

In an important way, this was the real beginning of the secret war between America and the Iranian revolution. Ambassador Sullivan and officials of the Bazargan government approved a secret mission to Kapkan. It flew February 28 in a C-130, piloted by a surly but finally compliant Iranian. Among the passengers were the U.S. defense attaché in Tehran, Col. T. E. Shaefer; one of his aides, Capt. H. F. Johnson; two loyal Iranian civilian employees; and 30 million Iranian rials in cash, worth about $200,000 at the time.

In the early morning hours, they left from a strip near Tehran and landed near Kapkan. There, in effect, they ransomed the twenty-two American technicians by giving the Iranian staff their wages. The Iranian military was now left in charge of both Tracksman 1 and Tracksman 2. Their monitoring capabilities were lost to the United States, perhaps for good.

The Cost of Spying on the Soviets

Professor James A. Bill is a seasoned Iran-watcher who foresaw the American catastrophe in Iran long before others. In his carefully reasoned book, *The Eagle and the Lion*, Bill points out that the CIA was weak in Iran because it had to devote most of its intelligence-gathering energies there not to studying the situation inside the country but rather to spying on the Soviets. The CIA was weak despite its "enormous reputation among Iranians, who considered it the all-knowing force that shrewdly and surreptitiously directed Iranian affairs while pulling the strings of the Pahlavi puppet."[21]

Bill mentions that an "informed American intelligence officer" wrote him that the Tracksman sites had been "absolutely critical" for two decades in enabling the United States to detect and properly evaluate Soviet ICBM testing activities. Loss of other sites in Turkey and Pakistan had been harmful, but this was catastrophic. The sites had been established only by oral agreement between the Shah and the CIA. CIA officials feared that if the Shah grew angry at the United States because an American president stressed human rights or otherwise irritated him, he would close them.[22]

American policy was to lean over backwards to avoid such annoyance. The United States even avoided contact with dissidents and opposition elements who could have helped it understand more about opposition sentiment as well as the Iranian mentality and temperament, which seemed to escape nearly all the Americans trying to deal seriously with Iran.

Repercussions were soon felt inside Turkey, Iran's Western neighbor (and former alliance partner of the Shah) and NATO member. According to a study by William Arkin and other U.S. defense consultants in 1985, there were just short of five hundred American nuclear weapons stored inside Turkey (probably never the case in Iran). For the Soviets, the five nuclear-armed U.S. air bases in Turkey were uncomfortably close. The main American combat and supply base for the Middle East is at Incirlik, Turkey. The Turkish government did allow the United States to stage an airborne intervention force there during the civil war between Jordan and the Palestinian Liberation Organization (PLO) in 1970; but they did not permit the United States to use the base for reinforcing marines or other personnel guarding military installations in revolutionary Iran. In 1990–91, during the American and allied buildup of Desert Shield in preparation for the Desert Storm hostilities with Iraq, U.S. F-111 fighter-bombers were moved to Incirlik. Turkish president Turgut Özal cut off pipelines exporting Iraqi oil through Turkey, called up Turkish reserves, and apparently promised the United States that his country would play at least a defensive role in Desert Storm, all in hope of favors such as membership in or association with the European Economic Community (EEC) and a guarantee of Turkey's continued role in NATO.

There were a number of other U.S. and NATO intelligence sites in Turkey. Probably the most important was Pirinçlik, in eastern Turkey, temporarily shut down in the 1970s when Congress embargoed U.S. arms to Turkey. When Tracksman 1 and 2 were lost in Iran, would Pirinçlik, though lacking the line-of-sight advantage in "watching" Tyuratam (there were mountains in between) that Kapkan enjoyed, become available again to support large tracking radars? These were a vital part of a net of surveillance on Soviet missile testing. Pirinçlik was also an important ground station for watching satellites of all types and nations.

The Carter administration, accused by many Republicans of "losing" the Shah's Iran, was determined not to lose Turkey as well. Relations had been seriously strained by the congressional arms embargo of 1974, lifted in 1978. By May 1979, the question of whether Turkey would allow the continued operation of Pirinçlik and other installations on its soil was being linked to new Turkish requests for American aid.

On May 22, members of the Carter team sighed with relief. The U.S. Senate voted to provide Turkey with $50 million in military grants. During a visit by U.S. Deputy Secretary of State Warren Christopher just before the vote, Turkish Prime Minister Bulent Ecevit had insisted on more aid and a firm commitment by the United States to meet Turkey's arms needs.

Another sensitive issue precipitated by the Shah's fall and the loss of U.S. sites in Iran was that of American reconnaissance flights by U-2s and the newer, far swifter, high-flying SR-71 Blackbirds. These aircraft flew over the Soviet Union from Turk-ish airspace and bases.

With the SALT II arms-limitation treaty nearly ready for signing, the question of verification focused on intelligence gathered by satellites and overhead reconnais-sance flights. Turkish officials made it known in early 1979 that they would allow flights to pass over Turkish territory only if the Soviet Union did not object. The Turkish Foreign Ministry confirmed this on May 14.

The next day, Ecevit said Turkey was "prepared to help make SALT II work" but could not accept the flights that would "jeopardize" Turkey's security without Soviet approval. Turkish commentators were quick to point out that Powers's doomed flight in 1960, when he took off from Pakistan, had originally been based in Turkey. That flight had strained Turkish-Soviet relations.

Ecevit's rightist political opponent, Süleyman Demirel, claimed that allowing the U.S. flights would put Turkey "in front of the gun barrel." A visiting Soviet official avoided a direct demand that Turkey reject U-2 flights but did say the Soviet Union would "receive positively" such rejection.[23]

Eventually, the United States was able to use its relations with China, which had begun to improve with President Richard Nixon and with Henry Kissinger's secret visit in the mid-1970s, to obtain two new secret monitoring sites in western China's Sinkiang-Uighur autonomous region. This is a story too long and complex to tell here, and many details are still secret. But there is one point to make here. In 1989–90, President Bush was reluctant to antagonize Chinese Communist govern-ment officials, many of whom he had come to know during his ambassadorship in China in the 1970s and during his administration of the CIA. This raised loud objections by human rights activists, who mourned the thousands of Chinese killed in the student uprising in Beijing's Tiananmen Square in May and June 1989. Bush's reasons were many, but one principal one was surely to keep the two secret Chinese monitoring sites, believed to provide coverage of Tyuratam and other Soviet centers nearly as good as that provided by the former sites in Iran.

Misguided U.S. Policy

Dr. William Polk, a Mideast adviser to both Presidents Kennedy and Johnson, once highlighted for me the effects of the intelligence community's electronic spying on U.S. foreign relations in general. One trouble, he said, was that very few members of any American administration have access to the sensitive products of such espi-onage. Since many policymakers lack the information, each has to go his own way. The result is the development of many different policies.

"Take our policy to assist Turkey, Iran, and Pakistan," Polk recalled in a phone conversation in March 1987. "We committed hundreds of millions of dollars. The responsible AID [Agency for International Development] officials had to design the programs." Some of this went to the Shah's Iran before the oil boom that would take care of Iranian finances:

[AID] would do a study on transportation, for example, that showed Pakistan needed, say, $50 million in U.S. aid. That would go with other programs to make an overall package. But, to put it crudely, much of our "aid" program was payment or rent for intelligence facilities. During the Kennedy and Eisenhower administrations, almost no one in the AID programs was cleared for that sort of information. Or the U-2 flights. So, when the aid official came up with his program and had costed it out, he would be patted on the head, so to speak, and told that several times that amount was to be committed. He was unlikely to learn why, until he read it in the papers or saw it on television.

After the U-2 incident, when U.S. ambassadors wanted to urge new policies on rulers like the Shah, the rulers would go to their independent U.S. intelligence contact and threaten American overflight rights or listening sites. The director of the CIA, recalled Polk, would then go straight to the president and say, "Mr. President, this is a national calamity. You cannot change your policy toward X country. If you do, we will lose information that is absolutely and utterly vital to the very survival of this country. Why, we won't even know if the Soviets set off nuclear weapons or fire missiles. We can't afford to antagonize these countries for anything."

In Iran, Polk felt, it should have been easier to avoid this dilemma. Except for the Tracksman stations, which very few people in the government knew about, there was much less intelligence activity there than in Turkey or Pakistan, "but everyone felt the Shah had us with our hands tied."

Indeed! The obvious point, which U.S. administrations between the time of John Kennedy (1960–63) and Ronald Reagan/George Bush (1981–) often ignored, was that the cold war with the Soviet Union should not have been the only theme of American foreign policy. Instead of keeping a huge presence in a country like Iran simply to gather intelligence, the United States should have emphasized Middle Eastern issues. In other words, Polk believed, the United States could keep a huge American presence, if it must, in a country like Iran, but not just to monitor the Soviet Union; it had to show the Iranians that the United States cared how they lived and were ruled, and understood that they aspired to better things.

This the United States did not do. Instead, it let the struggle with the Soviets determine priorities. Both adversaries and friends were able to exploit this. How one leading ally of the United States, Israel, was able to do so is our next subject.

3

From Babylon to Moshe Dayan

Embassy Under Siege

November 4, 1979—the day America's conflict with Iran erupted in human as well as strategic terms. In many ways, too, it was the day Israel's ambivalent, ancient relationship with Iran began to weigh heavily in American foreign policy.

Christine Powell, a journalist, left her flat in a small but quiet downtown Tehran street fairly early. It was an overcast Sunday morning, mild for November, although snow already streaked the Alborz mountain wall looming high over the Tehran cityscape. Christine's first stop on her rounds that day was a noisy student rally at Tehran University. In speech after speech, activists called for the seizure and return of the ailing Shah. After intensive lobbying by such illustrious friends of the Shah as Nelson Rockefeller and Henry Kissinger, President Carter had admitted the Shah to the United States for cancer treatments. The Tehran University crowd howled their protests. Christine, bored with the repetitious slogans, left the campus.

Outside, she met a Dutch colleague. Rain began to fall. They hurried through traffic-choked streets to a restaurant run by a Korean couple. It served good Oriental food. More important, bootleg whiskey and vodka were poured discreetly from fine porcelain teapots. Since the implementation of Khomeini's stern edicts banning drinking in public, the restaurant was popular, especially with foreigners.

By now it was 12:30 P.M. local time. Before eating, Christine phoned Reuters

News Agency to check on the news. The dwindling community of foreign journalists stuck together and helped one another whenever possible. The bureau chief, Christine thought, sounded harassed. "There's something going on at the American Embassy. Can you check it out?" Christine looked at the steaming rice dishes and the tempting teapot and decided they would have to wait.

The embassy was only two blocks north on Takhte Jamshid (Persepolis) Avenue. Everything appeared normal there. There were neither chanting crowds nor burning flags, as there had been two days earlier, to protest the deposed Shah's presence in a New York hospital. The gates were chained shut, but groups of Iranians walked around the parking area. The young men and women outnumbered the usual scruffy Iranian sentinels who formed a kind of semiofficial security force, remnants of the one-day occupation of the previous February. But now the gate-house was unmanned, and none of the embassy marine guards were in sight.

Christine called out to one of the young men. Would he let her in? She said she had an appointment with Barry Rosen, the U.S. press attaché who happened to be one of several Jewish Americans on the embassy staff. Good-natured arguing with the young guardian of the revolution did no good: The answer was no. "Come back later," said one of his companions. "We'll explain everything." Christine was reminded of the embassy break-in of the previous February. She headed for a nearby telephone to pass on the news.

Six hours later, at 7:00 P.M. Tehran time, a group of foreign reporters, outnumbered four to one by the locals, was still lined up waiting to get in. Though they scarcely realized it, headlines around the world were proclaiming the shocking news: The embassy had been captured, and over fifty American diplomats inside were prisoners. Somewhat later, the first television pictures were shown to numbed Western audiences. These included a blindfolded diplomat, displayed like a captive animal groping his way among jeering captors.

The captors carefully checked the credentials of Christine and her colleagues. They were admitted to the embassy that evening and given a short account, mimeographed in English, of how the compound had been taken without much resistance, despite whiffs of tear gas fired by the marines. The hostages, they were told, were fine and having dinner. Afterward, if the captives wanted to sleep, they could sleep on the floor. Chanting outside made it clear that unless the Shah was sent promptly back to Iran, the Americans would stay locked up in their embassy.

Enemies of God

As the days wore on into weeks and months, Americans, their families, and other foreigners flowed out of Iran, fearful for their lives. The young, uncertain faces of the self-styled "students following the line of the Imam" (Khomeini) gave way to older, tougher-looking Iranians, many of whom were to become the hardliners of future Khomeini and post-Khomeini regimes. They were more articulate in their denunciations of the United States. They amplified these with diatribes against

"Israel and the Zionist clique who are the lackeys of the Americans." Flags were burned, Israeli and American. Leering cartoons of the absent Shah, President Carter, and Israeli Prime Minister Menachem Begin were hoisted onto improvised gallows.[1]

One Iranian especially upset about what was going on was Simon Farzima. In prerevolutionary Tehran, Farzima was not a man who stood out in the crowd. He was one of the ancient community of about eighty-five thousand Jews who, at the outbreak of the revolution, lived, worked, and for the most part prospered in Iran. I remember him as a short, genial man with silver-gray hair and a pink complexion. Diplomats and many foreign journalists in Tehran had treated him with deference and even affection.

There was good reason. Farzima, who dressed meticulously in three-piece suits and looked for all the world like a pre–World War II French schoolteacher, was editor of the French-language *Journal de Tehran*. This was the smaller and more modest brother of the much-read English-language *Tehran Journal*. Both were published by the big Persian-language newspaper and publishing house, Etelaat.

Farzima was an endless source of tips, anecdotes, and useful information. He supplemented his income by doing translations for embassies. No matter how modest some of the jobs he performed, you never forgot, from his quiet but gentlemanly and humorous manner, that he was the son of an illustrious Iranian ambassador.

The Khomeini regime hanged Farzima in the summer of 1979, shortly after executing several other "enemies of the state," including Jews and Baha'is.

The crackdown on "enemies of God," as Khomeini's judges often referred to their victims, also targeted a prominent Jewish businessman, Habib Elghanian. He was known as Iran's plastics king because of his large plastics enterprise. An Iranian firing squad shot Elghanian to death on May 9, 1979, a few days before Farzima's hanging. He was accused of spying and raising funds for Israel, "to be used for killing Palestinians." During the same period, an American Jew, David Rebhan, who had been a pilot for Jimmy Carter when the latter was governor of Georgia, was arrested. He had been trying to start up a toy factory in Iran with an Iranian partner. Rebhan was denounced for fraud and thrown into prison without trial. Though attorneys got him out once, he was taken again in late 1979 or early 1980. In November 1989, a cellmate described Rebhan as "still held in total isolation, looking gray and sick."[2] In 1990, after a brief improvement in treatment, he was released from prison and sent home to the United States. Many foreigners in Tehran felt that Rebhan's Jewishness had more than a little to do with his long imprisonment.

Israeli Prime Minister Begin did not do much to help the cause of Rebhan, Elghanian, or any of the other Jews remaining in Iran (fifteen thousand had fled in the months before the revolution). After Elghanian's execution, Begin claimed publicly that he had been "a good Zionist and one who helped Israel." He denounced "the executions of this murderous regime." Much milder was the U.S. State Department's rebuke to Khomeini. It was disturbed, a spokesman said, because Elghanian "was a member of a minority community."

Farzima had not been condemned for trucking with Israel but for helping the Americans. What was more, he admitted this publicly. The "students" who took over the embassy in November 1979 found records of payments the embassy had made to him for translating new Iranian laws and decrees from Farsi into English. These together were enough to tar Simon Farzima as a CIA agent and get him killed.

Compared to Baha'is, communists, members of the leftist Mujaheddin, and followers of many other political and sectarian groups opposing Khomeini's tyranny, relatively few Jews were executed. However, for Israeli analysts, one thing seemed certain: they were killed *because* they were Jews.

The Ayatollah Rants

The relationship between Iran's rulers and the Jews of the Middle East has always been ambiguous. It led the Shah into a close and secret partnership with Israel. Today, it helps to explain why Israel and the Iranian Jews became key players— middlemen of a sort—in the game of secret warfare between Iran and the United States. The Jews in both countries played one role publicly and another, totally different one privately.

The main reason Israel and the United States "had different agendas" in Iran, as U.S. Defense Secretary Caspar Weinberger was to put it, was implicit in the reaction to killings of people like Simon Farzima. This reason was simple: Israel was determined, at all costs, to get as many of the remaining sixty-five thousand Jews it could out of Iran and into Israel. This would mean ransoming them, sometimes. The main payment would not be in money; it would be in arms deals. The secret, bilateral Iranian-Israeli arms deals, begun as early as September 1980 while U.S. embassy staffers were still held prisoner in Tehran, would eventually drag the United States into the quagmire of arms-for-hostages transactions with Iran during both administrations of President Reagan (1981–88).

Israel's desire to rescue the Iranian Jews, who had lived relatively peacefully with the Iranians since the reigns of the ancient Persian emperors, was publicized after the May 1979 executions. It was not Israel but the U.S. government that disseminated this news. There can be no doubt that this publicity furnished new fuel for the resentment that drove Khomeini's theocracy to challenge the United States.

On May 12, 1979, three days after Elghanian was shot, U.S. news media reported that Aryeh Dulzin, director of the Jewish Agency and the World Zionist Organization, had warned Iran not to harm the sixty-five thousand Jews remaining there. Israel was prepared "to take action" to protect them. One of Dulzin's aides suggested that Israel might undertake operations, "both orthodox and unorthodox," to help the Iranian Jews emigrate.

Three days later, probably on the advice of Ibrahim Yazdi or another of his American-educated advisers, Ayatollah Khomeini grudgingly received a delegation of visiting Iranian Jews. They and their coreligionists would be treated fairly, he assured them. Tehran radio dutifully reported that the Jewish delegation had said that it regretted "plots of Zionism."[3]

Pierre Salinger, reporting the hostage crisis, often conferred with his friend West

German Ambassador Gerhardt Ritzel. Salinger observed that Ritzel's popularity with the new regime of Khomeini was due to considerably more than just good contacts. Ritzel told Salinger that he had an "irrational German reputation" in Iran. There were two aspects of Adolf Hitler's Third Reich that these new Iranian rulers admired. The first was its war against Great Britain, which helped to loosen that country's hold on Iran. The second was the "final solution," Hitler's massacre of the Jews.[4]

The Ayatollah Khomeini had earlier expressed severe anti-Semitism. In 1968 an Australian tourist set fire to the Al-Aqsa Mosque, or the Dome of the Rock, in Israeli-occupied East Jerusalem barely a year after the Israeli conquest. Khomeini from his exile in Iraq's holy city of An-Najaf, called upon faithful Muslims to let the damage remain unrepaired as testimony to "Israeli desecration" of the holy shrine. The Shah, however, followed the example of other Muslim rulers. He opened a subscription to collect money for repairs. "In this manner," Khomeini ranted in a pamphlet that later became part of his book-length testament, *Islamic Government*, the Shah "fills his pockets and coffers and increases his assets. After the mosque is repaired, he will have covered all traces of the Zionist crime." The Shah increased taxes to "purchase Phantom [U.S.-made McDonnell Douglas F-4 fighter-bombers] aircraft so that the Israelis may be trained on them. . . . Whoever helps and supports [Israel] is in a state of war with the Muslims."

Iranian bazaar merchants were then complaining, as they often did, about unfair competition from abroad. Khomeini attributed this to "the Israeli influence in our country. . . . [T]he Israelis use our lands for their bases and as their markets, and this is something that will gradually lead to the decline of the Muslim markets."[5]

Like other Muslim leaders, Khomeini acknowledged that Muslim disunity was largely responsible for Israeli successes. He wrote that Muslims should heed the Koranic phrase, "Prepare for our foes all the force and all the horses you can muster so that you may scare away the enemies of God and your enemies." Had they done this and been ready to fight at the right time,

> It would not have been possible for a handful of Jews to occupy our land and to damage and burn our Al-Aqsa Mosque without being faced with any resistance. . . . Had the current Muslim rulers tried to implement the laws of Islam . . . putting aside their disputes and their divisions . . . the bands of Jews and the puppets of America and Britain would not have been able to reach what they have reached.[6]

Khomeini also recalled that Islam in its early years fought other sects and that "the prophet, may God's peace and prayers be upon him, annihilated the Bani Qurayzah Jews [in Arabia] to the last man because of the harm he realized they were causing the Muslim society, his government and all the people."[7]

In a contemporary note, Khomeini berated the Jews for

> tampering with the Holy Koran and distorting its phrases in new editions which they have published in the [Israeli-] occupied territories and other parts. We must

expose this treachery and must shout at the top of our voices, so that we may make
the people realize that the Jews and their foreign masters seek to share Islam and
pave the way for the Jews to dominate the entire world. . . . Because of our
weakness, we may awaken one day to find a Jewish ruler ruling our country. God
forbid![8]

Christian property and some of the meeting places of the Baha'i faith, which most
Shi'a and Sunni Muslim clergy consider a heretical offshoot of Islam, had already
been desecrated by Shi'a revolutionaries. Khomeini made the threat formal: "Christian, Jewish and Baha'i missionary centers are spread in Tehran to deceive people
and to lead them away from the teachings and principles of religion. Isn't it a duty
to destroy these centers?"[9] When Pope John Paul II asked Khomeini to act hu-
manely toward the American hostages, the Ayatollah replied in a Friday prayer
sermon in Qom:

You [the Pope] shouldn't worry about what is going on in Iran. Instead you should
look at everything that is going on in America! Why didn't you get upset when
Jerusalem was conquered by the Jews? That would have been the time to open your
mouth. When the Jews made themselves into the enemies of all religions, the Pope
kept his mouth shut! The Pope kept quiet, because the Americans wanted him to.
America spoiled everyone. . . . The rulers of the world are America's serfs—the
Pope too![10]

An Ancient Relationship

Such was the attitude of Khomeini and his followers toward Iran's Jews and the state
of Israel. But the relationship between Persia and the Jews, between Iran and Israel,
has another side, a colorful one that goes back to Old Testament times. The Bible
must always be taken into account when considering the thinking of Israel's leaders.
Most of them, from the late David Ben-Gurion and Moshe Dayan to present-day
authors like Israeli novelist Amos Oz, take their Bible extremely seriously and tend
to interpret historical actions in biblical terms.

Nebuchadnezzar, the conquering king of Babylon, first invaded Syria and then,
in 598–97 B.C. and 589–87 B.C. mounted expeditions against Judea, the Israel of the
Old Testament. His exploits ended with the destruction of Jerusalem and the
captivity of a large part of the Jewish people, who were taken eastward to Babylon,
in today's Iraq.

Soon afterward, the Persian Emperors Cyrus, Darius, and Artaxerxes returned
the Jews from their Babylonian captivity to Jerusalem. There, they encouraged
them to rebuild their temple, destroyed by Nebuchadnezzar's armies. With the final
defeat of Babylon, about 539 B.C., came the establishment of the Persian Empire.
Jews, for a time, were honored if not wholly equal partners under the Persian and
Median rulers. These were the Jews who had chosen not to return to Jerusalem.
Their descendants, direct or indirect, lived in Babylon until the exodus from mod-

ern Iraq encouraged by Israel after its creation in 1948. Babylon was a mainstay and
became a center of Jewish culture for 1,500 years.

Despite Cyrus' approval of the Jews' return to Palestine in 538 B.C., it didn't work.
Many Jews who had remained in Palestine resisted the appearance of these more
affluent settlers and prevented them from raising the walls of Jerusalem.

The Babylonian Jews and their Persian patrons tried resettlement again in 520
B.C. and managed to rebuild the temple in Jerusalem. In 485 B.C., the resettled Jews
were reinforced by a third wave. Then the prophet Nehemiah, a Perso-Jewish
official, led forth another large group of immigrants. The emperor granted Nehemiah the governorship of Judah and the authority to build it into an independent
political unit within the empire. This fourth wave stabilized the resettlement of the
Jews in Palestine. Jerusalem was rebuilt in fifty-two days and nights of around-the-
clock work, an accomplishment that would inspire the pioneers of modern Israel.[11]

From 400 B.C. to 200 B.C., the Jews and the Persians seem to have gotten along
without major difficulties. There were no Jewish revolts against Persian rule; Jewish
mercenaries even helped to put down a rebellion against the Persians in Egypt. Jews
practiced their faith freely throughout the Persian Empire. The Jewish settlers
brought back to that area a body of rigidly orthodox religious rules, which had
grown in the Babylonian captivity, and spread it throughout the emperor's domin-
ions as well. Jerusalem prospered as an essentially Jewish city: its population had
reached 120,000 by the third century B.C. It was, perhaps, no wonder that Jewish
prophets, in retrospect, echoed the earlier praise of Cyrus the Great by their elders
as a kind of messiah. Discord and anti-Semitism, however, began to grow during
the period from 332 B.C. to 200 B.C. During that time, the Jews came to be ruled
by Greeks (the Ptolemies in Egypt), and after 200 B.C. by the Seleucids, Hellenized
Persian rulers.

This entire era has remained stamped upon the Jewish national consciousness,
and to a much lesser extent, upon the Iranian one as well. The Jewish prophets left
behind a bold concept. This was that the Babylonian imperialists, whom today's
Israelis identify with Iraqi dictators like Saddam Hussein, were fulfilling some kind
of divine intent in destroying the ancient kingdom of Judea, for thereby they paved
the way for the rise of a new order. The Persian imperialists who let kidnapped Jews
return to Palestine made the new kingdom viable. Moreover, Persia's peaceful
policies and highway construction gave Jews the opportunity to spread throughout
an area stretching all the way from the lower valley of the Nile in Egypt to the basins
of the Oxos and Ixartes rivers.

By the time of Christ, Babylonian Jewry had been weakened by severe economic
and social crises. About A.D. 600, when the prophet of Islam Muhammad appeared
in Mecca, the Persians launched a powerful offensive against the new empire of the
Byzantine Greeks whose capital was Constantinople. The Jews of Antioch, in Syria,
revolted against their Byzantine ruler, killed the Greek patriarch there, and helped
the Persians capture Antioch. History repeated itself: the Persians invaded Palestine
and again permitted the Jews, banished by the Roman Emperor Hadrian between
A.D. 128 and 132, to return to Jerusalem.

The perennial Jewish dream of rebuilding the temple there was soon dashed. This time the Persian army was driven from Palestine by the Romans, who repressed the uprisings of the Jews. (It was no historical accident that in the twentieth century the Ayatollah Khomeini talked of regaining Israel.)

In the seventh century A.D. Jews sided with Muslims when the latter conquered the Middle East and north Africa from Christian Byzantines.[12] By persecuting Jews, along with Christian heretics and other minorities, Christian bishops had alienated possible allies and thus made it easier for the Muslim tide to sweep over them.

Religious Roots Entwined

Looking back at this period, so crucial to Judaism as well as to Christianity and Islam, illuminates today's complex love-hate relationship between Tehran and Tel Aviv, which in turn heavily influences American attitudes and policies. In fact, a little more attention than the average American or European is willing to pay is rewarded by an understanding of how closely interwoven these three great religions are, despite their sects, their schisms, and the actions of their zealots. Muhammad himself noted that the Christians and Jews in Syria believed in one God, as well as salvation, damnation, freedom of will, and other matters set down in the Koran as divine revelation.[13]

While first receiving the revelations of the Koran, Muhammad looked toward Jerusalem during his prayers, not toward Mecca. Only after the Jews (unlike most of the Christians in the path of his armies) refused to be converted to Islam did he order that prayers be said facing the Kaaba, the sacred black stone in Mecca.

Muhammad died in A.D. 632. The Caliph Abdel Malik ibn Marwan (A.D. 685–705) resolved to make Jerusalem a main center for Muslim believers. Before building a mosque there, he consulted a Koranic scholar, al-Zuhiri. The scholar testified that Muhammad himself had considered the three holy places—Mecca, Medina, and Jerusalem—as of equal rank. One year before Muhammad traveled from Mecca to Yathrib, he had seen a dazzling light above a stairway coming from heaven. This is said to have been the start of his Koranic revelation. He went to Jerusalem and mounted to heaven, then returned to Mecca. A gray rock was erected on Mount Moriah, the site of Muhammad's ascension; it is known as the Dome of the Rock. Since Abdel Malik was not successful in making Jerusalem a main target of Muslim pilgrimages, he sent his Syrian army to conquer Mecca.[14]

The Sunni-Shi'a hatred that so divides Muslims today, and gives Tehran's efforts at religious hegemony such a strongly sectarian flavor, was already operating then. The Shi'a believed that command of the Muslim movement should remain in the family and not be subject to election, as the Sunni or orthodox group believed. Shi'a historians claim that Abdel Malik's son poisoned the fourth Shi'a imam, Zain al-Abidine, under orders from the rival Sunni dynasty in Damascus, the Ommayads, around 712.[15]

As Iranian Jews, like their coreligionists in Syria, Mesopotamia, Palestine, Egypt, and North Africa, began to emigrate to Europe, Jewish communities dwindled steadily in size.[16] In the days of the Shah Abbas of Iran (1587–1621), however, one Christian traveler found about fifty thousand Jews in that country, a sizeable number.

Their widespread belief in witchcraft prompted one Jewish renegade to allege that they used formulae found in the Kabbalah, a body of esoteric teaching, to harm the shah. Therefore, in 1620 the shah issued a decree that these and many other sacred books should be confiscated and burned. When the Jewish community of Isfahan objected, he ordered their leaders to convert to Islam by force. The order was later extended to all the Isfahani Jews and remained in force until 1628.

Further persecutions of the Iranian Jews continued under Shah Abbas II (1642–66). The Jews were expelled from Isfahan, and eventually, in 1656, all Jews were ordered to be converted by force. The forced converts were freed from the poll tax and the obligation imposed on the Jews to wear special dress, and they received gifts of money. But they kept their religion in their hearts. Five years later, they were allowed to revert openly to Judaism provided they return the gifts of money and pay the poll tax.[17]

Persecution of the Iranian Jews peaked in 1839, when the entire Jewish community of the Shi'a holy city of Mashhad was forced to convert. A Muslim youth accused a Jewish woman of vilifying the Shi'a faith on Ashoura, the solemn day of mourning for the Imam Hussein, the grandson of the prophet Muhammad. A fanatical mob demanded death or forced conversion of all Jews. Some thirty-five Jews were killed in the rioting that followed. This time, the converts in Mashhad were not allowed to return to Judaism. For three generations after this, most of the Iranian Jewish community had to pose as Muslims while they secretly observed Jewish laws. Many crossed into Afghanistan. Some of these, including the Marannos of Mashhad, had fled Persia in earlier centuries.

Recent History

The Bolshevik Revolution of 1917, which resulted in the overthrow of the czar, was condemned in Iran, especially by the Shi'a clergy, as immoral. Spiritual leaders in the holy city of Qom saw the revolution as a plot by Russian Jews to destroy Islam. This was the same kind of truncated polemical reasoning that made Nazi theoreticians in the Germany of the 1920s and 1930s profess to see a gigantic Jewish conspiracy to destroy their country's moral values and society. The idea of the Bolshevik Revolution as a Jewish plot was impressed upon Ayatollah Khomeini's mind during his studies and perhaps contributed to his anti-Semitic pronouncements.[18]

In the late forties, both Israeli and U.S. intelligence agencies cooperated in a joint effort to help Jews escape from Iraq and at the same time to gain the Shah's recognition of Israel. Large sums were paid to "sweeten" Iranian politicians. Moshe

Tchervinski, a high official of Mossad, the Israeli secret intelligence service, said, "it was possible to achieve almost anything in Iran" through bribery. [19]

In their history of Israeli intelligence, *The Imperfect Spies*, Israeli journalist Yossi Melman and CBS correspondent Dan Raviv trace clandestine cooperation between Israel and modern Iran to Zion Cohen, an agent of Aliyeh-B, a forerunner of Mossad concerned with illegal Jewish emigration to Israel. In 1949, the Shah's government recognized Cohen as a de facto representative of the Israeli government, then headed by David Ben-Gurion. Iran's national airline agreed with Cohen to fly Jewish refugees, who had crossed the border clandestinely from Iraq, directly from Tehran to Tel Aviv.

One of the early Israeli secret agents in the Middle East, Yaacov Frank, was half American. He served in the underground Haganah, the paramilitary terrorist group that operated against the British mandate authorities in pre-independence Palestine. After escaping a British dragnet, Frank worked for the Institute for Aliyeh-B. As an American soldier in the Pacific, Frank fought the Japanese and was wounded in the Philippines in 1944. In 1948 he was able to return to Israel with his U.S. military pension. Two Israeli recruiting agents persuaded him to become a covert agent in Iraq, on behalf of Mossad, to help speed the emigration of Iraqi Jews to Israel.

Frank flew from Tel Aviv to Tehran in 1951 with a false Israeli passport in the name of Yitzhak Stein. Under the supervision of Zion Cohen, the Mossad station chief in Tehran, he was equipped with a new passport in the name of Ismail Tashbakash, a supposed rug merchant from Bahrain (Frank was certain that a much better cover would have been a British or American identity, since he *was* American). On April 20, 1951, some smugglers Frank had bribed got him across the border from Iran to Iraq. There, Shlomo Hillel, later a cabinet minister in several Israeli governments, was posing as British businessman Richard Armstrong. Hillel used his experience in running Operation Magic Carpet, flying Yemeni Jews to Israel in 1948–49, to organize a similar operation from Iraq, using the so-called American Near East Transport Corporation. Iraqi Jews were being allowed to leave, provided they gave up Iraqi citizenship; many descendants of the proud community of Babylonian Jews chose to leave.

Iraqi Prime Minister Tewfik al-Sawidi was chairman of Iraq Tours and an agent for American Near East Transport. The airline gave a maintenance concession to Iraqi Airways, run by Col. Sabah as-Said, son of the Iraqi statesman and future pro-Western prime minister Nuri as-Said. Through the concession, the Israelis kept Nuri "sweetened."

A smaller Israeli operation was run by Mordecai Ben-Porat, a journalist who also worked for Mossad. He smuggled Jews overland from Iraq to Iran, then out to Israel. The Iraqis arrested Ben-Porat several times and brutally interrogated him. Another Israeli who worked with him, Yehuda Tajar, could not maintain his cover as a Persian merchant because he did not speak Farsi. Tajar, a veteran of the pre-independence Palmach, the part of Haganah that specialized in guerrilla warfare and Arab pogroms, had been sent to Baghdad to run with Iraqi Jewish agents collecting intelligence for Israel. The Iraqis caught him. He was sentenced to life imprisonment but was traded in 1959, when Mossad gave Iraqi dictator Abdel Karim Kassem information on Iraqi dissidents who opposed him.[20]

American CIA operatives Kermit Roosevelt and Miles Copeland and British counterparts had arranged for the overthrow of the nationalistic Iranian Prime Minister Muhammad Mussadeq and the return of the Shah from his brief exile in 1953. All the parties then agreed that they needed more collaboration among intelligence services, including those of Israel. It took some time to get things organized. Finally, in September and October of 1957, senior Mossad officials, led by the current chief, Isser Harel, and his deputy, Yaakov Karoz, met in Paris and Rome with the first chief of SAVAK, Gen. Taymour Bakhtiar. Israel's main goal with regard to Iran was to encourage pro-Israeli and anti-Arab views in Iranian government circles. This was in keeping with U.S. and U.K. advice to cultivate a "peripheral" strategy of alliances with Turkey, Iran (the "northern tier"), and certain black African states (the "southern tier"). These states formed a ring encircling the Arab world.

From 1957 on, Mossad helped to train SAVAK, especially in interrogation techniques and clandestine work. Other Israeli agencies helped to train the Iranian gendarmerie. This was a role until then largely monopolized by Americans, especially the famous Gen. Norman Schwarzkopf, father of the victorious American military commander of the same name in Operation Desert Storm. Mossad aided SAVAK in various phases of the Kurdish rebellion in Iraq, another operation shared for a time with the Americans. The Israeli intelligence community was also put in charge of various civilian aid projects in Iran. Members of the Shah's own family and certain of his key aides personally watched over these operations and often profited from them.[21]

In addition to the joint ventures, arms deals, usually promoted by retired Israeli senior officers, brought as much as $225 million in 1978. In that year, Mossad began to warn the U.S. government that the Shah would not survive the rising tide of revolution. One of those final Israeli arms shipments consisted of Uzi submachine guns for the Shah's imperial guards. By the time the revolution began, Iranian fighter aircraft were maintained by Israel Aircraft Factories. Iran was then the largest supplier of oil to Israel. The Shah's relatives made deals with Israeli firms and set up such operations as the Trans-Asiatic Shipping Line, running oil tankers from Abadan, Iran, to the Israeli port of Elat. The same company also pumped oil through the Elat-Ashkelon oil pipeline inside Israel. Iran was part owner.[22]

Iranian intelligence support for covert Mossad operations was occasional but effective. On August 19, 1966, for instance, a few months after I took up my assignment as the *Monitor*'s Mideast correspondent, Beirut news bureaus were shaken by the news that after long preparation a Christian Iraqi pilot named Munir Rodfa had flown a Soviet-made MiG-19 to Israel. At the time, this plane was of great interest to the United States and NATO, as well as to Israel. Rodfa was rewarded with money and a new identity by an American girlfriend working for Israel. Mossad paid him through a Swiss bank account. Rodfa's family was smug-

gled out of Iraq into Iran, with the help of Kurdish rebels who regularly worked for
Israeli agents. The Mossad station in Tehran then flew the family to safety in
Europe, enabling them to join Rodfa in Tel Aviv.[23]

Events such as these, known to the elite leaders of the Iranian revolution though
not to the world, nor even widely in the West, had set the stage. During the
1980–88 Iran-Iraq War, Israel's military-industrial complex aided the Persian state
in its ancient conflict with the Arabs. How that conflict continued to develop was
to set a new and often erratic course for America's own confrontation with Iran.

4

The Roots of Irangate

A House Built on Sand

It was President Nixon, during the early 1970s, who built the Shah's Iran into what looked like a solid pillar of the *pax Americana* in the Middle East. Another pillar of that edifice was Israel. What few Americans realize, however, was that the huge U.S.-Iran deals of the Nixon era, concluded mainly by Secretary of State Henry Kissinger with the Shah, also set a seal, strongly imprinted with an American eagle, on the Iran-Israel relationship.

In 1966, the Shah met with Kermit Roosevelt, the senior CIA operative who had helped put Pahlavi back on the throne during the Mussadeq interlude in 1953. The two reviewed the reasons Iran had become indispensable to America. The main one: the imperial Iranian government was one of the few regimes in the region still willing to support and help Israel.

When President Lyndon B. Johnson came to power in November 1963, the Shah again stressed his support for Israel. For Johnson, far more than for his predecessor Kennedy, the Jewish state was the primary pillar of U.S. policy in the Middle East.

On February 18, 1975, the Shah took time out from one of his winter skiing holidays in Switzerland to meet Kissinger in Zurich. At this meeting, the Shah agreed to sell Israel Iranian oil over and above what it was already getting. Apparently feeling that he must do something for his friend, Egypt's President Anwar al-Sadat, the Shah set one condition: Israel must agree to Kissinger's plan to retreat from the Egyptian oilfields in Sinai, which it captured in 1967 and had been exploiting ever since.

By this time, Iran had been supplying Israel with oil for about a decade. The multinational oil companies themselves, especially in the British-led consortium that extracted and marketed Iran's oil, handled the trading. This gave the Iranian side plausible deniability when asked whether the Iranian *government* was selling oil to Israel. "It's the *companies* that market the oil, you know," the Shah would tell visitors who questioned him on this. "What they do with it when it leaves Iran is their business."

Once in Israel in the early 1970s, when I referred in an outgoing cable to supplies of oil going from Iran to Israel's port of Elat, the Israeli military censor politely but firmly asked me to delete that. "Why?" I asked, affecting an innocent air. "How does that harm Israel's security interests?"

A bit embarrassed, the censor, an affable and scholarly reservist, answered, "Well, actually it doesn't. But, you see, we have a deal with Iran not to talk about it. So we don't, and you can't." After the Iran-Iraq War ended in 1988, Iran resumed oil sales to its old customer Israel.

One good deal between friends often leads to another. Two weeks after the meeting in Zurich between the Shah and Kissinger, Hushang Ansary, Iran's minister of economy and finance, signed an agreement with Kissinger worth $15 billion, the largest of its kind ever signed between the United States and Iran. It committed Iran to spend $15 billion on American goods and services over the next five years. This included construction of eight large nuclear power plants to provide Iran with a total of 8,000 megawatts of electricity.[1]

The plants were never built. Later, the French and West Germans began construction of nuclear plants, likely, in the post-Khomeini era of the 1990s, to provide the basis for a military nuclear arm. The Kissinger commitments, however, did make it possible for the Shah shortly before his fall to obtain advanced and highly sensitive laser-enrichment technology from the United States for a secret nuclear weapons program, of which more later.

U.S.-Iranian-Israeli trilateral cooperation also helped the Kurds. For Israel and Iran, this was a way of weakening their mutual enemy Iraq. But it was also part of a grand strategic design.

In the 1950s, both the U.S. and the British governments had advised Israel to find ways to participate, if only secretly, in the northern tier of alliances tying together Iran, Turkey, Pakistan, the United States (as an observer in the so-called Central Treaty Organization, or CENTO), and Britain. Before the overthrow of the Ethiopian Emperor Haile Selassie, Israel and the United States were similarly bound to Ethiopia. The United States had a military reason. In Eritrea, a northern province that was still fighting in 1990 for independence from Ethiopia, the United States operated a top-secret electronic intelligence and monitoring station at Kagnew, near Asmara. It was like the ones in Iran but more tuned to communications eavesdropping than to monitoring missile tests. Israeli instructors and advisers were present in Ethiopia, and at various times Israelis have operated secret facilities in Ethiopia's Dahlak islands in the Red Sea to monitor Arab traffic and arms movements.

What Iran, Turkey, Ethiopia, and the rest of this disparate collection of allies had in common was a fear of both the Arabs and the Soviet Union. The Soviets were then established in the southern tier as well as on the Iranian border. There were Soviet naval and air bases in Aden and on Socotra Island off southern Arabia.

In December 1957, Turkish Prime Minister Adnan Menderes met Israeli emissary Eliyahu Sasson. This was followed up in 1958 by secret visits of Israeli intelligence officials, headed by Reuven Shiloah, a former (though no longer serving) chief of Mossad. David Ben-Gurion himself flew to Ankara to meet Menderes, and Golda Meir held equally secret meetings with Turkish officials in Istanbul. At that time, Kurdish minorities living in Iraq, Iran, Turkey, Syria, and the Soviet Union had already struck a troublesome and potent note of discord throughout the area.

Reuven Shiloah reached an agreement between Mossad and the Turkish National Security Service (TNSS), Ankara's equivalent of the CIA, for cooperation in many fields. The Turkish agency was already deeply concerned about stirrings of Kurdish nationalism in eastern Turkey, along the borders with Iran, Iraq, and Syria. Around the same time, Mossad concluded its formal cooperation agreement with SAVAK. At the end of 1958, all three agencies set up a group called Trident and agreed to hold meetings of their service chiefs every six months. Mossad was thus able to share intelligence being collected by the Turks and Americans in Turkey on Soviet clandestine operations there. In exchange, the Israelis were able to inform the Turks about Soviet or East bloc operations against Turkey from elsewhere in the Middle East. Turkey, in turn, helped to keep Israel informed about Syria's intentions toward that country. Israeli instructors trained Turkish secret agents in espionage, counterespionage, and the use of high-technology equipment.[2]

Mossad's joint operations with SAVAK were probably even more extensive than those with TNSS. In the 1960s, there was a constant exchange about Egyptian President Gamal Abdel Nasser's crusade for Arab unity and his subversive operations throughout the world. Close attention was paid to Iraq, the Iraqi Kurds, and various communist operations in Iran. The latter also inevitably called for close attention to the Kurds.

Especially during the Nixon administration, helping Iraqi Kurds in their fight against the Arab armies of Iraq, a central objective of Israel, became an important American goal as well. After several private agreements between Kissinger and the Shah, the United States channeled $16 million in CIA funds to the Kurdish Democratic Party of Mullah Mustapha Barzani, the aging, formidable leader of Kurdish partisans in Iraq.[3] "It is not enough, this little aid you Americans send," one of Barzani's sons, Massoud, told me during my visit to Kurdistan in March 1973, "but it helps to keep us and our fight going."

Israel had also been helping the Kurds, mainly through the intelligence channels explained above. This made the Kurds a favorite on Capitol Hill. Senators Jacob Javits, the New York Democrat, and Richard Stone, along with Congressman William Lehman, led support for the Shah because of the Israeli connection. On the House floor in February 1979, Lehman confused Iran with an Arab country, calling the Iranian revolution an example of Arab instability and stressing the strategic importance of Israel to the United States.[4]

Senator Javits sponsored or supported some cultural and economic projects in the Arab world, such as help for the increasingly beleaguered American University of Beirut (AUB), but he was not enthusiastic about American arms aid to the Arabs. He maneuvered to delay sales of Sidewinder missiles and other equipment to Saudi Arabia, while agreeing to massive weapon sales to imperial Iran. In 1976, it became public that his wife, Marian Javits, had accepted a $67,500 retainer to do public relations for Iran Air, the Iranian state airline. This was part of the public relations firm Ruder and Finn's $500,000 to promote the Shah's image. However, in early 1979, when Israel's own leaders were privately considering if and how they could continue their prerevolutionary cooperation with postrevolutionary Iran, Javits sponsored a congressional resolution hostile to the Iranian revolution.[5]

Economic Fallout of the Revolution

Against this contradictory background, by 1980 the two allies—Israel and the United States—saw a multiple threat posed by events in Iran, Iraq, and the Gulf. First of all, in February 1979, PLO chairman Yassir Arafat, archenemy of Israel's leaders, was welcomed to Iran by the new revolutionary rulers as the first foreign head of state. The historical irony was manifest: First, Arafat was treated as a hero and promised support (a support later diverted to Arafat's extremist Palestinian foes, like Ahmed Jibril of the Popular Front for the Liberation of Palestine–General Command [PFLP-GC]) in a country where Israelis had helped to train the secret police. It was also the country where Israeli pilots had trained on American-supplied Phantom F-4 fighter-bombers, which frequently bombed Palestinian targets in Lebanon and elsewhere in the Arab world. Finally, Iran had supplied much of Israel's oil, although this had already begun to change: in 1977 Israel foresaw the Shah's fall and in 1977–78 undertook negotiations with Nigeria, Mexico, and other oil producers.[6] At the same time, as Israeli supporter Michael Ledeen reported, Israel's Mossad station chief in Iran at the time of Khomeini's return had convinced the Israeli government to alert Iranian Jews about leaving. Washington found the Israeli assessment "alarmist."[7]

Arafat arrived in Tehran on February 17, 1979, and met with senior aides of Khomeini, though not with the Ayatollah himself. Iran's supreme leader did give Arafat a pledge of Iranian support for the PLO once the revolution had been consolidated. On February 18, 1979, Iran formally broke diplomatic relations with Israel. All remaining Israeli diplomats, trade mission representatives, and citizens were ousted from the country, and Iranian diplomats were recalled from Jerusalem.

In a statement issued on February 18, Arafat proclaimed, "Today Iran, tomorrow Palestine. . . . Every Iranian freedom fighter is represented in the Palestinian revolution." The revolution had "changed completely the whole strategy and policy in this area. It has been turned upside down." Arafat then claimed the former Israeli mission building and the next day inaugurated it as PLO headquarters in Tehran. In Jerusalem, Israel's elder soldier-statesman Moshe Dayan, then foreign minister, expressed regret at Iran's decision to break diplomatic ties. Simultaneously, he warned that if the Khomeini regime cooperated with "the PLO physically, it will be another matter and one very serious for us."[8] And so it turned out to be.

Within days, the PLO was operating its mission in Tehran as an embassy. It had also moved missions into Ahwaz and Khorramshahr in the heart of Iran's main oil region. As its first representative in Tehran, the PLO selected Hani al-Hassan, a member of the conservative Muslim wing of al-Fatah. This choice was intended to appeal strongly to the Ayatollah, although the proclaimed leader of the main branch of Shi'a Islam had little time for Sunni Muslim leaders.

From the perspective of both Tel Aviv and Washington, the PLO was now positioned strongly near the heart of the industrial West's main oil reserves in Saudi Arabia and the Persian Gulf states. PLO radicals saw themselves closer to realizing Arafat's implied promise after the Camp David peace conference in September 1978 to erode the U.S. position in the Middle East. A few months after the signing of the Camp David treaty in Washington on March 26, 1979, this threat was made more explicit by the PLO.

PLO leaders had marked the Shah, despite some token financial aid he had given to al-Fatah and his pro-Arab contingent in the UN, as Israel's strategic ally. At first, then, they considered his fall a major victory for the Palestinian cause. Later, after the Israeli invasion of Lebanon in 1982, Iranians proved to be embarrassing and cumbersome allies because they supported the extremist anti-Arafat Palestinian groups like Ahmed Jibril's PFLP-GC.

Some Palestinian leaders, like George Habash or Ahmed Jibril, had helped to train Iranian revolutionaries and their sympathizers. Members of Khomeini's elite, such as Saddeq Ghotbazadeh, foreign minister during the embassy hostage crisis but later executed for plotting against Khomeini, had known Palestinian leaders in Lebanon. New revolutionary leaders in Tehran such as Rafik Mohsen-Dost, the redoubtable leader and minister of the Revolutionary Guards, were soon to establish firm links with the Syrians and the Palestinian extremists and to set up radical pro-Iranian and anti-American forces in Iran like Hezbollah, the Party of God. Khomeini was to prove indifferent to later PLO overtures on behalf of U.S. Embassy hostages in Iran, and Arafat's initial success in gaining freedom for several women and blacks among the hostages was not repeated.

It was in the economic sphere that Israel and the United States felt the first consequences of the revolution. Trade between Iran and Israel ceased, and Iranian oil shipments to Israel were cut off. In their peak year of 1977, Israeli exports to Iran, though only partly compensating for the value of Israeli oil imported, were as much as $230 million.

Israel therefore made sure that the Camp David accord of March 1979 would guarantee its oil supply for the next fifteen years. This increased the already massive American commitment to Israel's security. Under Khomeini, the National Iranian Oil Company (NIOC) solemnly promised before the war with Iraq began to boycott any international oil company known to be providing crude oil to either Israel or South Africa, even if it came from non-Iranian sources.[9] This promise was apparently never put into effect. Once the Iran-Iraq War had begun in 1980, Iran could no longer be choosey about what oil companies it dealt with.

In the wake of the Iranian revolution, American and multinational companies filed huge compensation claims for assets and business lost in Iran. Israel and its new partner in peace, Egypt, were also under growing economic pressure from the revolution. The strains resulting from this pressure were to be absorbed ultimately by the U.S. administration, Congress, and the American taxpayer.

By mid-1979, the Khomeini regime had announced that it would comply with the Arab boycott and blacklist of firms dealing with Israel. This was administered by the Arab League boycott office in Damascus. Western businesses trying to operate in Iran discovered that contractors were banned if they still operated in Israel. Similar prohibitions were applied to foreign marketing, manufacturing, and trading firms with projects in the Jewish state. Iranian dock workers, customs officials, and others involved in foreign trade had already shown that they were ready to follow the example of workers in Iran's oilfields, mainly of Arab origin, with strikes. There had long been a PLO economic intelligence unit that followed up on boycott measures in Arab states such as Syria and Iraq. American companies were more affected than others because of U.S. antiboycott legislation forbidding them to comply with Arab boycott provisions. Many firms and merchant ships on the Arab blacklist did a large portion of their Mideast business in Iran.[10]

After the Camp David accord, Arab League states began to apply boycott measures against Egypt as well. The Shah had made a major foreign aid commitment to his close friend Sadat, estimated at about $1 billion. Much of it was for work in clearing the Suez Canal of war wreckage. An unspent $500 million was now withheld. Also, there was a total freeze on Iranian investments in Egypt, and Egypt had to look to American and, to a lesser extent, other Western backers to make up the difference.

Roots of the Secret Arms Deals

It was the military impact, rather than the economic consequences, of the Palestinian-Iranian alliance that was to lead to the secret Israeli arms deals with Iran and so deeply affect the course of the covert conflict between that country and America.

When I went to Israel with Defense Secretary Harold Brown in February 1979, at the height of the Iranian revolution, Israeli Defense Minister Ezer Weizman told us that even as Egypt had been removed from the roster of Israel's enemies, Iran would probably be added to it. Gen. Aharon Yaariv, retired military intelligence chief who had taken over the Institute for Strategic Studies at Tel Aviv University, said, "Iran is not going to field an army or send its F-14s against us tomorrow. But in the long run, we have to count the Iranians . . . as a member of the hostile

Arab-Islamic coalition." Iranian officers of the revolutionary armed forces proudly told Arab newsmen that Iran now considered itself "a confrontation state with Israel."[11]

By September 2, 1980, when Iraqi armed forces began their full-scale invasion of Iran, that country's land, sea, and air forces were a shambles. In 1979, they had been demobilized and dispersed, and remobilization was slow to get under way during the months before the war. An estimated $12 billion in orders for U.S. military equipment, from jet fighters to sidearms, had been canceled by the revolutionary government. Supplementing the efforts in Tehran of General Huyser (see chapter 2) were those of Erich von Marbod, a senior U.S. defense official sent by Secretary Brown. His task was to identify the revolutionary military officials and then persuade them to sign a memorandum agreeing to terminate the major U.S. foreign military sales program with Iran. He succeeded. This gave the United States, at least from the standpoint of American law, a basis for cutting off billions of dollars of advanced weapons and defense systems in the supply pipeline.[12]

The first to benefit was Israel. It received fifty-five General Dynamics F-16 fighter planes. These were part of a $3.5 billion order canceled in February 1979 by Iran, which could no longer make payments or train enough flight and maintenance personnel to keep the planes operating. As we saw earlier, seventy-eight Grumman F-14 Tomcats, paid for by the Shah's government, were guarded at air bases near Isfahan and Shiraz by politically purged personnel of the Iranian air force. However, as early developments in the 1980–88 Iran-Iraq War were to show, there were not enough fully trained Iranian pilots to fly these planes, let alone to service or fly the five squadrons of McDonnell Douglas Phantom F-4s that had been operational before the revolution. Moreover, there was a terrible lack of spare parts. Most notably, the F-4s lacked tires. Finally, for eighteen months before the Iraqi invasion, Iran's ground forces had been bogged down in mostly low-intensity fighting with Kurdish, Turkoman, Baluchi, and Azerbaijani separatists demanding full autonomy or more.

These were all considerations weighed by Israel's leaders as the Iran-Iraq War cast its shadow over the Middle East in the fall of 1980. Documents left behind by the Israeli mission in Tehran during its hasty evacuation in early 1979 showed that Israel Defense Forces (IDF) and the Shah's armed forces had been secretly collaborating on the development of surface-to-air tactical missiles designed to carry conventional or nuclear warheads up to 125 miles. The collaboration was codenamed Flower. One of the few weapons the United States had refused the Shah was the Pershing intermediate-range ballistic missile (IRBM), deployed in Western Europe as part of NATO's nuclear deterrent. The United States and Iran both had obligations under the 1968 Nuclear Non-Proliferation Treaty (NPT) not to allow nuclear or nuclear-capable weapons to reach Iran. The Shah therefore turned to Israel for help. As early as 1977, Iranian Defense Minister Gen. Hassan Toufanian had attended the test-firing of Israel's latest version of the Jericho intermediate-range missile, the prototype for Flower. The joint missile project was part of a secret Iranian-oil-for-Israeli-arms deal concluded in the summer of 1977 between Toufanian and Shimon Peres, then Israel's defense minister.[13] The Iranian revolution cut this short, and Flower never bloomed.

Israel was the first country to come to the rescue of Iran's beleaguered armed forces in the days immediately following the Iraqi invasion of September 1980. Iran was glad enough to welcome this secret help, which it carefully shielded from the eyes and ears of its only real Arab ally, Syria.

The American hostage crisis, still in full swing, precluded hope of U.S. help. On June 18, 1979, L. Bruce Laingen, the American chargé d'affaires in Tehran had taken command of the U.S. Embassy and tried to improve or at least expand relations with the government of Prime Minister Mehdi Bazargan. Later, the State Department's veteran Iran specialist Henry Precht and old Mideast negotiating specialist Harold Saunders met Iranian Foreign Minister Ibrahim Yazdi and other Iranian emissaries in the Iranian UN mission chief's residence in New York City. The problem of past and future U.S. military supplies was brought up, but nothing was resolved.[14]

President Carter had halted nearly all American trade with Iran. The Iraqi invasion touched off speculation about whether the administration would now trade military equipment that Iran desperately needed for American hostages. On September 19, 1980, less than three weeks after an "Islamic" government had been installed in Tehran under Prime Minister Muhammad Ali Rajai, two relatives and a close aide of the Ayatollah Khomeini met in Tehran with West German Ambassador Gerhard Ritzel. The object was to outline terms for a settlement of the hostage crisis.

When Ritzel conveyed the Iranian terms to the Americans, the latter found them surprisingly mild. As was often the case, the Iranians' private discourse failed to match the fiery anti-American rhetoric they spoke publicly. There was no demand for an apology for past American crimes against Iran and no repetition of public demands for a trial for the hostages.[15] On September 12, 1980, Khomeini repeated similar terms in a public speech.

It was at this point that President Carter delegated Deputy Secretary of State Warren Christopher, one of the most skilled diplomats in the U.S. foreign service, to meet with an unidentified Iranian official in West Germany. Christopher chose his negotiating team carefully. Members were senior U.S. officials who had either been involved in the hostage crisis from the start or who had the legal and administrative knowledge as well as the power to deal with it effectively. They included Lloyd N. Cutler, counsel to the president; U.S. Navy Capt. Gary Sick, from the National Security Council staff; Harold Saunders, assistant secretary of state for Near Eastern and South Asian affairs; Arnold Raphel, special assistant to the secretary of state; Robert Owen, State Department legal adviser; Deputy Secretary of State Robert Carswell; and Assistant Attorney General John M. Harmon. Douglas Dworkin, a special assistant to Christopher, was also part of the group.[16]

Christopher and his team asked the West German government for assurances from Iran that whoever was sent to meet them would have authority to speak for his government. The response was that the representative would indeed speak for

Khomeini himself and that Khomeini's four demands—U.S. noninterference in Iran's internal affairs, return of frozen Iranian assets, cancellation of U.S. claims against Iran, and return of the Shah's wealth—would be on the table.

The U.S. response, which governed Washington's position for months to come, was, first, to agree to the nonintervention pledge. As for the assets, returning them would involve complicated judicial procedures that could not be reversed by simply rescinding President Carter's freeze, but something might be done. Robert B. Owen believed that of the $4.8 billion in offshore assets (plus accrued interest) on deposit in branches of U.S. banks in Europe, some $3 billion could be released once the hostages were freed. Another $2.5 billion in gold bullion and securities that the Iranian government had deposited with the Federal Reserve Bank of New York could probably be released too. Thus Christopher told the Iranians they could have about $5.5 billion back if the hostages were freed. The rest of the frozen assets could not be released until Iran's borrowing from U.S. commercial banks was sorted out and a solution found for the problem of Iranian assets claimed by U.S. claimants.

Khomeini's third demand to cancel all claims could not be met, Christopher and his team felt. Cancellation of "valuable commercial claims by the U.S. government" would, in Owen's words, "surely have been regarded as a payment of ransom, conferring a multi-million dollar financial benefit on Iran at the expense of U.S. nationals."[17]

As for Khomeini's final demand for return of the Shah's wealth, the U.S. position was that Iran would have to resort to American courts. The Carter administration could only agree to facilitate this, while keeping the right to block removal of any Pahlavi assets until the matter was settled.

Early on September 14, 1980, Christopher, Carswell, Saunders, Owen, and Raphel flew to a West German air base. Four government Mercedes limousines whisked them to Schloss Gymnich, a palace surrounded by formal gardens and well-armed security guards. The Iranian negotiator was twenty-four hours late in arriving. He turned out to be Saddeq Tabatabai, whose sister was married to Khomeini's son Ahmed. The Christopher team codenamed him the Traveler and the name stuck. Because he was traveling alone, Tabatabai asked that West German Foreign Minister Hans-Dietrich Genscher attend the meeting. The Americans agreed.

On September 15, Christopher, Raphel, Genscher, and Tabatabai met secretly at a small West German safehouse outside Bonn. After Christopher explained the responses to Khomeini's demands, the Traveler wanted the United States to waive any claims that it or the hostages might want to raise against Iran as a result of the embassy seizure. These included personal damage claims concerning health or career. Christopher refused this. Tabatabai, moreover, was unwilling to accept the American argument that the U.S. administration could not affect court rulings in regards to restoring the Shah's private wealth to Iran.

Most crucial for the future, the Traveler asked whether after the hostages' release the United States would supply spare parts for the Iranian military arsenal of American equipment. Christopher "parried" this demand, Owen recalls, and it was later shelved temporarily by the Iranians after the Algerians began to play a crucial role in the hostage mediation.[18]

The question of billions of dollars of equipment and services purchased by the Shah and paid for but not delivered by the United States was to prove dramatic. At that time, the undelivered items—from fighter planes and submarines to software and hardware for training programs—lay stored in military warehouses throughout the continental United States. Before the Bonn talks, when the Iranians had asked through Genscher's office for a detailed inventory of what the Shah had ordered but had not received, a vague U.S. memorandum was supplied. "The objective," one of the drafters recalled with satisfaction, "was to whet their interest without relieving their ignorance."[19]

The Iranians and American negotiators held a second series of meetings, then flew home September 17 for consultations. Some of the American negotiators were left with the impression that they had the makings of a deal. The impression was fleeting. The outbreak of war on September 22 prevented the Traveler from going to Europe again, and the negotiations were suspended. There was a grim bottom line here for Iran. As Saddam Hussein's motorized legions and combat-eager Iraqi air force began what they thought would be a blitzkreig of a few days or weeks to bring Khomeini to his knees, the Americans would not come to the Ayatollah's aid. For that Khomeini would have to wait four years, after pro-Iranian forces had once again taken American hostages—this time in Lebanon.

Secret Arms Shipment Network

Israel, the Zionist state that Khomeini had so reviled, not only came to his aid but did so with a carefully selected program of military aid applied where it would do the most good.

Preparations began in Tel Aviv, Jerusalem, and European capitals during the first few days of the war. While Christopher and his American team were still reporting to President Carter on their secret talks in West Germany, Iran was moving. On October 5, 1980, the Iranian government set up a front company called Interparts. Its purpose was simple: to buy everything possible for the Iranian war effort on the world arms market. In Athens, an intermediary called the All Trade Projects Company was set up. Its Paris representative was a Lebanese arms dealer named Ahmed Haydari, who carried with him to France a letter authorizing him to buy arms and equipment for the Iranian Defense Ministry. A complicated trigger mechanism was put in place so that Iranian funds from Iran's Bank Melli Paris branch could be transferred to the Banque de la Mediterranée, also in Paris. Israeli and other arms purchased by All Trade Projects for Iran were to be inspected and certified by Iran's chargé d'affaires in the Iranian embassy in Madrid, Muhammad Behnam. He provided false end-user certificates.

Israel's first known shipment to revolutionary Iran was made on October 24,

1980. It came only four days after Carter, in an election campaign speech, had spoken of the possibility of supplying spare parts and unfreezing Iranian assets if the U.S. hostages were released.

Meanwhile, Iraq's Soviet-made MiG and Sukhoi aircraft and French-made Mirage combat planes were blasting Iranian military positions, cities, and troops almost unopposed. For the Iranian high command, it was essential to get some of the already aging squadrons of American Phantom F-4 fighter-bombers into the air to fly missions against the Iraqi invaders.

The Israeli and Iranian arms intermediaries managed to find 250 retreaded tires for the F-4s. Some $500,000 was paid by Iran through a secret account in the Algemene Bank Nederland in Zurich. Documents in my possession show that funds were paid into the Israeli Purchasing Mission's account with Israel's Bank Hapoalim in Zurich.[20] A Luxembourg air charter firm, Cargolux, was hired to fly the tires, as well as a secret shipment of engines from Britain through Italy for Iran's British-made Scorpion tanks, spare parts from Italy for U.S. M-60 tanks, and battlefield radios from Spain. This materiel was flown from Nimes, France, to Tehran, all under false bills of lading.

By December 1980, Interparts had expanded its business with Israel and others. Now a contract could be signed with Interparts, described as "an Iranian trading company residing at Varahram Street, No. 25, Tehran," for no less than $73.5 million. Rocket launchers and huge quantities of ammunition were among the items covered. Over fifty Americans were, of course, still held by Iranian captors, undeterred by the Carter administration's freeze on U.S. weapons deliveries.

Israel's end of the new and booming business with Iran was handled mainly by retired Israeli Col. Yacov Nimrodi. He conducted the business from International Desalination Equipment Limited at 49 Ibn Givrol Street, Tel Aviv. By July 24, 1981, more than six months into the Reagan era, secret business with Iran had escalated to the point where Nimrodi and a Col. K. Denghan were able to sign a $135.8 million contract for Lance missiles, 155mm cannon shells, Copperhead missiles, and sixty-eight Hawk antiaircraft missiles. All items were badly needed by Iran, which was fighting the Iraqis to a standstill and preparing for a counteroffensive.

Born of a family of Iraqi Jewish émigrés in Jerusalem, Nimrodi had served as the last Israeli military attaché in Tehran under the Shah and as an aide to Gen. Ariel Sharon during the 1967 Arab-Israeli War. He retired in 1975, by which time he already spoke fluent Farsi and dealt with top members of the Shah's military establishment on a first-name basis. During the late 1970s, he returned to Tehran as a "businessman," then as a government official.[21] Later, in the heyday of Col. Oliver North and Vice Adm. John Poindexter's covert arms operations with Israel, Iran, and the Central American contras, Nimrodi played a central role.

Like Mike Harari, the former Israeli colonel and Mossad agent who did important business for Panama's Gen. Manuel Noriega, Nimrodi belonged to a tough breed of Israeli military men who, upon leaving the defense force, found themselves with nothing to do. Lucrative business deals abounded for men with their experience, and the Iran-Iraq War brought many such opportunities.

Another Israeli associated with the Iranian business was Zvi Reuter, former military attaché with Israeli missions in Amsterdam, Copenhagen, and Oslo. At the time of the Iranian revolution, Reuter became assistant director of an Israeli agency whose Hebrew acronym is SIBAT (known to American insiders in Israel as the Foreign Defense Assistance and Defense Export Organization, or FODADE). SIBAT handles a large share of Israel's multibillion dollar export business, mostly arms. "We send cheaper and better goods than our competitors," Zvi Reuter commented, ". . . and we deliver without political conditions. We're not expecting favors from anyone. . . . He just has to pay, and pay immediately. . . . [T]hat helps our arms industry to survive." Moshe Mandelbaum, who ran the Israeli state bank, went so far as to say that income from Israeli arms sales to countries like Iran helped the state of Israel itself to survive.[22]

The business supervised by Nimrodi and SIBAT, insofar as it involved American-made equipment—and most of it did—was subject by law to U.S. authorization. Late in 1980, Morris J. Amitay, executive director of the powerful American Israel Public Affairs Committee (AIPAC), approached Ronald Reagan's campaign manager, Richard V. Allen (who later became the president's first national security adviser). How, Amitay asked, would the incoming administration view Israel's shipment to Iran of wheel and brake assemblies vital to keeping that country's F-4s in the air? Allen's answer is not on record, but no such shipment appears to have been made around that time.[23]

While Israeli tires and spares kept at least part of Iran's air force in the air, flying isolated but carefully chosen missions against targets such as Iraq's Fao oil terminal in the Persian Gulf, Israel and the Khomeini regime kept up their network of secret communications. About a hundred Israeli advisers and technicians flew to Iran on civilian flights. They were sheltered in an isolated and heavily guarded camp on the northern outskirts of Tehran. They remained throughout the war and were reported still there after the August 1988 ceasefire.[24] This happened despite U.S. involvement in the war against Iran and despite the fact that since 1982 Hezbollah, the terrorist party created by Iran in Lebanon, had been involved in anti-Israeli and anti-American activity.

Shortly after President Reagan's inauguration, when the American hostages had finally been set free, Secretary of State Alexander Haig belatedly gave Israel permission to do what it had already been doing since September 1980: ship U.S.-made spare parts for fighter planes to Iran. David Kimche, another old Iranian hand from Mossad and now the director-general of the Israeli Foreign Ministry, had been discussing this issue with Robert C. McFarlane—at the time a counselor of Haig at the State Department and soon to become national security adviser.[25] McFarlane would play a central part in both the covert arms-for-hostages deals with Iran and the U.S. military effort against Iran, Syria, and their allies in Lebanon.

Iran made prompt payments. In early 1981, after the Haig authorization, the

Bank Melli sent a letter of credit worth over $73.5 million to Paris, some $53 million of which went to Ahmed Haydari for arms purchased on the open market. Israel received $20 million, probably through the Athens firm, to pay for 106mm recoilless cannon and ammunition. El Al flew cargo flights to Lisbon on March 21 and May 23, 1981. Arms cargoes were transferred to Iran Air flights in Lisbon on March 25 and May 25. Other money known to have been allocated for arms purchases seems to have vanished.

A misadventure on July 18, 1981, lifted the veil that had so far covered Israel's arms supplies to Iran. On that day, an Argentine CL-44 turboprop cargo plane en route from Tel Aviv to Tehran strayed over the Soviet-Turkish border and was apparently shot down by Soviet jets. The pilot, a Scot named Stuart Allan McCafferty, is presumed to have died in the crash. In a deal negotiated in London, McCafferty had been hired to deliver 360 tons of tank spares and ammunition. His Swiss partner, Andrew Jenni, leaked the information that the CL-44 was on its third of a projected twelve runs on the Tel Aviv–Larnaca–Tehran route.

McCafferty was intercepted on his return run. Some aviation experts believe the Soviets lured him into Soviet airspace by sending fake navigation signals, for the plane made a sudden right turn before disappearing from Turkish monitoring screens. Newsmen who had met him said McCafferty, a former cargo-loading supervisor at Amsterdam's Schiphol Airport, had come out of a modest retirement in Miami to fly the secret missions from Israel to Iran.[26] The sudden demise of one more soldier of fortune was, of course, not enough to halt Yacov Nimrodi and his enterprising Israeli arms exporters: less than a week after the crash, Nimrodi and Colonel Denghan signed their hefty $135.8 million agreement.

By early 1982, the Reagan administration was already aware that Israel was preparing the invasion of Lebanon. It came in June 1982, resulting in the near-destruction of Syria's air force, the defeat of Syrian ground forces in Lebanon, and President Hafez Assad's fateful decision to allow Iranian Revolutionary Guards into his country. By this time, as later U.S. intelligence studies show, Israel was shipping arms (not of American origin) to Iran, and men like Yacov Nimrodi and middleman Manuchehr Ghorbanifar were arranging private deals involving U.S. arms. McFarlane was to testify that the CIA had never told him of these Israeli deals. Following that testimony, he cabled Secretary of State George Shultz that it was obvious the Israeli channels had long existed. A National Security Council (NSC) staffer said that McFarlane discounted the reports because there was no conclusive evidence, and Israeli Prime Minister Shimon Peres had assured the United States no such trade was going on.[27]

Much later I spoke with General Aharon Yaariv, who in 1989 was running a somewhat dovish Israeli think tank called the Institute for Strategic Studies at Tel Aviv University. What, I asked him, was the sense of covert Israeli arms supplies to an Iran whose leader had proclaimed his intention to destroy Israel? Already, I reminded him, Hezbollah was organizing suicide attacks on Israeli troops in southern Lebanon. Yaariv shrugged.

You're right, of course, at least for the present. But you and I both know about Israel's strategic interest in keeping Iran friendly and helping it to survive the attacks of our common enemies—today the Iraqi Arabs, three millennia or so ago, King Nebuchadnezzar and the Babylonians. Besides, plenty of people, including Israelis, have made a lot of money on the arms deals with Iran.[28]

By the time Iranian forces entered Lebanon to confront and help to drive out the U.S. Marines and French troops of the multinational peace force, the Tehran–Tel Aviv axis was functioning effectively.

5

The Road to Mecca:
Saudi Oil,
American Defense

Saudi Requests for Aid

Friday, September 26, 1980, 10:55 P.M. President Carter's national security adviser, Zbigniew Brzezinski, was trying to relax at home after a day of coping with the steadily worsening Mideast situation. Iraq had invaded Iran. Suddenly, the telephone rang. It was the duty officer in the White House Situation Room. A few hundred miles north of the Saudi oilfields, key to the continued economic prosperity of the United States, there was serious mischief afoot.

For the past seventy-two hours, Washington had been buzzing with reports of an impending Iraqi attack on Iranian ports, oil facilities, and military and naval installations along the Gulf coast.[1] There was nothing surprising about this. After all, the two countries were at war. What worried King Khaled ibn Saud of Saudi Arabia, guardian of the holy cities of Mecca and Medina and the main ally of the United States in the Arab world, was that Iraq's dictator, President Saddam Hussein, was planning to use the territory of some of the Persian Gulf emirates for the attack.

In addition, as Pentagon officials and a reliable private source at one of the Arab embassies in Washington whispered, the Iraqis hoped to land helicopters and use

47

places like Dubai and Oman's Musandam Peninsula, directly on the Strait of Hormuz, as bases for their gunships. Among some of the immediate Iraqi objectives were offshore oilfields owned or operated by American companies and three small but strategic islands near the straits: Big and Little Tunb and Abu Musa, which I had visited aboard one of the Shah's warships in 1971, shortly after Britain had relinquished control in the area to the Shah.

What Brzezinski heard that night from the White House duty officer was that the Saudis had urgently repeated requests for the deployment of American AWACS (airborne warning and control system) planes, air defense reinforcements, and greater intelligence backing.[2] The latter probably included a request for greater access to U.S. intelligence satellite and SR-71 Blackbird reconnaissance photos.

The next day Brzezinski called a meeting of the Security Coordination Council, an inner cabinet body dealing with sensitive issues. In a note to President Carter, the Polish-born Brzezinski, an intrepid cold warrior in the contest then raging with the Soviet Union, wrote:

> September 26, 1980: Iran-Iraq. It is important to differentiate between short-run danger to the oil supplies, which we are right in *minimizing*, and the longer-range threat to the region—which we should not underplay. The country must understand that the long-term effort in the area requires fortitude and sacrifice to accomplish what Truman did in Europe.[3]

All of this served as a pointed reminder that the United States shared with Saudi Arabia at least two major security interests that were on a par with oil security. One was the perceived threat from the Soviet Union, which had already invaded Afghanistan; the other was the perceived menace from the revolution of Shi'a masses in Iran, which Khomeini hoped to export.

Between September 27 and October 7, 1980, at a series of crisis meetings, Defense Secretary Harold Brown and Brzezinski advocated what the latter called "an immediate and positive reaction to the Saudi request" for help. Arguing for a go-slow policy were Secretary of State Edmund Muskie and his deputy, Warren Christopher, by now already deeply embroiled in the Iranian hostage crisis. Vice President Walter Mondale seemed to lean toward the caution of Muskie and Christopher, who wanted to avoid provoking the Soviets, the Iranians, and the Iraqis. There was also concern that if the Soviets were asked to cooperate in reaching a settlement, it would legitimize their position in the Gulf, something the administration's cold warriors opposed.

On September 28, President Carter opted for Brzezinski's view that America's special relationship with Saudi Arabia should have priority. An order was soon issued to deploy the AWACS planes to Saudi Arabia, where American crews would fly them with Saudi insignia. The order was preceded by some acrimony between Brzezinski and Muskie, who worried at one point that it might cause World War III. President Carter also sent a message to French President Valéry Giscard d'Estaing proposing a joint U.S.-French naval presence to keep open the Strait of Hormuz, something the French agreed to and discreetly implemented as time went on.[4] In the meantime, American pressure was applied directly and through the Saudis on the smaller Gulf states to remain neutral, preventing both Iraqi and Iranian military operations in their territories. Finally, however, Saddam Hussein and his military commanders desisted from the attack on Iranian installations. This was one campaign in America's conflict with Iran that never had to be fought.

Heated discussions continued into October 1980 about how and how much the United States could contribute to defending the security of the Persian Gulf and, directly and indirectly, the security of the Saudi throne itself. President Carter agreed with Brown and Brzezinski that Saudi-U.S. military cooperation should increase. A new military-diplomatic team was sent to beef up the several hundred U.S. military advisers who had long been operating in the kingdom. During their final weeks in office and despite past battles with congressional friends of Israel and the powerful American Israel Public Affairs Committee (AIPAC), Carter administration officials began planning to upgrade further U.S. military assistance to Saudi Arabia.

The loss of Iran—so it was regarded in Washington by now—and Soviet military moves in Ethiopia, South Yemen, and Afghanistan led to what was called the arc of crisis. This concept referred to Soviet- or Iran-influenced aggression or subversion threatening U.S. friends from the southern tip of Africa to the Pamir Mountains in Afghanistan near the Soviet and Chinese frontiers. In terms of U.S. security planning, there were now three areas of vital importance: Western Europe, the Far East, and the Middle East.[5]

It was now clear to Washington strategists that there was one key Arab player in the confrontation, whether they liked it or not. That player was the Kingdom of Saudi Arabia.

The Saudi Connection

In 1981, Dr. William Quandt, a distinguished scholar and Carter administration official who was mainly responsible for drafting the Camp David peace treaty, tried to imagine what might happen to American interests if any one of a series of imaginary events were to occur during the 1980s. His hypotheses also apply to the 1990s, as the United States approaches the year 2000 with growing dependence on Saudi Arabian oil. Suppose, suggested Quandt, that radical military officers overthrew the Saudi royal family. In the turmoil to follow, Saudi oil production could virtually stop and ARAMCO personnel would have to flee the country. Another scenario would be hostile aircraft—Iranian, Israeli, Iraqi, or Yemeni—knocking out a substantial part of Saudi Arabian oil production.

These and other hypothesized events did not take place during the eight years of war between Iraq and Iran. But something equally disturbing for the Saudi rulers did happen, and the United States could do nothing about it. In July 1987, during the pilgrimage of millions of Muslims to the holy cities of Mecca and Medina, several hundred people were killed in a clash between militant Iranian pilgrims and

Saudi security forces. Khomeini's propaganda machine shouted that King Fahd, who had replaced the late King Khaled ibn Saud in 1982, had embraced a traitorous form of American Islam and no longer deserved to have the guardianship of the holy places (this role had been added to the Saudi king's official title, Protector of the Holy Shrines).

Americans, as Quandt pointed out, had benefited enormously from the long and close relationship with the Saudis, nurtured by America's need for their oil and their need for U.S.-provided security. American oil companies had continued to make enormous profits because of the phenomenon that appeared well before World War II: to get oil out of the Arabian Peninsula cost a tiny fraction, sometimes one-tenth or less, of the cost of production in the United States and most of the rest of the world. U.S. companies, moreover, had the lion's share of the huge Arabian Peninsula market. American military and diplomatic officials played extremely important, if often low-profile, parts in the unfolding drama of growing Saudi power.

Add to all this the strong anti-communist thrust of the Saudi royal family, and you have what was perceived as a great advantage for Western policy. Many Saudi operations targeted the Soviet Union and its adventures in the Third World. Well-funded Saudi think tanks supported propaganda and scholarly publications on Islam and ethnic nationalism among the Muslim people of Soviet and Chinese central Asia. Secret Saudi funds went to some of the Eritreans fighting the rule of Marxist Ethiopia. This was partly because most of the Eritrean leaders were Muslim and opposed the considerable Israeli influence in Ethiopia, because they were anti-communist and anti-Soviet, and last though not least, because the Saudis regarded their efforts on behalf of the Eritreans as also serving the interests of their ally, America.

Saudi—as well as Kuwaiti—aid and loans, given both directly and through various Arab multinational banks, bolstered poor countries in Africa and Asia to prevent their regimes from "going communist." Hundreds of millions of dollars in Saudi funds were pumped to Muslim mujaheddin rebels in Afghanistan, even after 1989 when the Soviet invaders left that country in a shambles. In this the Saudis were supporting U.S. anti-Soviet policy and also countering the influence of Khomeini in Afghanistan. To gain a strong foothold there, Iran had been supporting Shi'ite factions among the mujaheddin with propaganda, arms, and money.

Such factors as Saudi support for Afghanistan, during the Reagan and Bush administrations especially, inflamed the mullahs of Tehran. American Islam, as several hard-line Iranian leaders such as former Prime Minister Mir Hussein Mussavi called it, was an enemy to be destroyed in Saudi Arabia. Meanwhile, some private Saudi citizens such as the multimillionaire tycoon Adnan Kashoggi operated in international markets favoring U.S.-supported causes in Central America, notably that of the Nicaraguan contras. Paradoxically, other Saudis, who could scarcely have been acting without approval from their king, helped to promote the clandestine arms-for-hostages deals that provided weapons during the Iran-Iraq War for Saudi Arabia's and America's declared enemies in Tehran.

The Game of Power Poker in the Arabian Peninsula

The nature and full extent of the American commitment to Saudi Arabia, and the consequential Iranian challenge to America in the Saudi kingdom, are poorly understood in the United States and other Western industrial countries. To grasp the huge game of power poker between the United States and Iran in the Arabian Peninsula, it is necessary to recall a few basic facts about the origins of American involvement on the Arabian Peninsula.

In the nineteenth century, the presence on that peninsula of a huge underground lake of petroleum that would transform the West's industrial establishments and the world economy had been long suspected. Searching for it were such wheeler-dealers and adventurers as Baron Julius von Reuter, the first European financier to win mineral and oil concessions in Iran; Calouste Gulbenkian, who came to be known as Mr. Five Percent for the fabulous commissions he collected; and William d'Arcy, founding father of the Anglo-Iranian Oil Company, who lost millions in fruitless oil prospecting before he succeeded in Iran. In this century, it took a major depression and a new world war to bring home to the leaders of the United States the importance of the treasure trove of oil that in the 1930s was discovered in Saudi Arabia by the forerunners of ARAMCO.

In 1930, as the Great Depression nearly paralyzed American and European economies, Saudi Arabia's founding monarch, King Abd al-Aziz ibn Saud, invited Charles R. Crane to visit him. Crane was a wealthy American philanthropist who in 1919 had led a commission to investigate the controversial future of the lands of the ex–Ottoman Empire, including Palestine. During his visit, Crane promised to send the Saudi king an American mining engineer to examine the country's water, agriculture, and mineral resources. The engineer was Karl Twitchell, described by ARAMCO historians as a Vermont Yankee. In 1931–32, Twitchell crisscrossed Arabian deserts in search of water sources (essential for any work undertaken in the desert), mineral outcrops, and oil. Two geologists of Standard Oil of California (SOCAL) soon struck oil in Bahrain, an emirate under British protection, and SOCAL recommended new efforts to find it in Saudi Arabia.

With the help of Twitchell and British author and adventurer Harold St. John Philby (father of the British double agent Harold ["Kim"] Philby, who defected to the Soviet Union from Beirut in 1963), SOCAL's team negotiated a deal with the Saudi government. The United States had gone off the gold standard (gold was the only currency appreciated by Arab rulers at the time), and President Roosevelt had closed U.S. banks. Crude oil was selling for less than fifty cents a barrel. After weeks of close bargaining, SOCAL's lawyer, Lloyd N. Hamilton, signed a concession agreement in Jidda on May 29, 1933. SOCAL agreed to loan Saudi Arabia about $250,000 in gold and pay royalties of four shillings (about one dollar) per ton of oil produced. The government would get another quarter million dollars in gold once oil was found in commercial quantities. In return, SOCAL got the exclusive right to prospect for and produce oil in eastern Saudi Arabia and the preferential right (that is, the right to additional areas by matching others' offers) in most of the rest of Saudi Arabia. The sixty-year agreement was later extended to the year 2002.

Prospecting began almost at once, and SOCAL applied its Texas experience by bringing to Saudi Arabia a Fairchild 71 high-winged monoplane with photographic equipment. Without delay, SOCAL's intrepid prospectors ran afoul of Muslim bureaucracy: they were, at first, restricted to flying high without using the radio. Eventually, they were allowed to take pictures and coordinate work with geologists on the ground. After some disappointments with wells near Dammam, geologist Max Steineke and paleontologist Richard A. Bramkamp, working from their base camp at Dhahran, succeeded in drilling the first commercially viable well, Dammam no. 7. It soon proved to be the largest known oilfield in the world.

In 1935 SOCAL and the Texas Company (Texaco) combined their interests between Egypt and Hawaii, forming a new operating group called Casoc and providing funds to enlarge the oil operation in Saudi Arabia. On May 1, 1939, as the clouds of World War II gathered in Europe and Adolf Hitler's logistics specialists eyed the new Mideast oilfields from afar, King Abd al-Aziz ceremonially opened a valve into the first tanker at the new port of Ras Tanura, near Dhahran.

Hitler and his Axis partner, Benito Mussolini, were determined to knock out Western oil enterprises in the Gulf. Wehrmacht Marshal Erwin Rommel led an Axis offensive across North Africa, which failed to reach the Allies' (America was still neutral) main oil and communications artery, the Suez Canal in Egypt. On the night of October 19, 1940, after the fall of France, Mussolini struck at the American oil enterprise in Saudi Arabia, mistakenly thinking that he was hitting the British one.

Four big Savoia-Marchetti S-82 Italian seaplanes took off from the Mediterranean island of Rhodes, flew the long course to the Gulf without refueling, and targeted the Bahrain Petroleum Company (BAPCO) refinery in that British protectorate. On the way, one of the Italian pilots lost contact with his mates, saw the lights of Dhahran below, and released his bombs, thinking he was hitting Bahrain. No real damage was done, but everyone in the Casoc establishment knew then a war was on.[6]

Soon U.S. warships were moved into the Gulf. (From that day until the advent of Operation Desert Shield and Desert Storm in 1990–91, there has been a U.S. commitment to defend Saudi Arabian oilfields from any military or political encroachment.) Possible aggressors were seen to be the Soviet Union, Iran, and finally Iraq. Meanwhile, a great deal of American and British commercial rivalry led to bad feeling over oil concessions.

After Hitler attacked the USSR in June 1941 and Japan struck Pearl Harbor on December 7, 1941, resupply of the Soviet Union through Iran became a major task for the Allies. This led to the Anglo-American-Soviet occupation of Iran and a muting of Anglo-American rivalry. The Soviets made it clear that they coveted oil concessions that the Anglo-Iranian Company, to say nothing of American oil companies, was eyeing.

The U.S. government became increasingly worried about the rate of domestic oil consumption and the vast amount of petroleum needed for the war effort. When final victory was at hand, U.S. Secretary of Defense James V. Forrestal made an accurate prophecy:

> Within the next twenty-five years the United States is going to be faced with very sharply declining oil reserves and because oil and all its byproducts are the foundations of the ability to fight a modern war, I consider this to be one of the most important problems of the government. I don't care which American company or companies develop the Arabian reserves, but I think most emphatically that it should be *American*.[7]

By war's end, the recently installed Muhammad Reza Shah Pahlavi was concerned with safeguarding his kingdom's oil resources as well as developing them. He did not share the concern of the Saudi king, his potential rival, for the fate of Palestine. At the time, Palestine was still a territory under British mandate. Jewish nationalists, however, were making life difficult for the British military administration while they planned the creation of a Jewish state.

It is arguable that the Saudi-American relationship, which some cynical commentators might call the $64 billion misunderstanding, began not in the Gulf, Iran, or Saudi Arabia, but in Egypt. In February 1945, aboard U.S. Navy cruiser *Quincy*, anchored in the Great Bitter Lake of the Suez Canal, King Abd al-Aziz had met President Franklin D. Roosevelt. The two reaffirmed the preeminence of the United States in developing Saudi oil resources as well as in defending those resources and the kingdom. In March 1945, the king followed up this meeting by declaring war and siding with the Allies. In a letter to the president, Abd al-Aziz stated that all countries should receive and assist the Jewish victims of the Nazi holocaust, that Palestine could not be expected to bear the full burden alone. Implicitly but strongly, the Saudi king expressed the view of the other Arab rulers that there should be no Jewish state in Palestine.

Roosevelt, in his reply, reminded Abd al-Aziz of his personal assurance at their meeting that the U.S. government would make no change in its policy toward the Palestine question (this policy did not yet support a Jewish state) without full consultation with both Arab and Jewish sides. Roosevelt promised to undertake no action that might prove hostile to the Arab people. Two weeks later, as ARAMCO's official history records, Roosevelt told the U.S. Congress:

> Of the problems of Arabia, I learned more about the whole problem, the Muslim problem, the Jewish problem, by talking with Ibn Saud [King Abdel-Aziz] for five minutes than I could have learned in the exchange of two or three dozen letters.[8]

Herein lay the great misunderstanding between the United States and Saudi Arabia, one that lay at the heart of the Arab-Israel dispute: the Arabs tended to believe, or wanted to believe, that subsequent U.S. rulers would honor Roosevelt's promises. William Quandt points out that while the Saudi king was adamant in opposing a Jewish state, Roosevelt's "own views were flexible." Harry Truman, Roosevelt's successor, was often to be reminded during the three turbulent years that followed—the state of Israel proclaimed its independence on May 15, 1948—that Roosevelt had "assured Abd al-Aziz that he would not help the Jews against the Arabs and would not take any steps that were hostile to the Arab people." There was also the question of his promise of consultations on the Palestine problem before making any final decisions—such as President Truman's immediate decision to recognize the new state of Israel.[9]

What the Arab world as a whole and individual Saudi rulers with more or less emphasis have since spoken of as Truman's violation of Roosevelt's commitments became the main bone of contention between three generations of American administrations and Muslim rulers. Added to the latter's ranks, since 1979, are the leaders of the Islamic republic of Iran. They have chastised Saudi rulers for not holding the "Great Satan," America, to promises like those made by President Roosevelt.

Fourth of July in Jidda

As war between Israel and the Arab states loomed for the third time since 1948—this time triggered by the desire of President Anwar al-Sadat of Egypt and President Hafez Assad of Syria to recover territory lost to Israel in 1967—I experienced the realities of the Saudi-American dilemma over oil and Palestine.

It was July 4, 1973, Independence Day for Americans. I found myself observing it in Saudi Arabia's sweltering west coast port of Jidda. Jim Hoagland of the *Washington Post* and I were driven by government car up horseshoe turns to the much cooler town of Taif, Saudi Arabia's summer capital. Our purpose there was to get an interview with King Faisal.

Almost twenty years earlier, on November 9, 1953, King Abd al-Aziz had died after a remarkable life's work of unifying and modernizing his country. The reign of his son, King Saud, lasted until 1964 and saw some of the kingdom's most turbulent events: a temporary break with Britain and France when they joined Israel to attack Egypt in the Suez War of 1956; the gradual hardening of the kingdom's opposition to the program of militant Egyptian "socialism" (conducted in neighboring Yemen and elsewhere with strongly messianic and expansionist overtones); and financial, economic, and social difficulties as spending exceeded oil revenues.

In November 1964, Saud's health and grip on affairs failing, the kingdom's elders persuaded Crown Prince Faisal, his younger brother, to take the throne. Faisal was an educated, traveled statesman who became respected even by Saudi Arabia's adversaries for his courage, integrity, and devotion to religion. He was abstemious in his personal life and a tireless worker, not characteristics typical of the Saudi ruling family. As Saudi UN delegate, he made a speech during the 1947 UN debate on the Palestine question and stated his opposition to the partition of that territory into Jewish and Arab states. Many at the time gave him a large share of the credit (or responsibility, depending on the viewpoint) for the partition's defeat. At home, Faisal pushed for unpopular fiscal, administrative, and educational reform. He was the first Saudi ruler to ordain the creation of girls' schools, and he ordered the army to surround and protect the first such school from the fury of hard-line tradition-alists.

On that July 4, Jim Hoagland and I were aware that Faisal had been telling numerous Americans, including Frank Jungers, chief executive of ARAMCO, that unless America was willing to pressure Israel into withdrawing from the occupied territories, Saudi Arabia could no longer be taken for granted as the free world's major supplier of oil. In other words, for the first time in the Arab-Israel conflict, Saudi Arabia—the biggest and most important of the Arab oil producers—was putting Western leaders on notice that oil would be used as a weapon, if necessary. After a short wait in Taif, Jim and I were informed that we could make a courtesy call on King Faisal, but only that—no interview and probably no pictures. If I remember correctly, we were not allowed to bring a tape recorder either. As it turned out, the king was holding a traditional *majlis*, which in the absence of anything resembling a parliament in Saudi Arabia was his main means of contact with his population.

In one corner of the hall where Faisal sat modestly enthroned in an armchair, his interpreter and chamberlain standing by, we spotted two Lebanese magazine writers whom we knew in Beirut. Notebooks and ballpoints in hand, with a still camera or two, they were ready to take down anything said during our courtesy call. They would probably make up an interview—common practice, alas, among our Leba-nese colleagues from Beirut in those days—or embroider anything given to us for their own purposes.

We sensed that one of Faisal's famous lectures was coming, and it did. For about forty-five minutes, in eloquent Arabic, he repeated his familiar idea equating Is-rael's state doctrine of Zionism with communism. Both, he insisted, were part of a global conspiracy to frustrate the Palestinians in particular and to cheat the Arabs in general of their birthright. Faisal followed this with pointed warnings that if the United States considered itself a friend and ally of Saudi Arabia, as it always maintained, it would do the right thing in regard to the Israeli question. Otherwise, the kingdom could no longer go on meeting America's oil requirements or acting as a close partner in other domains.

We jotted everything down as fast as we could, then drank cups of strong, spiced coffee served by a dignified retainer who clinked his cups in various rhythms to indicate what stage of protocol we had reached. When the audience ended, we were greeted by a familiar figure dressed in a flowing white robe. He was the kingdom's leading commoner: Sheikh Ahmed Zaki Yamani. Educated at Harvard Law School and New York University's Law Institute, among other places, and absolute master of Saudi oil policy, he was a man to whom Faisal, as well as presidents, kings, energy ministers, and executives of multinational oil companies, listened carefully.

In his courteous and always good-humored way, Yamani greeted us. We had each met him before (I when first visiting Saudi Arabia with the late Professor

A. J. Meyer of Harvard, a consultant, friend, and guru to many American-educated Saudi economic strategists and planners).

"King Faisal's words weren't well translated," Yamani told us. "Come to lunch at my home and I'll explain what he said, and pass on a couple of other items as well."

Lunch at Yamani's simply but tastefully furnished villa in Taif was delightful as well as informative. The approaching war between Israel and the Arabs, to which King Faisal and probably Yamani were privy, was then mentioned only as a hypothesis by Yamani. After the war broke out in October 1973, we knew that his words had been prophetic. The message he left with us, and which we hastened to send to our newspapers in Jidda over long-distance telephone lines then still in need of modernization, was as valid in the age of the Iranian revolution as it was then, on the eve of the October 1973 war:

> If another war with Israel comes, we suppose that you Americans, as always in the past, will help Israel with arms and whatever.
>
> We do not like to use oil as a weapon. We don't want to do that. But if war comes, even if we deployed the entire Saudi regular army and National Guard around the oilfields, we could *never* defend them against small, highly trained and fanatical groups of commandos and explosive experts determined to sabotage them.
>
> Therefore, if war comes, *we will have to cut off the flow of oil*. This will mean production cutbacks, at the very least, and embargoes. Please tell your government and your readers to think, and think again, about what is in America's own interest.

By fanatical groups Yamani meant Palestinians. But his remarks apply equally to the Iranian-influenced saboteurs who, here and there, did do some damage to oil installations during the Iran-Iraq War. Before and during Desert Storm in 1991, Saddam Hussein's Iraqi saboteurs were feared, too.

When we appeared later in the evening at the traditional Fourth of July reception hosted by the U.S. ambassador, we tried to pass on the remarks of Yamani and the king. We suggested that they had taken the time and the trouble to convey to us what sounded like a very serious message.

"Ah," said the ambassador, with a dismissive wave, "they've been trying to peddle that kind of stuff for months now. It's just their line. They don't really mean it." Those were the last words Jim and I ever heard from that ambassador.

War began with Egypt's successful crossing from the Suez Canal into Israeli-occupied Sinai on October 6, 1973. Two weeks later, Saudi Arabia, which sent a few troops and supplies to the Syrian front, embargoed oil shipments to the United States and the Netherlands because of their support for Israel. The big oil companies gave up trying to sound off in public about U.S. policy; executives shrugged their shoulders and switched to Indonesia, South America, and other sources to buy oil supplies. For Iran the embargo, which ended in 1974, was a bonanza: the Shah was able to increase both his sales and his prices at the same time. Years later, Yamani was unwilling to humor King Fahd's unrealistic wish to do the same and keep both production and prices high on an increasingly glutted world market. So Fahd dismissed him on October 29, 1986.

Yamani, said to have been playing cards with friends at home, heard of his firing on the radio before receiving the news directly from the king. He shrugged, the story goes, heaved a sigh of relief that the crushing responsibility had been lifted from his shoulders, and began winning—not only at cards. Yamani would go on to launch a successful series of private business ventures[10] and, later, in London an important think tank dealing with energy questions.

Bolstering Saudi Defenses

Brzezinski's recommendation after the outbreak of the Iran-Iraq War that the United States beef up Saudi defenses has a long background. The United States and Saudi Arabia never had a formal alliance. In 1946, King Abd al-Aziz, mindful of the U.S. military presence in nearby Iran, then threatened in Azerbaijan and Kurdistan by Soviet expansion, granted the United States an important concession.

The U.S. Air Force was allowed to exercise temporary "unrestricted air traffic rights" at Dhahran Air Base and later at Dhahran International Airport. During the Korean War, the air base at Dhahran, later greatly enlarged by the U.S. Army Corps of Engineers, became part of a global network of American bases ringing the Soviet Union. In 1990–91, it was the center of the biggest overseas airborne supply operation since World War II and the rear base for Operation Desert Shield/Storm.

In the late 1950s, the Saudi-American relationship soured because of Arab pressures on the Saudis to stop cooperating with an ally of Israel. Failure of the United States to join—indeed, its decision to oppose by diplomatic means—the Anglo-French-Israeli attack at Suez in 1956 helped to sweeten the Saudi mood, although there was considerable argument over extending for a final five years the U.S. lease at Dhahran Air Base. Although they were unable to back the Saudis in regard to Israel, U.S. administrations did give them some moral and diplomatic support in a dispute with Britain over Buraimi Oasis. At this remote corner of the kingdom, where the Saudi–Abu Dhabi–Oman borders were uncertain, the British-officered Oman Trucial Scouts sometimes skirmished with U.S.-trained and -equipped Saudi troops.

New Saudi-U.S. strains arose over the civil war in Yemen, which flared up at various times between 1958 and 1967. The Saudis supported the Yemeni royalists and sometimes flew in foreign correspondents like myself to investigate the depredations of the Yemeni Republicans and their Egyptian military supporters. There was a regular Egyptian expeditionary force that at times consisted of over 100,000 men and included the most modern jet fighter-bombers Egypt had in its Soviet-supplied arsenal.[11]

One reason Saudi-U.S. relations cooled during this period is that the Saudis believed the United States was trying to placate not only their enemy Israel and their neighbor Iran but also their ideological, antimonarchist foe, President Gamal Abdel Nasser of Egypt. The Americans recognized the Republican regime in North Yemen in 1962, part of the Kennedy administration's efforts to understand President Nasser and to induce Egypt and Israel to talk peace. The Saudis were shocked, regarding a Yemen with an aggressive (as they saw it) Egyptian military presence as a serious threat.[12]

From 1962 until Desert Shield/Storm in 1990–91, the Saudis were unwilling to give the United States direct use of their air base except for reconnaissance and other missions felt to be in the Saudis' interest. Sometimes, as during the Iran-Iraq War and even after the ceasefire in August 1988, the Saudis let the Americans link these flights, especially reconnaissance missions, to U.S. naval units in and near the Gulf and the Indian Ocean.

None of this reticence about a direct American military presence, which, as we have seen, existed for many years before the Iranian threat to Saudi Arabia, prevented the Saudis from calling on the United States to modernize and strengthen their armed forces. Before 1970, little was done to update or reinforce the Saudi military. The air force and navy were almost nonexistent. The royal family shared the traditional distrust of monarchs, especially Arab ones, of military men. It had learned by bitter experience that the military is inclined to stage coups d'état. Neutralizing the threat from the regular armed forces was the Saudi National Guard, used extensively against Iranian-inspired terrorism after 1978. National Guard officers were generally chosen for personal loyalty to the crown prince. Their units would be stationed near Riyadh, Jidda, and Dhahran. The regular army and air force, often with few supplies, were kept away from major centers. This arrangement continued even after the Iranian military threat emerged at the outbreak of the Iran-Iraq War.

Until France in the early 1980s won important contracts for training and equipping the fledgling Saudi navy, most of its equipment came from the United States. By the time the Iranian revolution erupted in 1979, the Saudis had signed over $6 billion in sales agreements for U.S. construction, training, and weapons. Saudi military spending rose along with oil revenues—just as Iranian arms shipping had grown under the Shah's rule.

Thousands of Saudis from the regular army and the National Guard have trained in the United States, and since 1951 the U.S. Military Training Mission has worked in the kingdom. The expansion of Saudi defense forces that began after the Iranian threat emerged in 1980 found a willing partner: the U.S. Army Corps of Engineers, which had already planned or begun construction of military bases and other major works worth $20 billion by that time. The forward Saudi land forces' base near the Iraqi border houses about seventy thousand Saudi servicemen and their families and hosts three armored brigades. It cost upwards of $8 billion.[13]

There were precedents for President Carter's decision to grant the Saudis airborne aid with E-3A AWACS planes in 1980. At least one such plane, for example, had been deployed at Saudi request in the spring of 1979, not because of Iran but because of a perceived threat along the border with Yemen. These deployments helped to arouse the Saudis' appetite to buy E-3As of their own. The so-called Saudi Air Defense Enhancement Package involved the sale of five such planes and eighteen ground radar installations to go with them. The U.S. Senate didn't back the sale, however, until October 28, 1981, after a long and bloody battle with Israel's supporters in Congress and skillful lobbying by the Reagan administration.[14] Delivery of the planes did not begin until 1985. Meanwhile, other equipment of the package including ground radar and computers were occasionally used during deployments by U.S. Air Force AWACS in Saudi Arabia.

An Uprising at the Grand Mosque

November 20, 1979, 5:20 A.M., was the first day of the Muslim year 1400. It was also the first day of real crisis for the Saudi Arabian royal family. Mecca, the Holiest of Holies, and the desert around it were bathed in the gentle light of dawn. Both foreign pilgrims and the citizens of Mecca were waking up for the morning prayer. The Grand Mosque's loudspeakers boomed out the call, "*Allahu al-akhbar! Allahu al-akhbar!*" (God is great!) As he finished the prayer, Sheikh Muhammad ben Subayyal, imam of the Grand Mosque, was seized by armed men inside its walls. They shot another Sunni cleric dead.

The gunman, a former religious student and a Sunni fundamentalist rabble-rouser named Juhaiman ben Muhammad Oteibi, brandished an AK-47 assault rifle and grabbed the microphone. The loudspeakers carried his first message of the revolt: "The mahdi and his partisans seek protection and aid in the holy mosque, for they are everywhere persecuted and have no other refuge." The mahdi, Oteibi subsequently pronounced, had returned in the person of his brother-in-law.

The mahdi, or chosen one, is a messiah-like figure who is supposed to return to the earth at the end of time. He occurs in both the Shi'a and Sunni sects. There have been historical mahdis, like the Sudanese Muhammad Ahmed ben Abdallah. In 1881 he declared he would save Sudan from British colonialism and then conquered Khartoum in 1885, defeating an Anglo-Egyptian army. A more powerful symbol, however, is al-Iman al-Mahdi, a half-historical, half-mythical figure who was born Muhammad Abdel Kassim in Baghdad in A.D. 872. He is the vanished imam of the Shi'ites, who disappeared without a trace and who will reappear, like the Sunni mahdi, in the last hours of the earth when mankind is ready for divine judgment. One of the legends about this mahdi that made the move of Oteibi and his group of fanatical tribesmen doubly dangerous is that he is waiting in the Radwa Mountains near Mecca, guarded by a lion and panther, until his second coming.

During its rise to power, the Royal House of Saud had faced revolts by fundamentalists claiming kinship with the Ikhwan, or Brothers. The Ikhwan were founders of the austere Wahabi faith that had provided religious and ideological nourishment for the rising Saudi dynasty. In 1929, King Abd al-Aziz defeated one such revolt led by Sultan ibn Bijad ibn Humaid. His defeat and disgrace still rankled Oteibi's native village in Al-Qassim province. Even as a child, Oteibi considered television, photography, and the influx of American culture as the work of the devil.

Viewing what he regarded as the corrupt ways of Saudi Arabia's increasingly rich rulers, Oteibi had long planned his rebellion. At some point in his early career, possibly after being dismissed as a corporal in the Saudi National Guard, he had heard the fiery lectures of Sheikh Abdel-Aziz ibn Baz. A blind, charismatic theologian who in 1969 became rector of the Islamic University of Medina, the sheikh taught that the earth was not only full of corruption but also flat. In the early 1960s, a group of his followers, mostly students from Arab countries outside Saudi Arabia, drew unfavorable attention from Saudi authorities and was dissolved. The foreigners were expelled.[15]

This crackdown, not well understood nor much heeded by the Americans, was the work of King Faisal. Barely two years after my audience with him in 1973, he was killed by his nephew Prince Musaad al-Faisal. Musaad was a dreamy, unstable character who had spent nine years in the United States studying some of the time, most of the time drinking, gambling, and romancing. He had been arrested once for possession of drugs.

Musaad's brother, Khaled, had been shot dead by a policeman when he tried to storm a Saudi television station, saying it defied Islamic law. Musaad petitioned King Faisal to have the policeman executed and was refused. So Musaad appeared one day at the king's public audience. His membership in the royal family got him past the armed guards without a challenge. As the king greeted him, Musaad pulled a revolver from under his robe and fired three shots, shouting, "Now my brother is avenged!" After long and intensive questioning, in which U.S. authorities reportedly took part, he was beheaded by the traditional blow from the executioner's sword.

King Faisal was replaced by his half-brother, King Khaled, an amiable but none-too-resolute man. Once and for all, Khaled and his close relatives closed ranks against the fundamentalists.[16]

Consequently, what happened after Oteibi's proclamation in Mecca that morning of November 20, 1979, was catastrophic. The young preacher's fanatical partisans had spent weeks infiltrating the mosque and its sacred inner precinct, storing a huge supply of munitions, food, and water there. From a gallery dominating the courtyard and its central monument, a sacred black stone hung with canopies where devout pilgrims pray, they opened fire. Iranian accounts insist that the snipers' first targets were Saudi policemen posted at surveillance points to watch the crowd. The Prophet Muhammad forbade arms in the mosque.

During and after the first fifteen-minute shoot-out, hundreds of faithful were forced into the mosque's enclosure and taken hostage by the gunmen. There they were forced to listen to a sermon broadcast by Oteibi over the loudspeakers. He announced that the hour of Islam's final triumph had arrived. He demanded the overthrow of Saudi Arabia's "corrupt" rulers, the "princelings" who had "abandoned Islam a long time ago, as soon as they saw the golden-haired women of the West and the glittering dollars of ARAMCO."[17]

While Oteibi's speechmaking continued in the mosque, bombs were exploding at sensitive points in Jidda, Riyadh, Mecca, and Medina, among other places. The

Qahtan and Oteiba tribes went on rampages. Demonstrations erupted in many towns, especially in Shi'a centers on the Gulf coast in and around ARAMCO oilfields. An American banker acquaintance of mine recalled that "roadblocks were up everywhere, and for days you could scarcely drive anywhere."

Thousands of the Mecca visitors were Iranians. The Saudi security forces at first concentrated their efforts against them, even though the revolt was clearly an internal Saudi affair. Muhammad ibn Abdallah al-Qahtani, Oteibi's brother-in-law, joined him now in exhorting the faithful to fight the armed mosque guards who were opposing them.

Sheikh Muhammad ben Subayyal tore off the robe that marked him the official imam and ran to the nearest telephone booth to call for help. King Khaled was awakened with the news at 7:00 A.M. Ill health had caused him to cancel his own appearance at the new year prayers, saving him from assassination or worse. Newsmen around the world found international telephone and telex connections severed by official order from Riyadh—a desperate attempt to prevent fifth columns of revolutionaries from communicating with one another. Not even Crown Prince Fahd, in Tunis for an Arab League meeting, could find out what had happened.

Muslims from Baghdad to Brooklyn were excited and horrified by the vague news of "trouble in Mecca." From Al-Azhar University in Cairo the Grand Sheikh of the Sunni persuasion broadcast an appeal to the Islamic world to defend Mecca's holy shrines against the "sinful aggression" of heavily armed apostates. In Tehran, Ayatollah Khomeini not only disavowed responsibility; he blamed the revolt on "criminal U.S. imperialism and international Zionism." Although scarcely more than two weeks had passed since the capture of the U.S. Embassy and its staff, the biggest anti-American demonstration since the Shah's overthrow followed in the Iranian capital. Largely as a result of the hateful Tehran broadcasts, the U.S. Embassy in Islamabad, Pakistan, was stormed and partially burned down by a huge, chanting crowd. Pakistani army reinforcements flew in on helicopters to save the staff.

Oteibi's band, barricaded in the mosque and on its grounds, shot at everything that moved outside. Fifty government soldiers trying to storm the mosque without heavy weapons support were killed the first day (November 21). The Saudi authorities were determined to avoid major damage to the holy places. By early afternoon, Hercules C-130 transport planes, some probably piloted and crewed by Americans, had airlifted in at least six hundred members of the elite security forces. On the second day, reinforcements attacked at 11:30 A.M. and again suffered heavy losses. Bodies littered the sacred enclosure. On the third day, King Khaled ordered an assault led by twelve M-113 armored personnel carriers and five helicopter gunships with three thousand troops. This time, an M-113 and a helicopter were destroyed before government forces beat a retreat. Acting under a religious authorization issued by the *ulema*, a group of Islamic scholars advising the king, Prince Sultan, the minister of defense, set up headquarters near the mosque and directed a two-week siege. The tactics involved returning fire but not taking the initiative to attack with heavy weapons, which would further desecrate the mosque.

Apparently King Khaled decided that the Americans—even more exposed since the riots in Tehran and Islamabad than before—were not the power that could save him this time. He appealed to the French instead. After contacting French President Giscard d'Estaing, Captain Barril and two noncommissioned officers of the elite attack arm of the French National Gendarmerie flew to Saudi Arabia November 23. Barril, a non-Muslim, was given special dispensation to enter Mecca. French intelligence provided Barril with detailed maps of the 1,400-year-old vaults of the mosque, which the Saudis themselves lacked. He assessed the situation and advised crushing the rebels by neutralizing those in the cellars, protected by thick walls.

Barril's superiors in Paris sent him tear gas, sprayers, plastic explosives, fuses, and gas masks. Although 2,500 regular army troops, 600 men from the National Guard, and 125 parachutists surrounded the mosque, and its electricity had been cut, the rebels continued to shoot anyone they saw moving outside. Slowly, government troops managed to infiltrate upper passageways of the mosque. They drove the rebels out of two towers and into the main building. Then, despite the clouds of tear gas they sprayed, the king's men were stopped cold again.

Meanwhile, in the eastern province, Shi'ite villages were already burning and echoing with gunfire and explosions from the heavy weapons of the security forces. It was the tenth day of the holy month of Muharram, when Shi'ites parade and flagellate themselves. By the time the demonstrations were put down, sixty were dead, three hundred wounded, and banks, shops, and police stations had been wrecked. Broadcasts from Iran fanned the flames, calling upon the faithful in Saudi Arabia to end the rule of the traitors, the heretics, and the Americans.

Finally, on December 1, at 8:41 P.M., a Caravelle transport containing chemical warfare materials and gas masks arrived from France. Sixty Saudi soldiers and thirty officers had been specially trained for the attack. It began December 4 at 10:00 A.M. "In the name of Allah, forward!" The defenders responded with the cry, "Under God's command!" Door by door, gallery by gallery, the government forces advanced, releasing a total of two tons of gas against the machine guns and terminal fervor of the zealots.

Mid-morning on December 4, the hand-picked elite troops, with French advisers and Prince Sultan observing close by, assaulted the last insurgent position. In the final attack forty-five Saudi soldiers were killed. Later, the Saudi government said the number of dead rebels was 117, among them the mahdi, whose corpse was photographed and filmed as proof that he lacked divinity. The wild-eyed, long-haired Oteibi and his followers were shown in chains; the official Saudi media referred to them as mutinous gangsters and terrorists.

On January 8, 1980, after an intensive investigation, sixty-three rebels were taken to eight Saudi cities. King Khaled instructed his interior minister, Prince Nayef, who denied any foreign participation in the repression, to "kill those whose names are contained in this announcement, in order to be pleasing to Allah, to defend the holy consecration of the Kaaba and its worshipers, and to free the Muslims of their anxiety."[18]

Of the sixty-three men beheaded, forty-one were Saudis; ten, Egyptians; six,

South Yemenis; and three, Kuwaitis—one each came from North Yemen, the Sudan, and Iraq. This, at least, was what the official Saudi news agency reported. Many others found in the mosque with weapons or serving as lookouts were jailed. Women who had carried food and water into the mosque were given two-year sentences and apparently received religious instruction in jail. Several teenagers were sent to reform school. Some thirty-eight people were reported released.

Only two days after the siege ended, King Khaled returned to the Grand Mosque to lead prayers. The Ministry of Religious Affairs ordered all mosques to condemn the insurgents in their prayers. Various government agencies and the controlled media went to great lengths to disguise the anti-American and antiroyalist nature of the Mecca revolt.

Many newsmen, including me, watched the Mecca uprising and its aftermath only from afar. For the fifty thousand or so Americans then living in the Saudi kingdom, it was an unsettling experience. Aware of the mass exodus of the American community in Iran, they began to feel, if not similarly threatened, at least like a foreign minority that needed protection.

Saudi Arabia had pretty much calmed down by the beginning of 1980, the year President Carter decided to commit to its defense new American resources. But Iranian revolutionaries still holding American diplomats hostage in Tehran helped to light a few more fires, this time in Shi'a villages in Saudi Arabia's eastern province near the oilfields. The villages lay deep in the heart of what recent American adminstrations have called the crescent of crisis—that area in which Khomeini and his cohorts unfurled the banner of the Islamic revolution.

In the meantime, the Iran-Iraq War and the continuing Iranian revolutionary efforts had spilled westward into another area where American cultural and educational values had changed history: Syria and Lebanon.

6

Islamic Revolution in Lebanon

The Kidnapping of David Dodge

On July 19, 1982, as invading Israeli forces hammered Lebanon in Gen. Ariel Sharon's campaign to break the power of the Palestinians there, a new and deadly hostage crisis erupted between Iran and the United States. That crisis, unlike the earlier one that had ended with Jimmy Carter's presidency, was not solved within months or years. It persists into the early 1990s. In the secret warfare among Iran, the United States, and their allies and proxies, no other episode has had such repercussions on the two countries.

That July day, a few days before I arrived in Beirut to cover the battle between Israeli and Palestinian forces, was hot and sultry. Artillery thundered sporadically on the city's outskirts. Israeli fighter-bombers hit the PLO-controlled southern suburbs in a few desultory strikes. Sharon's ground forces had encircled the city a month earlier, after invading Lebanon by land and pushing steadily northward.

Western newsmen were grouped in the PLO-controlled Commodore Hotel because of its ample supplies of water and electricity and its communications facilities in a West Beirut otherwise deprived of these. They were trying to find out just what progress Lebanese-born Philip Habib, President Reagan's special peace negotiator, was making in his mediation efforts. They would go to the mansion of Saeb Salem in West Beirut's leafy, once tranquil Musseitbe quarter for coffee and briefings each morning. Saeb Bey, as he was affectionately nicknamed, was the intermediary between Habib and PLO Chairman Yassir Arafat.

On this particular day, Salem had his perpetual carnation in the buttonhole of an expensive suit, which set him apart from the dusty men in battle fatigues who guarded him. He awaited the American answer to a PLO suggestion that beleaguered Beirut guerrillas should move temporarily to northern Lebanon. This was supposed to bring a peaceful end to the siege, while talks settled on a permanent destination for the PLO forces in Lebanon. King Faisal of Saudi Arabia and Foreign Minister Abdel Halim Khaddam of Syria, whose token-size troops were still battling in Lebanon despite Israel's crushing blows in early June in the Bekaa, were to present the same idea to President Reagan in Washington the next day.[1]

One of Saeb Salem's American friends, David Dodge, acting president of the American University of Beirut (AUB), was preoccupied that day. The American University was the oldest and probably most enduring American institution in the entire Middle East. Its survival depended on a return to peace. All the major decisions about AUB now lay on Dodge's shoulders. In the afternoon, walking home from his office, Dodge was reflecting on the crisis. Suddenly, a Renault station wagon whose driver had somehow bluffed his way past the Lebanese gate guards, jerked to a halt in Dodge's path. Two gunmen jumped out, hit him with a pistol butt, and shoved him into the car. Within seconds, it had sped past the guards and disappeared into the maze of streets surrounding the campus.

Lebanese authorities quickly sounded the alarm. Every policeman and gendarme who could be spared from defense duties was put on Dodge's trail. There were persistent rumors, never confirmed, that the kidnappers had studied at AUB. Perhaps the abduction had been an "inside job."

Dodge's captors held him first in South Beirut, in or near buildings controlled by the Iranian embassy. Then, drugged and blindfolded, he was taken to the Bekaa Valley and handed over to a detachment of Iranian Revolutionary Guards. The guards were there because President Hafez Assad of Syria had decided to cast his lot with Iran and the Ayatollah, the enemy of Assad's own personal adversary, President Saddam Hussein of Iraq. It suited the Ayatollah and his acolyte, President Bani-Sadr of Iran, to export the revolution to the underprivileged Shi'ite minority in Lebanon. It suited Assad (or so the Syrian leader believed) to allow this to happen. Therefore, a force of between eight hundred and twelve hundred Revolutionary Guards had entered the Bekaa Valley. They moved in from their main rear transit and training base at Zebadani, Syria, near the Lebanese frontier. In 1986, when I last visited the camp area, it appeared deserted but still flaunted Iranian flags and Khomeini portraits outside the gates.

The guards made their headquarters at the Sheikh Abdallah Caserne, a Lebanese army and gendarmerie base outside the ancient city of Baalbek. An annual summer theater and music festival held among its majestic Roman temples and Phoenician ruins had made the city famous during Lebanon's decades of peace. David Dodge and most of the other Americans living in Lebanon had spent many happy days and nights there. Now he was drugged and wrapped like a mummy, stuffed in a car trunk, and driven to Damascus Airport. There Revolutionary Guard Minister Rafik Mohsen-Dost passed Dodge through Syrian checkpoints and shipped him as an item of Iranian military cargo—immune from Syrian security or customs controls—to Iran.

Dodge was held in Evin Prison in northern Tehran. He was not tortured, but neither could he communicate with his distraught family or anyone else until his final release, through Syrian pressure, in July 1983. During much of his captivity, he was submitted to senseless interrogations about himself and other "suspects" among his colleagues, just as the American diplomats in Tehran had been.

Why was Dodge selected as the first of a long string of American and other Westerners to be kidnapped by Iranian and pro-Iranian elements in Lebanon? And what was the significance of the timing?

The second question is easier to answer than the first. Dodge's abduction was partly an act of retaliation. This he made clear to me after his liberation. At the time, Iran wanted, and in 1990 still demanded, the return of four Iranians kidnapped by Samir Geagea's Maronite Christian militiamen in early June at a roadblock outside Beirut. Dodge was held, initially at least, as a hostage for their return. The most important of the four was Ahmad Motevasselian. The official Tehran announcement called him an embassy political officer; actually, he had been commander of the new Revolutionary Guard detachment in Baalbek. With him were two embassy staffers and an Iranian newsman. Within days of their kidnapping, the consensus of the Beirut rumor mill was that the four Iranians had been murdered by their captors after interrogation.

The Influence of American Education in the Middle East

As Robin Wright suggests in her excellent book, *In the Name of God: The Khomeini Decades*, Dodge was probably taken because he was the most senior American then in Lebanon; but there were more concrete reasons as well.[2] These lie anchored in the century-old American presence in the Middle East epitomized by AUB. In the nineteenth century, the impetus AUB gave to learning and the parallel growth of a free press saw the rise of Arab nationalist movements against Turkish rule. They attracted a strong following, especially among Christian Arabs, and as such were bound to incur the wrath of Muslim fundamentalists.

By 1875, a small group of Syrian Protestant College alumni had organized a secret society dedicated to the expulsion of Ottoman rulers from all of Syria, including Lebanon. For want of support from local Muslims, the group barely lasted a decade.[3] The revolution spawned by American education, however, was spreading throughout the Middle East. In Egypt, Americans helped to found the American University in Cairo and Assiut College. There was an American school at Aleppo, Syria, and an American school for girls at Smyrna (later Izmir), Turkey. At the university level in Lebanon, Christians generally (at least until the 1960s) surpassed Muslims in terms of percentage of attendance.

The years 1918 to 1945 marked the peak of the European colonial period in the Middle East. During that time, the United States was the only power present without colonies and no political ax to grind. This made America and American education popular. When the King-Crane Commission, an American group, surveyed the sentiments of Arabs, Jews, and others under French mandate rule in post–World War I Syria and Lebanon and under British mandate rule in Palestine, the people indicated a preference, along with independence, for some form of American protection.

Under Kemal Atatürk, who founded the modern Turkish republic in the 1920s, the trend was secular and progressive. Some aspects of Islam, such as the use of the Arabic alphabet and the wearing of turbans, were strictly forbidden. Education was a critical weapon in combating the old order. Atatürk and his heirs also encouraged technical and vocational training and the education of women. In Iran, Reza Shah, father of the late Muhammad Reza Pahlavi, tried to secularize too, but with much less success. Rather than see the brightest Iranian students drained off to AUB and other foreign institutions, he opened the new University of Tehran in 1934. In Egypt, Cairo University was founded in 1908 under the influence of the so-called Young Turks. The Egyptian state assumed full control of the university in 1922, when British control had loosened. In Jerusalem, the Hebrew University was opened in 1925 to serve the Jewish community.[4]

Despite these efforts, more and more students from the Mideast flowed to America and Western Europe. Learning in Iran continued to be traditional; in the 1960s and 1970s, higher education meant secularization and especially training abroad. Millions of Iranians traveled to schools in the United States. Then came the Khomeini revolution, which had a devasting effect on education. In 1979, the year of the revolution, Iranian scientists contributed 404 research papers to institutions abroad. Some eighty-two institutions contributed one or more publications. But by 1983, at the height of the campaign to drive Americans out of the Middle East, the number of publications had fallen to 103. These were the product of research in only twenty-eight institutions. Women came under strict dress regulations, and mixed classes were forbidden. Meanwhile, the war with Iraq gave rise to a great deal of military-related research and development, as it did in Iraq.[5]

In neighboring Saudi Arabia, things were different. There, men like David Dodge, who headed the Trans-Arabian Pipeline Corporation for many years, had left the mark of American culture and technology. By 1985, the kingdom was connected with the world by telecommunications networks superior to those in Iran, which had deteriorated under Khomeini. In that year Saudi Arabia's new Arabsat corporation launched two communications satellites. The second one, Arabsat 1B, was carried aboard an American space shuttle and launched to a work station 39,500 miles above Africa on June 18, 1985. Carrying out scientific work aboard, including surveys of his country's mineral and water resources, was Saudi Prince Sultan al-Saud, the Arab world's first astronaut. This Saudi-American space mission laid the groundwork for future intelligence coordination during Operation Desert Shield/Storm, when satellites fed around-the-clock information to the allied forces on Iraqi military movements and military-industrial installations.

The Arabsat network was used to relay live television coverage of Muslims at prayer, sporting events, and news. By 1990, Arab states were receiving twenty-four-hour Western television news via Arabsat. Intellectuals could be comforted by reminders that Arabsat operated on scientific principles discovered by Arab astronomers during the classical Arab age between the ninth and fifteenth centuries A.D. But they realized that it was Western and largely American technology that had put those principles into practice.[6]

At the center of the U.S. network of culture and technology, in particular medical science, that had spread from Beirut over the entire Middle East, was AUB. By 1974, when I was privileged to audit courses at AUB and make the acquaintance of David Dodge and many of the faculty there, the university was a beacon of light in the political darkness surrounding Lebanon. It was a secular university. The campus had about fifty classrooms and laboratory buildings and an enrollment of over two thousand. Its medical school and the American University Hospital (AUH) were famous worldwide. Emergency treatment at AUH, often done at gunpoint and under threats from patients' relatives or fellow militamen, was to save thousands of lives in the years of strife that lay ahead.

AUB was always, and despite everything still may be, the most influential center of learning in the region. Financed by revenue from an endowment fund whose American source had largely dried up by 1990, AUB was to survive shelling, sniping, and the assault of assorted militias and gangsters. It paid a terrible price.

The AUB charter required it to have an American president. By the mid-1980s, especially after President Malcolm Kerr's murder in January 1987, much if not all of the American faculty and staff had been replaced by Arabs. There was an acting Lebanese president. Other AUB staffers had been kidnapped—such as Thomas Sutherland, a dean, and Joseph Cicippio, an AUB controller—by pro-Iranian Shi'ite groups. Some were murdered by design or by "accident." Ms. Suha Tuqan, editor of AUB's university press and a distinguished painter, was shot at a roadblock by militiamen in 1987 when she tried to swerve and avoid the kidnapping of a Frenchman riding with her.

"The Islamic Republic of Lebanon"

There had never been a time when the ten thousand or so Americans living in Lebanon felt more threatened than during the Islamic invasion and siege of Beirut in summer 1982. Up to then, U.S. administrations had managed to keep American military forces out of Lebanon. There were some American officers assigned to UN peacekeeping and observer forces in southern Lebanon and Israel, but the only notable exception was the U.S. Marine force stationed in Lebanon in 1958. Their mission was to bolster President Camille Chamoun's government against a Muslim uprising inspired by President Nasser of the then United Arab Republic. Another reason for the U.S. military action was the Iraqi military uprising of July 1958, which had seen the overthrow of King Faisal and his pro-Western Prime Minister Nuri al-Said.

The marine intervention on the shores of Beirut did not directly relate to Arab-Israeli hostilities or the Palestinian conflict. However, the events of 1982 that plunged U.S. forces into what strategists like to call low-intensity warfare with the forces and surrogates of Syria and Iran were directly related to both.

The 1982 conflict was triggered by the attempted assassination by Abu Nidal's rogue Palestinian terrorists of the Israeli ambassador to Great Britain, Shlomo Argov, in London on June 3, 1982. They were acting not on Yassir Arafat's orders but apparently on those of Saddam Hussein's Iraqi intelligence. Three days later, Prime Minister Begin of Israel ordered a land, sea, and air attack on Lebanon. The announced purpose was to destroy PLO strongholds inside Lebanon within a twenty-five-mile radius of the Israeli border and so secure peace for Galilee, Israel's northern region. Prior to a strictly enforced ceasefire with the PLO since June 1981, Galilee had been subject to PLO guns and rockets. By June 10, 1982, Israeli forces had pushed northward to East Beirut. There they were welcomed, in accordance with secret agreements, by Maronite Christian militias and politicians.

After fruitless efforts to arrange a ceasefire, President Reagan announced on July 6, 1982, that the United States would send a small military force to Beirut as part of a multinational peacekeeping force. On July 10, France announced it would also contribute soldiers to help its favorite former colonial possession, Lebanon.

On July 16, after Westerners sent persistent reports that Israel was not only using prohibited cluster-bomb artillery shells but also dropping booby-trapped objects, including toys, in Lebanon, the U.S. Department of State announced that it would hold up shipments of cluster bombs to Israel. That country insisted it was using the bombs in ways consistent with U.S.-Israeli agreements.

On August 12, following an eleven-hour Israeli air attack on West Beirut that those of us who witnessed it will never forget, an uneasy ceasefire began. The PLO agreed to begin withdrawing August 21. President Reagan also announced on that day that the first contingent of marines would arrive on August 25. About three hundred members of the French Foreign Legion, who hadn't seen much action since the Algerian war of 1954–62, had already arrived in Lebanon from Corsica. I watched as East Beirut residents cheered them and threw flowers at their jeeps. "France is coming to save us," screamed one enthusiastic Maronite woman. Lebanese memories were still strong of French military intervention on behalf of the Maronites in the 1860s, when they were locked in warfare with their ancestral neighbors and enemies, the Druze people. Meanwhile, in Moscow, the Soviet media muttered warnings about U.S. troops in the Middle East; but there was no Soviet action. Most of the world scarcely noticed when a token Italian force of company strength followed the French to Lebanon.

The Americans and Italians joined the French at onshore observation posts. Others stayed aboard their warships to observe the evacuation of the PLO forces. An initial four hundred PLO partisans left aboard a Greek ship, defiantly signaling victory and waving their banners. The last group departed September 1. Those who had left included about fifteen thousand Palestinians and the troops of the Syrian commando regiment.

Arafat himself sailed for Greece August 30. Most of the PLO fighters and bureaucrats went to Syria. After some U.S. urging, Tunisia agreed to be the site of the new PLO political headquarters. By September 10, the U.S. Marines who helped to supervise the departure had embarked on their ships.

Within nineteen days, they were back, after a series of shocks in Lebanon. There was the Israeli invasion, then the summer war, and above all the initial unleashing of extremist forces that would eventually tear Lebanon, and with it, the American presence, to shreds.

Even as the PLO fighters were leaving Beirut, Bashir Gemayel was elected the new president of Lebanon, replacing Elias Sarkis, a pliant pro-Syrian Maronite Christian who retired quietly. Bashir was the tough, determined son of Phalangist leader Sheikh Pierre Gemayel. His election was made easier by the Israeli occupation of East Beirut and much of its mountain hinterland. Before the invasion, the Israelis had agreed with Gemayel to establish pro-Israeli and pro-Western Maronite hegemony over the whole of Lebanon. Occupation gave them leverage to encourage pro-Gemayel voters among the aging Lebanese parliamentarians, whose constitutional task it was to meet and choose the new president.

But on September 14, Gemayel was killed by a bomb planted at Phalangist headquarters by a man subsequently believed to be acting for Syrian intelligence. His death precipitated the Israeli invasion and temporary occupation on September 15 of West Beirut, much to the consternation of the U.S. government. The Israelis advanced into the city with little resistance. The next day, Phalangist forces under Elie Hobeika's command raided the Palestinian camps of Sabra and Chatila, under the eyes of and with some logistical support from surrounding Israeli forces. Many hundreds of Palestinians were slaughtered; nearly all were women, children, and old men left behind by the PLO forces.

I arrived in West Beirut as part of an ABC News investigative team. For the Outlook documentary we produced on the massacre, we interviewed Palestinian, Lebanese, and Israeli eyewitnesses. They told us a tale that horrified the world and provoked massive antiwar and antigovernment demonstrations in Israel.

Yassir Arafat and a half-dozen members of the PLO executive committee, now back in Damascus, were sickened when they viewed tapes and heard recordings of the vengeance killings. They rightfully claimed that U.S. negotiator Philip Habib had, in the final agreement with Arafat, promised that "the United States will provide its guarantee [of the safety of Palestinian civilians] on the basis of assurances received from the government of Israel and from the leadership of certain groups with which it has been in touch."[7]

Though the American pledge was not cast in concrete, Habib and other Reagan administration officials had relied on Israel and the now-dead Gemayel to prevent revenge killings. To the delight of Gen. Ariel Sharon, Israeli defense minister, U.S.

Marines of the multinational force had been swiftly withdrawn from Lebanon once the PLO was out. Israel, for three weeks, had had a clear field of maneuver.

Certainly, the Sabra and Chatila massacres marked the start of the decline of American power, prestige, and presence in Lebanon. This is why the events of that dark September 1982 proved to be such bad news for Americans who, from the founding of AUB on, had done good works in the Middle East.

Within a few days of Sabra and Chatila, the U.S. Marines were on their way back to Lebanon. Habib and his senior aide, Morris Draper, were furious with the Israelis for having taken over Beirut International Airport, from which the Phalangists had marched into the Palestinian camps. They signaled Washington to keep the marines offshore until the Israelis left the airport. Reluctantly, Sharon pulled his men back to positions a few hundred yards down the road. This caused a three-day delay in the marine landing.

Finally, on September 29, 1982, thirteen hundred men of the E and F Companies of the Thirty-second Marine Amphibious Unit waded ashore across the road from the airport—the same location where U.S. forces had arrived during the earlier, happier landing of 1958. Then, the Lebanese who greeted them were blithely peddling Coca-Cola and ice cream. This time, the atmosphere was charged with menace. Some of the ragged survivors of the Sabra and Chatila killings watched as the marines splashed ashore and prepared bivouacs near and on the airport grounds. There the Americans set up their first, absurdly exposed positions.

In a letter to Congress, President Reagan defined the marine mission: ". . . To provide an interposition force at agreed locations and thereby provide the multinational presence requested by the Lebanese government to assist it and the Lebanese Armed Forces." In a message to the speaker of the House of Representatives and the president pro tem of the Senate, he offered the assurance that "our agreement with the government of Lebanon expressly rules out any combat responsibilities for the U.S. forces."[8]

As it turned out, the two messages were a contradiction in terms. Eventually, assisting the Lebanese government had to involve the marines directly in hostilities. They could not operate outside the terms of reference of the Multinational Force Agreement, which called for the protection of Beirut and no more. Near the airport were the mountains of Aley, a stronghold of Maronite militias and the Lebanese army, and the Shouf Mountains, where the pro-Syrian Druze militia was master. Between them, these two hostile forces dominated the airport and held it at the mercy of their artillery. The marines were thus violating one of their own main tenets—"Always take the high ground." However, marine commanders, according to conversations I held with several, believed that they were in stronger positions than the 1,500 French and 1,200 Italians stationed further inside the city, or even the tiny, 100-man British contingent bivouacked a short distance from the airport.

The day after their arrival, the marines experienced their first casualty. Twenty-one-year-old Cpl. David L. Reagan of Chesapeake, Virginia, was killed and three other marines were wounded while clearing away an unexploded cluster shell, a

155mm artillery round containing thirty-eight bomblets. Israeli forces had left it behind when they withdrew from the airport. The use of cluster weapons, except for strictly defensive purposes, had been prohibited by U.S.-Israeli agreements.

Even as the marines were mourning their first casualties and digging in amid some euphoria that at last an American solution for Lebanon might bring everything to a happy end, Amin Gemayel, Bashir Gemayel's elder brother, was elected president of Lebanon. Voting him in were the same aging deputies who had hopefully elected the late Bashir August 23. Amin Gemayel was acclaimed as a messiah, the man who would unify Lebanon and deliver it from its foreign occupiers. Last, and for Israel and the United States most important, Amin Gemayel wanted to make the entire country a permanent part of the Western political bloc. The American military men had not yet heard of the extremist Hezbollah or the more moderate Shi'ite militia Amal (meaning "hope"). Some believed this was going to be a pleasant military operation, marred only by accidents like the one suffered by Corporal Reagan.

Amin Gemayel, as Israeli military commentators Zeev Schiff and Ehud Ya'ari observed, "was his brother's opposite in many ways—rigid where Bashir was wily, aloof where Bashir was magnetic—and strove to assume a completely different political image."[9] I had spoken with both Gemayels, and the contrast was dramatic. Once, following a private meeting he had addressed in Washington, I reminded Bashir that the Phalangists had looted everything that would move from the Beirut port in 1976, the first year of the civil war. When I mentioned that because of this my family and I had lost most of our possessions, including a three thousand-book library, Bashir misunderstood.

"It's true," he muttered in French. "They did take everything, didn't they?" (The "they" referred to his own men.) "Listen," he went on, "we can't discuss this kind of thing here. The next time you're in Beirut, come by and see me about it." Bashir, thinking in line with the Lebanese jungle law that had emerged with the civil war, thought that I wanted a handout for my lost possessions.

Amin, however, was a different kettle of fish. He was cautious and measured in all his interviews and statements. He always managed to give at least lip service to Arab nationalism, the Muslims of Lebanon, and Lebanon's "Arab role." Israeli observers like Schiff suspected that, whereas Bashir constantly coordinated everything with Israel, Amin preferred to inform President Hafez Assad in Damascus of what was going on. "The man in the white suit," as some of us called him, stood on the Green Line between East and West Beirut proclaiming reunification, not only of divided Lebanon but "of the hearts."[10]

One thing certain about President Amin Gemayel was that he feared the Iranian threat, not only to Lebanon but also to Western values and institutions, far more than his brother. Bashir had been murdered before he could fully apprehend the significance of the Revolutionary Guards and the rise of the militant Shi'ite militias. Often, to be sure, he had conferred with Nebi Berri, the lawyer who took over the secular leadership of Amal. Born to a Lebanese Shi'ite émigré family in West Africa and educated in France and the United States, Berri told me he had informed Amin that the Ayatollah Khomeini's plans for an Islamic revolution in Lebanon did not meet his approval.

Amal was created in 1974 by an extraordinary, charismatic Iranian, Musa Sadr, or the Imam, as people called him. Tall, with magnetic gray-green eyes, he persuaded most people who met him of his sincerity. He became the champion of the underprivileged Shi'ite tobacco and truck farmers of southern Lebanon. Amal was formed as a self-help organization to guide them in their efforts to escape the feudal relationship with the big landlords and political bosses. One of Sadr's main adversaries was the clan of Kamal al-Assad, who had dominated the Shi'ite political scene in Lebanon for many years as speaker of parliament. Sadr was also an adversary of the Shah of Iran, whose SAVAK had marked Sadr as a dangerous man.

After the Palestinian guerrillas began moving into southern Lebanon in 1970–71, Sadr saw the need to create an armed militia. Sadr told me during a meeting with him in 1976 that Amal needed it for two reasons: First, to resist Israeli reprisal attacks on Shi'ite villages and hamlets located among or near PLO camps; and second, Sadr knew that some day, despite his own and other Shi'ite leaders' sympathy for the Palestinian cause, the time would come when Shi'ites and Palestinians would fight each other for Lebanese turf. This happened, in fact, in the south in 1977–79 and again on a much worse scale at Palestinian camps outside Beirut after 1984.

By 1975, Amal was training its militia groups in the Bekaa Valley and elsewhere with Syrian support, discreet at first but considerable later on. By 1966, the Imam had established the Council of the South to coordinate development projects. In this way he wrested control of his Shi'ites from the hands of the Sunni religious establishment in Beirut and Sidon. Soon afterward, Sadr developed a political line midway between the pro-Palestinian Sunni Muslims and the anti-Palestinian Maronite Christians. In October 1978, Musa Sadr disappeared in Libya after a stormy argument with Col. Muammar Qaddafi.[11] This made him into a legend among the Shi'ites. Since his disappearance, many deeds both of charity and of terrorism have been committed in his name.

Nebi Berri, who in his own modest way tried to assume Amal's political if not religious mantle, was different. An American ambassadorial cable to Washington had described Musa Sadr as "one of the most, if not the most, impressive individuals I have met in Lebanon. . . . His charisma is obvious and his apparent sincerity is awe-inspiring." The official impression of Berri, on the other hand, was of a moderate functioning within the framework of Lebanese politics who wished to curb the power of the Christian minority and bring the Shi'ite majority to its rightful position.[12]

The problem for the United States, its institutions like AUB, and its people in Lebanon was now stark and clear: not the cautious, moderate Berri but Hezbollah's sheikhs, backed by Iran, had assumed the mantle of Musa Sadr. Their purpose was to eradicate the influence of the United States by demolishing American institutions and kidnapping and killing American citizens. Thus would they mold the ruins of the tolerant, relatively democratic society of Lebanon into a new totalitarian theocracy—a satellite of its big sister, the Islamic republic of Iran.

7

America Versus Iran— in Lebanon

Najeeb Halaby

The sectarian tide that began to wash over Lebanon after the influx of Iranian ideologues in 1982 was well understood by one American, Najeeb Halaby. His daughter, Lisa, is Queen Noor of Jordan, the fourth wife of King Hussein.

The Halabys, father and daughter, and King Hussein himself have always been keenly aware of the challenge posed to men of good will in the West by Islamic Iran's more extreme revolutionaries. During a private conversation in 1987 at the height of the Iran-Iraq War—when Hussein was sending aid to Iraq—the king told me that Jordan must at all costs avoid Lebanon's fate of being "crushed between opposing steam-rollers." For Jordan, the danger of Israel's seemingly permanent colonization of the West Bank and East Jerusalem, lost to Jordan in 1967, was equal to and perhaps surpassed by the threat from the Ayatollah Khomeini.

Najeeb Halaby and King Hussein, both enthusiastic pilots, have been friends since the 1960s, when Halaby was involved with the fate of AUB. He struggled to keep it an open institution representing the best in American educational values.

To understand the position of Halaby and AUB, as well as that of King Hussein and Queen Noor (whom newsmen in Beirut had known as a free-lance photographer), you have to trace Halaby's extraordinary career. In 1900, his father came to the United States from Zahle, Lebanon, as a steerage passenger and became suc-

74

cessful peddling Mideastern copperware, jewelry, fabrics, and rugs along the East Coast. Najeeb was born in Dallas on November 19, 1915. His brilliant academic career took him through Stanford University and the University of Michigan Law School and won him honorary degrees from Yale and Allegheny College. Traveling with his parents abroad inspired in him a love of airplanes. During World War II, he became a test pilot for new jets. He made a secret transcontinental solo flight in an incredible five hours and forty-five minutes (most DC-3 airliners then did it in twenty-two hours).

Halaby worked with U.S. Defense Secretary James Forrestal at the time of the founding of Israel. Hounded for his outspoken opinion that its creation would eventually lead to disaster for the United States in the Middle East, Forrestal put a strong political stamp on Halaby's life and career. Halaby also served as head of the Federal Aviation Administration under President John F. Kennedy. Like others who worked for both Kennedy and Lyndon Johnson, Halaby believed that had Kennedy lived, his administration might have succeeded in reaching a settlement of the Palestinian issue.

In 1965, Halaby became chairman of Pan Am Airways. Palestinian terrorism began to dog him on Labor Day weekend, 1970, in a prelude to the major effort by Palestinian extremists to overthrow King Hussein of Jordan. While weekending at his summer home on Fisher's Island off the Connecticut shore, Halaby received a coded message from Pan Am in London: AFTER DEPARTURE AMSTERDAM FLIGHT 93/06 SEP SUFFERED 9052 REPEAT 9052. The 9052 was a code designation for hijacking. Two gunmen from the PFLP had seized a New York–bound flight and taken it to Beirut. Halaby refused the hijackers' demand that they fly to Cairo with a demolitions expert. He ordered a Pan Am truck to block departure of the jumbo jet from Beirut Airport, giving way only when local Pan Am and U.S. Embassy personnel warned of danger to the passengers and crew as well as to the precarious peace then prevailing in Lebanon. The plane was flown to Cairo, and there the PFLP disabled it with a bomb.

Halaby left Pan Am in 1972. He became a chairman emeritus of AUB and served as a member of the university board in New York. In that capacity, he grew concerned about AUB's future and even more about the future of the American presence in Lebanon as a whole. Events that took place when U.S. troops were stationed there in 1983–84 were to prove his apprehension well placed. On January 18, 1984, during skirmishes between Shi'ite and Druze militiamen and the U.S. Marines positioned at Beirut Airport, Malcolm Kerr, who succeeded David Dodge as president of AUB, was killed. As he emerged from the elevator to begin his working day, two gunmen shot him. Within hours, Islamic Jihad, a name often adopted by the Hezbollah, publicly claimed responsibility for the deed. Their goal, they announced, was to "drive all Americans from Lebanon."

In Damascus, Syrian Foreign Minister Farouk al-Sharraa, with whom by chance I had an appointment that morning, literally paled at the news. "This," he told me spontaneously, "is a terrible act of terrorism against AUB and against all humane values. Syria can only condemn such a criminal act."

Kerr's assassination deepened the sense of crisis at AUB. As Najeeb Halaby and many other people knew, after David Dodge had been released from captivity through Syrian pressure in July 1983, one of his first acts was to telephone Kerr long distance and warn him about his safety. Always keep a bodyguard, he advised Kerr. During my last interview with Kerr at AUB in late 1983, he said that always being accompanied by a bodyguard had grown to be a nuisance. He had made off-campus trips without one, especially after reconciling himself with President Amin Gemayel. Their hostility had apparently been based partly on AUB's reluctance to move some of its operations to East Beirut and then on Kerr's reputation as a scholar who had shown serious interest in, if not sympathy for, the late Gamal Abdel Nasser and his brand of Arab nationalism.

The assassination was a terrible blow to Najeeb Halaby, who had handpicked Kerr for the job. Halaby had returned to assume active chairmanship of the university board shortly before it happened. From then on, AUB's faculty and staff, especially Americans, felt more than ever like marked men.

The U.S. Embassy Assault

April 18, 1983, was the day Khomeini's offensive against America in Lebanon began in earnest. If having your life saved by a friend's hospitality shows you have divine protection, it should also have been the day I returned to the Episcopalian faith drilled into me as a small boy by a zealous grandmother.

It began as a sunny day. Viewed from my former neighborhood in seafront Ain Mreisse, the Mediterranean was slate blue, shadowed only by a distant thundercloud. I walked out of the ABC News office just in front of the American University Hospital. I had made an appointment to see someone in the press section of the U.S. Embassy, a few hundred yards from the apartments I lived in during an earlier residence in Beirut. The appointment was not until 1:00 P.M., and it was only 11:45. There was plenty of time to walk down the old steps that skirt one corner of AUB and descend into a street, scarcely more than an alley, leading to the embassy and the sea. Deciding to visit a nearby camera shop, I walked past the hospital entrance to where so many casualties of Beirut's fratricidal fighting were taken each day.

Suddenly, I spotted a Lebanese friend, Kamal al-Khoury. "Come and have a coffee," he said. I was delighted to see Kamal again—as chairman of the Litani River Authority, he had been tremendously helpful in arranging access for a series of reports on the water situation in southern Lebanon—and gladly accepted.

Kamal was one of the countless Lebanese who wear many hats and moonlight to make ends meet. He was coproprietor of Standard Stationery, a shop just behind the university hospital. We sipped Turkish coffee in the back room of his shop. My embassy appointment was temporarily forgotten, I was so engrossed in our conversation.

And then it happened. The time, as I remember, was 1:03 P.M. An explosion like a tremendous thunderclap rattled the shop, sending echoes around the hospital and the narrow streets behind it. Kamal and I raced outside. I had two thoughts at once.

First, *that must have been a thunderbolt, and the lightning must have struck close by*. But there was no hail or rain falling. Second, *I was minutes late for my embassy appointment*.

Shouts, cries, and the sound of ambulance and police sirens drowned out Kamal's shouted warning not to run downhill to the embassy. Within seconds, a mushroom cloud of brown and black smoke rose from the seafront to the ABC News building as I dashed down the stairs.

The U.S. Embassy in West Beirut had been blown up by a suicide bomber. Though I gave it scarcely a thought until the first shock had subsided, Kamal al-Khoury's invitation for coffee had saved my life. Normal walking speed would have put me in front of the embassy, or just inside it, at 1:03.

When I reached the embassy, U.S. Marine guards who had survived the attack and Lebanese army forces were already trying to open a path through a horrified crowd for the rescue squads and ambulances. Ambassador Robert Dillon, who had escaped being one of the sixty-three dead because he was high in his penthouse office, was temporarily pinned under a wall. All seven stories in the center of the building had collapsed, leaving furniture, wires, and limbs dangling in air from less-damaged wings. The victims on the lower floors had been crushed. It was as if some giant had hammered part of the building and pulled down the rest of it.

What had happened was this: a young man in a black leather jacket drove a pickup truck with a ton of TNT to the driveway of the embassy from the seafront boulevard. He then pressed the pedal to the floor, ignoring the Lebanese guards and their few sandbags, and crashed into the main entrance of the building, detonating the TNT.

Thirty-three of those killed were embassy employees. About fourteen were visitors or passersby. The heaviest-hit portion of the embassy was its CIA station. Robert C. Ames, most senior of the agency's Mideast analysts, and seven other CIA operatives including Station Chief Kenneth Haas were killed. A member of the U.S. Army's Delta Force, assigned as Dillon's bodyguard, also died.

President Amin Gemayel appeared during the afternoon. Viewing the smoking debris, he voiced the hope that "those responsible for this crime have joined in death innocent Lebanese and Americans, and strengthened the determination of our two countries to continue to work together." President Reagan, in a statement at Andrews Air Force Base, intoned, "This criminal attack will not deter us. We will do what we know to be right. . . . Let this serve notice to the cowardly, skulking barbarians of the world that they will not have their way."[1]

Late that afternoon, when I visited the Agence-France Presse office, they had already received a phone call from the Islamic Jihad claiming responsibility for the "mighty blow against American imperialism." A leftist newspaper, *al-Liwa*, was told by a caller that the U.S. Embassy attack was "part of the Iranian revolution's campaign against imperialist targets throughout the world. . . . We shall keep striking at any imperialist presence in Lebanon, including the so-called Multi-National Force."[2] Although some rumors suggested a bomb had been pre-positioned in the embassy snack bar with the connivance of Lebanese employees, evidence pointed to the pickup truck as the culprit. A similar method had been employed against the Iraqi Embassy in Beirut in December 1982.

The West Beirut embassy assault was only the first of a long series of Iranian-inspired suicide attacks against American, French, Israeli, and other foreign targets in Lebanon. In many ways this attack, although it caused far fewer casualties than the bombing of the U.S. Marine barracks the following October, was the most serious for U.S. policy. The best Mideast CIA analysts had been destroyed. The United States had been humiliated in the eyes of Lebanese, Syrian, Israeli, Palestinian, and other regional observers. Weeks later, as I lunched with a prominent Shi'ite banker in Geneva, a man I had first known as a professor at AUB, he shook his head sadly. "John," he said, "the identification of the United States with Israel, and your own American policy blunders, are only now catching up with you." By "you," he meant, of course, "you Americans."

Accounts published by many of the players have established that before the embassy assault the U.S. National Security Agency (NSA), probably through a British monitoring station in Cyprus, intercepted and decrypted messages from Tehran to the Iranian Embassy in Damascus. They hinted of a major attack on the multinational force in Lebanon. Officials in Tehran had transferred $25,000 to Iranian Ambassador Muhammad Mohtashami. Requests were made for Syrian officers to help twelve Iranians move through Damascus to Lebanon—the reverse route of that used to abduct David Dodge.

A CIA security officer, Keith Hall, assisted Lebanese army intelligence in interrogating four suspects in the bombing. One was a Palestinian who worked in the embassy. Hall and the Lebanese agents beat the suspects up; the CIA fired him when this became public. The Palestinian confessed that his job had been to inform the terrorist high command that Ambassador Dillon was inside the embassy so the assault could start. The other three suspects admitted helping to load explosives into the pickup truck in South Beirut's Shi'ite suburbs. Lebanese investigators then found a fifth man who acknowledged recruiting the others. He claimed he had escorted a Syrian intelligence officer into Beirut to wire the explosives.

Rifaat Assad, brother of President Hafez Assad, summoned the American ambassador in Damascus, Robert Paganelli, to deny energetically the charge that Syrians had facilitated the operation. A Syrian intelligence officer then telephoned the Iranian embassy in Damascus to complain that Iran should not have ordered the bombing without Syria's approval. Men like Noel Koch, the top counterterrorist official in the Pentagon, argued that this call was staged for the listening NSA and for American policymakers to get Syria's Rifaat and Hafez off the hook. Others, believing Syria's protestations of innocence, fixed most of the blame on Iranian Ambassador Mohtashami.[3]

Weeks later, in July, Rifaat and Hafez Assad took a leading role in freeing David Dodge from Tehran's Evin Prison. President Assad made a phone call to Khomeini's office, an unprecedented intervention on behalf of an American and probably repeated only in the case of American newsman Charles Glass before he escaped his Hezbollah captors in August 1988.

Syrian emissaries went to Tehran to convince Dodge's captors that they could not win freedom for the Iranians who had vanished in Lebanon in 1982. Then, in a frightening melodrama, a young Syrian intelligence officer managed to bluff his way through a crowd of Revolutionary Guards who wanted to prevent Dodge's "rescue." "Neither he nor I was sure that we'd really made it out safely until the Syrian plane they had sent was out of Iranian airspace and on its way to Damascus," remembers Dodge.

After the briefest stop in Damascus to thank the Assad brothers publicly, Dodge flew to Westover Field, Massachusetts, in a U.S. Air Force plane. His wife and children, their hundreds of friends, Najeeb Halaby, and the rest of the AUB board rejoiced, with many weeping tears of joy.

President Assad, through his assistance in Dodge's release, had proven (as he was to prove on future occasions) that when it was in Syria's interest, he could exert maximum influence on Iran. And his brother, soon to become Syrian vice president, a man who had been accused of many transgressions by the Western media, earned brownie points with the United States. After all, Rifaat Assad might some day succeed his brother as Syria's supreme leader.

Neglecting Security in High-Threat Areas

The embassy attack caused Gen. Willie Y. Smith, commander in chief of the U.S. European Command in Stuttgart, West Germany, to conclude that something was seriously wrong with U.S. military security in Beirut. This was the European Command's responsibility, and General Smith selected the very best man he could find to deal with it: Col. William Corbett. Smith's special assistant for security matters, Corbett was a former Green Beret and a hardened Vietnam War veteran with a balanced and profound grasp of America's politico-military problems and what caused them.

Three days after the attack, U.S. Assistant Secretary of State Lawrence Eagleburger led a team from Washington to Beirut to represent President Reagan at a memorial service and to bring back the bodies of Americans killed at the embassy. Corbett joined the party in Frankfurt, West Germany.

Corbett's mission in Lebanon was tough but much better defined than that of the marine contingent there. He was to review the antiterrorist security of the 130-man strong, Beirut-based U.S. Office of Military Cooperation (OMC), headed by Col. Arthur Fintel. OMC was equipping and trying to retrain the Lebanese army to become a national rather than a sectarian force.

Corbett was appalled by what he saw and heard at ceremonies and news conferences devoted to the aftermath of the attack. "One would have thought that a victory, rather than a disaster, had occurred," he wrote. Ambassador Dillon had singled out for praise the conduct of the embassy's regional security officer: *after the attack* he had worked twenty-hour days to secure the area, recover classified documents, and help with the cleanup.

Nor were Corbett and some other security people pleased when Assistant Secretary Eagleburger told newsmen that American embassies abroad "don't hide behind steel doors and peek out through peepholes." Corbett had heard that kind of talk before, following terrorist blows against American targets. What was wrong with providing simple antiterrorist protection against the Ayatollah's partisans and other enemies? "As far as I am concerned," Eagleburger told his audience in Beirut, "this embassy [which lay in ruins barely a hundred yards away] has done its job and more than done its job." How, thought Corbett, could a professional diplomat of Eagleburger's stature, standing near the ruins of a major disaster, compliment those responsible?[4]

Once Eagleburger and his party had left, Corbett and Colonel Fintel checked out the physical security of the OMC. It was headquartered in the seafront Cadmos Hotel, where newsmen, diplomats, and others in Beirut had once partied. Corbett was dismayed to find no less than 120 U.S. military personnel concentrated there. The entrance to the underground garage opened directly onto a major street, and it had no door to prevent entry. One more bomb-laden vehicle like the one that had blown up the embassy, Corbett reflected, would take out the Cadmos and most, if not all, its occupants. If anything, it was an easier target than the embassy.

Fintel insisted that he had lobbied the embassy to authorize the erection of physical barriers around Cadmos. Without its authorization, he finally managed to put up barbed wire, sandbags, and fifty-five-gallon drums filled with sand as "minimal measures."[5]

By nightfall on the day of Eagleburger's departure, Corbett had established antiattack barricades and defenses all around the hotel. During the following weeks, personnel in the Cadmos were dispersed among other hotels in Beirut. This removed the political value of such targets as the Cadmos for the Tehran-directed terrorists.

In a report to the European Command on April 17, Corbett warned that the bombing had removed "any doubt of terrorist threat to U.S. interest in Lebanon." He pointed out that identification of the bombing as "against U.S. policy" or the "U.S. military presence" was meaningless from a security viewpoint.

> Since such [terrorist] organizations are motivated by an ideology seeking long-range ends, a single, random act of terrorism against U.S. interest in Lebanon is nonsensical. More applicable would be a series of terrorist acts, each, if possible, more spectacular and costly than the previous.

Corbett, in effect, prophesied the coming slaughter of the marines at their vulnerable airport base: "Following the U.S. embassy attack, U.S. military forces represent the most defined and logical terrorist target. . . . U.S. interests in Lebanon can expect an attack more spectacular than the action against the U.S. embassy."[6]

In June 1983, Corbett tried to warn Col. Timothy Geraghty, the U.S. Marine commander at the airport base, of the threat. Corbett was not even aware that 350 marines were living in a single building only a hundred yards or so from where their talks were going on. That was the battalion landing team (BLT) headquarters building, used as a billet and for artillery spotting. Very soon, the marines became partisans in the growing warfare between the mainly Maronite army units of President Amin Gemayel and the pro-Syrian and -Iranian forces in the nearby mountains.

Colonel Geraghty, who was public-relations conscious, often permitted newsmen, camera crews, and their technicians to watch and record skirmishes in the nearby hills from the roof of the BLT building. Once I watched a U.S. Army officer visually spotting artillery targets and relaying the information on a hand-held walkie-talkie, apparently to Lebanese army outposts. Near one of our favorite camera positions was a huge apparatus under a tarpaulin marked "Danger, Attention Laser." A laser range-finding device, surely?

Syrian, Iranian, and other hostile intelligence spotters could easily have mingled with Lebanese newsmen, who were occasionally allowed on the BLT roof that fatal summer. What there was to observe and record up there would have convinced Ambassador Muhammad Mohtashami, Revolutionary Guard minister Rafiq-Dost, and others directing anti-American operations that the BLT was a legitimate military target.

Unaware of all this, and unable to pull rank on Geraghty (they were both full colonels), Corbett tried hard to persuade the marine commander to authorize up to one hundred members of Colonel Fintel's OMC to move inside the defended perimeter at Beirut International Airport. Corbett says that he found Geraghty fully aware of the dangers and in possession of intelligence reports about the "Syro-Iranian threat," as one U.S. Embassy political officer called it. As Corbett saw it later, the problem was not a failure of U.S. intelligence; it was a failure of "commanders and managers neglecting their responsibility for securing their personnel in high threat areas, against repeated, proven attack techniques."[7]

Syria and Iran: Uneasy Allies

The conflict between the United States on one side and Iran, its ally Syria, and their surrogates on the other was soon to become two battles: a war of kidnapping and terrorism, and a brief but intense, mostly one-sided shooting war between the U.S. military and their adversaries. In Lebanon, Iranian involvement straddled the murky boundary between a shooting war and terrorism.

Khomeini's offensive there did not, strictly speaking, begin with the assault against AUB and the kidnappings and murders of its officers and staff. It began a few weeks after the capture of the U.S. Embassy in Tehran. In December 1979, a force of three hundred Iranian "volunteers," led by Ayatollah Muhammad Montazeri, set out for Damascus planning to obtain a springboard into southern Lebanon. The Iranians were offering to help the Shi'ites of southern Lebanon resist Israeli reprisal attacks and related pressures from Christian militias.

Syrian president Hafez Assad was given no warning of the Iranians' arrival. President Elias Sarkis of Lebanon, who would scarcely send his wife outdoors without requesting Syrian permission, phoned Assad. "Please," he begged, "don't let the Iranians into Lebanon. We have enough problems already with the Palestinians, the Israelis, and the other foreigners." Alarmed that Syrian forces might be dragged into unwanted and losing battles with Israel, Assad promptly had the Iranians assigned to a PLO training camp outside Damascus.

To the Iranians, this seemed unjust. After all, many of the revolutionary leaders, including the Ayatollah's son, Ahmed Khomeini, had been trained with the Palestinians and especially with Yassir Arafat's al-Fatah in Lebanon. Scores of Lebanese Shi'ites in the Amal had gone to Iran and played active parts in the revolution.[8] For Iranian militants to bring the revolution back to Lebanon would only be fair play.

For the time being, the militants had to wait. In the meantime, Syria and Iran tightened their ties in other ways. Assad, who opposed the Iran-Iraq War but who felt compelled to help the adversary of his bitter enemy, President Saddam Hussein of Iraq, closed the border with Iraq in March 1982. He also shut down the pipeline carrying Iraqi oil across Syria to the Mediterranean coast. Linked to this act was a comprehensive trade pact with Iran that secured oil for Syria at highly preferential rates, virtually for free.

Iranian revolutionaries with impeccable credentials, especially black-shrouded war widows and mothers of fallen men, were given periodic package tours to Syria via Iran Air. Most went to say prayers at the Shi'ite shrine of Sayidah Zaynab, the prophet Muhammad's granddaughter. Soon a market and an Iranian Revolutionary Guard center had sprung up around the mosque.

Then came more concrete Syrian support for Iran. In May 1982, Syrian troops were concentrated on the Iraqi border. This forced Iraq to move its forces from the Iranian front to the new western front with Syria. Although that front remained quiet, the Syrian action helped Iranian counteroffensives to drive the Iraqis back from the international frontier and bring the Iranians to within a few miles of Basra and other Iraqi population centers. During Operations Desert Shield and Desert Storm in 1990–91, Syria joined the allied military coalition to force Iraq out of Kuwait.

The Israeli invasion of Lebanon in June 1982 gave Khomeini an opportunity to prove that he meant what he said about the Muslim reconquest of Jerusalem. For Iran, Lebanon became a western front against the United States and Israel; disadvantaged Lebanese Shi'ites, now instructed and encouraged by the Revolutionary Guard, would be the Islamic revolution's spearhead in Lebanon. Within hours of the Israeli onslaught, a senior Iranian delegation arrived in Damascus to show solidarity with Syria and to plan action against Israel. Before the *majlis* on June 10, 1982, Prime Minister Mir Hussein Mussavi announced "war until victory in Jerusalem." He asked the deputies to fund the war "until the liberation of Palestine," which he called "an inseparable part of the Muslim motherland."[9]

On August 1, 1982, when I arrived to help reinforce the weary ABC News team covering the war, fifteen hundred Revolutionary Guards had been dispersed in

Baalbek and several villages in the Bekaa Valley. They moved into former Lebanese army barracks at the Sheikh Abdallah Caserne and began to work with a breakaway segment of Amal called Islamic Amal. This was a suicide attack unit led by Hussein Mussawi, former commander of the military wing of Nebi Berri's Amal (and not to be confused with Iranian Prime Minister Mussavi).

The unit was sometimes called Brigade 110. Its members were volunteers from various Arab states. They would carry out many kidnapping and guerrilla operations under the auspices of Hezbollah against American, French, Israeli, and other foreign targets in Lebanon.

Hezbollah was started by a group of Shi'ites that took as their motto the Koranic verse that says, "Those who form the party of God will be the victors." It operated Mussawi's Brigade 110 and other units under a variety of names: Islamic Jihad, Islamic Amal, the Revolutionary Justice Organization, the Oppressed of the World, and the Islamic Jihad for the Liberation of Palestine. Hezbollah's leaders in the Baalbek region were Hussein Mussawi's brother, Sheikh Abbas Mussawi, and Sheikh Subhi Tufayli. In Beruit, Hezbollah was spearheaded by a man who became the principal adversary of the United States in Lebanon, Sayyed al-Amin. He was the organization's spokesman and coordinator of Hussein Mussawi's suicide unit.

The spiritual guide for all of Hezbollah was and is Sheikh Muhammad Hussein Fadlallah. When Lebanon's civil war surged over Nabaa in 1976, Sheikh Fadlallah left there for the more hospitable southern suburbs and wrote many books on religious and legal subjects. His utterances and writings showed him to be a shrewd tactician. He oversaw Hezbollah along Iranian lines, guaranteeing the supremacy of the religious over the political by putting mullahs in command of the organization. Although Fadlallah referred to Lebanon as part of the "world Muslim nation," he saw no immediate possibility of converting it into an Islamic republic, however desirable that goal was. Like Nebi Berri, he called for social equality among Lebanon's sects. Fadlallah seemed to understand that the Christians, the Druze, and Sunni Muslims were determined to prevent Shi'ite rule of the country, and that Syria's President Assad would also stop short of allowing this.

Syria's Sunni majority tried many times to destabilize or overthrow Assad, who himself belongs to the Alawi sect, which might be classed as Shi'a. This gave Assad the role of gatekeeper: the more logistical support he allowed into Lebanon for Iran and Hezbollah, the more he risked destabilization of his own country.

None of this, of course, prevented Iran and Iranian Ambassador Mohtashami in Damascus from joining forces with Syria to expel the three "Satans"—Israel, the United States, and France—from Lebanon. With the help of Hezbollah and other new friends and surrogates, the first step was getting President Gemayel to repudiate an agreement for peace and normalization signed on May 17, 1983. This agreement involved a partial Israeli withdrawal from Lebanon but still far too much Israeli influence there for Syria's liking. After a campaign of diplomatic pressure reinforced by terrorist activity, President Gemayel was forced to repudiate it on March 5, 1984.

The ISA's Recommendations

Meanwhile, the American military in Lebanon found themselves being drawn more and more into a shooting war they had not wanted, had no mandate to fight, and to which they could make only a limited or "low-intensity" response. Knowing your enemy is the first role of any successful defense force. However, this presupposes that you know your own mission on the ground, in the air, and on the sea. The American forces in Lebanon knew none of these things. They and the United States would be made to pay dearly for such ignorance. As for intelligence, Colonel Corbett's prediction after the bombing of the embassy in West Beirut that "U.S. interests in Lebanon can expect an attack [even] more spectacular" did set bells ringing in Langley, Virginia, the headquarters of the CIA.

The loss of Robert Ames, probably as competent a Mideast analyst as the United States ever produced, was a U.S. intelligence catastrophe. During the late 1970s, Ames had handled the CIA's secret contacts with the PLO. Through Ali Hassan Salameh, or Abu Hassan, as he was known, Yassir Arafat kept Ames informed of terrorist threats against Americans. A few American newsmen knew Abu Hassan as a good-looking, intelligent, often hard-drinking, and amiable man with whom it was possible to swap gossip and sometimes important news. Few if any of us (certainly not I) knew of the close PLO-CIA relationship that flowed like an electric current through Ames and Abu Hassan.[10]

The Israelis knew of the U.S.-PLO relationship, of course. Their determination to destroy it may have been one of the motives behind Abu Hassan's assassination in Beirut in 1979. (Israel also blamed Abu Hassan and the Black September, a maverick wing of al-Fatah, for the massacre of eleven Israeli athletes at the Munich Olympic Games in 1972.) Abu Hassan was murdered, along with some innocent bystanders, by a car bomb in Beirut in 1979. This was not at all to the CIA's liking and those in a position to know say that CIA-Mossad relations deteriorated afterward. Three years later, during Israel's war in Lebanon, Gen. Yekutiel Adam, a skilled military man who had worked with Mossad and the Americans, was killed in battle. Relations between the American and Israeli intelligence services fragmented even further.

General Adam had been tipped to succeed Yitzhak Hofi as chief of Mossad. Now Hofi's deputy Nahum Admoni was chosen as the new head. Admoni was the first career intelligence officer to become chief. He had been educated in the United States and, having served Mossad for twenty-eight years in such posts as Washington, D.C., well understood the need to improve relations with the CIA.[11] As much as anyone, Admoni was anxious to work with the Americans against their common adversaries in Lebanon.

One problem for the United States, however, was that although the NSA could intercept radio messages from places like Tehran and in most cases interpret them correctly, the Israeli dismantling of the Lebanese PLO network had wiped out many of the CIA's "assets" in the terrorist underworld.[12]

Sensing the need for backup intelligence for the beleaguered marines, now the targets of snipers and occasional mortar shells, the Pentagon sent a team from the army's Intelligence Support Activity (ISA). Officially, the unit did not exist. Actually, it had been created after the failure of the Iran hostage rescue mission in 1980. The ISA leader was that mission's deputy director of operations, Lt. Col. William V. Cowan, a former U.S. Navy man who knew satellite and computer technology. Cowan arrived in Beirut on May 26, 1983, and became acquainted with William Buckley, the CIA station chief. Much of the embassy staff was hostile toward Cowan, who had let his beard grow to blend in with his Lebanese environment.

Cowan and his fellow ISA men soon got to know Beirut's labyrinthine layout. They recommended to General Smith at the European Command that the best way to frustrate Iranian Revolutionary Guard and other terrorist operations would be to set up a "fusion center." This would filter and evaluate the welter of conflicting intelligence reports from informers and other sources. The European Command's only response at first was to assign one intelligence officer to Colonel Fintel's OMC.

Noel Koch was an assistant secretary of defense responsible for counterterrorist operations. The European Command's indifference to ISA recommendations, he said, "reflected adversely on people who outranked them [the ISA's operatives]. . . . This led to denials, ass-covering, and all-around outrage that the [ISA's] survey had been done at all. . . . It was decided that there were no problems and that even if there were, they had been fixed."[13]

The extent to which they had not been fixed was to emerge at dawn on the morning of October 23, 1983.

8

"New Jersey!
New Jersey!"

A Mountain Interlude

September 18, 1983, I was with a television crew in the northern Shouf Mountains of Lebanon. Our driver charted an uphill course through the fragrant pine trees, his old Mercedes smoothly shaving the corkscrew bends of the road.

It was mid-afternoon of the first day of direct U.S. involvement in Lebanon's civil war. President Amin Gemayel's U.S.-supported army units were fighting off a direct threat to the presidential palace and the Lebanese Defense Ministry in Baabda. Druze and Palestinian fighters supported by Syrian artillery were pressing the Gemayel loyalists hard in the mountain village of Souk al-Gharb, a few miles below and to the west of us. Shells had begun landing along nearby ridges. What we did not know at that moment was that U.S. Sixth Fleet units off the coast had finally joined the battle. To discourage the Syrians and their allies, the missile destroyer *John Rodgers* and the cruiser USS *Virginia* were pumping shells into the high ridges.

At the U.S. ambassador's residence in Baabda, President Reagan's national security adviser Robert McFarlane and his staff had been hearing horror stories from Lebanese army commanders. One, possibly untrue, was about Iranian guerrillas who had stormed a hill at Souk al-Gharb and used axes to hack a company of the Lebanese Eighth Brigade to pieces.

U.S. Brig. Gen. Carl Stiner, the JCS representative traveling with McFarlane, urged that U.S. forces be allowed to defend U.S. Marine positions, the U.S. ambassador's residence at Baabda, and, if necessary, support Gemayel's army.

McFarlane agreed. He sent his famous "The sky is falling" cable to Reagan, saying that U.S. fire support was crucial to preserving the American presence. Among other things, he urged using tactical aircraft from the Sixth Fleet. It was foreigners fighting Lebanese, McFarlane argued, not Lebanese fighting Lebanese. Forces in the previous night's attack had been "comprised of PLA [Palestine Liberation Army] brigade and Iranian elements. The battle was savage and included ax fighting and hand-to-hand fighting of a brutality equal to the worst atrocities of Vietnam." The Lebanese government, McFarlane found, was "threatened with impending takeover by an uncivilized foreign force."[1] Reagan's national security staff read this as a clear warning that Syria, a satellite of the Soviet empire, and Iran, another foreign adversary, were threatening a country under U.S. protection.

Col. Timothy Geraghty, commander of the U.S. Marines ashore, had to decide whether to open fire. For a week, fearing for his men in exposed positions at the airport, he had held off. Then on September 18, General Stiner visited the Lebanese Eighth Brigade command post and its commander, Michel Aoun. Aoun's assessment of the situation, imbued with a sense of panic, had impressed Stiner. Since 10 A.M. the guided-missile cruiser *Virginia* had been hurling 5-inch shells into the wooded ridges above Souk al-Gharb.

Our drive through those same wooded ridges had been peaceful and uneventful despite the battles raging nearby. With typical Lebanese disregard for trouble in neighboring houses and villages, people in the big town of Aley went about their business. A troop of uniformed schoolgirls walked in a chattering file by the roadside, shepherded by their teacher. And from the slopes above the town of Hamama, we saw pines and firs spreading over the valley in a scene worthy of a Lebanese tourism poster. The battle around Souk al-Gharb was nothing but a series of dull, echoing rumbles.

Then, as soon as we rounded a hairpin bend in the road, a Syrian soldier was waving us down. Parked in the trees nearby, along with a weapons carrier and a jeep, was a Syrian army truck. It was painted green-brown, masked from overhead American reconnaissance by trees of the same color. Our driver braked instantly. His first thought was that we had come upon a Syrian artillery position, not a healthy place to be on this day. But he was wrong. Apparently it was a signal unit, for the truck and weapons carrier were stuffed full of communications gear.

In command was a tall, slim, mustachioed Syrian with captain's pips on his battle jacket. He strolled over to our car and glanced at our passports. "Journalists," we explained. Neither the captain nor his subordinates showed much interest in us. After the usual request not to film any faces, he even let us set up our camera at the roadside within sight of the unit but at a discreet distance.

About four minutes went by. We were almost ready to take some "beauty shots" of the mountain terrain when panic broke out in the little encampment. The soldiers piled their equipment into the truck and jumped in after it. The captain ran over to us. "Go, go fast!" he said. "Get out of this place. There is danger!" He ran to his jeep, and as soon as he was in the seat, all three vehicles roared off into the mountainside behind us.

Within seconds, we threw our camera, tripod, and gear into the Mercedes and headed downhill. As we rounded the bend just below the one where we had encountered the Syrians, we heard a whistle and a roar. The place we had been parked erupted in a geyser of black smoke, red clay, and fractured pine trees. Seconds later, another explosion, upslope from the first, spewed underbrush and rocks over the mountainside.

Somehow, the Syrians' early warning system had saved us from two 5-inch shells sent our way by one of the American ships. We remain grateful to the warning of that Syrian captain, for whom we were probably troublesome interlopers but also fellow human beings.

Enter the *New Jersey*

Many months later, in June 1985, two zealous Lebanese Shi'ites hijacked TWA Flight 847 on its way from Rome to Athens with 153 passengers and crew. The pilot, Capt. John Testrake, shuttled the plane between Beirut and Algiers until, finally, with help from the crew, he faked engine failure and managed to land in Beirut. After killing a U.S. Navy diver, Robert Stethem, and brutally beating other U.S. military personnel aboard the aircraft, the kidnappers finally released all but the three crew members and thirty-six American male passengers. Spirited off the aircraft under cover of darkness, these hostages were held in small groups around Beirut. Eventually Syria, aided by the speaker of the Iranian parliament, Ali-Akhbar Hashemi Rafsanjani, secured their freedom.

According to passengers' statements, immediately after Stethem's murder, one of the two hijackers ran up and down the plane's aisle screaming, "New Jersey, New Jersey!" What, wondered several of the passengers, did he have against the state of New Jersey? Later on, they found out.

The U.S. battleship *New Jersey* had become both a symbol and a piece in the game of revenge and retribution played out between the United States and its Mideast enemies.

Out of Mothballs

Although we in the Mercedes escaped retribution for the Sixth Fleet's shelling that September day of 1983, the U.S. ambassador's residence in Baabda, which had served as a makeshift embassy since the destruction of the West Beirut embassy complex in April, did not. Shells rained down directly on it. By late afternoon everyone had to be evacuated. A marine guard and several communications men remained behind, hunkered down behind sandbags and concrete blocks. For the first time, marine reports referred to the anti-Gemayel forces as "the enemy," that is, the enemy of the United States.

To mark the end of the marines' peacekeeping role and the beginning of their direct engagement, McFarlane flew to Damascus for the last of a series of meetings with President Assad that had begun following the Israeli invasion of Lebanon. The conversations were as futile as the earlier ones. Just before leaving, McFarlane said, "By the way, President Reagan asked me to let you know that the battleship *New Jersey* will be arriving in a few days."[2]

The *New Jersey* was more than a floating museum piece of the U.S. fleet; she was one of its leading legends. Her 16-inch guns had first blazed in action during World War II. She had seen battle in Korea and again in Vietnam before being mothballed. In 1981, having been reactivated for the battles that the Reagan administration anticipated on the fringes of the Soviet empire, she was ordered to Lebanon.

On September 15, 1983, four days before our brief encounter with those 5-inch shells in Lebanon, Rear Adm. Richard D. Milligan relieved his predecessor as the *New Jersey's* commanding officer in a brief ceremony off Puerto Rico. When the battleship arrived off the coast of Lebanon, Vice Adm. Edward Martin, commander, Sixth Fleet, came aboard to brief some of the senior officers on the new mission.[3] The battleship's presence, it was hoped, would intimidate and deter Syrians, Iranians, and other adversaries who might have further designs on U.S. forces. If need be, its huge guns could offer fire support to the Lebanese army and protection to the multinational peacekeeping force.

To the Americans on the scene, the *New Jersey's* strong medicine seemed to be working at first. A new cease-fire was arranged onshore. From the ship's bridge, Admiral Milligan surveyed a strip of Beirut coast through his binoculars. It could have been the coast of any peaceful resort, with sunbathers, motorboat races, a carousel near the water's edge that seemed to revolve perpetually, day and night.

Barely hundreds of yards away, however, there was sniping and rocket fire. Now and then, mortar and artillery shells hit the vulnerable marine compound at the Beirut Airport. The marines were taking casualties.

The Attack on the Marine Compound

There had been plenty of intelligence warnings of a major attack. According to William Corbett's reports to his superiors in the European Command, both Lt. Col. Howard L. Gerlach, the battalion commander, and Col. Timothy Geraghty, the Marine Amphibious Unit commander ashore, were guilty of "professional failure" in not preparing better defenses. "Here is a case," wrote Corbett, "of responsible commanders, in a combat area, fully aware of the terrorist danger and preferred method of attack, warned of the high possibility of attack, but [who nevertheless] assembled 350 of their men in a single, lightly guarded building." What was more, Corbett might have added, overhead intelligence had observed truck and car bombs near the Iranian Revolutionary Guards barracks outside Baalbek. Newsmen of various nationalities also had full access to that building to observe, film, and record the hostilities.

"Even the greenest of second lieutenants are taught and understand," Corbett went on, "the tactical imperative of dispersal and cover when in a hostile fire zone. Had these commanders performed in such an unsatisfactory manner during a graded field training exercise, they would have been relieved of command."[4]

On the morning of October 23, 1983, marine Lance Cpl. Eddie DiFranco was on guard in a sandbagged post outside the battalion landing team (BLT) building. He saw a yellow Mercedes truck crashing through a 5-foot-high roll of concertina wire. On orders from above, DiFranco's M-16 rifle was not loaded. By the time he had loaded it and was ready to fire, the truck was tearing past him. The driver was a young man with bushy black hair and a mustache. He looked into DiFranco's face and smiled.

The driver shifted, picked up speed, and passed through an open gate in the chain-link fence surrounding the barracks. Sgt. Steve Russell, in the guard shack at the barracks entrance, saw the truck heading towards him at 30 mph. He raced through the lobby and out the back door, shouting "Hit the deck! Hit the deck!" The truck smashed into the barracks and halted in the middle of the lobby. The last thing Russell saw was an orange-yellow flash at the front of the truck; then he was hurled through the air by a horrendous blast.

The gruesome carnage was described in detail by many who saw and survived it. FBI experts said it was the largest non-nuclear blast ever, equivalent to 12,000 pounds of TNT. The bomb scooped out an 8-foot crater in a 7-inch floor of reinforced concrete, lifting the whole building and severing its support columns. Bodies, severed limbs, clothing, and gear rained down on the wreckage. A total of 245 lives had been lost.

At the time of the attack, Col. Arthur Fintel, the Lebanese army's U.S. adviser, was sleeping in his Beirut apartment five miles away. He thought what he heard was the Cadmos Hotel, supposedly secured by Corbett's efforts, going up in smoke. But when he leaned over the railing of his balcony, he saw a "huge mushroom cloud. . . . Then, right in front of me, there was a flash and a big cloud of black smoke [which was] was the French going up."[5] Another suicide truck bomber had blasted a multistory structure in downtown West Beirut, the barracks of a paratroop unit that formed the core of the French peacekeeping force. Fifty-nine French soldiers were killed.

A report by the Long Commission, headed by retired Adm. Robert Long, summed up several different investigations of the marine disaster. It recommended punishment of both Gerlach and Geraghty for "failure . . . to take the security measures necessary to preclude the catastrophic loss of life"; the secretary of the Navy gave "letters of instruction" to both.[6] Rear Adm. John Butts, director of the Office of Naval Intelligence (ONI), found that available information should have made it possible to predict the attack. Despite all the talk in the United States about fighting terrorism, however, ONI had not assigned a single analyst to study the threat to the marines in Lebanon. Gerlach was in a Veterans Administration hospital being treated for spinal injuries when he received his letter of instruction. He was more concerned about recovering the use of his arms and legs than he was about his career.

In the end, President Reagan took full responsibility on himself. This headed off any court-martial or other legal proceedings that might have told the story of the disaster in greater detail.[7]

William Corbett found that the attack, aside from being a major human tragedy, "was also a military debacle of a magnitude not seen since World War II. . . . [It]," he wrote his superiors,

> is incomprehensible that no disciplinary action was taken against those responsible for the horrendous failure to secure military personnel in an active hostile fire zone, especially when knowledge of the threat, preferred terrorist attack methods and techniques [vehicle bombs had been used three times in Lebanon since 1980] were known to all.[8]

Aboard the *New Jersey* and other U.S. warships, there was grief and rage. Ships went to general quarters. Their commanders feared terrorist attacks by speedboats, frogmen, and even light airplanes that Iranian and Palestinian guerrillas were known to possess. On November 4, the *New Jersey* was released from its frustrating no-shoot patrol duty long enough to steam to Alexandria, Egypt, for a four-day port call. Shortly after Admiral Milligan returned from making courtesy calls ashore, orders came through from the commander of the Sixth Fleet to return to Lebanon.[9] The guerrillas had struck again. This time they had sent a suicide truck into the Israeli military governor's headquarters in occupied Tyre, killing fifty-six Israelis and their Lebanese prisoners.

Plans for Retaliation

Both American and French military commands began planning reprisals against the forces of Hezbollah and their Iranian mentors, the Revolutionary Guard. What did U.S. and French intelligence know, or what did they think they knew, about their attackers? Quite a bit. Islamic Jihad claimed responsibility for both attacks, announcing in the Beirut newspapers, "We are the soldiers of God and we crave death. Violence will remain our only path if they [the multinational force] do not leave. We are ready to turn Lebanon into another Vietnam. We are Lebanese Muslims who follow the dicta of the Koran."[10] The dark-haired, mustachioed truck driver who had so cheerfully sacrificed his life at the marine barracks was said to be a member of a group called the Suicide Commandos of Hussein (referring to the Hussein of the Koran and his martyrdom at Karbala).

The NSA had decrypted cables from Tehran to Muhammad Mohtashami at the Iranian Embassy in Damascus urging him to organize a heavy blow at the Americans. NSA information also showed that the Revolutionary Guard in Baalbek had asked the embassy for permission to carry it out. One week before the bombing, a central figure in the capture of the U.S. Embassy in Tehran, Hussein Shekholislam, who had become Iran's deputy foreign minister, stopped off in Damascus. He checked out of the Sheraton Hotel there on October 22, the day before the attack.

Plans for retaliation included both conventional warfare and terrorism. Conventional responses would be carried out by U.S. Navy forces off Lebanon. Along with the *New Jersey* were several cruisers, among them the *Virginia* and the high-tech Aegis cruiser *Ticonderoga*, and two aircraft carriers—the *Eisenhower* and the *Kennedy*. Support ships of all types cruised offshore. The carrier *Independence*, scheduled to replace the *Eisenhower* in mid-November, was temporarily diverted to Grenada in an effort by President Reagan to bolster U.S. prestige and his own popularity by invading the Caribbean island two days after the marine barracks bombing in Beirut. The plan was for at least two carriers to be on station at all times off Lebanon. Until Operation Desert Shield in 1990–91, the firepower amassed off Lebanon was greater than any since World War II. The commander of this huge conventional force was a tough, diminutive workaholic, Rear Adm. Jerry O. Tuttle. Commander of Battle Group Two, Sixth Fleet, he also held command of Carrier Task Force 60—impressive fighting forces. However, in the words of the *Washington Post*'s veteran defense correspondent, George Wilson, who visited the force off Lebanon: "Tuttle often found himself a Gulliver pinned down by Lilliputians."[11]

Following the attack on the marine barracks, hundreds of intelligence warnings reached the force about something even more terrible being perpetrated on land, at sea, or in the air. Time after time, the *Kennedy*'s air wing was sent out to chase attacks that somehow never materialized. One of the threats came from Swedish-made speedboats operated by the Revolutionary Guard naval division. To counter this threat, the *Kennedy*'s A-6 attack planes carried special bombs to strew bomblets over acres of territory, destroying anything in their path. They were supposed to be used only in night raids; during the day, when greater precision was possible, single-warhead, high-explosive bombs were preferred.

Newsmen invited aboard U.S. naval units escorting reflagged "American" tankers owned by Kuwait later became accustomed to the ships' weapons: 50-caliber machine guns, manned on a twenty-four-hour watch, and heat-seeking antiaircraft Stinger missiles, which were to fight off kamikaze attacks by light planes or gliders. Helicopter crews and marines were trained in night antiboat operations. Carrier planes also had to stay above the buffer zone of 3,000 feet or else they would be shot down by their own ships.

To launch an F-14 Tomcat fighter or an A-6 bomber, an entire airborne support system was needed: KA-6D tanker for midair refueling operations, rescue helicopters circling the carriers' sterns in case fliers crashed, and often E-2C Hawkeyes (a smaller navy version of the AWACS) to give fighters target guidance. The result was that American taxpayers shelled out billions of dollars for operations that served an uncertain mission in an unknown cause. "The mightiest armada ever assembled," wrote George Wilson, "was in danger of being worn out by phantoms . . ." because the United States was never sure what was going on in the shadowy world of the terrorists."[12]

To Admiral Tuttle, the biggest threat in the air appeared to be the Syrian air force, or what was left of it. The Israelis had downed more than eighty Syrian planes in 1982. Hit-and-run raids by Syrian MiG-23 and -25 and Sukhoi fighter bombers, however, were always a possibility. So Tuttle split the airspace off the Lebanese coast and its extension to Cyprus into five ambush stations manned by carrier-based F-14s. They were armed with AIM-7F radar-guided Sparrow missiles, AIM-9L Sidewinder missiles, and a 20mm cannon. Thousands of hours of flying time were racked up by the two carrier wings. As time went by and no enemy appeared on their heads-up combat displays, the Red Rippers, as the F-14 pilots called themselves, grew progressively more bored.

While all this frenetic activity continued, planning began in early November for a strike to avenge the marines. When the *Kennedy* arrived off the Lebanese coast, Admiral Tuttle summoned Cdr. John J. Mazach of Air Wing 3 and asked him to bring along a strike planner. Mazach brought Cdr. Paul Bernard, executive officer of an A-6 squadron called The Buckeyes. At a meeting on the carrier, Tuttle reviewed with his air-group commanders a set of top-secret plans for the first air strike ever by the United States on an Arab country.

The immediate target, however, was not Arab, it was Iranian. They wanted the Sheikh Abdallah barracks outside Baalbek, once used by the Lebanese army and gendarmerie, now in the hands of the Iranian Revolutionary Guards and their Hezbollah allies. Hitting this was supposed to fulfill President Reagan's requirement that retaliation should punish terrorists alone, not civilians—in Pentagonese, that it should avoid "collateral damage."

According to George Wilson, the original strike plan for Baalbek called for the use of eight A-6 bombers—later increased to twelve—each carrying twelve 1,000-pound bombs. The idea was to flatten the barracks in fifteen minutes. The columns of Baalbek's fabled Roman and Phoenician ruins, where many theater and music enthusiasts had attended summer festivals, were supposed to make it easier for the A-6 bombardiers to get into position before releasing their bombs.

Syrian antiaircraft defenses—Iran's Revolutionary Guards had none of their own—were thought to be sparse in that area at night. Nevertheless, the A-6 pilots would rely on night-vision devices and electronic countermeasures to deliver their bombs and escape safely. The F-14s from the *Kennedy* would patrol the night of the attack to take care of any Syrian fighters that might challenge the A-6s. Helicopters from the USS *Guam* with marine rescue crews were tasked to fish lost fliers from the water. Air controllers aboard two EC-2 Hawkeyes would direct the operation.

On several nights, A-6 crews aboard the *Kennedy* were awakened, ordered to don flight and survival gear, briefed, and actually sent to their planes. But each time the higher command called off the raid. Eventually the *Eisenhower* redeployed to the United States, and on November 17, Admiral Tuttle made the carrier *Independence* his flagship for the intended revenge strike.

During that period, I was working with an ABC News Closeup team on a documentary about Syria. Early on November 18, I drove with the crew to the Syrian mountain resort of Bludan. At the top of the mountain near Bludan, on a clear day, you can see Baalbek's ruins. The Revolutionary Guards' supply trail meanders through the Bekaa Valley and the hills below, leading from the Syrian base at Zebadani and into Lebanon. Sometimes it is called the drug trail because large quantities of hashish, morphine-based heroin, and other contraband pass over it. What we were half expecting that day, however, was not a drug or arms shipment but an air strike from the U.S. Sixth Fleet. The Israeli air force had hit Hezbollah training camps in the Bekaa Valley the day before, retaliating for the suicide assault on their Tyre military headquarters. Arab newspapers predicted American action would follow. From first light that morning, we watched the gray-blue clouds over Lebanon for intruders. None came, so we had an early lunch at a mountain inn and drove back to Damascus.

About the time we reached the city limits, the French naval air arm mounted a surprise strike on the very area we had been watching. As Hezbollah and Revolutionary Guard casualties of the Israeli raid were being buried, fourteen French Super-Etendard jets took off from the Mediterranean-based French carrier *Clemenceau*. They streamed over the Bekaa Valley toward the very target the Americans had been planning to hit: the Sheikh Abdallah barracks on a hill above Baalbek. Another target was Islamic Amal's headquarters in the Khawam Hotel.

This was intended to be France's retaliation for the loss of their fifty-nine paratroopers in Beirut on October 23. It was an almost complete fizzle. One of the few fatalities was apparently a Lebanese shepherd; neither the barracks nor the Revolutionary Guards themselves seem to have suffered any setback. "They woke up the gardener," one officer of the French strike force commented after the fact.[13] Later, a Syrian photographer found a small hole in the ceiling of a top-floor room in the old Palmyra Hotel. A shrapnel fragment had penetrated the bedroom of an International Red Cross worker.

What the French and Israeli raids and the growing U.S. reconnaissance flights did manage to do was to raise the Iranians and their Hezbollah allies to new heights of zealotry. Kamikaze volunteers had already performed their funeral rites and were prepared to meet their maker. "America, France and Israel started the war. Our fighters wear their death shrouds," intoned Hezbollah cleric Sheikh Subhi Tufayli.[14] Meanwhile, the French and Israeli strikes called for a new command decision by the Americans. Clearly, the Sheikh Abdallah barracks would be much better defended now.

But by December 3, the U.S. Navy had not rethought its plan. It was instead prepared to try some aggressive new reconnaissance probes against Syrian antiaircraft flights. This was the decision that would kill one of the most popular "top guns" among U.S. Navy fliers and lead to the capture of another. It would result in an outstanding political and public relations coup for American politician Jesse Jackson and President Assad of Syria, and would kindle new criticism of the senior members of the U.S. military.

The Lieutenant Goodman Affair

On the morning of December 3, 1983, an F-14 equipped with a precision camera was sent out. It swept over marine positions on the coast and the hills beyond, trying to get high-resolution tactical pictures. These would show where the enemy was and how he could be targeted. Another F-14 flew shotgun on the wing of the first plane with hostile challengers. From the hills, antiaircraft guns flashed and winked at the F-14s. Telltale traces of smoke rose like corkscrews. These were the signatures of SAM 7 heat-seeking missiles, easily able to hit the aircraft as they streaked across western Lebanon at an altitude of 3,500 feet. But the planes returned safely. Admiral Tuttle filed a report that reached the White House.

The JCS recommended to the president that planes from both the *Kennedy* and the *Independence* bomb Lebanese antiaircraft sites manned by the Syrian army. Use of the *New Jersey*'s 16-inch guns was rejected. The chief of naval operations, Adm. James D. Watkins, said later that air strikes were decided upon as a "response in kind . . . a tit-for-tat kind of thing." The *New Jersey*'s big guns, they felt, would bring too much "collateral damage."[15]

Among those scheduled to fly the strike were Lieutenants Gil Bever, Tom Corey, Bill Davis, Mark Lange, Mark McNally, and Robert Goodman. A Naval Academy graduate from New Hampshire, Goodman sported "lucky socks" from his father, a retired air force lieutenant colonel.

At 3:45 A.M. on December 4, the lieutenants were awakened for a briefing on what most thought would be another of the innumerable drills they had conducted off Lebanon. Each two-man A-6 crew, a pilot and a bombardier, were given maps and target descriptions to study in their ready rooms. They were told to be prepared for launch at 7:30 A.M. Apparently this word was not passed to all of the ordnance teams, some of whom had not unpacked the correct mix of bombs from their cases in time. Notably absent were the Rockeye cluster bombs, which were supposed to take out several Syrian antiaircraft positions. Other ordnance was intended for a large white building housing Syria's main antiaircraft data base for Lebanon. The *Kennedy*'s E-2C Hawkeye observation plane was launched before the bombers to coordinate the raid by radio. Its call sign was Close Out. Two EA-6B electronic-warfare planes were also sent out. Their mission was to jam Syrian fire-control radars and spoil the aim of the ground gunners. Five A-6s and thirteen A-7s from the *Independence* joined ten other bombers from the *Kennedy*. Because they took off too long after sunrise, the pilots found themselves flying directly into the sun, which inhibited their search for small ground targets and their attempt to survive antiaircraft fire. On the way out, a tardy plane from the *Independence* broke the order of radio silence to ask for guidance to the main strike group—possible tipoff for the Syrians. Meanwhile, about half a mile off the port side of the *Kennedy*, the inevitable Soviet electronic trawler was watching, listening, and possibly alerting the Syrians about the mission.

Scarcely had the first planes crossed the coast when the ack-ack (antiaircraft artillery, or AAA) bursts of white smoke and spiraling tracks from the surface-to-air missiles (SAMS) greeted the American fliers. Over their headphones, the *Kennedy's* bombers behind them heard, "SAMS! SAMS! SAMS! . . . I'm hit . . . I'm hit!" And seconds later, "Honiak out of here!"—a signal that Cdr. Ed ("Honiak") Andrews was ejecting from his burning A-7. Rescue helicopters took off instantly from the *Guam* as he parachuted into the bay.

A Lebanese fisherman and his son pulled Andrews into their boat, then gave him over to a motorboat full of French newsmen as eager for a scoop as they were for a rescue. A French military Zodiak boat took Andrews away from them and got him ashore. A Lebanese helicopter then flew him to the soccer stadium, whence he was conveyed by a U.S. Marine helicopter back to his home carrier, the *Independence.*

The other aircraft began firing antiradar missiles and going after their targets. Thankfully, most of the hostile ordnance was exploding well below their 12,000-foot altitude. One missile did, however, manage to strike the A-6 piloted by Mark Lange. Robert Goodman was his bombardier. The two men ejected from their flaming bomber. Lange's chute opened just in time to break his fall, but a metal object or fragment severed his leg on impact. According to navy doctors who later performed an autopsy, the A-6 pilot bled to death. Goodman hit the ground hard, breaking some ribs and injuring his left shoulder and knee. He was captured by Syrian gunners who reportedly roughed him up without inflicting serious harm. Newsmen and cameras were summoned from Beirut to take pictures of Goodman and his disabled plane. The triumphant Syrians then whisked Goodman to Damascus along with Lange's body. Goodman, hospitalized, became President Hafez Assad's prize American prisoner.

Realizing that their raid had failed, the rest of the A-6s and A-7s limped home safely. George Wilson, who toured the *Kennedy* after the last plane returned, encountered "rage, bitterness, sadness, rationalization and protest." Earlier talk of "bombing Lebanon back to the Stone Age" was heard no more. One pilot, a Republican who had been a staunch Reagan supporter, proclaimed, "I'm going to vote Democratic because of the way [the Republican administration] micromanaged this raid." Another told Wilson, "If the American people ever find out that we sent ten airplanes over there . . . to do what one plane could do, they'll never forgive us. I'm embarrassed. Vietnam taught us how to do it without losses. . . . I wonder if we learned anything at all from Vietnam." Others complained that after months of training to hit the Iranians at Baalbek, targets were changed at the last minute, briefings had been inadequate, and the wrong ordnance had been chosen.

After interviewing everyone he could in connection with the December 4 raid, George Wilson concluded that those involved had not had the time they needed to prepare the mission for "minimum risk and maximum effectiveness." President Reagan wanted to send a political message, and he sent it before crews or planes were fully ready. "The fact that men were ordered to risk their lives to carry out such a flawed plan," Wilson wrote, suggested "that the American military command structure is broken and must be fixed. If it is not fixed, the United States is in real danger of losing any next war."[16]

Lange was given a shipboard memorial service on December 9. Less than a month later, Jackson, after spending several days in Damascus as an unofficial lone-ranger diplomat, received custody of Lieutenant Goodman. Goodman had partially recovered from his wounds after some good Syrian medical care (there are said to be more doctors in Damascus than there are truck drivers). Jackson's stateside supporters were delighted that their leader had extricated Goodman from the tangled web of Mideast politics in the wake of the White House failure to do so. The release, well covered by the media, probably gave U.S. ambassador to Syria Robert Paganelli grim satisfaction. During the comings and goings of presidential envoy Robert McFarlane and his successor, Paganelli had warned repeatedly that air raids, the naval gunfire, and the losses of military personnel in Lebanon were getting the United States nowhere and could lead to worse trouble. His warnings fell on deaf ears.

The *New Jersey* Unleashed

On the ground in Beirut, too, things were going from bad to worse. On December 4, 1983, the day of the ill-fated air strike, eight more Marines were killed at the Beirut Airport. Ten days later, the Pentagon finally decided to unleash the *New Jersey*.

She was ordered to fire her huge 16-inch shells ("as big as Volkswagens" was the popular description used by the news media crowd in Beirut) as a signal rather than in blanket retaliation. "I think," Captain Milligan said, "it was primarily an attempt to send a pretty strong message that, when we send the F-14 aircraft in for reconnaissance missions over Lebanon, we don't expect them to get shot at. This is going to be the price."[17] For, flushed with their recent successes, Syrian gunners now fired every time a U.S. reconnaissance flight appeared on their screens.

The shells traveled sixteen to eighteen miles over the ridges beyond Beirut, blasting craters as big as tennis courts and inflicted plenty of "collateral damage" on farms, villages, and civilians. I have never heard any confirmation of Syrian, Iranian, or other military targets being hit. There were no airborne observers to spot for the *New Jersey*; carrier-based reconnaissance flights were now giving the deadly Syrian AA and missile batteries a wide berth.

Later that winter, Robert Fisk, the award-winning correspondent and author of *Pity the Nation: Lebanon at War*, visited a woman who was lying in her hospital bed recovering from cuts and burns inflicted by the *New Jersey*'s shelling of her village. Her brother-in-law had been killed. Some of the survivors bore flash burns that had turned their skin pink and purple. In the forest outside Tibiyat, Fisk and several other journalists found craters five feet deep and fifteen feet wide left by the battleship's shells. Militiamen told them that naval shelling had killed twenty-four civilians and wounded 115 in the thirty-square-mile area of the Metn mountains and Shouf foothills. No one could verify rumors that there had been Syrian casualties.[18] Sadly for the image of the United States, the *New Jersey* became a watchword in the area for the application of mindless, brute force.

Aboard the *New Jersey* herself, the sagging morale of a bored ship's company was revived. Between December 15 and Christmas, a succession of entertainers visited the ship. On December 15, the day Wayne Newton performed on the battleship's fantail helo platform, she opened fire with her smaller 5-inch guns, lobbing forty rounds in support of the beleaguered marines. On December 24, Bob Hope appeared with Brooke Shields. They were followed by Cathy Lee Crosby, Ann Jillian, Julie Hayak (Miss USA, whose name convinced some Lebanese newspapermen that she must be of Lebanese origin), Vic Damone, and George Kirby.

Meanwhile, in Lebanon's tired mountains, the *New Jersey*'s victims nursed their wounds and buried their dead.

The United States Blinks in Lebanon

From a diplomatic perspective, much of America's warlike activity along the Lebanese coast had been in support of President Amin Gemayel and the unfortunate Israeli-Lebanese agreement of May 17, 1983. It was meant to initiate withdrawal of Israeli troops while preserving Israeli influence in Lebanon. Syrian President Assad, who wanted to play a leading role in the hapless little nation's affairs, continued to insist that the agreement had to go. Presidential envoy Donald Rumsfeld was well aware of an intelligence report about growing Iranian influence on Lebanese Shi-'ites, but he was hampered in his efforts to juggle the players. The Reagan administration had promised Israel that Rumsfeld would not be permitted to propose amendments on his own to the May 17 accord. Rumsfeld could raise with Assad only those ideas Israel wanted to discuss. A dispute was raging inside the U.S. administration. What could it do about separating the deteriorating Israeli and American positions in Lebanon? Both were under attack, and both were crumbling. Public support for the confused Lebanon campaign had begun to wane in the United States even before the assault on the marine barracks. On September 29, Congress had grudgingly extended the mandate of the marines another eighteen months. In exchange, the Democrats insisted that the Reagan administration not expand the role of the marines, move them from Beirut Airport, or further change their mission without congressional approval.

The marines and the navy fliers had been badly bloodied. The big guns of the U.S. Sixth Fleet had exacerbated antagonism against the United States everywhere. Defense Secretary Caspar Weinberger, already deeply worried over the related and intensifying war between Iran and Iraq, gave a warning to his more hawkish subordinates. To defeat the Syrians and drive the Iranians out of Lebanon, he said, "we'd have to put in about fifteen divisions."[19]

Little by little, the administration, in its planning and policy papers, began identifying America's position in Lebanon with that of Israel. The first step toward clearing the way for Israel to fight it out with Syria and Iran was an American withdrawal from the country. This was something the Ayatollah in Tehran as well as President Assad in Damascus had been working for.

The United States had blinked in Lebanon. As a result, the Ayatollah's surrogates and friends there—the Party of God and its like-minded supporters—were preparing new attacks. These were aimed at the buildings and key personnel of the U.S. State Department and the CIA.

9

Beirut Addio

A Morning in Beirut

On February 6, 1984, at first light I drove a friend's car across the dangerous Green
Line into East Beirut to find some friends whom I had not been able to reach by
telephone. I zigzagged frantically at the main crossing point near the Lebanese
Museum. Much of the city, east and west, was under shellfire from Walid Jumblatt's Druze forces and from the Amal (Shi'ite) militia. The Lebanese army loyal to
President Amin Gemayel had been returning the fire but was by now in pell-mell
retreat. Offshore, the great gray ghosts of the U.S. Navy cruised slowly back and
forth, powerless to prevent the fall of the politician many American officials had
been calling "our guy."

Two hours later, after I'd found my friends safe but frightened, I left my friend's
car in East Beirut, as arranged, and a taxi took me back to West Beirut. The driver
dropped me a block from the Commodore Hotel. We could not approach too close
because of sniping nearby. Meanwhile, Associated Press bureau chief Terry Anderson and Associated Press (AP) reporter Scheherezade Faramarzi (an Iranian) were
on their way back from visiting the besieged marines at the airport, where they saw
hooded gunmen and uniformed militiamen attacking Lebanese troops in street
battles.

Outside the Moscow Narodny Bank near the Lebanese prime minister's office,
Robert Fisk, then with the (London) *Times*, came across a thinly bearded militia-
man wearing a Koranic quotation on his battle jacket. Below it was embroidered a
white, curved Arabic sword. "Our new protectors had arrived," Fisk mused grimly.[1]

Amal, with Hezbollah fighters already among its ranks, was advancing steadily into the western part of the city. Posters of Imam Musa Sadr and Ayatollah Khomeini appeared all over West Beirut. Despite the furious bombardment, Beirut traffic crawled bumper to bumper past the Commodore. Drivers shouted curses and leaned on their horns. The din was almost too loud to hear the *crump-crump* of not-too-distant mortars.

Just as I reached the Commodore's steps, there was the deafening *wham!* of an exploding shell in the street behind me. Blue sparks flew from overhead wires and scattered cindery fragments through the air, already rustling with tiny shrapnel fragments. The force of the blast threw me to my knees. Stunned, I inched my way up the steps on my belly, shards from the hotel's glass door cutting my arms and hands. One of the Commodore's front desk men helped me into the lobby. Camera crews filming the Shi'ite advance backed out of the lobby and into the restaurant, expecting the worst.

The Allies Say Goodbye

That night, I nursed my cuts and tried to write some broadcasts that would make sense, while the Lebanese army unleashed the worst bombardment of West Beirut, now wholly in militia hands, since the Israeli siege of summer 1982. Nearly a hundred civilians were killed that night; I think I succeeded in sleeping for a total of one-half hour. At dawn, from the hotel roof, we filmed the burning city and tried to describe what was going on. Muslim militiamen were already looting shops, smashing up bars, and pouring bottles of alcohol into the streets. Only two days earlier, President Reagan had spoken of the need for Americans to stand fast in Beirut and not "turn our backs on our friends and cut and run." This would be "sending one signal to terrorists everywhere: they can gain by waging war against innocent people."

It was clear now, as we stood on the roof of the Commodore Hotel, that the original peacekeeping mission of the marines and the multinational force had ended. Later that day, on BBC World Service broadcasts, we heard an announcement that most of the U.S. Marines would be redeployed to their ships in the Mediterranean. A few would be left to guard Lebanese shore installations but not the airport. Tehran radio broadcast triumphant announcements.

Of the multinational force, the token British contingent left first. Without notifying their allies on the ground, they drove at high speeds to the port of Jounieh and abandoned equipment on the quay for the Phalangists. Most French troops pulled out, though a few remained with the UN force in southern Lebanon. The Italians stayed longer, gradually reducing the guards that had faithfully protected Palestinians in Sabra and Chatila from Phalangist killers. Driving past the southern suburb of Ouzai some days later, I saw painted in huge letters, "BEIRUT ADDIO" (farewell). This was for the Italians.

The United States and Britain airlifted their civilian citizens who wanted to leave by helicopter to warships that carried them to Cyprus. Unlike evacuations to Cyprus and Athens before 1982, which had been safeguarded by PLO forces, this one was protected by U.S. Marines. They would not let us take pictures of American civilians leaving. When Associated Press correspondent Don Mell asked the U.S. Embassy press officer why, he answered, "The reactions to the photographs might be dangerous—or—I don't know how to put it—damaging to the foreign policy or something like that."[2]

During the evacuation, an American student, a young woman from New York, started an argument with marines who stayed behind to guard the U.S. Embassy in West Beirut. "You wasted your time here," she told several of them. "You failed in everything you did." When a sergeant insisted to her that they were fighting terrorism and that she was being evacuated for her own safety, the woman shouted, "You're not! You came here and turned my friends into my enemies and my home into a place of fear."[3]

The *New Jersey*'s Last Hurrah

Offshore, the *New Jersey* was again put on alert. Since the new year began, the battleship had fired its 5-inch (not the big 16-inch guns) twice at hostile artillery positions, shooting thirty-two rounds on January 15 and seven rounds on February 7. February 7 was the day of Reagan's "cut and run" announcement, as it came to be known among locals.

Early on the afternoon of February 8, I sailed from Beirut, which was again under fire, aboard one of the big ferries that managed to carry passengers to Cyprus during the airport's closing. A haze hung over the sea just to our south. Suddenly, the big guns began to boom again. We could not see the ships firing through the haze, but shipboard observers on the *New Jersey* heard Captain Milligan announce on the public-address system, "The *New Jersey* has a fire mission. Man your gunnery stations." Finally suspended from their sentence of boredom, crewmen cheered and banged gleefully on the bulkheads.

In a terrible crescendo of explosive fire, the *New Jersey* vented the rage and frustration of the Reagan administration at America's failure in Lebanon. She unleashed 288 rounds, cutting a wide swath of destruction through the Lebanese mountains. Harpoon missile stations aboard ship were alerted to meet threats from land or sea, including the Revolutionary Guard speedboats already encountered in the Persian Gulf. But no attacks came. The *New Jersey*'s SH-2 helicopter, whose mission in other parts of the world had been over-the-horizon targeting, now flew constant surveillance patrols to watch for hostile ships among the many merchant vessels using neighboring Mediterranean sea-lanes.

Commander, Task Force 60, ordered all U.S. Navy ships in the eastern Mediterannean to general quarters. Men dropped their knives and forks at mess and reached for steel helmets. The Americans expected retaliation for the shelling, which continued until 11 P.M. that night. But the only real shipboard damage was caused by concussions from the thunderous 16-inch salvoes: a water pipe in Captain Milligan's sea cabin burst, soaking his bunk.

Scuttlebutt had it that the cannonade took out several Syrian gun emplacements, a few rocket launchers, and a command post with some of its personnel including a general. If so, Syria never made public complaint.

The *New Jersey* resumed patrolling in the final days of the marine deployment. Starting on February 21, men and equipment were moved from the Beirut Airport compound to the Sixth Fleet's amphibious warfare ships. On February 26, the transfer to sea of the Twenty-Second Marine Amphibious Unit was complete. Only a few guards remained ashore. That same day, militia forces opened up on what was left of U.S. reconnaissance flights. Again the *New Jersey* responded, now for the last time, with thirteen rounds of 16-inch shells. The crew was rewarded for their long vigil at sea with a seven-day port visit and shore leave at Haifa, Israel. There they were treated to a USO show that included the Dallas Cowboys cheerleaders.

On April 2, the *New Jersey* once again off Beirut, Captain Milligan informed his crew on closed-circuit television that they would continue their mission until the battleship *Iowa* arrived to relieve them. Only ninety minutes later, a radio message ordered the ship to depart Beirut at once and head for Naples.[4]

And so the lurking gray ghost that had spewed fire and thunder at Lebanon's mountains was gone. In Tehran, the Ayatollah Khomeini could chuckle with satisfaction.

Protecting Americans Left Behind

While U.S. Marines and the men of the Sixth Fleet enjoyed shore leaves in Mediterranean ports more friendly to Americans than Beirut, planning by Iran's Revolutionary Guards and their guerrilla allies proceeded apace. The Americans were now unmistakably on the run. This certainly coincided with the launching of fresh attacks on Persian Gulf shipping and new Iranian land offensives against Iraq.

In Beirut, Col. William Corbett was only too aware of the danger to remaining Americans. Now only about a hundred marines protected American diplomats and the remnants of military and intelligence teams sent in so hopefully less than two years before. Following the October 1983 bombing of the marine compound, Corbett's responsibilities had been extended to antiterrorist security of U.S. forces in Lebanon, including the U.S. Embassy and what was left of the marine position at the airport.

The new marine commander ashore, Brig. Gen. Jim Joy, was not an antiterrorist expert. He was, in Colonel Corbett's words, "a professional of the highest order who understood well the military mission of securing his force and of preparing to fight if necessary." In other words, Joy knew what he was doing and set out to do it—until U.S. Ambassador Reginald Bartholomew had some basic differences with him, as well as with Corbett and the other senior military commanders.

In May 1984, U.S. European Command headquarters in Stuttgart, Germany, responsible for U.S. military personnel in Beirut, was informed that Ambassador Bartholomew wanted to split up what remained of the U.S. Embassy. This was housed in the British Embassy building on the seafront. Bartholomew's idea was to move one section to East Beirut and maintain another in West Beirut. To Corbett, responsible for the physical security, this meant moving from one totally secure location—the British Embassy was protected by formidable barriers, tanks, fences, and firepower—to two separate and vulnerable locations. This seemed like "returning to square one."

Corbett had long advocated moving all marines out of Lebanon. While the embassy complex itself was secure, Corbett felt that the marines guarding it were not. The guard force could not stay hunkered down inside like the embassy staffers. They had to be outside to inspect vehicles and watch traffic leaving and entering the embassy area. Since the only remaining rationale for keeping warships offshore was to protect Americans ashore—the Gemayel government was now scarcely master of the presidential compound in Baabda, let alone of Beirut—Corbett advocated replacing the marines with a State Department security force. The other option was for the Lebanese government to provide a guard force in keeping with the international practice of host countries protecting foreign embassy and diplomatic personnel.

Corbett and his fellow officers, unhappy about the idea of splitting the embassy, had a suggestion: The State Department should hire the security personnel. The military in Beirut would then integrate them into the marine force and train them.

Ambassador Bartholomew did not accept this offer. He preferred to split the embassy compound. Some of the twenty-seven personnel were getting cabin fever in the barricaded West Beirut complex. Bartholomew's idea was that by opening the embassy annex in East Beirut, personnel suffering from claustrophobia or siege mentality could live in relatively safe apartment complexes in East Beirut, near the new annex. They could bring their dependents back to Beirut and enjoy a reasonable life-style, if not the dolce vita of old.

General Lawson agreed with Corbett's theory that it would be unsafe and wrong to split the embassy into two separate parts. However, if the ambassador, who had the final word, insisted on the split, the military would defend the U.S. Embassy in West Beirut until the ambassador was satisfied with the security arrangements at both locations.

Armed with these orders, Corbett returned to Beirut from Stuttgart. On June 2, he met with Ambassador Bartholomew, his deputy, and regional American military chiefs. Bartholomew lectured Corbett about knowing his job and his mission. The marines, he said, were doing a good job. He would continue to use the existing embassy security staff and would keep them divided between the two new locations as long as he felt necessary. Bartholomew stressed that he had the Washington connections and leverage to force through this decision against military objections. The West Beirut location, near the old one, would still be the main embassy office. Near the new site in East Beirut, restaurants were open and shops were usually better stocked. Only six or seven U.S. employees would be working there and on a rotating basis.

Corbett said the European Command wanted the marines eventually replaced by a fully trained State Department guard force. The Command did not want to split up the marine guard force or move it intact to any new location. It simply was not wise to abandon the well-protected West Beirut compound. Moving, he felt, would reduce security and invite attack.

Bartholomew seemed to understand the military's position. He insisted he could make the move almost at once; in mid-June he wanted the embassy personnel in East Beirut to commute by helicopter between the two embassy compounds until the East Beirut annex was ready for use.

To Corbett and other military men at the fateful June 2 meeting, this meant that the real purpose of the move was to get embassy personnel up to full strength again and improve their life-style—a far cry from the later State Department claim that security was the only reason for the move.

The U.S. marine commander agreed to cooperate. He would provide locally recruited security trainees with on-site instruction. Service attachés and training commanders helped acquire weapons from the Lebanese army, as well as training areas and firing ranges. At Ambassador Bartholomew's request, Corbett agreed to conduct a security survey of the two sites with the embassy regional security officer and the marine commander and his assistant.

Chosen for the West Beirut embassy was a place about two hundred yards down the seafront from the old Anglo-American site. For those of us who had lived on the Beirut seafront and knew it, the location looked highly vulnerable. There were open fields on two sides, and high apartment buildings and a hotel nearby from which direct gunfire could be delivered on the embassy. Herculean efforts would be needed to make it secure. As the military men saw it, the building would be wide open to a repeat performance of the April 1983 embassy and October 1983 marine bombings.

The military and the embassy both approved the proposed East Beirut building—a six-story structure sitting isolated on a hillside and with a commanding view of its surroundings. This made a car-bomb attack look unlikely and gave its defenders a platform to mount automatic weapons on the roof.

Corbett then left Beirut for good. When he retired from the U.S. Army on August 1, 1984, he continued to watch developments from Germany as a private consultant. Ambassador Bartholomew received the help he had requested from the marines, although he made no further attempt to split up the guard force. Corbett left two recommendations with the embassy's regional security officer: use temporary but adequate antivehicle barricades (concrete "dragon teeth," still stockpiled at the marines' old airport site but somehow never moved to East Beirut), move in disabled vehicles as barricades, and dig antivehicle ditches, among other devices. [5]

By mid-September 1984, Bartholomew and his staff were moving into the new annex. Before leaving, Corbett had recommended a number of interim security measures to protect the unfinished East Beirut annex, but few had been taken.

Royal Military Police to the Rescue

Iran's operatives in Lebanon presented the bill for American neglect on September 20, 1984. It could have been higher—the United States owes a debt to the then–British ambassador to Lebanon, Sir David Miers, and his staff that it was not.

On the morning of September 20, Miers arrived at the East Beirut annex to call on Ambassador Bartholomew. With him was a team of five RMP (Royal Military Police) bodyguards. All five were corporals. Their usual team leader, a staff sergeant, was away on temporary duty in Britain. One of the corporals stayed with Miers as he took the elevator up to see Bartholomew on the fourth floor. Another corporal stood on an embankment at the edge of the parking lot, eight feet above the approach road, which gave him a good view.

The soldier spotted a Chevrolet van moving through the embassy checkpoint about a hundred yards to his right. The van stopped at a barbed-wire barrier. There was a shot, after which the vehicle headed toward him.

Unlike marine sentries at the Beirut Airport before the October 1983 disaster there, the RMPs carried loaded guns. The corporal moved the switch of his HK-35 pistol to automatic. When the van reached his level, he fired five rounds into the left door. The driver slumped forward and his van careened to the right, rebounding off a parked vehicle and rolling another ten yards or so. Then it blew up, sending a thunderous blast all over the city. The new embassy annex partially collapsed in a repeat of the disaster at the West Beirut embassy on April 18, 1983.

If that quick-thinking RMP had not fired when he did, the van—probably targeting the embassy's underground parking lot—could have pulverized the building, killing hundreds of people inside and out. As it was, fourteen people were killed and scores injured, including the corporal, who was blown across the parking lot and left with permanently impaired hearing.

U.S. and British experts who checked the wreckage afterward concluded that a "dead man's hand" device had triggered the bomb. Several seconds after the driver released it, the bomb exploded; the terrorist driver, meanwhile, had been shot dead.

Two of the RMPs worked their way through the dust and smoke into the building. The prescient corporal who had shot the terrorist now radioed the British Embassy for help. As people ran in helter-skelter fashion, screaming, Phalangist militia began arriving. The two RMPs reached the fourth floor and found Miers and Bartholomew in what remained of the latter's office. One of the walls had collapsed, and Ambassador Bartholomew's legs were pinned beneath a steel girder. Miers, unhurt, refused to leave or let anyone else do so until Bartholomew, in pain, was freed. The RMPs pried Bartholomew loose after a few minutes; then one of them carried him down the rubble-strewn embassy stairs. They commandeered a passing civilian car for an ambulance. In true Beirut style, Phalangist militiamen drove their escort vehicles madly through the streets, firing weapons in the air to clear the way to the hospital. One of the British team remained behind to help the American survivors and their Lebanese assistants give first aid to the injured.[6]

Lessons Not Learned

In West Germany, William Corbett was stunned. How could it have happened again? He discovered that none of the essential security devices against car bombs had been in place. Barricades had been poorly positioned, making it easy for a vehicle to maneuver through; no automatic weapons covered the barricades or approaches. Corbett was dismayed with the official explanation that there had not been enough time to procure, ship, and erect all of the security devices. No one questioned why the move to East Beirut was approved in high places or why the move was made before the building was totally secured.

Corbett commented as follows:

> Professional failure starts with the Ambassador [who, fortunately, recovered from his injuries]. . . . [Because of] his desire to expand staff and operations and create a normal life-style in a totally abnormal environment, [the embassy] vacated a proven, secure position for uncertainty and danger. [His] reasons are starkly similar to those given by the Marine commander who moved 350 men into a single building [at the Beirut Airport]. . . . When will we learn that hostile areas are not . . . suburban Baltimore . . . ecosystems?

After the September 20 attack, twenty-six nonessential embassy employees were returned to the United States, reducing the staff to thirty—about the same number that had been safely fortified and supplied at the seafront West Beirut building. The consequences were another destroyed building; more expenses to the long-suffering U.S. taxpayer; and, after a further rash of exultant propaganda from Islamic Jihad and its Tehran mentors, the embassy was back where it was before. As Corbett remarked, the embassy security officer, severely injured in the attack, had the "single mission to defend the Embassy and its personnel. Awaiting custom-manufactured steel gates, electronic surveillance equipment, and other James Bond devices, he neglected to block the road."[7]

Corbett and other critics pressed their questions repeatedly. Why had the embassy been moved in the first place, unless it was for better liaison with Christian Phalangists who controlled the eastern sector? Why wasn't the move, if necessary, delayed until there was adequate security? Why was the embassy staff in Beirut doubled when affairs had been sufficiently conducted for over a year by a smaller staff? Why were those antivehicle barricades not positioned to stop all traffic? And why were the approaches to the embassy not covered by American guards equipped with automatic weapons? In a situation where responsibility and failure seemed so evident, why was disciplinary action not taken against anyone?

And finally, why did the Long Commission's report on the bombing of the U.S.

Marines in Beirut fail even to mention the assault on the West Beirut embassy and the attendant problems?

Again the payback was blowing in the wind of hate from Tehran. The terrorists it influenced were turning to a deadlier phase of their secret offensive: capturing hostages. Some of them were Americans, bearing the most responsibility for maintaining the Western presence in Lebanon.

10

Hostages to Misfortune

The Shi'ite Assault on Kuwait

December 12, 1983. In a well-planned though poorly executed operation, suicide bombers struck the American and French embassies and various strategic targets in Kuwait. Kuwait and its government were the primary targets; America and France, for their actions in Lebanon and for their support of Iraq in the Gulf conflict, were secondary. Considerable damage was done, especially to the U.S. Embassy. About nine people were killed there and eighty-six injured. A veritable holocaust at a gas plant in the Kuwaiti oilfields was narrowly avoided when a truck bomb stalled short of its target.

The Kuwait attacks resulted from the collusion of Lebanon's Hezbollah and a resuscitated underground organization, al-Dawa ("the call"). Founded by Iraqi Shi'as, al-Dawa was telecommanded from Tehran to unleash the revolution in the Gulf emirates. The bombings in Kuwait would also be a pretext, a trigger, and a motive for future kidnappings of Americans in Beirut.

From the beginning of the Iranian revolution, the war against America was waged in the Gulf as well as in Lebanon. Of wealthy Kuwait's heterogeneous population of over one million, there were more than twenty-five thousand Iranian and almost ten times that many Iraqi Shi'as. Kuwait's ruling family, like the ruling families of Saudi Arabia and the other Gulf emirates, is Sunni Muslim presiding over a population made up mostly of Sunnis. They mistrust the Shi'ites.

Shortly after the start of the Iran-Iraq War in 1980, al-Dawa suggested in a report to a senior cleric in Tehran that Kuwait was "ripe for revolution."[1] The report claimed that many if not most Sunnis would either flee or submit to a Shi'ite regime in the event that a Tehran-inspired Islamic revolution succeeded in Kuwait. Some 300,000 Palestinians in Kuwait, many in senior jobs and prosperous, would not risk their lives to defend the Kuwaiti ruling family (a prediction that came true when Iraq invaded Kuwait in 1990). The 200,000 Shi'as would overwhelm the Sunni majority with their revolutionary zeal.

The December 1983 bombings, then, were intended to start a revolution in Kuwait. The prelude began in January 1982 with attacks on cinemas, restaurants, libraries, and girls' schools—places considered by the Shi'ite zealots as centers of sin and corruption. Some women wearing slacks or Western dresses were stabbed in the street. Cars of pro-Iraqi businessmen were fire-bombed. Kuwait's leader, instead of getting tough with Iran, turned the other cheek and sought dialogue instead. The Kuwaiti branch of Hezbollah spread its propaganda throughout schools and Koranic study centers, the latter of which developed into hotbeds of revolutionary indoctrination.[2]

This well-established pattern of Shi'ite subversion made it relatively easy for the Kuwaiti authorities to identify and apprehend the conspirators behind the December 1983 attacks. Seventeen men were arrested: fourteen of them were members of al-Dawa; the other three were followers of Hezbollah in Lebanon.

One of the seventeen prisoners was a man named Mustapha Youssef Badreddin, a ringleader of the suicide bombers. Badreddin was the cousin and brother-in-law of another prisoner, a young Shi'ite Lebanese leader of Hezbollah, Imad Mugniyeh, known as one of that organization's toughest and most feared gunmen and organizers. Badreddin was sentenced to death. Another of those sentenced to death was Hussein Youssef Mussawi, a cousin of Hussein Mussawi of Hezbollah's Lebanese chapter. Neither was executed, however. The ruler of Kuwait, Sheikh Jaber al-Ahmed al-Jaber al-Sabah, had been threatened by al-Dawa; if he carried out death sentences on Badreddin and two other prisoners, American and other foreign hostages in Lebanon would die in reprisal.

Almost two years later, in May 1985, Shi'ite guerrillas threw bombs at the emir of Kuwait's car. They failed to kill him but did murder four other people, including one of the ruler's bodyguards. In July 1985, bomb attacks were made on two popular Kuwait cafés that allowed men and women to eat together—"wounds in the heart of Islam," the revolutionaries called these places. The café bombings killed at least twelve people and injured over a hundred more. But the emir would not sign death warrants for those sentenced to death, not even for the men who had tried to take his life.

Two of the seventeen al-Dawa prisoners were released in February 1989 after serving their sentences. The remaining fifteen escaped from prison when, on August 2, 1990, as Iraqi troops invaded Kuwait, their guardians abandoned them.

They evaded Saddam Hussein's forces, and some, with the help of Iran, managed to return to Lebanon.

Kidnapping, Inc.

In 1984, soon after the U.S. Marines left Lebanon, the kidnapping of Americans began in earnest. The first victim was a professor of electrical engineering at AUB, Frank Regier. He was one of the hardy few who had chosen to stay on after David Dodge's kidnapping and Malcolm Kerr's murder. Imad Mugniyeh's Hezbollah gunmen captured Regier on a West Beirut street on February 10, 1984, the day before the trial of the al-Dawa prisoners opened in Kuwait. Five days later the kidnappers cast their net again. This time they snared Christian Joubert, a French engineer, near the French Embassy in West Beirut. Miraculously, both men were freed when Nebi Berri's Amal militiamen, acting on a tip, raided a house and found them.

Amal, Hezbollah, and Walid Jumblatt's Druze had become the dominant organizations in West Beirut. On March 7, at 8:15 A.M., CNN correspondent Jeremy Levin, a Jewish American who had only been in Beirut a few weeks, walked to the CNN offices opposite the Commodore Hotel. Approaching the Saudi embassy at the end of Rue Bliss, not far from the AUB campus, a man tapped him on the shoulder and shoved a handgun into his stomach. He forced Levin into a car and threatened to kill him if he opened his eyes. For four hours, at a house somewhere in West or southern Beirut, Levin lay blindfolded as a rough voice accused him of being a CIA or Israeli spy. He denied his tormentors the satisfaction of anything but rebuttals. Next, he was blindfolded and gagged with brown wrapping tape, wound so tight it almost stopped his circulation. He was then loaded onto what seemed to be a truckbed.

After a lengthy journey, he arrived at his place of captivity: a tiny room in a house on a mountain. Levin's ordeal and the efforts of his wife, Sis, to free him are related in her book *Beirut Diary*.[3] Later, Hezbollah was to insist that it had deliberately allowed Levin to slip out of his chains and escape down the mountainside on the morning of February 14, 1985, something Levin stoutly refutes. Syria formally handed him over to the United States in Damascus immediately. This was a brief peak in the periodic ups and downs of Syria–U.S. relations.

The next kidnapping of an American in Lebanon shook the Reagan administration to its foundations. It was a major failure for U.S. intelligence and specifically for the CIA, then directed by William Casey. At the same time, it demonstrated both the lengths and the limits of the secret war between America and its Mideast adversaries.

Casey's Man in Beirut

At 7:00 A.M. on March 16, 1984, William Buckley woke up in his Beirut apartment and breakfasted to a background of classical music. His 343d day in Beirut, Buckley had plenty of reasons to take special precautions. Buckley's cover was embassy political officer, but it was well known that CIA Director William Casey had sent him to Beirut as CIA station chief after former station chief Kenneth Haas and eleven other U.S. intelligence personnel died in the 1983 suicide attack on the West Beirut embassy. For some unknown reason, however, Buckley had told his driver-guard not to show up that March morning.[4]

Tension in West Beirut hovered at standard levels. Amal and Hezbollah militiamen were operating freely in the streets. Only two days earlier, a truckload of explosives was detonated before a Lebanese "action," or intelligence, team (officially disavowed by the CIA) could kill Sheikh Muhammad Hussein Fadlallah. Then, a car bomb had exploded in the street below Buckley's window. Buckley had been fixing cocktails for an American couple just arrived from the States. Glass fragments flew all over the apartment. He insisted that the couple stay in his guest bedroom that night. In the morning, he summoned a U.S. Marine patrol to escort them to their quarters.

On the last morning of his freedom, fifty-eight years old but still fit for his age, Buckley took the elevator as usual to the parking lot in the basement of his apartment building. The shadow of the Iranian-inspired offensive against AUB hung over him. Sheikh Fadlallah, after the attempt on his life—he proclaimed it on a large banner hanging in front of his house, "MADE IN THE U.S.A."—had issued new warnings. This time they were addressed to the Lebanese prime minister: AUB should be closed because its teaching undermined Islam. Buckley was supposed to deal with the problem during calls that morning at the Lebanese Foreign Ministry in East Beirut.

With a "burn bag" chained to his wrist—a twist of its key in the wrong direction was supposed to ignite special gas burners inside, destroying the case and its contents in an emergency—Buckley said good morning to a woman tenant he knew. A well-dressed man entered the elevator one floor below Buckley's, also carrying a briefcase. As Buckley left the elevator on the garage level and headed for his car, the man hit him from behind with the case. A CIA investigation later found that it contained rocks. Then a white Renault appeared with a driver and one other man. The female tenant, now standing at a bus stop outside the garage, saw this and screamed for help, but it was too late. The Renault tore off through the side streets of West Beirut toward the Fakhani district. It was controlled largely by militias, including Hezbollah.

Casey was awakened at 3 A.M., March 17, in Washington with the news. He drove immediately to his office at Langley and convoked a breakfast meeting attended by many of the agency's senior Mideast executives. The word went out to get Buckley back alive, at all costs. Payments were authorized for information; the trimmed-down Beirut station—nearly all the American CIA officers were ordered out of Lebanon at once—was told to work with whatever assets it had left.

Hezbollah and their Iranian mentors, having pieced together much of Buckley's background, well knew the importance of their captive. In the 1960s in Vietnam and Laos, Buckley had helped organize the hill tribes, the famous Montagnards, into private armies not unlike the ones now operating in Lebanon—except that in

Southeast Asia they had been mobilized into the service of the CIA. Buckley's next big assignment was in Zaire. There he is supposed to have had knowledge of a CIA-organized conspiracy to kill Patrice Lumumba, the leftist president. According to one account, it was Buckley who was chosen to take Lumumba's file to Montreal, where CIA "black operations" expert Sidney Gottlieb was conducting mind-control experiments with poisons of various kinds.

Again, in Rome on May 13, 1981, Buckley happened to be the man on the spot. Mehmet Ali Agca, former member of a right-wing Turkish group called the Gray Wolves, shot and seriously wounded Pope John Paul II before a crowd of about 250,000 pilgrims in St. Peter's Square. At the time, Buckley was on vacation from training duties with Egyptian President Sadat's bodyguards in Cairo. He is said to have suggested that Ali Agca, after his arrest, showed signs of being drugged and perhaps "programmed." Many believed that the real culprit was the Bulgarian secret service acting on orders from the KGB, for the stubborn Polish pope had been publicizing his native country's struggle for independence from Moscow.

On October 6, 1981, at a military review before Sadat, several soldiers broke ranks and gunned down the president. His bodyguards hesitated before returning the insurgents' fire, and they also failed to form the kind of human wall that Buckley had earlier demonstrated to them in training films. Buckley himself was present at the assassination; in fact, he drew his revolver upon seeing the soldiers break rank. "He's dead as a dodo," shouted Buckley later on the phone to CIA headquarters in Langley.

After what some in the agency might have regarded as Buckley's tragic failure in Cairo, Casey sent him to Canada to collect background on a list of plaintiffs suing the CIA for the alleged mind-control experiments. Buckley wrote up a long report on torture, especially medical torture, around the world, cataloguing among other things amputations, electroshock "noise rooms" where victims were subjected to high-intensity sound until they became permanently deaf, and psychiatric drugs. Buckley accused not only enemies of the United States of abuse but also friends such as Turkey, Saudi Arabia, Egypt, Israel, and the Philippines. Much of this information was leaked to Amnesty International, the London-based human rights organization, which used it in reports over the course of the following years.

During a brief period of service in El Salvador, before his Beirut assignment, Buckley saw a man torturing a prisoner by dripping sulfuric acid, drop by drop, into an open wound.[5] Experiences such as these equipped him to understand rationally, at least, the kind of fate possibly awaiting intelligence operatives falling into the hands of captors as ruthless as those who held him from that morning in March 1984.

One of these men, according to the accounts of several intelligence services and a few liberated hostages, was Imad Mugniyeh. Mugniyeh was one of the few Hezbollah leaders who trained with the PLO's al-Fatah. A tough, good-looking, bearded man, intelligent and shrewd, he worked for awhile with Nebi Berri's Amal but preferred Hezbollah and became a confidant of its "spiritual adviser," Sheikh Muhammad Hussein Fadlallah. He rose to the head of Hezbollah's special operations branch, the duties of which included kidnapping, hijacking, and other acts of terrorism.[6] Securing freedom for his brother-in-law, as noted earlier, an al-Dawa prisoner being held at the time in Kuwait, became one of Mugniyeh's central goals.

Buckley's Confession

In the efforts to locate Buckley, the main Lebanese operator was Col. Simon Cassis, chief of Lebanese military intelligence. According to several pages of Buckley's confession, probably authentic and no doubt extracted under torture—it was passed on much later by intermediaries—Buckley had worked closely with Cassis. They had "at least weekly contact" during which "we discussed the security situation, future training programs and many other things that were of interest at the time. . . . I had a liaison relationship with Colonel Cassis, which meant that he passed information to me with the knowledge of his government and I in turn passed the information to the Embassy." One matter they discussed, says the document, was schooling Lebanese personnel in the orderly processing, filing, and retrieval of information so that it could become useful intelligence.

The confession's poor transcription makes some of Buckley's alleged words illegible, but not all: "I am primarily a trainer and instructor," he said, "having been one almost all of my life as opposed to being an intelligence officer. I found delays in training [the document blames this on Lebanese Defense Ministry bureaucracy] very frustrating, particularly when they necessitated having to send messages to the United States, requesting that training teams be rescheduled or canceled." Once, the confession says, Buckley had accompanied Cassis to the United States "so that he could brief analysts at the CIA on the situation in Lebanon . . . as government forces lost control of the leadership."[7]

According to the transcript, Buckley also worked with Lt. Col. Luis Cassis, brother of Simon Cassis and officer in charge of Amin Gemayel's presidential security guard. In general, Buckley complained about there being "too much information" abroad in Beirut—a gripe certainly shared by newsmen and diplomats bewildered by the plethora of rumors and disinformation. But support for the presidential guard and general information gathering were banal, routine activities for a CIA operative in a station as critical to the United States as Beirut was then. And Buckley's Shi'ite captors did not consider him a routine operative. They had in their grasp the man they thought was most responsible for keeping what was left of Lebanon and its government in the Western camp. They felt Buckley stood directly in the way of Khomeini's directives to erase American influence from Lebanon so that it could be turned into an Islamic republic.

Buckley was passed, it is presumed, to progressively higher echelons of Hezbollah and the Revolutionary Guard until finally he was confronted with interrogators from Iranian intelligence. These men probably operated under orders from Muhammad Rayshari, the dreaded military judge and prosecutor who had sent many of Khomeini's opponents in Iran to their deaths. The decision was made to transfer

Buckley to Tehran. This guest was not like mild-mannered American educator David Dodge; this guest, the Iranians believed, would yield valuable secrets and command a high price when the Americans tried to recover him.

Buckley, it appears, was flown from Rayak Air Base, former Lebanese air force headquarters in the Bekaa Valley, now under Syrian control, to Damascus Airport. Rafik Mohsen-Dost, Iranian minister in charge of the Revolutionary Guard, happened to be on an official visit to Syria at the time of Buckley's transfer. He may have personally supervised the movement of the drugged and blindfolded American from Damascus to Tehran, either in a regular Iran Air jumbo jet, probably in the cargo hold, or in an Iranian military C-130 cargo plane.

One of his first prisons in Tehran was a secret dungeon in Fereshte Street, close to the Iranian state television and radio building.[8] Undoubtedly, Buckley was tortured atrociously there. What his captors were probably most eager to wring from him was his knowledge of U.S. contingency plans for meeting new terrorist attacks and of U.S. tactics to be used by special forces in response to hijackings and kidnappings.

The Search for Buckley

In Washington, William Casey mobilized all of the available resources of the American intelligence community in a huge search for Buckley. The CIA, the NSA, and the Defense Intelligence Agency (DIA) pooled their resources and "called in all favors from friendly organizations." Two months after the kidnapping, the CIA's national intelligence officer for the Middle East sent a five-page memo to the NSC and the State Department suggesting conciliatory moves to reach Iranian moderates who might want to improve relations with the United States. It was never clear whether the memo was prompted by the need to save Buckley from Iranian clutches, or the timing was a coincidence. In any case, the memo was one of the basic documents used to justify the arms-for-hostages deal with Iran that emerged during the final months of Reagan's second term.

Early U.S. efforts in Lebanon to find Buckley were handicapped by the paucity of human intelligence (HUMINT) on the ground. To understand this, one must follow the history of the U.S. Army's Intelligence Support Activity (ISA), headquartered at Fort Belvoir, Virginia. ISA was the successor to the Foreign Operating Group (FOG), set up specially to rescue the U.S. Embassy hostages from Tehran in 1979. FOG had initiated American counterhostilities in the secret war with Iran by sending four Special Forces soldiers disguised as civilians into Tehran to collect such information as the type of locks on the gates of the U.S. Embassy compound where the captives were being held. FOG also rented trucks in Tehran for the ill-starred 1980 rescue attempt. In 1981, the ISA made its debut in Lebanon by conducting a joint operation with the CIA, spiriting the future Lebanese president and terrorist victim, Bashir Gemayel, back into Lebanon after he had visited the United States.

ISA was less successful in arms trading. During the furious Iraq-Iran tank battles of 1981–82, it tried in vain to obtain the most up-to-date model of the Soviet T-72 tank in return for self-propelled artillery, which the Iraqi army needed to stem Iranian advances.

After the debacles at the American embassies and the marine barracks, the ISA set to work in Lebanon mapping out the routes U.S. teams would use to rescue any new embassy hostages. A 1982 memo written by then–Deputy Secretary of Defense Frank Carlucci ordered the ISA disbanded because it had become "like Topsy, uncoordinated and uncontrolled . . . an organization that is unaccountable." Carlucci left the door open for its survival by requiring a workable operating plan. One seems to have been developed. In 1985, when the Reagan administration hoped to use the ISA to rescue Buckley, it had 287 employees and separate sections for administration, operations, training, and signal intelligence (SIGNIT).[9]

But before the ISA or other covert organizations could be sent after Buckley, the U.S. government desperately needed basic information. The CIA was light on the ground in Beirut: its senior operatives had been massacred in the U.S. Embassy attack in West Beirut in 1983. One of the first moves, therefore, was to offer large sums of money to locals for information. Sheikh Fadlallah, would-be victim of the car bomb arranged by Lebanese intelligence chief Simon Cassis, issued a stern warning against anyone accepting such offers. Two boys of eleven and twelve captured by Hezbollah at Beirut's museum checkpoint were found with some of the money. After interrogation, they were promptly shot in the head. Another man who gave information about Buckley, or who Hezbollah thought had done so, disappeared at Larnaca Airport in Cyprus on his way back from a trip to Greece.

Some French and American specialists, despite PLO offers to help in locating Buckley, persisted in believing there had been Palestinian involvement in the kidnapping. However, by March 20, 1984, Italy's own central intelligence agency, DIGOS, was confident enough of Hezbollah's guilt to report this in a teletype message to Interpol (International Police Organization), headquartered in Paris. In the United States, the FBI, usual recipient of such information, passed it on to CIA headquarters. Casey sent a CIA team to Beirut. His members questioned the woman witness who had last seen Buckley in the parking lot. They concluded that he was still in West or southern Beirut.[10]

In Washington, various suggestions were forthcoming from the intelligence establishment. One was to spray a short-term, nonlethal but incapacitating nerve gas over large areas of West Beirut, then send in a rescue team. This idea was quickly rejected. The United States had just protested (though not too loudly) Iraq's use of poison gas against Iranians. How could nerve gas be limited to the zone where hostages were held? And what would the Soviets, let alone U.S. allies, say if their embassy staffs were knocked out? Memories of Vietnam were revived within the Reagan administration by the unwelcome news that an overzealous member of the Beirut CIA team had tortured to death one Hezbollah suspect with a portable electroshock machine. The operative was returned immediately to the United States and fired.[11] The incident, however, gave Hezbollah and Iran one more reason to escalate their pressure on Buckley and any other American hostage they might care to subject to the same tactics.

Casey's deputy, John N. McMahon, flew to Tel Aviv and asked Mossad for help. Various Israeli think tanks made their computerized files available. Martin Kramer, the Dayan Center's expert on Shi'ites, flew to Langley for consultation. At about the same time, Mossad reportedly sent the CIA its opinion that a successful rescue mission in Lebanon would be impossible. The CIA and the ISA, as we shall presently see, did not at first accept this premise.

Buckley Appeals for Help

In Athens, Monday, May 7, 1984, just fifty-three days after Buckley's kidnapping, the U.S. Embassy received a video cassette mailed from Athens and addressed to the ambassador. The tape was of a cheap East German make sold widely in the Middle East. A CIA officer in the embassy phoned Casey. Within hours, at CIA headquarters in Langley, Casey was viewing the video with McMahon and a senior operations officer who had served in Beirut earlier. According to one account, the video showed Buckley naked and being tortured while clutching a secret document, supposedly evidence that his burn bag had not done its job. Enhancement of the film showed signs that Buckley had been drugged, for there were puncture marks in his skin.[12]

Twenty-three days later, the U.S. Embassy in Rome received another video wrapped in Italian newspaper. The CIA concluded from it that Buckley had continued to be horribly tortured. On this take, his voice was slurred, and he seemed to be in the sort of stupor induced by psychotropic drugs. His hands and legs shook frantically as he pleaded to be exchanged under a deal removing all American and Israeli influences from Lebanon.[13]

Then a third video was mailed from a post office in the Heliopolis district of Cairo. It arrived at the U.S. Embassy in Cairo on October 26, 1984, 224 days after Buckley's kidnapping. At the time, there was a heightened sense in the Western world of terrorist danger. Muslim fanatics had recently attacked the U.S. Embassy in East Beirut, and an attempted assassination by the Irish Republican Army of Prime Minister Margaret Thatcher in Brighton, England, raised fears of a new worldwide alliance of terrorists.

In the new video, an emaciated Buckley showed documents to the camera and stammered out defensive comments about his captors and Lebanon's right to self-determination. His statements were punctuated by screams. CIA medical men and psychologists suspected, after conducting computer analysis of his voice patterns, his eye movements, and his physical appearance, that he might be considering suicide.[14]

Psychological warfare between the United States and its Iranian and Lebanese tormentors intensified. On January 22, 1985, Sheikh Fadlallah said he had evidence that eleven years earlier, the "Great Satan" had built a center in California

for exercising mind control over the Muslims of North America by inserting electrodes into their skulls. Apparently, someone had given Fadlallah a highly distorted
version of an old idea of Ronald Reagan's. As governor of California, he had
harbored the notion of building a psychiatric "violence center" as a way to control
violence in the cities of his state. The plan never materialized.[15]

By this time, Casey and other top officials of the Reagan administration were
ready to authorize almost anything to get Buckley back. Two U.S. Drug Enforce-
ment Administration (DEA) agents covering Lebanon—which was by then aug-
menting the flow of Latin American drugs to the United States with its own cocaine
and heroin exports from the Bekaa Valley—were told by one of their informants,
apparently a Canadian citizen, that a ransom of $200,000 could get two American
hostages out of Lebanon. One of them would be Buckley. Lt. Col. Oliver North of
the White House national security staff met with the two DEA men and probably
their "asset" as well, and the job of raising $200,000 was subsequently given to
National Security Adviser Robert McFarlane. He flew to Texas to see the million-
aire champion of patriotic causes, H. Ross Perot. The money was paid to the asset,
who promptly disappeared, leaving no trace. In May 1986, despite this disappoint-
ment, Perot answered a new appeal from Colonel North, sending one of his own
men to Cyprus with a sum probably totaling about $2 million. This was deposited
in a bank account. (North and his operatives would later draw on this money to
reward contacts in Beirut who were demanding money for hostages.) Perot's emissary waited in Cyprus for seven days, but no one showed up to claim the money
or offer hostages.[16]

Helping Khomeini's Enemies

Buckley's plight provided fresh impetus for Israeli activity in the arms-for-hostages
industry. This, in turn, would lead various high-ranking Reagan administration
officials to the Israelis to explore new ways of winning over the minds, if not the
hearts, of Iranian "moderates." There was a curious prelude to this new chapter in
the affair of the Tudeh party militants and Soviet agents in Iran.

Since 1982, the CIA had been running a covert operation to keep Soviet influence
out of Iran. The idea was to provide a role for the United States in case Khomeini
should be toppled by his Iranian enemies, either the Iraqi-backed leftist Mujaheddin
Khalq guerrillas or various right-wing groups. Some of the latter were monarchists
who advocated the return of Crown Prince Reza Pahlavi, the Shah's son.

Rear Adm. Ahmad Madani, former commander of the Iranian navy who had
been court-martialed by the Shah for his "antigovernment attitude," was one ben-
eficiary of the CIA's largesse. He claimed to control six thousand to eight thousand
Iranian exiles in eastern Turkey, having fled there after a brief term as first defense
minister in the Khomeini regime. The CIA provided several million dollars to
Madani's forces.[17] Another unit of less than two thousand men, most based in Iraq,
was commanded by Gen. Bahram Aryana. He had served under the Shah as army

chief of staff. By aiding these groups, the United States hoped to ensure that it could harass the flanks of any Soviet armed invasion of Iran and perhaps protect moderates or pro-Western elements that might take power in Tehran.[18] Such was the pipe dream of Washington planners.

American concern about Soviet moves southward could be traced back to Stalin's 1946 invasions of Azerbaijan and Kurdistan. Thus when the Soviets invaded Afghanistan, it only heightened Washington's fears about interference in Iran. The United States, its ally Saudi Arabia, and Iran all opposed the Soviet takeover of Afghanistan. These three unlikely bedfellows proceeded to help the Afghan mujaheddin. (The Iranians, of course, gave preference to the Shi'ites among them.) In early 1983, just after Khomeini's crackdown on the Soviet-backed Tudeh ("communist") party, the United States provided Iran with detailed information about Soviet agents and collaborators in that country. The United States hoped thereby to ease Iranian pressure on Saudi Arabia, Kuwait, and other Gulf states.

On May 4, 1983, Khomeini used the information to arrest no less than two hundred suspected Tudeh agents, as well as the principal Soviet contact in Iran, Abbas Zamani, operating under the name Abu Sharif. This former ambassador to Pakistan was serving in the sensitive post of Iran's deputy director of intelligence. The result was the expulsion of eighteen Soviet diplomats, the execution of two hundred suspects, and the imprisonment of the Tudeh party leaders.

If Khomeini thus dealt a mortal blow to the Little Satan—the Soviet Union—in Iran, he nevertheless continued his offensive against the Great Satan who had so obligingly provided the information. This incident was one of the highlights of the waning cold war. Meanwhile, America's war in the Middle East raged on, as the kidnapping of Buckley and other American hostages demonstrated.[19]

Ghorba Enters the Scene

Manuchehr Ghorbanifar—Iranian merchant, former intelligence agent, man of many aliases, and intermediary with the Israelis—well understood the importance of captive William Buckley. Shortly after Buckley was seized, Ghorbanifar told a CIA agent in Frankfurt, West Germany, that Mohsen Kangarlou, an Iranian deputy prime minister who supervised covert operations overseas, was behind the kidnapping. One of several polygraph tests given to Ghorbanifar indicated that he had lied.[20] Nevertheless, Ghorbanifar, seeing profitable arms deals ahead, stayed on Buckley's case.

On July 26, 1985, Ghorbanifar met in Israel with State Department adviser Michael Ledeen, Israeli Foreign Office and former Mossad official David Kimche, and Israeli arms dealers Al Schwimmer and Yacov Nimrodi. Ghorbanifar claimed that in exchange for five hundred TOW missiles the "Western-oriented moderates" in Iran would get Buckley or others released. Ghorba, as his companions in commerce were already affectionately calling him, phoned Mohsen Kangarlou in Tehran from Nimrodi's house in Israel. Kangarlou, said Ghorbanifar, did not want to pay money for the missiles; he considered the release of the "big one" (Buckley) to be fair payment.[21] Later, it became clear that Iran would have to pay money for the missiles. TOWs would become some of the most sought-after commodities in the forthcoming arms-for-hostages deals.

What Ghorbanifar did not know, and what Kangarlou did not tell him at that point, was that William Buckley had probably been dead since June 3.[22] Buckley's execution, as it was called, was not announced by Islamic Jihad until October 3, 1985. The communiqué claimed the action as retaliation for the Israeli air force attack on PLO headquarters in Tunisia on October 1. Many reports and rumors of Buckley's torture and supposed death had leaked out.

By late 1984, it had become known to the CIA and other interested parties that Imad Mugniyeh, by now desperate to get his brother-in-law out of jail in Kuwait, was the moving force behind the kidnapping of Buckley. William Casey may have made a secret trip to Damascus to discuss the possibility of kidnapping Mugniyeh. Meanwhile, the U.S. ambassador to Kuwait, Anthony Quainton, who had headed the State Department's terrorism office, was encouraging the Kuwaitis to hold firm against Islamic Jihad's demands to release the al-Dawa prisoners.

In Lebanon, hostage Jeremy Levin escaped in early 1985. Presbyterian minister Reverend Benjamin Weir, kidnapped May 8, 1984; Peter Kilburn, librarian at the American University of Beirut, taken December 3, 1984 (and murdered April 17, 1985, after the U.S. air raid on Libya); and Father Lawrence Jenco, the Catholic priest and social worker kidnapped January 8, 1985, had been held with or near Levin. Their captors moved Weir and Jenco to new locations. Before they left, Jenco and Weir reported they heard (they saw nothing, being blindfolded most of the time) a voice saying, "I am Buckley . . . William Buckley. Who are you?" And apparently Jenco had seen Buckley earlier. At the time of this sighting, Buckley exhibited no signs of torture. But, Jenco and others said, Buckley sometimes talked with a guard named Said, reminding him that Said owed him favors. His reminders went unheeded.

On August 20, 1985, the Israelis sent Iran ninety-six TOW missiles built by Hughes Missile Systems in California. Ghorbanifar flew aboard the aircraft with the missiles, traveling from Ben Gurion Airport through Turkish airspace to Iran. No hostages were forthcoming as a result of the delivery—despite all the negotiations conducted in Tehran the previous May by McFarlane and North and all the transactions that had followed that visit. Ghorbanifar was quoted in official reports as saying that the Iranians had wanted *all* of a shipment of five hundred TOWs at once. "Do you want the Iranians to send an arm and a leg of Buckley as an advance?" he asked at a meeting with his American and Israeli colleagues.

The Revolutionary Guards at Tehran Airport seized this first shipment of missiles, despite the polite fiction within the U.S. administration that they would go to the more moderate armed forces to Iran. The idea of getting arms only to Iranian "moderates" (whatever that meant), so that the United States could have influence there after Khomeini died, was termed by Secretary of State George Shultz "perverse" and by Defense Secretary Caspar Weinberger, who, like Shultz, knew of the deals, "almost too absurd to comment on."[23] Meanwhile, hostages would be freed, Ghorbanifar insisted, only if the remaining four hundred missiles were shipped from Israel. David Kimche then said to McFarlane, "We can't deliver . . . [so] we can expect only one hostage. Which one do you want?"

McFarlane, forced to choose, said Buckley. Ghorbanifar replied that he was too ill to be moved. Instead, Benjamin Weir was released, through Damascus, on September 18.[24]

AUB hospital director David Jacobsen was kidnapped in Beirut eight months later, on May 28, 1985. Again, there were strong indications that his abduction was the work of Imad Mugniyeh's branch of Hezbollah. Jacobsen was released just as the arms-for-hostages scandal was breaking in early November 1986. According to his own account, he witnessed Buckley's last hours on or about June 3, 1985.

Blindfolded, Jacobsen found himself in the same room with a man who was obviously sick.

> He was delirious. He was regurgitating . . . running a very high fever. The guards came to me because I was a hospital director and said, "What can we do?" And I said, "You better take him . . . to hospital or get a doctor to him." They said, "We can't do that." I could not see him. . . . There was just a long, long silence. When you're in a small room . . . there are certain noises that are associated with death. . . . I firmly believe that William died the evening of June 3.[25]

Buckley apparently did not receive any care at all for his deteriorating heart condition or for pneumonia. Oliver North later said that Buckley probably died of pulmonary edema: "He had been kicked so brutally in the kidneys that his lungs filled with fluid and he basically suffocated."[26]

Although Islamic Jihad issued a hazy photo of Buckley's corpse after announcing his "execution" in October 1985, no U.S. negotiator or agency, at the time of this writing, has been able to secure the return of Buckley's body or, to this author's knowledge, the actual tape of his confession. William Buckley—a hero to his friends and colleagues and a symbol of American defeat to adversaries in Iran and elsewhere—remains the most noteworthy casualty of America's secret war with Iran.

The Abduction of Terry Anderson

If William Buckley symbolized America's secret war with its Mideast adversaries for U.S. officialdom, reporter Terry Anderson came to epitomize the plight of the hostages for many in America and the West as a whole.

March 16, 1985, began with Beirut still under the shadow of the attempt on Sheikh Fadlallah's life. There had been a rash of tumultuous clashes between the militia factions. Terry Anderson, who lost his freedom on that day, was equipped emotionally and intellectually to cover Lebanon. A veteran war correspondent who had served six years in the marines and worked as a service reporter in Vietnam,

Anderson had arrived in Beirut in 1983 as one of the most expert Beirut-based journalists. As chief Mideast AP correspondent, this expertise had been displayed in his coverage of the Lebanese Shi'ites.

The morning of March 16, Anderson was driving home from a tennis match through my old neighborhood of Ain Mreisse. His kidnappers were parked at an intersection near a statue of Egypt's late President Gamal Abdel Nasser. They blocked Anderson's car, pulling guns and forcing Anderson's passenger, photographer Don Mell, out. While one gunman held Mell against a wall, the others dragged Anderson from his car into theirs. He was wearing tennis shorts, tennis shoes, and a Commodore Hotel T-shirt. Mell recalls trying to force his way through the gunmen to stay with Anderson, but they told Mell that they would kill him if he kept fighting. Both Mell and Anderson knew that the latter was joining Buckley in captivity.

Mell watched the kidnap car speed away toward the Shi'ite strongholds in South Beirut with his friend and colleague aboard. The next day, Islamic Jihad claimed responsibility in a telephone statement to the French News Agency. It also admitted kidnapping two others, Geoffrey Nash and Brian Levick, on March 14 and 15. Both Nash and Levick were released at the end of March and reported that they had apparently been mistaken for Americans.

Two weeks before the March 15 truck bomb attack on Sheikh Fadlallah, the state of alert was already such that thirty-six Americans assigned to the UN Interim Force in Lebanon were evacuated. On March 12, the United States antagonized Muslims by vetoing a UN Security Council resolution condemning Israeli policy and practices in southern Lebanon. The Islamic Jihad statement to the French News Agency on March 17 said the abductions of Anderson, Nash, and Levick "come within the framework of our continuing operations against Americans and their agents." All three, it said, had been moved from Beirut.

As of this writing, Terry Anderson is still in captivity, the longest held of any of the hostages. Since the kidnapping, his common law wife, Madeleine, worked for many months with the ABC News bureau in Beirut, monitoring Arabic radio broadcasts. She bore Terry a daughter, Sulome Theresa Anderson, on June 7, 1985. Madeleine settled in a small house on a quiet street in Cyprus to bring up Sulome while awaiting Terry's release. On February 15, 1986, Terry's father died of cancer, and in June of that same year his brother, Glenn, also died of cancer. Four days before his death, Glenn made a videotaped appeal to Islamic Jihad from his hospital bed. Like the many appeals from his tireless, energetic sister, Peggy Say, it was broadcast over Lebanese television but apparently ignored.

Fellow hostages, later released, said Anderson knew of his daughter's birth. Some of his later messages showed that the news had helped greatly to relieve the terrible suffering and the endless tedium of captivity. However, his hostage companions added, he was not told about the family deaths.

About six months after Terry's kidnapping, Benjamin Weir was released. This followed the first completed arms-for-hostages deal between the Reagan administration and Iran. As a result of the secret negotiations, Khomeini's Iran had finally received the full shipment of arms, but Weir, not Buckley, had been freed. Weir reached Washington in September 1985, with a message that Anderson and five other American hostages would be killed unless the United States pressured Kuwait to liberate its Shi'ite prisoners.

The good news brought by Weir was that at least four of those six—Father Jenco, Thomas Sutherland (abducted June 9, 1985), David Jacobsen, and Terry Anderson—were alive. President Reagan, who worried a great deal about the hostages, was spared a confrontation with their families when they converged on Washington for meetings with Weir and demanded to see him as well. Reagan was at Bethesda Naval Hospital for a postoperative medical checkup. The task of meeting the families then fell to Vice President George Bush.

In Peggy Say, Bush found a formidable challenger. Say exploded at Bush for not showing more concern. [27]

"How can you accuse me of not caring?" was Bush's reply. "I'm a Christian man."

"You'll have to excuse me, Mr. Bush," Say said, "but don't tell me you're a Christian, show me." She recalled that when the hostages from the June 1985 TWA hijacking to Beirut had been released two months earlier, she "was in a hotel room watching the TV, waiting for my brother's face, and instead I got a call from some person in your office telling me he wouldn't be released with the others. The Christian thing would have been to call yourself."

"Maybe we've made some mistakes," Bush allowed.

"If you hadn't," Say interrupted, "you wouldn't be facing an angry mob." [28]

Later, the Reagan administration designated Anderson's birthday, October 27, as National Hostage Awareness Day in the United States. It was first observed on Anderson's forty-second birthday, in 1989. That day, in Anderson's upstate New York hometown, Batavia, his family and friends unveiled a statue of him with his hands bound in chains. After his release, the chains are to be removed.

The first photograph of Anderson in captivity was released on May 15, 1985. At the time, Islamic Jihad was claiming to hold him, Buckley, Weir, Jenco, and two French diplomats, Marcel Fontaine and Marcel Carton. Accompanying the photo was the usual set of demands, the chief one being freedom for the seventeen al-Dawa prisoners in Kuwait. It warned of "catastrophic consequences" if they were not freed. Ten other photographs of Anderson reached the media, mainly in Beirut, from then until the start of his fifth year of captivity in 1990. Many were apparently prints made from the same negative and were supposed to prove that Islamic Jihad was responsible for the kidnapping.

Television networks received the first videotape showing Terry Anderson on October 3, 1985. In it, Anderson and Jacobsen made a joint appeal to President Reagan to work as hard for their release as apparently he had worked for that of Nicholas Daniloff. An American correspondent for U.S. News and World Report, Daniloff had been imprisoned for a month in Moscow but was released after an informal U.S.–Soviet deal.

A second videotape of Anderson appeared on December 24, 1987. Looking gaunt and tired, he rebuked the Reagan administration for its failure to free him and the other American hostages, warning "there's a limit to how long we can last." One analysis of the videotape reportedly found indications that Anderson, at that moment, might have been held in the old jail in West Beirut's Muslim quarter of Basta, along with British negotiator Terry Waite, kidnapped on January 20, 1987.

If Terry Anderson is freed some day, his recollections may enlighten us about the details of his life in captivity. At the moment, it appears to have improved: in mid-1990, his captors showed him a videotape of his child, Sulome, which Lebanese television had broadcast on his thirty-eighth birthday. They also permitted him to send an eight-page letter to his family and his common-law wife. Parts of it were published:

> Madeleine, my love, my heart, I saw our daughter on TV the other night and I cried for joy. I only saw her for two or three seconds, enough to notice your black hair and beautiful, bright eyes. But I can't describe how it felt to end months of not knowing [what she looked like].[29]

An Unfinished Story

Peggy Say and Don Mell have often described the wild rollercoaster of emotions that comes of waiting for the release of a hostage—the glorious highs when some Mideast diplomat or politician holds out hope, then the plunging despair when that hope is dashed yet again. After his release, Weir recalled that about six months after Terry Anderson's kidnapping in March a guard told the captives one hostage would be freed. They themselves were to decide which one. The freed man would put Islamic Jihad's case to the Reagan administration. Fellow hostages Weir, Jenco, and Jacobsen agreed among themselves that Anderson, because of his media status and experience, would be the best choice. Perversely, it seemed, the kidnappers chose Weir instead.

The U.S. administration said nothing for five days after Weir's release. North and other members of the administration's hostage team believed more captives were to be freed. President Reagan phoned Israeli Prime Minister Shimon Peres and thanked him for Israel's contribution to the arms deal that freed Weir. Carrying a passport issued by the State Department in the name of William P. Goode along with a personal letter from President Reagan, North met Weir in Wiesbaden, West Germany.[30] Weir was able to recall the circumstances and timing of certain milestones, such as the death of Buckley in June 1985. No releases followed immediately after his. Peggy Say, Don Mell, and other hostage family members and friends plunged back into despondency.

In the spring of 1991, after the Operation Desert Storm had expelled Saddam Hussein's Iraqi invaders from Kuwait, Terry Anderson and four other Americans, as well as Britons Terry Waite, John McCarthy, and Jack Mann, were still held in Lebanon. The crisis in Kuwait and the Persian Gulf dominated America's consciousness. But the friends and relatives of Terry Anderson and his fellow prisoners had not forgotten them and never would.

11

Mass Destruction for Sale

A Close Encounter in the Gulf

The evening of February 12, 1988, several newsmen peered up into the cloudy sky, somewhere between Iran's Sirri Island and the coast of Abu Dhabi. Almost unnoticed, an airliner streaked overhead, its lights blurring. We were standing on the bridge of the U.S. guided-missile destroyer *Chandler*, trying not to get in the way of its commander, Capt. Steven Smith. He faced a split-second decision whose consequence would bear heavily on the future course of the Iran-Iraq War, now well into its seventh year.

A few minutes earlier, the *Chandler's* radar had picked up an Iraqi F-1 Mirage fighter-bomber. It had flown past us on a north-south track, bound for some nocturnal mission in the central or southern gulf, and had just turned back. The aircraft was quickly overtaking the northbound convoy of U.S.-flagged Kuwaiti tankers. The *Chandler*, along with the accompanying frigate USS *Reuben James*, was under orders to protect the convoy. This was the twenty-third such escort mission by the U.S. Navy since the summer of 1987, when the Reagan administration and Congress had agreed that such protection must be given. Some Americans thought that convoy escorts helped to wipe out the stigma of the U.S. defeat in Lebanon in 1982 and the vast embarrassment of the revelations of the arms-for-hostages and arms-profits-for-contras deals.

As the Iraqi bomber continued to close, Captain Smith had to choose: should he activate the *Chandler*'s rapid-fire, antiaircraft system or not? He recalled that in May 1987 the U.S. destroyer *Stark* had been struck by two missiles from a fast-closing Iraqi jet, which the *Stark*'s captain and crew believed to be a friendly aircraft. Thirty-seven crewmen had been killed and dozens of others injured. If Captain Smith opened fire now, he knew he could trigger a major clash with Saddam Hussein's Iraqi forces, which the United States was now supporting in a number of secret and semisecret ways.

Smith called his men to general quarters over the ship's loudspeakers. Our television crew members, veterans of a number of Gulf patrols, switched on their cameras and peered into the eerie greenish halo of their night-vision viewfinders. Then Smith radioed the approaching Iraqi pilot and urged him to turn back.

"He acknowledged my warning," the captain told us later. "But he didn't seem to understand English too well." The aircraft continued on course. Captain Smith had one last move before activating the *Chandler*'s multibarreled guns or launching any missiles. He ordered the ship's two 5-inch deck guns cranked up. Then he had two red flare shells fired in a final warning to the Iraqi pilot.

The bomber, veering away from the destroyer, unleashed two missiles whose orange tracks were unmistakable and, at first, running parallel to us. "Chinese-made Silkworms—an airborne version," one of the ship's intelligence officers said later. The *Chandler*'s watchers, peering into their night-vision scopes, followed the missiles' tracks. There was puzzlement, then relief: the weapons did not seem to be aimed at us or the convoy. . . . Then suddenly, one of the Silkworms turned toward the *Chandler* and streaked by her starboard side about eight miles away.

The horizon off the destroyer's starboard bow lit up with a flash. The missile had exploded, apparently in the sea. Antiaircraft fire rocketed up from Sirri Island, where oil facilities often came under attack. The Iranians would later claim that several U.S. helicopter gunships had been trying an assault on the island—an unlikely story. More plausible, in retrospect, was that the Iraqi pilot had fired at an Iranian frigate that was shadowing us.

A radio operator on the *Gas King*, a tanker in the convoy, asked, "Should we be concerned about that flash of light that just went by?"

"Not any more," replied the *Chandler*.[1]

The incident, banal compared to many that have occurred during the course of U.S. involvement in naval hostilities in the Persian Gulf, had one consequence: just as after the *Stark* incident, teams of Americans and Iraqis investigated how and why it happened. And for over two months, until the "decisive" Iranian-U.S. naval engagement of April 1988, there was a truce in the attacks on shipping on both sides in the Iran-Iraq War.

In the weeks before the *Chandler*'s brush with combat, during which I covered several U.S. Navy operations as a U.S. network-television pool reporter, Iraqi air strikes and attacks by Iran's Boghammer speedboats had taken out half a dozen ships of various nationalities and resulted in a number of casualties. West Germany had joined other NATO allies in supporting U.S. naval efforts in the Gulf. For several days in early January, U.S. Defense Secretary Frank Carlucci toured the Gulf emirates to reassure them that the United States was doing something about the Iranian threat and, in particular, that the United States cared about Kuwait's security. By February 16, five days after the *Chandler*'s close encounter, Carlucci and JSC Chairman Adm. William Crowe had approved the redeployment of four U.S. naval units.

Events in the war were confirming certain concerns Admiral Crowe had related to me at the Pentagon in June 1987, shortly before the reflagging and escort operations got under way. Iran's threat was three-sided: hit-and-run raids, land-based Silkworm missiles that could be launched from both northern and southern ends of the Gulf, and mine warfare—for which the U.S. Navy at that time was thoroughly unprepared.

All three threats were to play crucial roles as the United States was dragged farther and farther into open warfare.

Satellite Eyes Over the Gulf

During the Iran-Iraq War, the United States's best and most effective weapon was satellite intelligence (sat-int). Washington used its spies in the sky to learn the intentions of each side and the results of their battles. It passed on bits of this intelligence, usually to the Iraqis, often via AWACS links to the Saudis.

When the war was barely a year old, in September 1981, Iran had begun a massive counteroffensive using "human wave" and commando tactics to push the Iraqis back, wiping out nearly all of the initial gains they had made in the autumn 1980 blitzkrieg. Computer-enhanced sat-int photos revealed how Iranian armor had reinforced the beleaguered garrison at the oil port and refinery of Abadan. The pictures recorded the destruction of an Iraqi pontoon bridge over the Karun River and the opening of the Iranian highway south from Abadan to Bandar-e Khomeini, on the Gulf, for reinforcements and supplies. The pictures also indicated that the Iraqis withdrew to the devastated city of Khorramshahr. Iran claimed to have destroyed Iraq's 100th Armored Brigade, capturing all forty of its tanks and killing thousands of enemy troops. Selective sat-int information fed to the media in Washington, however, suggested that in a whole month of fighting, casualties had not amounted to more than five thousand killed and wounded on both sides.[2] Sat-int put overall Iranian casualties in 1981 at one hundred thousand.

Worse losses came in early 1982 during two Iranian offensives, Operations Fatah ("victory") and al-Quds ("Jerusalem"). Sat-int estimated that during this period, the Iraqis lost about thirty thousand and the Iranians about ninety thousand men. Heavier Iranian casualties were caused by the suicidal human-wave attacks of Revolutionary Guards and *baseej*, would-be teenage martyrs. They leapt onto Iraqi mines and fortifications with prayers on their lips and plastic "keys to heaven" dangling from their necks, avid to emulate the martyrdom of Hussein, Ali, and the other Shi'a founders and prophets.

In July 1982, Revolutionary Guards and *baseej* led new Iranian assaults northeast of Basra. Four divisions in all managed to break through the enemy's outer defenses. Iraqi helicopter gunships, armor, and infantry counterattacked. Sat-int pictures taken around July 26, 1982, showed that as the battle ebbed, the Iranians still held about two hundred square miles of Iraqi territory in that sector. The cost in casualties, U.S. estimates found, were horrendous for Iran: over one thousand dead on each day of a six-day battle. Iraq's casualties were about a third of that amount. Later, Iran admitted losing ten thousand men, claiming they had killed seven thousand Iraqis and taken fourteen hundred prisoners. Such heavy losses led Khomeini to order the Revolutionary Guards and the mullahs to cooperate more with Iran's regular army. For its part, the army was to take a greater offensive role.[3]

By 1983, the Iraqis were far superior in the air with their French-made Mirage F-1s and Soviet MiGs and Sukhois. The Iranians were able to fly their few remaining U.S.-made planes only with the help of the clandestine supply line developed by Israeli and some international arms merchants. Both sides now used aircraft formerly held in reserve. On January 18, Iraq, for example, announced "sixty-six bombing sorties" over Iranian military and civilian targets. Iran's newly delivered American Hawk missiles and reinforced antiaircraft artillery took their own heavy toll that day; the Iraqis admitted to meeting heavy resistance. Sat-int estimated that eighty Iraqi aircraft were lost in the battle.[4] Soon, despite sporadic Iranian forays by Phantom F-4s and the odd F-14 against Iraq's air bases, the Iraqis began their concerted offensive to knock out Iran's giant Kharg Island oil terminal, its biggest in the Gulf. Iraqi pilot performance, however, was never outstanding. Kharg was eventually crippled but never totally destroyed.

At the start of 1984, sat-int revealed many details of Iran's massive new deployment, equivalent to about thirty divisions and a total of three hundred thousand men and boys, from Kurdistan in the north to Shatt al-Arab in the south.[5] The Americans passed on at least some of this data to the Iraqis.

Following some feints, the main Iranian offensive was launched. Advance pictures being flashed from space indicated that its aim was to surround Basra and cut that city's land links to Baghdad. The Iranians advanced through the Hawīzah Marshes in a huge flotilla of small boats of all descriptions, capturing some villages in the southwestern area. The Iraqis, expecting a major frontal assault elsewhere, had left these undefended. After a series of huge battles, Iraq prevailed on land and in the air. Iraq allowed newsmen and television crews to come to the front and film thousands of corpses. Later, Iraqi television broadcast the pictures over and over on "freebees" (satellite video feeds without cost to the recipients) to Western television networks.

To repel the Iranian offensive, Saddam Hussein now deployed chemical weapons: mustard gas and sarin, a nerve agent developed by Nazi Germany in the 1930s but never used in World War II. Iraq achieved tactical surprise the first time it used sarin, but there was a payback: the wind changed and blew the nerve gas onto Iraqi soldiers. This new weapon would later prompt Iran to buy large quantities of protective gear and supply its soldiers with vials of atropine, an anti–nerve gas drug.

Iranians also received respirators, made in the same country that originally developed the poison and whose firms were now helping Iraq make its own gas: West Germany.

In March 1984, the Iranians went on the offensive again, this time on salt flats southwest of the marshes. Iraq opened canal gates and dikes to flood portions of the battlefield; Iranian combat engineers tried using pontoon bridges. Two full Iraqi army corps were thrown into the battle, which after new gas attacks turned the battle into a major Iranian defeat. Sat-int estimated over fourteen thousand Iranian dead; Iraqi casualties are not known but were almost certainly much lower.[6]

The Battle for the Crazy Islands

Deep within the marshes, about two miles inside Iraqi territory, lies an area called Majnoon, which means "crazy" in Arabic. There was nothing crazy about Iran's desire to seize the region, measuring about six by four miles, or Iraq's determination to keep it. Executives of multinational oil companies, especially those American companies still working under contract in Iraq, watched the battle for Majnoon as attentively as they did the tanker war in the Gulf. A prospecting team sent by Petrobras (Brazil's state oil company) in the 1970s, when Iraq began trading its oil for Brazilian arms, estimated reserves at over seven billion barrels, nearly one-fourth of Iraq's known reserves at the time. Drilling by Iraq's national oil company, which used foreign contractors, had sunk fifty-two wells—all capped when the war began in September 1980.

In early 1984, as we have seen, waterborne Iranian forces poured into Majnoon's marshes and captured small built-up areas left by the oil prospectors. At first, Iraq's two army corps were too busy defending the other approaches to Basra to be able to hold Majnoon. They did not launch a real counterattack until March 6. The Iranians held on to three-quarters of their Majnoon positions, including some of the oil installations. These they retained until 1988, when during the early stages of its final counteroffensive Iraq took them back. According to Saddam Hussein and his generals, this "won" the war for Iraq.

By the spring of 1984, U.S. AWACS planes were accumulating plenty of battlefield intelligence from a discreet distance (probably in Saudi or Kuwaiti airspace) to supplement sat-int. Together, this intelligence told the Pentagon that in the February–March 1984 marsh operations, at least twenty-seven thousand more personnel had been killed, twenty thousand Iranians and seven thousand Iraqis. Many of the casualties were caused by chemical weapons. In the three main battles, about half a million troops had been engaged.[7]

Red Alert Over Saudi Arabia

U.S. surveillance cameras and sensors came into their own in the sea war. This phase heated up with the beginning of the Iraqi air offensive against oil terminals and shipping owned by or supplying Iran. After one raid on Kharg Island on February 27, 1984, the Iraqi high command issued a formal warning, proclaiming an "exclusion zone" near Kharg where a "blockade is being imposed." Greek, Turkish, and Indian ships were damaged, and their crews suffered casualties in the days that followed. On March 28, 1984, an Exocet missile fired from one of the Super-Etendard aircraft the French leased to Iraq damaged a Greek ship about forty miles south of Kharg. An Iraqi war communiqué made first mention of the Exocet's use in hostilities.

A red alert for Saudi Arabia and its American protectors began in May 1984. Iran decided to test Saudi and American resolve and coordination by hitting shipping that used Saudi and Kuwaiti ports and oil terminals. Iranian aircraft and missile boats hit and set afire a Saudi supertanker inside Saudi territorial waters near the port and naval base of Jubail. The Saudis refused an offer of direct U.S. air or naval support, but accepted increased U.S. intelligence on Iranian movements via the AWACS surveillance system. This was based at Dhahran, which, during Operations Desert Shield and Desert Storm in 1990–91, would become the center of a far more comprehensive operation against Iraq.

The heightened AWACS surveillance worked. In May 1984, Saudi Arabia's air force, assisted by AWACS data links, began regular patrols off the Saudi coastline. On June 5, widely remembered in the Arab world as the anniversary of the Israeli attack that launched the 1967 Arab-Israeli War, two Saudi F-15 aircraft, forewarned by AWACS data, were lying in wait when two Iranian Phantom F-4s approached the Saudi coast. The Iranians probably intended to attack oil installations or shipping close to shore. The Saudi pilots fired their Sparrow air-to-air missiles, destroying one of the Iranian aircraft at once and hitting the other. Publicly, Saudi Arabia claimed only one kill, but AWACS surveillance showed that both planes crashed.

This U.S.-assisted Saudi victory—the American role got little, if any, public mention—had some impact on Arab public opinion. The kingdom had shown, at last, that it was willing to draw Iranian blood if necessary. Nevertheless, on the home front, the fiction was maintained that this feat of arms was only an isolated act of self-defense that had nothing to do with supporting Iraq's war effort. The names of the two Saudi pilots, potential heroes, were never released.

For years, in the words of a senior American diplomat, the Saudis "sought to conciliate the Ayatollah Khomeini rather than to confront him," just as they would try to placate Saddam Hussein before he invaded Kuwait in 1990. Saudi ministers avoided mention of U.S. military or intelligence support. They maintained consistently that their only dispute with Iran was over politics, for example, the intended ouster of Saddam Hussein by military means.

And so Saudi-Iranian diplomatic relations remained intact. However, the Saudis expected trouble from the Iranians during the annual Muslim pilgrimage to Mecca in 1984, and they prepared for it with help from American and other Western intelligence. From September 14 to 16, Iraqi and Iranian pilgrims clashed at Medina, and one pilgrim died. Meanwhile, Islamic Jihad claimed an attack against

Saudi expatriates in Marbella, Spain, playground and headquarters of many wealthy Arabs. One person died and another was wounded. Attacks such as this often flared up and were difficult for U.S. intelligence to predict or monitor.[8]

In 1985, discreet Saudi-Iranian contacts brought about the first visit to Tehran since the Iranian revolution by Saudi foreign minister, Prince Saud al-Faisl. This was a tacit expression of Saudi acceptance of the Iranian revolution or at least of the Arab need to come to terms with it.

U.S. observers in Riyadh reported to Washington that the Iranian threat had, in fact, affected Saudi relations with all of its neighbors. It became the paymaster of the Iraqi war effort, pouring billions of dollars into the seemingly bottomless Iraqi war coffers to pay for arms. This enabled Saddam Hussein to fight a war and also satisfy most of his citizens' material needs—including, for a time, new cars for families of casualties.

Arms, many from the Soviet Union, were consistently offloaded from neutral shipping at the little-used Saudi port of al-Qadhima and trucked across the desert to Iraq. (The same process went on from Jordan's Red Sea port of Aqaba, a result of King Hussein's firm support of Iraq.) Saudi oil proceeds went to Iraq after Iranian artillery and air attacks destroyed that country's limited oil-export facilities in the Gulf. A spur line was built for the trans-Saudi oil pipeline between Jubail and the Red Sea port of Yenbo. Eventually, the line's capacity was doubled to move Iraqi oil to markets safe from Iranian attack. This policy of aid antagonized Iraq's political and commercial rivals and adversaries. Then in August 1990, Saudi Arabia, at American behest, closed the pipeline as part of the international blockade and embargo against Iraq following its invasion of Kuwait. Saddam Hussein's honeymoon with the House of Saud was over.

In 1981, prompted by the Iran-Iraq War, the Gulf states of Kuwait, Oman, Bahrain, Qatar, and the United Arab Emirates joined Saudi Arabia to form the Gulf Cooperation Council (GCC). This largely consultative body was originally inspired by Kuwait. It was headed by an outspoken Kuwaiti nationalist, Abdallah al-Bishara. Iraq was not asked to join. Saddam Hussein, locked in his death struggle with Khomeini and almost totally dependent on Gulf money and logistical support, could only accede to the formation of the bloc that he might otherwise have tried to destroy. After invading and pillaging Kuwait in 1990, Saddam expressed nothing but scorn for the GCC.

The Gulf rulers, with some prodding from the Saudis in Riyadh where GCC headquarters was located, gave top priority to security; after that came economic integration. GCC members held joint military exercises. After much bickering, they formed a brigade-strength rapid-intervention force composed of elements from each member state and based in U.S.-built Saudi facilities at Hafar al-Batin, near Iraq and Kuwait. Here, too, largely through the Saudi link, they enjoyed some access to U.S. AWACS intelligence and sat-int.[9] With the start of Operation Desert Shield in 1990, the GCC force became a negligible, token military expression of a political dream. It was completely eclipsed in the allied offensive against Iraq in 1991.

Tension in the Strait of Hormuz

Despite the growth in regional cooperation, it was unilateral American reaction that turned the tide of events in the Iran-Iraq War. This came only after Tehran seriously challenged Western and Arab rights to move ships, oil, and men into and out of the Gulf.

At a meeting in Tehran of the Supreme Defense Council on February 14, 1984, Iran's leaders decided to occupy and fortify a disputed atoll named Goat Island, or al-Ghanem, in the Strait of Hormuz. Oman regarded Goat Island as part of its territorial waters. The United States then reaffirmed the Carter doctrine of American military action, if necessary, to ensure freedom of navigation through the strait. Iran's UN representative declared on May 15, "We cannot permit anyone to use the Gulf against us. It will remain free and open to us all—or nobody will be allowed to use it."[10]

The threat of hostilities in the strait had already alarmed Washington insiders at the outset of war in 1980. In 1982, after long and often difficult secret negotiations, the United States had signed an "access agreement" with Oman, which had six modern patrol boats and an army of about sixteen thousand men, many of them non-Arab. The commander was a British general who told author Edgar O'Ballance that Oman could probably resist a serious Iranian invasion for no more than forty-eight hours.[11] Although U.S. intelligence confirmed that Iranian dispositions might prove lethal to Oman, no attack or invasion took place.

Some of the major strikes of the war did take place within sight or sound of Oman. On November 25, 1986, Iraqi air force commander Gen. Hamid Shaban sent his French Super-Etendards on several Gulf missions. Once they hit an Iranian oil terminal on Larak Island, which lies just across the strait from Goat Island and opposite the Musandam Peninsula, an Omani enclave surrounded by the United Arab Emirates. This mission, a round trip of at least 1,560 miles, revived earlier speculation about Iraqi in-flight refueling capabilities. The Iranians accused the Saudis of allowing Iraqi planes to refuel on Saudi territory. Citing Pentagon sources, *Aviation Week and Space Technology* reported that an in-flight Iraqi refueling operation, perhaps using converted airliners as tanker planes, had failed and that the aircraft were obliged to land in Saudi Arabia on the return flight.[12]

War for the Waterways

Iran boasted that in the land battles of 1986 around Basra and at other points on the front, it had brought to the battlefield a mighty host of 650,000 regular troops, reservists, draftees, Revolutionary Guards, and *baseej*. Other guards and *baseej*, 400,000 altogether, were held in immediate reserve. Observing the guards via satellites, intelligence disclosed that incredible as these figures seemed, they were essentially correct.[13]

Sometime shortly before Christmas of 1986, the United States alerted Iraq to sat-int evidence of an imminent Iranian attack on Umm Rasas, a point on a sandbank island south of Basra. The Iranians later said that six hundred "special troops," apparently frogmen and marine commandos, surprised the Iraqis. Though warned by the United States, the defending Iraqis were at first pushed back. Then they trapped the attackers in a killing field of barbed wire and mines planted among date palm groves—the kind of killing field Iraq would prepare for allied forces in Kuwait in 1991. Iraqi Gen. Maher Rashid said that after thirty-nine hours of fighting, the enemy was annihilated: 150 Iraqis killed for 32,344 Iranian dead. Iranian prisoners-of-war and Western-made equipment captured from the Iranians including Soviet and Chinese weaponry, life jackets "made in the U.S.A.," and frogmen's wet suits tagged "Made in Britain" were shown to newsmen.[14]

Sat-int also helped to map the important water defenses that both sides installed, using a network of marshes, canals, and artificially dug ditches and lakes along the southern front. The Shatt al-Arab, historically the main object of contention between Iran and Iraq, remained Iran's principal obstacle. At the start of 1987, the Iranians decided to push closer to Basra along the Shatt's eastern bank rather than crossing the western one. They had advanced as far as Shalamsha, about twelve miles east of Basra.

During a visit I made to Baghdad in April 1987, an Egyptian engineering officer attached to the Iraqi forces sketched the water situation for me on a napkin at a diplomatic cocktail party. Beginning in 1982, the Iraqis diverted the course of several canals and flooded parts of the Shatt's east bank, creating the sixteen-mile wide Fish Lake. This formed the boundary between two Iraqi army corps. Along the length of the lake ran a deep channel half a mile wide, making it impossible for assault troops to wade across. Sat-int data released to the media (probably long after the Iraqi high command got it) confirmed what the Egyptian had said. Fish Lake had ample shore and underwater defenses, including submerged barbed wire, mines, electrodes, and sensors. A causeway across the lake's center was linked with other causeways in Iraq's marshland defense zone.

The Battle of Fish Lake

On January 9, 1987, the Iranians had about 200,000 Revolutionary Guards and 50,000 regulars deployed from the Fao Peninsula northward to Shalamsha. Four Iraqi divisions and several smaller units of Saddam Hussein's personal Republican Guards faced them. The Republican Guards were an elite force that, it was reported (probably falsely), had prevented the Iranian conquest of Fao.

On direct orders from Rafsanjani, the Iranians launched Operation Karbala-5. Throwing much of their force into action, they crossed Fish Lake to penetrate five successive Iraqi defensive arcs. Thousands of Iranians waded and swam into the lake, taking heavy casualties, while Iraq's amphibious armored vehicles got bogged down in counterattacks. On January 12, when Hussein, in his familiar uniform and beret, visited the battle zone, U.S. sat-int confirmed that the Iranians had broken through the first and second Iraqi arcs and were now stalled before the third. Another force of Revolutionary Guards, meanwhile, had used small assault boats to capture four river islets. Iranian artillery now began to pound the eastern suburbs of Basra.

The make-or-break land battle of the war had clearly begun. On January 17, Hussein summoned his senior commanders to his bunker in Baghdad to discuss how to win it. The next day, Rafsanjani flew from Tehran to the Iranian lines to inspect the forward battle himself. On February 22, while newsmen waited vainly in Baghdad for authorization to visit the front, the Iranians launched a final human-wave assault, breaking through the fourth defensive arc and seizing a few more square miles of flooded land.

On February 26, Tehran issued communiqués trumpeting that Operation Karbala-5 had been another famous victory. U.S. sat-int, however, estimated that the Iranians had lost at least another 10,000 dead and 20,000 wounded since January 9.[15]

What had actually happened was this: the Iranians had advanced about six miles in seven weeks in a small part of the front and were within six miles of Basra's outskirts. They occupied about forty square miles of flooded land after fire-blasting marshlands and date-palm groves. The remains of date palms protruded from the water in strange resemblance to the blackened stumps of dismembered enemy soldiers that their adversaries liked to show on Iraqi television satellite feeds. In a news conference at Ahwaz on January 25, the Iranians claimed to have taken 1,750 prisoners-of-war including 150 officers during Karbala-5. A captured Iraqi pilot also asserted that French and Indian technicians worked at Iraq's Nasiriya air force base.[16]

In April newsmen were finally permitted to leave for Basra. I spent the night in an ancient British hotel on the bank of the Shatt al-Arab, sandbagged against continuing artillery fire. The real battle for Basra was over. It had been won by the Iraqis. If one single factor turned the balance in their favor, it was the chemical warfare capacity sold to Iraq by Western companies.

The Chemical Threat: A Background

As early as February 1984, Iraq and Iran had been raining missiles with conventional warheads on each other's cities. The "war of the cities," as the missile activity came to be called, spread terror throughout urban areas. Psychologically, the worst fear was that the enemy would use mustard or nerve gas in his warheads.

Many years before the war of the cities, mustard gas had been made or stockpiled in Egypt, Syria, Libya, and probably Israel. During the civil war in North Yemen in January 1967, I traveled with a group of newsmen to the mud-walled village of Ketaf, held by Yemenis loyal to the ruling Iman Ahmed. Their enemy was Egyptian-backed "republican" regime in San'a. Because trigger-happy Egyptian pilots had strafed a rescue convoy of the International Committee of the Red Cross (ICRC), several ICRC doctors angrily broke the rule of confidentiality. They told us all they knew about gas attacks the Egyptians had made and showed us a burial ground near Ketaf. Experts said the victims apparently died from World War I–vintage phosgene and mustard gas, probably from old British stocks captured by the Egyptians during the British evacuation of the Suez Canal Zone in the early 1950s.

Words, even pictures and film recordings, failed to convince some U.S. viewers and readers that the Egyptians had done this. It was inconvenient just then for the U.S. government, still involved in a long flirtation with Egyptian President Nasser, to face the facts. Nasser, in fact, may not have known what his army was up to. Field Marshal Hakim Amer, his army commander in chief who committed suicide after the June 1967 defeat by Israel, almost certainly did.

After that, many Mideast leaders did make a determined effort to push the chemical genie back into the bottle. The trouble was that the genie had escaped much earlier and from more than one bottle. Since World War I, every confirmed use of poison gas has been against a Third World country lacking protection against chemical arms, as Iran was when Iraq first used them against it in 1981–82. Spain used chemical weapons against the Moroccan resistance leader Abd al-Krim in 1925. The Soviet Union followed in China in 1934, Italy in Ethopia in 1935–36, and Japan in China between 1937 and 1945. In each instance, as in the Iran-Iraq War, gas often proved an effective terror weapon to kill or force out civilians. And Western governments, despite their knowledge of the vast suffering caused by poison gas in World War I, had chosen to look the other way.

Israel has used nonlethal gas extensively to injure and demoralize the Palestinian rioters in the *intifada*, which erupted in the West Bank and Gaza in December 1988 and continued in 1990, just as the United States employed it in Vietnam. In many of these situations, and especially as used by Iraq in the Iran-Iraq War, it was effective in killing and defeating superior numbers of enemy troops.

So the genie spread. Egypt's use of chemical arms in Yemen spurred Israel to import gas masks for its schoolchildren during the 1967 war. Talk of Israel's nuclear capability, there is reason to believe, spurred Syrian efforts to assemble a chemical warfare plant in the mid-1980s. Perhaps this explains why in 1989–90 strange bedfellows opposed Syria and its Muslim supporters in Lebanon: Maronite Christian militias, mainstream PLO partisans, and Iraq's Saddam Hussein. In 1987, while being held hostage in Beirut's southern suburbs, Charles Glass was told by his captors of local suspicions about a fire that destroyed a "paint factory" in East Beirut. Local newspapers reported that Lebanese Christians had been receiving Iraqi funds for a small do-it-yourself chemical weapons plant in East Beirut.[17]

Israel's invasion of Lebanon in 1982 also seems to have given new impetus to long-range war planning throughout the Middle East. By 1990, through purchases from China and with technological help from Western Europe, Saudi Arabia, Egypt, Iraq, and Libya had all received or were developing medium- or long-range missiles. By 1991, these missiles could deliver poison gas to crowded cities like Haifa, Tel Aviv, Tehran, and Damascus, and to targets in even the most remote areas.[18]

Attempts to Capture World Attention

In Iraq, south of the ancient city of Samarra was one of the first and largest chemical warfare manufacturing complexes in the Third World. Iraq sought technical help from Western companies. An American firm in Rochester, New York, one of the first to be approached, was quick to report the event to the U.S. government. That firm did not respond. According to Kurdish émigrés, however, Soviet, West German, and other European specialists went to Iraq to help it develop a chemical capability. Pesticide plants and chemical warfare laboratories were erected at a number of well-protected sites around the country.

"From very early on," a senior American intelligence official told John Bullock and Harvey Morris of the London *Independent*, the plant near Samarra had been

> surrounded by air defenses and given maximum security on the ground . . . No one ever saw any pesticides produced there—because there weren't any. Right from the start it was designed to produce mustard gas and two nerve gases, sarin and tabun, and the only reason for calling it a pesticide factory was to ease the consciences of those concerned in building it. But no one was fooled; they all knew what they were doing.[19]

Arab and West German firms went ahead with the construction of their plants. Sat-int passed to various intelligence services confirmed what was going on; but no one did or said anything, and no one wanted to know about it.

Reports of the Iraqi use of poison gas were slow to surface before 1983. Then, on October 31, the Iranians claimed that the Iraqis had used nitrogen–mustard gas weapons in the fighting in Kurdistan.[20] On November 8, Iran formally complained to the UN Security Council and asked that a UN commission of experts investigate. During the final week of November, the Iranians held an international medical conference attended by five hundred delegates. Evidence of the use of chemical agents and several victims were produced. Since Saddam Hussein had already warned of a "secret weapon" he would use if Iraq was invaded, the conference concluded that the agent must have been nitrogen–mustard gas, a refined version of the crude World War I gas used against the Yemenis in 1967. Iraq was condemned for violating the Geneva Protocols of 1925, which both Iran and Iraq had signed.

On December 22, 1983, the British Defence Sales Organisation acknowledged that in 1981 it had supplied Iran with ten thousand kits of protective gear for use against chemical weapons. In 1984, Iran complained again to the UN Security Council that Iraq had used "chemical bombs on forty-nine occasions between May 1981 and March 1984," which had "killed 1,200 Iranians and injured 5,000." The

United States, to Iran's chagrin, gave no particular attention to the claims. This added one more grievance to the list the Iranians had already compiled against the Reagan (and later Bush) administrations. By contrast, Iranian poison gas victims were treated in hospitals and given publicity in Britain, France, Austria, and Sweden. On March 28, 1984, a UN team went to Iran and confirmed that the Iraqis had indeed used mustard gas. On March 30, the UN General Assembly called on both Iran and Iraq to abstain from using chemical weapons but did not name Iraq as the guilty party.

A U.S. government report came out in December 1983 saying that West German firms had supplied Iraq with the means to manufacture tabun, allegedly used that year. U.S. intelligence confirmed that Iraq was producing and storing nerve gas in five places, including a big chemical complex at Akachat in western Iraq and that mustard gas was stored at Samarra. (All of these were among the strategic sites the allies attacked in 1991.) On March 31, 1984, the U.S. government blocked a shipment of chemicals and equipment to Iraq after it used gas against the Iranian human waves in the marshes.[21] On August 7, 1984, the Bonn government said it would tighten export controls on chemical manufacturing equipment. It also ruefully admitted that it could not persuade two West German firms, Karl Kolb and Pilot Plant, to stop working in Iraq.

Iraq shopped abroad for thiodiglycol, a main ingredient of mustard gas. It appeared on an embargo list drawn up by nineteen industrial nations calling themselves the Australia Group, formed to control chemical warfare production. An American oil company, Phillips Petroleum, made a thiodiglycol delivery to Iraq in 1983 by way of an Iraqi middleman working through the Dutch firm of Krull Bunker Service. When the first public reports came out about Iraq's use of poison gas, Phillips halted the second scheduled delivery. In 1985, a Spanish textile firm acted as intermediary for a delivery to Samarra. According to a West German report, a U.S. concern called Alcolac smuggled another 500 tons of thiodiglycol to Iraq in 1987–88. The same company showed its evenhandedness by sending 90 tons to Iran through a businessman in Dusseldorf, West Germany. Altogether, Saddam Hussein's chemical engineers must have received 2,000 tons of thiodiglycol. That made a lot of mustard gas.

Hussein's April 1990 threat to "burn half of Israel" with his "binary" chemical weapon may have referred to the product of a new and secret chemical weapons plant constructed in Al-Falluja, northwest of Baghdad. It was supposed to be on stream by 1991, when it was destroyed by allied air raids. One of the main ingredients of this product, and a harmless one by itself, was hydrogen sulfide, known to high-school chemistry students as "rotten egg gas" because of its smell. The other ingredient was the less common compound called ethylene oxide, produced in a petrochemical plant near Basra called PC-1 and in another called PC-2 in Al Musaiyib. The two ingredients can be mixed together to make thiodiglycol.

Another Iraqi installation in Al Falluja reportedly produced basic ingredients for the nerve gases tabun and sarin, and possibly another agent called VX. These, according to West German experts, are highly toxic by-products of chemical pesticides. Breathed in or absorbed through the skin, they lead quickly and progressively to colic, diarrhea, loss of bladder control, vomiting, high blood pressure, garbled speech, cramps, crippling of the muscular system, and finally death by strangulation. Iraq used these gases in the later stages of the Gulf War against both Iraqi Kurds and Iranian troops.[22] This led to great fear and speculation that Iraq would use them again in Operation Desert Storm.

What finally compelled people in the United States and Western Europe to recognize, if not act against, Iraq's chemical weapons capability was the terrible slaughter in Halabja, a Kurdish village inside Iraq. On March 16, 1988, after a series of gas attacks in nearby valleys and in areas close to the Iraqi-Turkish border, Iran captured Halabja after the Iraqi garrison withdrew. Iraqi planes and helicopter gunships swooped down on the village, dropping hydrogen cyanide, mustard gas, and tabun bombs. Estimates of the dead ranged from hundreds to five thousand. The bodies were photographed by TV crews taken to Halabja by the Iranians. A Kurdish doctor later said, "One bomb contains a hundred liters of cyanide. It was cold on that day and the vapor spread rapidly. Those people had no chance."[23]

Even cynical editors used to pictures from the Iran-Iraq War fronts gasped at the film footage. The Halabja pictures showed parents struck down as they ran with children in their arms, or lying over children whom they had wrapped in plastic bags in the last seconds before death.

Some experts believed that Iran had also used chemical weapons at Halabja. It certainly possessed them by this time. Iran's sympathizers, however, said Ayatollah Khomeini had given direct orders against the use of gas, despite pressure from other Iranian leaders to retaliate in kind against the Iraqis and the Great Satan, seen as always lurking behind them. Khomeini declared that Iran was engaged in a "holy struggle" and must set an example to other Muslim countries.[24]

Blinders in Washington

Western governments, though alerted, nonetheless paid scant attention to the evidence against Iraq. The U.S. State Department did order members of its embassy staff in Ankara, Turkey, to photograph and interview Kurdish refugees at the Iraqi border. The CIA and sat-int provided reports from inside Iraq. After much hesitation and careful weighing of the evidence, Secretary of State George Shultz finally announced that the United States had evidence that Iraq had used gas against the Kurds. Eventually, some forces inside the U.S. Congress tried, in the face of opposition from the administration, to denounce Iraq and bring sanctions against it. In mid-September 1988, two staff members of the Senate Foreign Relations Committee, Peter Galbraith and Chris Van Hollen, flew to Turkey. There they found and reported "overwhelming evidence" to support the CIA and sat-int's reports of Iraq's use of gas against its Kurdish citizens. International acquiescence, they said, had been a major factor in Iraq's belief that it could do so with impunity.

In Washington, Democratic Senator Claiborne Pell, chairman of the Senate

Foreign Relations Committee, in October 1988 introduced the Prevention of Genocide Act, which the Senate passed as a unanimous resolution. Pell said the world had sat by quietly thus far because of "Iraq's great oil wealth, its military strength, and a desire not to upset the delicate negotiations seeking an end to the Iran-Iraq War." But silence was complicity: the world had also been silent when Hitler exterminated the Jews. Never again, Pell concluded, could the world play mute witness to genocide.

At this point, however, lobbyists for American business interests in Iraq added their voices to Pell's opposition in Congress and the administration. The Reagan White House said it found Pell's resolution "premature" and "counterproductive." A sanctions bill in the House of Representatives was watered down after Republican Representative Bill Frenzel—an opponent of government intervention in private business—said sanctions against Iraq would hurt American employers and American employees. (He did not seem to consider Iran, the hostages, or other American business interests in the rest of the Middle East.) A proposed compromise permitting limited sanctions on agricultural trade with Iraq was dropped in the last-minute rush to wind up congressional business before the 1988 presidential campaign.[25]

U.S. intelligence had valuable information about chemical weapons, which Arab states have come to regard as the "poor man's nuclear weapon," an answer to Israel's presumed nuclear capability. The trouble was that it passed this information to men and women in governments that either did not analyze it correctly or simply preferred to ignore it. Equally serious, perhaps, for American policy in the long run was the misuse of intelligence information—commonly called "disinformation"—in deception operations. As disinformation often does, it tended to backfire on the users.

12

America Enters the Iran-Iraq War

A Meeting with Saddam Hussein's Deputy

April 11, 1987, Baghdad. The AA crew on the gun tower near the Mansour Melia Hotel on the banks of the Tigris swung their gun around in an arc. The sky was cloudless. The Iraqi warning radar was probably working as well as it ever had, but surprises were always possible. Iranian missiles—possibly souped-up Soviet Scuds from the stock Col. Muammar Qaddafi of Libya recently supplied to Tehran—were known to drop out of the sky without warning. We had toured a devastated Baghdad street the day before and seen blocks of housing demolished by missile attacks in the reheated war of the cities. As in Tehran, on the receiving end of Iraqi attacks, a watcher might on rare occasions look skyward and discover a marauding enemy plane releasing silvery chaff designed to confound ground radar before it unloaded, with varying accuracy, its few large bombs.

Dr. William ("Bill") Polk and I could not stay around to watch the show from our hotel window that morning. After days of waiting in vain for a meeting with President Saddam Hussein, we were heading for an interview with his main deputy for military and security affairs, Vice Premier Taha Yassine Ramadan.

Bill and I were driven by a grim-faced, black-suited driver, not unlike the one who had taken me to my last meeting with the Shah in Tehran in September 1978. We passed innumerable checkpoints and skirted gigantic concrete slabs, savage saw-toothed street barriers, and a host of heavily armed guards who looked as ready to shoot as to wave us onward. Soon we were walking up the steps of the sanctum sanctorum, the Republican Palace on the banks of the Tigris where Saddam Hussein and his closest aides worked.

Moments later, we were ushered into a spacious, carpeted office. Ramadan—a zealous Baath party apparatchik, bull-necked and as intelligent and tough by reputation as he looked—awaited us behind a massive desk. His chief's ubiquitous portrait glowered at us from the wall behind him, one of millions of Hussein's portraits seen in all corners of Iraq. Ramadan waved an impatient gesture of approval when we asked to record our meeting with a small Video-8 camera on a tripod.

By this time, the full force of the secret Israeli and U.S. arms-for-hostages deals was being felt, militarily in the Middle East as well as politically in the United States. While the State Department was running Operation Staunch to induce governments around the world not to sell arms to Iran, the Reagan administration had been secretly selling it large quantities of armaments or approving their sale by other countries. The shocking news had been broken by *Al-Shiraa*, a small Lebanese newspaper, the previous November.

How, we asked Vice Premier Ramadan, did Iraq see all this?

"What was going on for more than one and a half years," he began, "was not only sending arms to Iran. It was part of a conspiracy, a dangerous conspiracy against Iraq."

How was that?

"There was coordination between the three parties—Israel, the United States, and Iran. It covered intelligence, communications, weaponry, and the quality of this weaponry." Ramadan seemed to be forgetting that the Iranians had bitterly complained about substandard arms supplied by Israel and the United States.

"Intelligence information from the United States," Ramadan charged, "had concealed the weaknesses of the Iranian armed forces. At the same time, the United States cheated Iraq by telling us that it had one policy toward the war [tilting toward Iraq] when in reality it had another. . . . All these things could be interpreted by us as part of a conspiracy to enable Iran to occupy part of Iraqi territory. . . ."

Ramadan leaned back in his chair and paused to reflect. Perhaps his mind was still in Kurdistan. The day before, he had returned from a trip to Mosul where, it had been whispered in diplomatic circles, there had been an assassination attempt against Saddam Hussein. Then he resumed his narrative.

"The conspiracy . . . began on December 24, 1986 [the start of the last big offensive against the Basra area]. For two months, they [Iran] wanted to reach one main objective: to cut off and occupy a portion of Iraqi territory.

"But the result was huge casualties and failure to achieve the objectives of that conspiracy. Of course, they . . . inflicted some harm upon us in weaponry, both on our air force and our armored forces. This did not make us restrict our capabilities, and the ability of the Iraqi armed forces to face up to the conspiracy and the Iranian aggression has been strengthened."

What about the Hawk missiles sent to Iran by the United States?

"In fact," Ramadan replied, "we bravely faced those batteries. We met the challenge . . . and now the Iraqi armed forces are in a better position than at any time before. . . .

"In the first statement made by President Reagan after the revelation of the weapons conspiracy, he said that all the United States had sent Iran would fit into a single airplane, and its value would not exceed U.S. $10 million. Later it was discovered that they sent missiles, spare parts, and even tanks and military equipment which would have cost U.S. $1.2 or 1.3 billion. . . .

"All the time," Ramadan went on, "the United States was telling us that it wanted to stop the flow of armaments to Iran, they were cooperating with Israel to send more arms. . . . The antiaircraft equipment was intended to offset Iraqi air superiority; the antitank equipment was to balance the superiority in armor."

Ramadan reserved his greatest scorn for what he said was American doctoring of sat-int and other intelligence supplied to Iraq. What he may not have known at the time of this interview was that at least once, in February 1986, the secret White House team had helped Iran in another way: it directly supplied Iran with photographic and intelligence information on the Iraqi military.[1]

Next, Ramadan complained about what had happened in connection with the taking of the Fao Peninsula. On February 10, 1986, the Iranians had launched a two-pronged operation to capture the Fao Peninsula. Fao, a kind of springboard toward Kuwait and the oil states on the western side of the Shatt al-Arab, was at the time Iraq's only real window on the Gulf. Frogmen and Revolutionary Guards first captured Umm Rasas Island to the north of Fao. Another commando-type operation won the Iranians a foothold in Siba, on the main Basra-Fao road. Within a short time, amid torrents of rain, the Iranians had ferried troops across the Shatt to reinforce their bridgeheads until a force of thirty thousand men was assembled.

At the same time, the Iranians began diversionary attacks north of Basra, toward Amara. The Iraqis, believing them to be the start of a new offensive, committed heavy firepower against these and two smaller attacks further south. Iran finally captured Fao and its environs on February 14 after a savage battle. It also took AA missiles stockpiled near the port and an Iraqi surveillance and control post used to direct air strikes against Gulf shipping. Using pontoon bridges and rapid overland movements to build up their positions on Fao, they kept the Iraqi defenders off-balance. Massive Iraqi counterattacks and the water barrier of the Khor Abdallah, a huge salt-water creek to the west of Fao, prevented the Iranians from either moving on to the Iraqi naval base of Umm Kasr or capturing the Iraqi ships bottled up in the Khor Abdallah.

With the conquest of Fao, the Iranians won control of around four hundred square miles of Iraqi territory and waters. Sat-int showed about thirty thousand Iranian casualties and seven thousand Iraqi ones. The Iraqis took four hundred Iranian prisoners of war. Although the Iraqi defenders used chemical shells, as confirmed by a UN investigating team, they had not offset the lack of initial preparedness.[2]

The Iraqis were unable to recapture Fao until the war began to turn against Iran. There was direct U.S. naval involvement in 1988.

Ramadan sat in his chair, blinking at the little video camera. He was thinking about the words he would use to blame the United States for the Iraqi disaster at Fao. "Two months before the Fao battles," he said slowly, "there was some information that the Iranian military buildup was not against Fao, but against the area east of the Tigris River. Information came to us through many sources, but we knew that the main, the direct source, was through the Americans. . . . We had the impression that the information was correct, because it was from an American source. But when it came, the Iranian aggression was really against Fao.

"Even while the aggression was going on, the flow of information from the United States of America kept coming. It said that Fao was not the main target, [that] the main target was the region east of the Tigris. Later, we [asked] the Americans, . . . What was the purpose of your flow of information?

"Their answer was that this was the only data they had about the situation. So, the question now is, is there a conscious technical process in the United States to give this false information? All this, together with the contradiction between what was publicly said about the American attitude toward the war . . . and what was actually done by them—the flow of arms to Iran—would make us question the information and the policy, as well as the purpose behind them. Of course, you can draw your own conclusions."

Ramadan could not resist a final dig. The United States and Iraq had resumed diplomatic relations in 1984, even after the fall of Fao. The United States had stricken Iraq from the list of countries deemed to support terrorism. After the war with Iran began, Ramadan reminded us, Iraq had expelled Abu Nidal's ultraterrorist al-Fatah Revolutionary Council from Baghdad and officially declared itself against all terrorism—Palestinian, Iranian, or otherwise. "At the same time," Ramadan concluded, "Iran is very well known all over the world as the terrorist state *par excellence*. Reagan himself claims that he is against terrorism. Well, isn't sending weapons to Iran really giving it the means . . . to support more terrorism?"[3]

The Vulnerability of Kuwait

Over two months after the interview with Ramadan, retired U.S. Navy Capt. Gary Sick, an Iran expert formerly with President Carter's NSC, expressed an American viewpoint on the same set of problems. Irangate, he told me, was an "unmitigated disaster. It penetrated the consciousness of the people in the Gulf in ways that really nothing had up to that point. . . . [C]ould they trust the United States? . . . They came to the conclusion that they'd better be very, very careful."

Tariq al-Moayyaed, the subtle and sophisticated information minister of Bahrain, expressed similar sentiments in a conversation I had with him in June 1987: "People in the Gulf were concerned that Iraq might fall in a triumphant new burst of the Iranian revolution."[4]

The question was how the United States could restore the trust of friends and allies. The Iran-Iraq War threatened oil supplies in Japan and Europe. And in Saudi Arabia and the Gulf emirates, the war posed the threat of religious, political, and military turmoil. Paradoxically, it was the Iranian threat to Kuwait, never quite as friendly to the United States as the other emirates, that was to provide the Americans with an opportunity to balance the scales of its involvement in the war. This time, America would intervene against Iran.

Ayatollah Khomeini's appeal in Shi'ite communities in the Gulf had been limited, but the risk of sabotage and terrorism by small, determined cells in Bahrain and elsewhere remained strong. As we have noted, in Kuwait, 30 percent of the population in 1987 was Shi'ite, many of them immigrants from Iran. Like the Palestinian immigrants in Kuwait, they held sensitive jobs in the oil, gas, and airline industries, and in technological fields such as sea water desalination.

Most members of the Shi'ite community did not respond to calls from Tehran to rise up against the dynasty of the al-Sabah family. However, there had been the major attack by the al-Dawa terrorists against the American and French presence in Kuwait in December 1983, in addition to lesser cases of terrorism and sabotage. By 1986, this had led to pressure from the Sunni majority to get Shi'ites out of key jobs.[5]

The U.S. Embassy in Kuwait understood the vulnerability of Kuwait's internal security. The Gulf emirate was a wealthy oil state without a strong military force. By the summer of 1986, Iranian attacks on shipping had begun to concentrate on Kuwaiti vessels. Iran hoped to dissuade Kuwait from giving further support to Iraq. In December 1986, Kuwait privately approached the United States to ask that a number of its tankers be placed under the American flag. The request was made public and formal in January 1987.

Initially, the United States responded that a decision would take at least six months to clear the ponderous machinery of Congress and the various executive departments. Then, on March 2, 1987, the Soviet Union's efforts to give some Kuwaiti ships Soviet-flag protection seemed near success.

The Soviets' bid to escort Kuwaiti tankers, preceding the American offer of protection, according to Gary Sick, was partly due to "Moscow's recognition of the power of Islamic fundamentalists in their area, and that they were going to be dealing with Iran as a new military superpower in their midst. . . . I think you can almost plot, in a sort of perverse way, the rise of Soviet *credibility*, not threat or presence in the region, but credibility, with the decline of American credibility."[6]

The Soviet offer galvanized Washington into action. On March 7, the Reagan administration notified Kuwait that if its supertanker fleet of eleven ships were to be put under the American flag, the fleet would be entitled to U.S. naval protection. On May 19, two days after Iraq's attack on the *Stark*, and following weeks of debate in Congress and the media over the wisdom of such a step, the Reagan administration announced that it had agreed to reflag the Kuwait tankers and have U.S. warships escort them through the Persian Gulf.

Weinberger Champions the Kuwaitis

Defense Secretary Caspar Weinberger became one of the most articulate partisans of the reflagging operation. One of his main arguments was that "if we don't do it, the Soviets will." Weinberger told critics that the United States had an important advantage over the Soviets that it should keep: the United States was able to maintain a force in the Gulf and the northern Arabian Sea. This was partly because Arab Gulf states, in particular Bahrain, where the U.S. Navy had enjoyed the use of facilities at Mina Sulman and Jufayr since World War II, guaranteed access and logistical support. Kuwait, Weinberger revealed, had become the main source of fuel for U.S. Navy aircraft and ships in the area. During the escort operations, the al-Sabah government bore some of the fuel costs for American ships and planes, just as it agreed to bear a large share of the huge costs of Operation Desert Shield after the Iraqi conquest in 1990.

The Soviets enjoyed nothing of the kind. Their closest base, other than limited facilities at Aden, South Yemen, was Cam Ranh Bay in Vietnam. However, Weinberger said, the Soviets would be eager to move into Gulf basing facilities, and a refusal or further hesitation from the United States would confirm the Gulf rulers' fears about its credibility and reliability.

To those who argued that the United States had enough oil and should not be concerned with protecting European and Japanese supplies, Weinberger replied that oil is "fungible"; that is, once it leaves port it ends up wherever the oil companies want it to be. Kuwaiti oil was then indistinguishable from American oil. Loss of oil to European or Japanese markets would affect the U.S. supply, too, because everyone would be competing for a smaller pool of oil. In addition, a large percentage of oil produced in the Gulf was shipped and refined by U.S. oil companies. Closing the Strait of Hormuz would hit "American companies that pay U.S. corporate taxes and employ U.S. citizens."[7]

A major issue in the reflagging debate—and later during Operation Desert Shield—was whether the War Powers Act should be applied to American operations in the Gulf. Passed in 1973 after many years of U.S. involvement in Vietnam, the act requires the president to consult with Congress before consigning U.S. forces to hostilities or imminent hostilities, and to report to Congress within forty-eight hours of so consigning them. After the Iraqis attacked the *Stark* on May 17, 1987, President Reagan refused to invoke the act for the incident was apparently an accident. Protecting shipping, the Reagan administration now argued, was defensive, not hostile.

The counterargument made by some congressmen was that to place U.S. forces in the midst of an escalating shooting war was to risk attack, either accidental or deliberate. There were also charges that the administration had avoided consulting Congress to escape public scrutiny of the reflagging operation and other U.S. plans. Both the Reagan and Bush administrations were successful in prevailing over their critics and in keeping them from passing legislation that would have invoked the War Powers Act.[8]

Another factor in American thinking was that while Iran claimed to be hitting shipping that supported the Iraqi war machine, in fact Iran was attacking mainly the tankers of nonbelligerent countries heading to and from Kuwaiti ports. Most of these ships were not carrying arms; Iraq was being supplied through Saudi Arabian and Jordanian channels.

The Iranians rarely stopped and searched ships to see if they carried arms. Only once did they stop a Soviet vessel, an arms carrier bound for the port of Bandar Abbas. Moscow, hearing that a Soviet ship had been seized and confiscated, dispatched a tank-landing ship with a complement of troops and an escort of several warships from Aden toward Iran. When a Soviet diplomat in Tehran ordered Iran to release the carrier, that country complied at once—even though the ship's hold was full of arms for Iraq. Under international law they could have claimed the Soviet vessel as a prize of war, but the Iranians chose instead to pick on less well-defended ships.[9]

Turmoil in Mecca

Every year since Khomeini's return to Tehran in 1979, Iranian pilgrims had tried to spread his revolution to Mecca and the other holy places. The 1979 revolt of Arab fundamentalists in Mecca had strengthened Saudi determination to keep the *hajj* a religious rather than a political event.

In July 1987, Saudi Arabia was on high alert. The U.S. and allied naval buildup had combined with the shipping war to raise tension. In addition, as the Saudis were aware, Mehdi Hashemi and other Iranian radicals close to Muhammad Montazeri planned to smuggle explosives into Saudi Arabia and bomb Iranian notables at Mecca during the *hajj*. The Iranian insurrectionists calculated that the Saudis would be blamed.

Saudi authorities granted permission for the 155,000 Iranian pilgrims, led by Mehdi Karroubi—a powerful cleric and parliamentarian who headed the lucrative Martyr's Fund for survivors of the war and their families—to hold a demonstration on July 31, 1987. Women and veterans marched in the vanguard. The demonstration soon developed into a pitched battle with Saudi security forces. According to Saudi figures, 402 people, including 275 Iranians, died, many shot or crushed to death in the panicking crowd. The Iranians were whipped into a near frenzy at the height of the battle when their cheerleaders announced that a U.S. helicopter had been shot down in the Gulf. There was also fighting in Tehran, stirred up according to the Iranians by Iraqi and Jordanian agents at the behest of the Great Satan. On this, the declared "Day of Hatred against America," street gangs controlled by Hezbollah stormed the Kuwaiti Embassy in Tehran.[10]

Neither Saudi-Iranian nor American-Iranian relations have quite recovered from the hatred and mistrust kindled during the *hajj* of 1987.

Increasing U.S. Cooperation

At the end of May 1987, Iranian naval forces seized seven of the Kuwaiti navy's high-speed patrol craft off Bubiyan Island, near the Iraq-Iran frontier. The Iranians charged that the boats were spying for Iraq.

"What they were really doing," an Arab official in Bahrain told me, "was guarding Bubiyan." Kuwait had managed to keep the island demilitarized despite the hostilities raging nearby. Now Kuwait felt that it was on the front line.

To meet the growing Iranian threat, and at the same time to deal with congressional opposition to helping Kuwait, Secretary Weinberger felt that the Gulf states, notably Saudi Arabia, needed to do more in their own defense. It was crucial that Saudi Arabia conduct its own AWACS flights to complement American ones supporting the escort program. Kuwaitis, Saudis, and the emirate rulers were still reluctant to cooperate in high-profile military operations with the United States. Little did they know that in 1990 Iraq would force them into it.

What finally clinched early Saudi cooperation was Weinberger's meeting with Prince Sultan, the Saudi defense minister, in a lush private villa on the French Riviera on June 4, 1987. By the end of the day, Weinberger had obtained Saudi consent to participate in American AWACS patrols and other operations and, despite the opposition of some top naval officers, to use barges as floating bases in the Gulf.

Kuwait financed and helped outfit at least three of the barges, which became bases for U.S. Army helicopters and U.S. Navy and Marine Corps crews. The choppers supplemented AWACS warning by detecting hostile Iranian activity, and they provided gunship support when needed. Besides being used as naval storehouses, the barges became bases for U.S. Navy sea-air-land (SEAL) teams, seaborne clandestine commandos that played an occasional role in America's naval operations against Iran and that would be fully mobilized in 1990–91 against Iraq.

U.S.-Iranian Naval Warfare in the Gulf

On July 24, 1987, the *Bridgeton*, a large tanker in the first U.S. escort convoy of Kuwaiti ships, struck a mine and suffered serious damage. Weinberger appeared to blame the Iranian mining attack against the first escort convoy on a Washington leak. He mentioned a briefing by himself, National Security Adviser Frank Carlucci, and Chairman of the Joint Chiefs of Staff Adm. William Crowe on July 14, 1987. Afterward, Representative Les Aspin, chairman of the House Armed Services Committee, briefed newsmen about it. Weinberger claimed Aspin disclosed details of the convoy, including starting time and place, number of ships, and other details—many of which were reported in the next day's *Washington Post*.[11]

The attack came only four days after the UN Security Council adopted resolution no. 598 calling for a cessation of all hostilities connected with the Iran-Iraq War.

This resolution would not be implemented until August 20, 1988, after thirteen more months of warfare and growing U.S. involvement. On July 22, Lloyd's insurance brokers in London published the casualty toll of the shipping war from August 1, 1986, to August 1, 1987: 118 reported attacks and 47 merchant seamen killed. [12]

In mid-September 1987, U.S. sat-int and SR-71 Blackbird reconnaissance patrols backed up by Saudi-supported AWACS planes discovered a 750-ton Iranian auxiliary, the *Iran Ajr*, laying mines near the Strait of Hormuz. On the night of September 21, an SH-60B Seahawk helicopter from the U.S. guided-missile frigate *Jarrett* directed a flight of U.S. Army AH-6 and MH-6 Cayuses to the *Iran Ajr*. With guns blazing they ambushed the vessel while it was laying mines in the first serious U.S. attack on Iranian shipping since the Kuwait convoy operation had begun.

While an MH-6 sensor platform equipped with Black Hole electronic suppressors hovered nearby, the AH-6s raked the *Iran Ajr* with 7.62mm machine guns and 2.75-inch rockets. According to U.S. Navy reports, the ship, though damaged, continued to lay mines. The helicopter gunships returned for another attack, this time landing assault forces—SEALs may have been involved, although the navy has never confirmed this—to capture the minelayer. In the ensuing action, four of the Iranian crew were killed, three wounded, and the remaining twenty-six captured. Pictures later released by the Pentagon were taken of prisoners and mines still aboard the *Iran Ajr*; then the ship was scuttled. The United States used the good offices of Oman to repatriate the prisoners to Iran. This incident was generally accepted as firsthand evidence of Iranian minelaying in international waters. [13]

Two weeks later, U.S. helicopter gunships patrolling the eastern Gulf near Farsi Island, a base for naval Revolutionary Guards, again clashed with Iranian craft. Iran's regular navy had little or no control over attacks by the guards. They used their high-speed Boghammer speedboats and other fast craft for hit-and-run raids on Iraqi and sometimes Western-owned oil platforms, as well as for shoot-em-up attacks on tankers and dry-cargo ships. Three or four of the Boghammers were sunk or put out of action in this incident, without American losses.

Beginning on October 8, the Iranians tangled repeatedly with the U.S. Navy. First, said the Americans, a Boghammer boat fired on a U.S. helicopter in international waters. Then American gunships sank three Boghammers and fished six Iranians out of the Gulf, two of whom died of their wounds. The four survivors were repatriated through Oman. The U.S. Central Command had no intention of keeping Iranian prisoners or exchanging them for hostages in the Middle East.

Wayward Stingers

On October 9, 1987, the Pentagon announced that spare parts for the deadly U.S. Stinger antiaircraft missile, used by the mujaheddin in Afghanistan to great effect against the Soviet air force, had been found in an Iranian boat. There was an immediate outcry in Washington, especially in Congress, where the Stinger missile was a highly sensitive subject. Since February 1986, Congress had turned down several major arms deals with the Reagan administration proposed for Saudi Arabia. The main reason was pressure from the pro-Israeli lobby, in particular, the highly effective American Israel Public Affairs Committee. In addition to requesting forty-eight F-15 fighters, sixteen hundred Maverick missiles, armor-piercing uranium bullets, and additional ground equipment for the crucial AWACS system, the Saudis had wanted eight hundred Stingers to protect their ships from Iranian attack. After a peak of $54 billion in 1980–81 American arms sales to the Saudis fell to only $636,000 in 1987.[14] Without the support of the U.S. Congress, the Saudis turned to the British government for over one hundred British and European-made Tornado combat planes and related air defense and training systems, worth well over $20 billion.

In the meantime, the Americans still had to answer that nagging question: how did the Stingers get into the hands of the Iranian Revolutionary Guards?

When U.S. investigators checked out the mujaheddin in Afghanistan, they discovered that two chiefs of the Hezbi Islami party had allegedly sold up to sixteen Stingers in May 1987 to Revolutionary Guards for a sum of about $1 million. Hezbi Islami party leader and protégé of America and Saudi Arabia Younis Khalis claimed that men under his command had been fired on by Iranian border guards when a Hezbi Islami convoy strayed accidentally from Afghanistan into Iran. The Iranians, he said, captured two of their trucks with Stingers aboard. Later, a Soviet political commissar maintained that Soviet military intelligence had evidence of thirty-three Stingers being sold by Afghan guerrillas to Iranian agents. Ten more, he said, went to Iranian drug smugglers. Each sold for about $300,000, or three times their market price. As James Adams reports in a recent book, the U.S. government publicly accepted Khalis's version of the border attack but privately recognized that the Afghans had sold the Stinger missiles without being coerced.[15]

The U.S. Navy Strikes Back

The appearance of Stinger parts may have accelerated the pace of U.S. involvement in the secret and overt conflict against Iran. On October 15 and 16, 1987, the Iranians fired several Chinese-made Silkworms from their base in Fao, missing a Kuwaiti oil terminal at Mina al-Ahmadi but damaging two other targets—a Liberian tanker operated by an American company and a reflagged Kuwaiti tanker, the *Sea Isle City*. In Kuwait, I joined a party of newsmen taken to see one of the offshore Kuwaiti oil platforms and the damage inflicted by another Silkworm missile during the same period.

The U.S. Navy then had a field day. After brief warnings, four U.S. destroyers poured hundreds of shells onto Iran's Basharat oil platform in the lower Gulf. This was followed by an effective demolition job, reportedly by one of the navy SEAL teams. On October 21, the Iranians charged that the United States was now engaged directly in the war on the side of Iraq.[16]

Undoubtedly U.S. naval successes humiliated the Iranians and increased their desire for revenge; however, they preferred to retaliate against Iraq and its Arab allies rather than risk a terminal clash with the U.S. Navy. Tehran threatened Iraq with new action, including missile strikes on Baghdad, if Iraq continued to target industrial and civilian areas in Iran. In turn, the Iranians heavily shelled Basra. A long-distance Iraqi air strike on five tankers in the Strait of Hormuz subsequently brought retaliatory Iranian missiles into Baghdad, in one case hitting a school and killing thirty-two people.

Iraqi propaganda goaded Iran by calling Ayatollah Khomeini a coward who did not dare take on the U.S. Navy. Iranian soldiers at the front were reported to have been so enraged by their country's failure to respond to the *Iran Ajr* incident that they had sent delegates in late September 1987 on a long march from the front to Khomeini's house in Tehran to demand action. Revolutionary Guard Minister Rafik Mohsen-Dost tried to assure his followers that "ways to confront the United States and retaliate against its mischievous acts" were under study; the United States would be dealt a heavy blow "in due course."[17] Analysts of the Pan Am Flight 103 bombing tragedy that took place in December 1988 could not help but remember this early warning of revenge.

The White House, sustained by Secretary Weinberger and Admiral Crowe, wanted to avoid escalation of the shipping war and so resisted suggestions by the U.S. command in the Gulf that protection for reflagged Kuwaiti tankers be extended to non-American ships under threat from Iran. Meanwhile, naval forces of other Western countries hurried to the scene to protect their own ships. By the early weeks of 1988, a force of over forty ships, mainly minesweepers, was operating in the Gulf alongside the American ships but without day-to-day coordination.

What led to this change of heart by formerly reluctant European allies was a series of mining incidents. In May and June 1987, while U.S. attention was focused on the *Stark* incident and reflagging procedures, the Greek merchantman *Ethnic*, the Soviet-flagged *Marshal Chuykov*, and two U.S.-owned, Liberian-flagged ships hit mines near Kuwait. In August, the unescorted *Texaco Caribbean*, under a Panamanian flag and carrying Iranian (not Arab) oil out of the Gulf, hit a mine. This happened at an anchorage near Khor Fakkan, a United Arab Emirates' port enclave on the Gulf of Oman, a rendezvous for ships waiting for escort to Kuwait. Attacks on the Italian merchant ship *Jolly Rubino* and the British freighter *Gentle Breeze* followed in early September—events that moved the Europeans to send their warships to or reinforce those already in the Gulf.

On November 23, Iranian gunboats set afire the Rumanian freighter *Fundulea* near Abu Musa Island, another naval Revolutionary Guards' base. On Christmas Day, American television networks got some spectacular footage when SH-60B helicopters from the U.S. Navy missile frigate *Elrod* and a Lynx from the Royal Navy frigate *Scylla* winched up to safety 20 members of the crew of the Korean tanker *Hyundai*, also shelled and set afire by Iranian gunboats.

Weinberger left office as secretary of defense on November 23, 1987. As he returned to private life, he reported that he was pleased that U.S. and allied forces had performed well in the Gulf and convinced that the United States "would never bow to any future Iranian intimidations."[18]

Operation Staunch, the worldwide effort to end the covert flow of arms to Iran, seemed to be enjoying at least moderate success (the arms-for-hostages deals had not yet leaked to the press). Weinberger's successor as defense secretary, Frank Carlucci, had toured Kuwait, Bahrain, and Saudi Arabia in early January, renewing the U.S. commitment to Kuwait's security. The major turning point in the war was near. For a time, the armada of American and allied warships seemed to help restore calm, with fewer ship attacks during the first weeks of the year. Some allied naval units even began to return to their European bases.

During February, however, heavy fighting flared up in Iraqi Kurdistan, and Iranian boats resumed attacks in the Gulf. Between February 29 and March 27, Iraq launched a new series of missile assaults against Iranian cities. By the end of March, a total of 142 missiles had been fired into Baghdad and Tehran, causing signs of panic and a mass exodus from the latter. Baghdad was less seriously affected for only about a fourth as many Iranian as Iraqi projectiles were reaching their targets. Between March 13 and 31, the Iranian offensive in Kurdistan resulted in the capture of Halabja, whose Kurdish population was wiped out by chemical attack.[19]

Then came the break that was to take the Iranian navy out of the war and assert U.S. power in the Gulf more decisively than ever before. On April 14, the guided-missile frigate USS *Roberts*, heading south in the gulf after a convoy northward, struck a mine. Ten of the crew were injured, and the ship was seriously damaged. The commander of the joint task force in the Gulf concluded from available intelligence that the mine had been freshly laid. In reprisal and intending to cripple a significant part of Iranian naval capability, early on April 18 U.S. forces again struck at Iranian oil platforms, this time in the Sirri and Sassan offshore fields.

U.S. Navy planners also wanted to take out one particular Iranian frigate, the *Sabalan*. Its skipper had a reputation for attacking unarmed merchant ships after seemingly friendly radio exchanges. When the April 18 operation commenced, however, the *Sabalan* was at the port of Bandar Abbas, safe against anything but a carrier-based air strike. This type of action the Americans wished to avoid.

Directly challenging the U.S. operation was difficult or impossible for the Iranians. Instead, Revolutionary Guard Boghammers attacked an American-owned oil rig in a United Arab Emirates' oilfield, an American-flagged tugboat, and a British tanker. Immediately, two A-6 Intruder bombers from patrols already in the air sank one Boghammer and drove off the other attackers. In the Sirri oilfield, the Iranian gunboat *Joshan* fired an American-made Harpoon missile, whereupon American units promptly sank the boat.

Next, the Iranian frigate *Sahand*, a sister ship of the *Sabalan*, opened fire on the two A-6 Intruder bombers. From near the vicinity of Bandar Abbas, the *Sabalan* itself joined the duel. One of the A-6s bombed the *Sabalan*, crippling it. The Iranian units then limped into port as the United States, on orders from the Pentagon, broke off the action and ceased fire. The events of this day left over a third of Iran's naval force destroyed. In all, six Iranian units, including a missile-launching patrol boat and two frigates, were sunk or crippled at a cost of one U.S. Cobra helicopter gunship. An official Iranian communiqué accused U.S. forces of having "entered into the war, in direct and flagrant manner, on the side of Iraq."

End Game in the Gulf

As Iranian outrage against the United States mounted, the Iran-Iraq War began to resemble a film that gradually speeds up with each successive episode. On April 30, the United States announced it would permit its thirty-three-ship force in the Gulf and the Arabian Sea to protect nonbelligerent ships serving nonbelligerent ports if protection was requested. On May 1, Tehran radio responded to this with a cliché, warning the United States against getting involved in a "new Vietnam."[20] Iran's conviction that the Great Satan was now throwing its weight decisively onto the side of the enemy had been strengthened by Iraq's reconquest of Fao on April 16 and 17, just before the decisive naval battle between Iran and the United States in the Gulf. Without Fao, Iran could not threaten Kuwait or shipping in the upper Gulf. Iraq opened a series of successful military campaigns from Fao that helped bring about the war's end.

On May 23, Iraq's defense minister borrowed a page from Iran's book of war slogans, proclaiming a new Iraqi offensive, Operation Count on God, on the Basra front. In a swift campaign, Iraq's Third Army Corps together with the Republican Guards freed about sixty square miles south of Fish Lake. During the second two weeks of June, a general offensive in Kurdistan cleared the Iranians from forty strategic heights. Baghdad was able to announce on June 30 that Iraqi armies had resumed control of the entire area. A parallel offensive gained ground on the central front. Finally, in the last week of June, the Third Army Corps and the Republican Guards moved to retake the oil-rich Majnoon area, occupied by Iran since February 1984.[21]

Iran's Payback to Weinberger

With defeat still looming on the horizon, Iran secured its payback for U.S. involvement in the Gulf conflict. On February 17, 1988, near the Lebanon-Israeli border, one of retired secretary Weinberger's most valued military aides was captured by Iranian-backed terrorists. Lt. Col. William Richard ("Rich") Higgins was a bright, decorated Vietnam War hero who had had access to the most sensitive classified material crossing Weinberger's desk from June 1985 to June 1987.

Higgins's Pentagon friends remember him as an enthusiastic man, easy to anger. Perhaps this had stood him in good stead in Vietnam and, coupled with his bravery, helped win him some of his combat decorations, among them the Defense Superior Service medal, the Bronze Star, and Meritorious Service medal. While serving as commander of the UN Truce Observer Organization (UNTSO) force in southern

Lebanon, however, his emotional volatility may have helped doom him. Whatever the case, Rich Higgins's abduction and death at the hands of his kidnappers remains one of the most stunning blows delivered by Khomeini's Iran at the United States. If, like William Buckley, Rich Higgins was horribly tortured and forced under drugs and duress to confess some of the Pentagon secrets he knew from his service with Weinberger, the Islamic Republic of Iran and its subordinates could—had they known how to exploit the information—have benefited enormously.

Rich Higgins had joined the Marine Corps in 1967, going to Vietnam with the infantry. After his term in the Pentagon as junior military assistant to Weinberger, Higgins served in southern Lebanon through the turbulent summer, fall, and early winter of 1987–88. Probably he had little if any access then to the high-level material about Gulf strategy he had dealt with in his Pentagon job before; but he could well have had knowledge, through U.S. rather than UN channels, of contingency plans made by Oliver North and others to rescue or ransom American hostages. It might have been Rich Higgins's real or presumed associations with secret U.S. initiatives on behalf of the hostages that brought about his fate.

On February 17, after meeting with a senior Amal official—he had excellent contacts with this pro-Syrian organization—Higgins was driving back to UN headquarters in Naqoura, on the Lebanese-Israeli border. Several other UNTSO officers drove ahead of his Jeep Wagoneer, clearly marked and flagged as a UN vehicle. About four miles south of Tyre, at the coastal village of Ras al-Ain, the leading officers rounded a bend. When they looked back, they noticed that Higgins was no longer behind them. His jeep sat empty at the roadside. They had broken an important rule of escort tactics: never lose sight of the vehicle or of the man under protection.

An account of what happened immediately after the abduction was given to the Associated Press by Amal's southern Lebanon commander, Daoud Daoud. (He was murdered during a street ambush in south Beirut on September 22 later that year.) The kidnappers, Daoud said on February 20, had run into one problem after another. The first car they used, a brown Volvo, got stuck in the mud from Lebanon's winter rains. They forced a bulldozer driver to push them out of the mud, but the bulldozer damaged their car and they had to change to a white Peugeot. Then this car collided with a truck laden with oranges southeast of Tyre. The car that finally took Rich Higgins to the kidnappers' hideout was a red Mercedes. During the hour-and-a-half delay, Amal, probably ordered by Syrian intelligence, sealed off all exits from the Tyre region south of the Litani River, the northern boundary of UNTSO's operational zone. According to Daoud, the kidnappers' leader sent four other brown Volvos as decoy cars through neighboring villages.

The search for Higgins—sometimes coordinated and sometimes not by Amal, Syria, the UN, and U.S. and Israeli intelligence agents—was the largest ever made in Lebanon for a kidnap victim. After all, Higgins was a key UN official and an American with a history to boot.

Syria and its surrogate Amal were concerned because Higgins had just left that friendly meeting with the senior Amal official in Tyre. Syria, moreover, was now anxious to win the approval of the United States after battling its presence in Lebanon only four years before. The United States, Britain, and the EEC had imposed sanctions following an incident in which a Palestinian, allegedly working for Syrian intelligence, got his pregnant girlfriend to board an El Al flight at London's Heathrow Airport; unwittingly she carried a bomb. Syria hoped to have the sanctions lifted and needed a spectacular success. Thus, Syria committed hundreds of its elite special forces, dressed in Amal uniforms, to search for Higgins alongside Amal.[22]

The strategy of the searchers was to guarantee that Higgins stayed in the relatively open country of southern Lebanon. Once in the maze of shacks in southern Beirut, a hostage could disappear for good. Equally, the Shi'ite and Iranian strongholds in Baalbek and other parts of the Bekaa Valley were places where captives could be guarded with impunity.

Hundreds of UN troops, Amal militiamen, and Syrians sealed off three hundred square miles of southern Lebanon with roadblocks and checkpoints of all types. The UN brought in German shepherds with police training and also used helicopters, but the rainy, miserable Lebanese winter with its low ceilings and sometimes zero visibility grounded them during the first three days of the search. Amal captured dozens of Hezbollah members and partisans, including (according to Daoud) an accomplice in the task of smuggling Higgins to Beirut. The searchers believed that Higgins had spent at least one night in the place he was taken in the red Mercedes. This may have been at the home of Hezbollah's Sheikh Abdel Karim Obeid, who was later accused of helping to plan the kidnapping.

Daoud said the mastermind behind Higgins's seizure, whom he refused to name, was still in southern Lebanon on February 20, three days after the kidnapping. The Christian-run Lebanese Broadcasting Corporation identified him as Abbas Reihani, Hezbollah military commander in southern Lebanon, and said he had worked under orders from Hezbollah's top security chiefs in Beirut, Imad Mugniyeh and Abdel Hadi Hamadi.

On January 18, 1990, following fighting with Hezbollah, Amal leaders showed Beirut newsmen a five-cell underground bunker they said had been used by Higgins's kidnappers. The entry was behind a false door in a car paint shop in a village thirty miles south of Beirut. Amal's security chief in southern Lebanon said the complex had been used for three years by Hezbollah as a prison, torture chamber, and terrorist base.

The Battle for Southern Lebanon

The first claim for the abduction of Weinberger's former aide came two days afterward, on February 19, 1988. A handwritten statement in Arabic and a photocopy of two identity cards, which the UN later confirmed were Higgins's, reached a news agency in Beirut. The statement said he would be tried "for his dangerous espionage role with the CIA." Both the UN and the U.S. government vigorously denied the espionage allegation. In return for Higgins's release, the statement demanded an Israeli withdrawal from the security zone in southern Lebanon, an end to American interference in the Middle East, and freedom for all Lebanese and Palestinian prisoners held by the Israelis.

On February 22, the kidnappers released a seventy-second video showing Higgins unshaven but apparently in fairly good health. He looked gloomy and wore the same dark-green sweater he had had on when kidnapped. He repeated his kidnappers' three demands. With the tape was a written statement insisting that Amal stop looking for Higgins and warning that it would continue to capture suspect Americans. White House spokesman Marlin Fitzwater replied, "We don't make deals with terrorists, period."

On March 1, a third statement, without a picture or another authentication, repeated the demands and the charges against Higgins. It added the claim that "an American-Israeli deal" was "being hatched" for southern Lebanon. Shi'ite clerics, it said, would get the details "once the investigation of Higgins is over."

Another statement with a black-and-white photograph of Higgins was issued on April 21, four days after the Christian Voice of Lebanon reported that he had been killed in Amal-Hezbollah clashes. The colonel, said the new statement, would be tried by the "Court of the Oppressed" for spying. Higgins, it specified, had been supervising the activities of a Pentagon team specialized in combating Arab organizations; he had also been filing reports on military and political affairs in southern Lebanon.

On December 12, a message from the kidnappers announced that Higgins had been sentenced to death following his trial by the Court of the Oppressed. He had, the statement added grimly, "made a full confession about his espionage activities."

Had Higgins been imprudent in his travel procedures, on and before the day he was taken? UN personnel in Lebanon were, since the onset of the kidnapping offensive by Iran's surrogates in 1984, subject to travel rules. Timor Goksel, the Turkish spokesman for UNIFIL (the UN Emergency Force in South Lebanon), said the day after Higgins's kidnapping that the American officer should have had a UN military escort. But the next day, a spokesman at UN headquarters in New York rejected this: "As did all his predecessors, he traveled freely in the area without escort. UNTSO observers throughout the Mideast, unlike [other UN] peacekeeping forces, do not carry weapons or move with armed escorts."

Travel rules aside, the worst was yet to come. The sequel would further damage U.S.-Iranian relations, if this were possible, and strain U.S.-Israeli ties as well.

The Sheikh Obeid Affair

In the small hours of July 28, 1989, Israeli airborne commandos landed near the home of Hezbollah's Sheikh Karim Obeid at Jibchit, a Shi'ite village in southern Lebanon often battered by both Israeli forces and Amal-Hezbollah fighting. The

Israelis seized Obeid and two aides, then flew them to captivity in Israel where they remain as of this writing, despite widespread international criticism. Obeid, the Israel said, was deeply involved in planning Hezbollah attacks against Israeli forces and had also played a major role in planing the kidnapping of Higgins.

The kidnappers' first reaction was a threat to execute Higgins, who, they indicated, was still living, albeit under the shadow of his earlier death sentence, if Sheikh Obeid were not returned by a certain hour on July 31. On that day, a Monday, Muslim areas of Lebanon observed a general strike called by the two main Shi'ite organizations, Amal and Hezbollah, adversaries now united in their protest against the abduction. Just before the deadline, Israeli planes swept over Beirut on a reconnaissance mission. But there was no news of Higgins. Israeli Defense Minister Yitzhak Rabin repeated a standard proposal: Israel would trade all the Lebanese Shi'ite Muslim prisoners it held for three Israeli servicemen captured in 1988 and all Western hostages in Lebanon.

Then, two hours after the deadline, a news agency in Beirut received a message claiming Higgins had been hanged at the stated time. A thirty-second video of the swinging corpse accompanied this document, but there was nothing such as a dated newspaper to authenticate the timing. The message was signed by a group calling itself the Organization of the Oppressed on Earth, linked to Hezbollah.

Among the acts of violence the group had previously claimed were the abduction of twelve Lebanese Jews in Muslim West Beirut since 1984; a bombing in Madrid on June 2, 1985; and the hijacking of a Middle East Airlines flight from Beirut to Larnaca on June 13, 1985. Until Higgins's capture, Hezbollah had officially denied involvement in kidnapping Westerners.

Higgins's hanging, said the kidnappers, would be "an example for the day of reckoning. We also renew our stance that the virtuous sheikh and his two brethren be immediately released because what is coming is greater and America and Israel will bear full responsibility for it." There was a pledge to "uproot the cancerous Israel" and "chop off the hands" of the "arrogant people, headed by criminal America, and to glorify the Muslim faith and the nation of Muhammad till the flag of Islamic unification flutters all over the world."[23]

The murder of Rich Higgins had most likely occurred much earlier, perhaps after his "trial" in December 1988 or during a later altercation or escape attempt. As in the case of William Buckley, the captors saved the announcement of his death for a major political occasion.

Not content with having inflamed Western, especially American, public opinion, the captors kept the crisis alive and brought within its widening circle Israel, the Lebanese militias, the UN, and Iran. The new threat? To kill another American hostage in Lebanon, Joseph Ciccipio, formerly of AUB's administrative staff. We will return to his story later.

13

Swords Sheathed, Daggers Drawn

The Death of Iran Air Flight 655

July 3, 1988, saw families all over the United States preparing to celebrate the Fourth of July weekend, complete with fireworks and outdoor spectaculars. Allies of the United States during the American Revolution, notably France, were being remembered and feted. Few Americans, however, had begun to focus on a tragic clash whose roots lay in another revolution, the Iranian.

Over the previous months, there had been great turmoil in Iran. It was losing the war with Iraq, and most of its people knew it. In March, Gen. George B. Crist, commander in chief, Central Command, responsible for American operations in the Persian Gulf and the Arabian Sea, had told a congressional committee that after the last drive on Basra Iran could no longer mount a major offensive. Constant pounding by the Iraqi air force and Iraq's medium-range anticity missiles, aggravated by Iraq's use of chemical weapons on the land front, had severely demoralized the armed forces and the citizens of Iran.

After Iraq recaptured Fao, the regular Iranian army and the Revolutionary Guards blamed one another. Senior commanders of both services were dismissed, including the Iranian army chief of staff. On June 2, Khomeini appointed Ali-Akhbar Hashemi Rafsanjani as acting commander in chief and gave him the impossible mandate of achieving military victory over Iraq within six months. On June 1 and

2, a number of the friends of Mehdi Bazargan—who had urged a ceasefire and the opening of peace negotiations and who had dared to criticize Khomeini himself as solely responsible for the war—were arrested. On June 3, reflecting Rafsanjani's determination to drive the war home to the enemy, an Iranian fighter-bomber raided the Iraqi village of Ouijeh, near the residence of Saddam Hussein's family. When, in late June, the Iraqi armies recovered the Majnoon region, Hussein reaffirmed Iraq's will for peace (its acceptance of UN Resolution no. 598) and accused the United States, almost certainly falsely this time, of giving Iran secret intelligence on Iraqi offensives.[1] This speech was a foreshadowing of the future Iraqi-American conflict.

On July 1, Pentagon planners were worried about an Iranian buildup at Bandar Abbas, where F-4s and F-14s were deployed, and at the Strait of Hormuz, where new Silkworm missile sites were spotted under construction. That same day, the Pentagon announced the arrival in the Gulf of the guided-missile cruiser *Vincennes*, commanded by Capt. Will C. Rogers. By first light on July 3, the *Vincennes*, equipped with the U.S. Navy's most sophisticated combat-control system, Aegis, had received the same intelligence as all other units of the Central Command: the Iranians might use the fourth of July, when U.S. command authorities were preoccupied with bicentennial festivities, to launch a surprise attack of some kind.

On the previous day, Iranian Boghammer boats had clustered around a Danish supertanker like a swarm of wasps, hitting it with rockets until a U.S. frigate intervened and drove them off. That evening in a televised interview, Rafsanjani gave one of the first public hints by the Iranian leadership that Iran might have to stop the war.[2]

Between 10:45 and 11:00 A.M. on July 3, an Iran Air A-300 airbus, designated Flight 655, took off from Bandar Abbas Airport. Its scheduled flight to Dubai through the cross-Gulf Amber 59 air corridor, as it was known in Gulf aviation parlance, would be 140 miles. It was a popular low-fare trip for many Iranians who went to shop in Dubai's well-stocked markets or to visit relatives in the large Shi'a community there. A total of 290 people, including 66 children, were aboard.

Thirty-five minutes before Flight 655 took off, one of the *Vincennes*'s helicopters drew fire from Iranian gunboats outside Bandar Abbas. The *Vincennes* and another cruiser, the USS *Elmer Montgomery*, engaged the boats, sinking two and damaging a third. Watchers at the *Vincennes*'s screens thought they saw an Iranian F-14 fighter descending toward the ship in aid of the gunboats that had been circling the cruisers. Captain Rogers radioed seven alerts to the unidentified aircraft. After getting permission to shoot from his area command—something he did not need, under the prevailing regulations for combat in the Gulf—Rogers still hesitated. The plane, according to air traffic controllers in both Bandar Abbas and Dubai, was on course at 12,000 feet, not descending. It had just received permission from Dubai to climb to its designated altitude of 14,000 feet.

Finally, after four minutes, Rogers gave an order to fire two Standard surface-to-air missiles, an action for which he would later take personal responsibility. At least one of the missiles hit the airbus, shattering it into thousands of fragments and killing everyone aboard. Most of the victims were Iranians, but there were also six Yugoslavs, an Italian, and six Indians aboard. Within minutes, Tehran radio announced that the United States had committed a "crime against humanity."

At home in London that day, I monitored the shortwaves and placed phone calls to Washington and different points in the Gulf. The attack provoked a torrent of invective from Tehran and largely stunned silence from the Arab side of the Gulf. At first, the Pentagon said that the *Vincennes* appeared to have shot down an Iranian F-14. Later in the day, the chairman of the JCS, Adm. William Crowe, said that "electronic indications on the *Vincennes* led it to believe" this was the case, but that the target instead had been Flight 655.

The Pentagon spokesmen referred repeatedly to the electronic wizardry of the *Vincennes*'s Aegis defense system, capable of simultaneous tracking of the course, speed, and radar signature of two hundred targets at a distance of up to 150 miles, and of attacking twenty targets at once. They admitted, however, that the head-on radar image of the airbus was hard to distinguish from that of an F-14, that Aegis had never been able to tell one aircraft type from another. Two days after the incident, Pentagon spokesmen said that the airbus had been emitting mode 2–frequency electronic identification signals, the kind used by military aircraft (mode 3 signals were used by both civilian and military flights). Later, as writers in technical magazines such as *Proceedings of the U.S. Naval Institute* pointed out, the mode 2 signals had apparently originated from sources other than the airbus.

"The purpose of the Aegis system," said Caspar Weinberger, "is primarily detection and tracking in a combat environment. . . . The tragic event underscores the risk that Iran was running by trying to conduct business as usual while engaged in hostile activities throughout the Gulf."[3] The official American view expressed by Weinberger and others, including Vice President George Bush, was that Iran, not the United States, committed a wrong act, or at best a "tragic error."

In Dubai, airline pilots (including one I spoke with over the phone from London) who wished to remain anonymous said that the *Vincennes* and other American ships had developed a reputation for playing fast and loose by issuing threats and warnings against civilian airliners. More than once, the Dubai control tower had to complain to the U.S. Embassy to get threats rescinded.

On July 15, Iran released a tape of communications between the airbus and air traffic controllers confirming that Flight 655's transponder had been "squawking" (sending out signals) on the approved IFF (identification friend or foe) frequency. Other pilots suggested that the airbus pilot might have been too busy talking to controllers in Bandar Abbas and Dubai to have picked up warnings and requests for identification from the *Vincennes*. Although Bandar Abbas controllers had delayed previous flights when Iranian naval commanders reported fighting at sea, this time the controllers did not seem to know, or perhaps to care, about gunboat attacks against the *Vincennes*.

One American critic of Captain Rogers, Capt. M. Eckhart, Jr., USN (Ret.), asked why the Aegis cruiser had been allowed to get into firefights with assault boats in the first place. "Hazarding a billion-dollar cruiser against spit kits, particularly in a situation that did not involve its unique capabilities, does not come out as a logical command trade-off," he wrote. The accompanying frigates, not the *Vincennes*, Captain Eckhart thought, should have engaged the gunboats. "Captain Rogers," he went on, "was left to guessing, and he guessed incorrectly." A kind of rebuttal came from Rear Adm. Frederick C. Johnson, USN (Ret.):

> The shoot-down was not an accident. It was an error, maybe, but not an accident. . . . The *Vincennes*'s Aegis system performed pretty much according to design. . . . [T]he ship's company went about their business, as professionally as any other combat-ready crew. . . . No one, senior or junior, should pronounce judgments unless they were on deck in that situation and were able to see it from the *Vincennes*'s vantage point.[4]

It was the latter view that apparently prevailed at the top levels of the U.S. Navy and the administration. Captain Rogers suffered intense mental anguish. At home in California, he and his wife, a teacher, were persecuted. She was banned from her school and underwent severe shock when a bomb destroyed her car. In early 1990, the hardship was mitigated slightly when the U.S. Navy decorated Rogers, an event noted bitterly in Tehran.

President Reagan expressed condolences and regrets to the victims' families and to Iran in a letter transmitted through the Swiss government on July 4. The White House indicated to news media that it considered the incident "closed." Families of the victims, although not Iran Air nor the Iranian government, would be compensated once machinery could be found to do this directly, an announcement in Washington said July 11.

Calls for Revenge

On July 3, as U.S. independence celebrations continued almost unruffled, Iranian television repeatedly showed macabre film clips of bodies floating in the Gulf. "The greatest war crime of our era," it proclaimed, denouncing the "criminals and murderers" and calling for assaults on U.S. targets. Ten thousand mourners at the official funeral in Tehran, a tiny fraction of the crowd that would turn out for the Ayatollah Khomeini's funeral in June 1989, put deep feeling into their chants of "death to America."

Only a few of Iran's leaders echoed the public call for revenge. President Ali Khamenei declared that the Islamic republic would use "all our might . . . wherever and whenever we decide."[5] Radicals like Muhammad Mohtashami were silent. At a news conference on July 15, as the Iranians sought to convoke a UN Security Council meeting, Foreign Minister Ali-Akhbar Velayati said Iran was demanding UN condemnation of the United States for violating international conventions and principles. He recalled Iran's frequent warnings of the danger in America's naval buildup in the Gulf.

U.S. allies were less supportive than usual. British Prime Minister Thatcher accepted the right of units like the *Vincennes* "to defend themselves," but she tempered her statement by expressing "profound regret for the loss of life" in "a tragedy for all concerned." Soviet reactions were routine and predictable. TASS called the incident a "tragedy" resulting from the U.S. forces' buildup in the Gulf. Libya and Syria spoke of "criminal" action and "terrorism."

On July 20, the UN Security Council passed a resolution expressing "'distress" and calling for "a full explanation of the facts of the incident based upon an impartial investigation" by the International Civil Aviation Organization at Iran's request. The council repeated calls for a cease-fire in the Iran-Iraq War as set out in resolution 598. The final Pentagon report of August 19 admitted to U.S. error but repeated the thesis that Iran should share the blame. It concluded there would be no punitive action, because Captain Rogers and his crew had been under severe stress.

The loss of the airliner and its passengers apparently convinced Rafsanjani and other leaders in Iran that pursuing the war further could "lead to extraordinary losses for our people and the Iraqi people."[6] Together, he and Ahmed Khomeini, the imam's son, went to see the old man, who was suffering from migraines and was said to be chewing plugs of opium for relief from the pain. The intelligence from all fronts was bad for Iran. U.S. warships were still clashing with remnants of the Revolutionary Guards' navy. From Iraq, the leftist mujaheddin, with an army several divisions strong, were pushing into Iranian territory. The presumption in Tehran (reinforced by the glossy propaganda brochures and triumphant communiqués of the mujaheddin) was that if the mujaheddin could establish itself in southwestern Iran, it would set up a government under Massoud Rajavi beholden to Baghdad for its power. Rafsanjani and Ahmed Khomeini are said to have told the Ayatollah that there had to be a settlement of war before Allah took his soul to paradise; otherwise, there would be a bloody struggle for the succession.[7]

The Ayatollah agreed with them. Effectively, the war with Iraq was over. The other, secret war of settling accounts with the Great Satan was now ready to move into a new phase.

On July 18, 1988, Rafsanjani made a radio announcement accepting UN Resolution 598 and the cease-fire. Two days later, Khomeini's own statement, in which he said accepting the cease-fire was like "drinking poison," was read on Tehran radio. All of the old fire was still there:

> We have been and are determined to expand the influence of Islam in the world and to lessen the domination of those who are devouring the world. Now if the servants of the United States call this policy expansionist . . . we will not fear this but will welcome it. . . . We must smash the hands and the teeth of the super-powers, especially the United States. We have two choices, martyrdom or victory. We regard both as victory.

As for the Saudis, Kuwaitis, and other Gulf Arabs, "all of you are conspirators in the adventurism and crimes of the United States. We have refrained from engaging in any action to submerge the whole region in fire and blood, making it totally unstable." The implication was that this could still be done.[8]

The Iraqis kept up the military pressure on Iran until the cease-fire of August 18. Mujaheddin forces drove deep into Iran, about ninety miles at one point, threatening but never capturing the city of Kermanshah. This "dagger stroke" into Iran during the dying weeks of the war rallied Iranian popular support for Rafsanjani. The remaining Revolutionary Guards and regular reserve forces fought alongside an armed populace, finally routing the invaders in a defeat from which the mujaheddin never fully recovered.[9]

Between August 8 and 20, the UN Security Council set up the peacekeeping machinery to patrol the more than thousand miles of cease-fire line between Kurdistan and the Gulf. A resolution on August 9 created the new UN Iran-Iraq Military Observer Group (UNIMOG). Some 350 unarmed observers from twenty-four countries, not including the United States, were deployed at posts along the cease-fire line between August 10 and 20.

After Iran declared, on August 19, that it retained rights under the cease-fire to inspect ships passing through the Strait of Hormuz, and the next day Iraq firmly rebuffed the Iranian declaration, the cease-fire took effect. The first phase of the peace negotiations began in Geneva from August 25 to September 15. Soon the talks bogged down on the question of sovereignty over the Shatt al-Arab, one that remains unanswered to this day.[10]

Preparations for Revenge

While the peace efforts got under way, the airbus tragedy still rankled the Iranian leadership, especially the radicals. Thoughts of revenge were openly voiced. I was part of an ABC news team that spent months investigating the events of 1988, and according to our intelligence reports, Speaker Ali-Akhbar Hashemi Rafsanjani became once again the leading voice of moderation and reason. Sometime between July 3 and 5, Rafsanjani chaired a meeting in Tehran of the "kitchen cabinet" of Ayatollah Khomeini. Present were Ali-Akbar Mohtashami, Khomeini's son Ahmed, and Mehdi Karroubi, the powerful politician who controlled the wartime Martyr's Fund. "There must be no revenge," Rafsanjani is reported to have told them. "The Americans are capable of doing something even worse. Iran is exhausted. We cannot fight America, Iraq, and all of their allies all at once. Let there now be peace and reconstruction."

One or two days later, according to the information we received, Mehdi Karroubi attended or chaired a second meeting of the same group, and this time Rafsanjani was absent. There Karroubi is reported to have advocated revenge for the airbus attack and to have offered a lucrative premium to the person or persons carrying out the first act of revenge.

Ahmed Jibril

Toward the end of July, a fatal five-month scenario began to unfold. It made Ahmed Jibril, leader of the PFLP-GC, a leading suspect but not, as of this writing, the indicted conspirator in the worst act of terrorism against American civilians ever committed in peacetime.

Ahmed Jibril was born in Palestine in 1937. He and his family joined the general Arab exodus from Palestine in 1948 and settled down in Quneitra, Syria, a city near the Golan Heights, in ruins since the 1967 war. He joined the Syrian army at the age of nineteen and reached the rank of captain in the engineering corps, specializing in explosives and demolition. Dismissed from the army for "revolutionary activities," Jibril moved to Cairo. Later he rejoined the Syrian army, from which he was again dismissed.

Jibril joined and quit a number of Palestinian terrorist organizations.

During the late 1960s, Jibril met George Habash, a Palestinian physician who had graduated from AUB and who had organized the radical Marxist-oriented Popular Front for the Liberation of Palestine (PFLP). Although they did agree on wiping the state of Israel from the world map as soon as possible, Jibril and Habash were soon at daggers drawn on almost every other issue. Within a year of joining Habash in the PFLP, Jibril, during fundraising trips to Kuwait, began to accuse Habash and his politically minded friends in the Movement of Arab Nationalists (MAN) of being wimps not really interested in fighting Israel and of trying to dominate the PFLP ideologically.

Habash gave me his own assessment of Jibril in 1972:

> The Jibril faction has no political feeling or ideology. We have been fighting for twenty-two years. You have to know how to fight. You have to have a total political doctrine and vision. Our relations with Arab governments have had countless complications because of this attitude of Jibril.[11]

In 1968 Jibril set up a small fighting outfit called the Popular Front for the Liberation of Palestine–General Command. The PFLP-GC perpetrated several infamous terrorist attacks from its base in Damascus, including the raid by three Palestinian hang gliders that killed six Israeli soldiers and wounded seven others in November 1987. This event helped spark the Palestinian *intifada*, or uprising, in the occupied territories. Jibril also had a penchant for attacking airliners. For example, on February 21, 1970, about 15 minutes after Swissair Flight 330 left Zurich for Tel Aviv, a barometer-triggered explosion—the first of its kind—destroyed the baggage compartment of the plane. It crashed in a Swiss forest, killing all forty-seven passengers and crew members. On the same day, a similar bomb placed by Jibril's operatives aboard a Frankfurt-to-Vienna Austrian airlines flight exploded at 10,000 feet, blowing a hole in the plane. Nevertheless, the pilot was able to make an emergency landing at Frankfurt. Only one person was hurt.

Investigators later found that both bombs had been built into transistor radios assembled in East Germany and mailed in airmail parcels from Frankfurt.[12]

Jibril had also been involved in the taking and exchange of Israeli prisoners. During the 1982 Israeli invasion of Lebanon, his men captured three Israeli reserve soldiers. The Israelis kidnapped one of Jibril's nephews in Lebanon to pressure him. But Jibril, with the help of the International Committee of the Red Cross, managed in an operation completed May 20, 1985, to trade Israeli soldiers for 1,150 Palestinian, Syrian, and Lebanese prisoners in Israeli jails. One of those freed then was Jibril's faithful friend and deputy, Hafez Kassem Delkamouni.

The only enemy Jibril probably hated as much as Israel was Yassir Arafat, chairman of the PLO and since the 1970s advocate of a negotiated peace with Israel. Jibril's men repeatedly ambushed, wounded, and killed Arafat's men, and they retaliated against him. One of Arafat's top security aides told me in Tunis in November 1988, "Jibril, for us, is the most dangerous man in the Arab world. He wants to replace Arafat"—who was about to be proclaimed President of the State of Palestine by a session of the Palestine National Council, the PLO's top body, in Algiers that November—"as supreme leader of the movement."

Jibril's antipathy to Arafat was personal, to be sure, but it was also extremely ideological. He believed that a free Palestinian state, created on the West Bank and in Gaza after an Israeli withdrawal from those lands, could never coexist with a Jewish state. Jibril was ready to fight to the death or until the Palestinians liberated their homeland.

It is easy to understand why, three weeks after the U.S. cruiser *Vincennes* shot down the Iran Air flight over the Gulf, Western intelligence officers grew uneasy. Both Iraqi agents, who were protective of Arafat, and Israeli agents, watchful always over Palestinian activities of any sort, had spotted Ahmed Jibril in Tehran.

Western agencies knew that Jibril had one major problem not shared by Arafat's well-endowed mainstream PLO organizations: Jibril lacked money. Syria provided him with bed and breakfast, so to speak; his headquarters, training camps, and other activities, such as a hospital and a school for Palestinian orphans, were located in Syria. But Syrian intelligence gave him little operating money. Earlier Libyan support had trickled away to nearly nothing in the mid-1980s after Jibril refused Qaddafi's efforts to reconcile Jibril and Arafat.

Jibril's sighting in Tehran was enough to prompt Mossad, Israel's secret intelligence service, to warn the United States of a terrorist attack motivated by revenge for the airbus. Some weeks after Jibril's visit, another of his henchmen was spotted in the Iranian capital: Delkamouni, the one-legged veteran of frontier raids against Israel. By the time he visited Tehran, Delkamouni was thought to be in charge of all external PFLP-GC operations.

To many knowledgeable Arabs, Delkamouni seemed an odd choice for this job. He had spoken publicly against attacking civilians and disapproved of going after non-Israeli targets, or so it was said. His family also claimed that he disagreed with Iranian extremists who wanted the airbus avenged by an assault on an American target. This may or may not be true; certainly Delkamouni's responsibility for two bomb attacks on American troop trains in West Germany—an offense for which he was jailed in Germany in 1991—is accepted by most West German and American investigators.

Such observations would have looked irrelevant in the summer of 1988. Israeli intelligence expected revenge for the airbus. Jibril needed money, Jibril and Delkamouni had both been seen in Tehran. Yet Israeli, Arab, and Western intelligence services worked separately to find out what Delkamouni was up to and how Jibril was marshaling his forces for what many insiders believed would be a savage blow at Israel, the United States, or both.

At the end of July, Jibril contacted Marwan Khreesat, his accomplice in bomb attacks on airliners in the early 1970s, and said he needed his services again. An informant for Jordan's intelligence service, Khreesat reluctantly agreed to leave the quiet family life he lived in Amman with his Syrian wife and children, after he notified Jordanian intelligence, and to go back to work with Jibril.

Jibril told Khreesat that El Al was using a new security device, the barometric chamber. Installed at high-risk airports, the chamber simulates conditions of an aircraft in flight. A bomb, set to detonate when a plane reaches a certain altitude and air pressure drops accordingly, would explode in the controlled environment of the chamber rather than later on in the aircraft. So, the barometric chamber had to be thwarted. Jibril expected Khreesat to find a way.

The Five Multiple Barometers

Khreesat and the other bombmakers in the Middle East had no problem obtaining plastic explosives. Renegade Americans had shipped tons of C-4 explosive to Qaddafi in the 1970s. Between 1979 and 1981, a munitions factory outside Prague was to provide no less than 960 tons of the explosive Semtex-H to Libya for $6 million. That amount was small change to Qaddafi in the halcyon years when Libyan oil revenues were bringing in $20 billion a year.

In 1984, a special operations group directly under the command of the Czech Interior Ministry conducted clandestine tests to discover how much Semtex it would take to blow an airplane out of the sky. The information was kept strictly within Czech channels, but later it was learned that the testing installation was adjacent, and actually part of, a school for Third World guerrilla operatives, including Iranians and Palestinians. In any case, the Czech tests determined that it would take at least 200 grams of Semtex to cause an explosion powerful enough to bring down a large plane. [13]

Khreesat went shopping in the "Smuggler's Souk" near Damascus, where travelers stop to inspect tobacco products, whiskey, and other contraband smuggled from Lebanon and on sale for cash. In a dusty secondhand electrical shop, he bought five used radio cassette recorders, apparently Toshibas. Working with these and some explosives brought from Libya by intelligence couriers, Khreesat made five multiple barometers. Attached timers sensitized the barometers to react to changes in air pressure. A timer would be set for, say, thirty-five minutes. After that period, if cabin pressure did not change, the timer would close an electrical circuit and explode its bomb. Any change in pressure *before* the thirty-five minutes was up, indicating that the plane was descending, would reset the timer to zero. This enabled Khreesat's bombs (or so he told Jibril) to outwit El Al's pressure-chamber simulators.

This also meant that the devices could fly on short feeder flights before exploding aboard the aircraft that was targeted. Provided the preset air pressure levels were maintained for less than thirty-five minutes, the bomb would be safe; but if the plane flew at a predetermined altitude, say 30,000 feet, for longer than this, the bomb would be detonated.

On June 8, 1988, Khreesat was told to submit his handiwork for inspection to a senior PFLP-GC bomb expert, known only as Abu Elias, at Jibril's base camp outside Damascus. Abu Elias questioned Khreesat closely, looked at the devices, and then told him to hand them over to him for later use. At the start of August 1988, Khreesat was told to head for the village of Krusevac in Yugoslavia, the base first known for the PFLP-GC's terrorist projects in Europe. But when one of Delkamouni's lieutenants, Abdel Fatah Ghadanfar, was barred from entering Yugoslavia, that scheme collapsed.

Israel's Mossad tightened surveillance of the group. This provoked friction between Mossad and the German intelligence services. Mossad apparently penetrated the PFLP-GC, using Ramzi Diab, a young, well-educated Druze Arab from Israel who joined the PFLP-GC. He disappeared soon after the West Germans broke up the cell's preparations.

Marwan Khreesat arrived at a safe house in Neuss, West Germany, on October 13. There, Delkamouni had him reassemble the bombs he had already made in Damascus. In each he hid a charge of Semtex, which, because of its chemical composition, was not easily detectable by X-ray gear then in use. Barometric triggers would detonate the bombs when any aircraft carrying them reached a certain altitude.

The first target was to be Iberia Airlines Flight 888 from Madrid to Barcelona and on to Tel Aviv. Other bombs Khreesat reported making to his Jordanian intelligence case officer, who kept the West Germans informed, were intended for cargo holds of Israeli El Al flights. A Frankfurt nightclub frequented by U.S. service personnel was also on the target list.

More terrorists began arriving, and surveillance grew more difficult. So on October 26, 1988, the West German federal police raided fourteen apartments and made seventeen arrests of known or suspected PFLP-GC members or their accomplices. They seized arms, ammunition, and Spanish documents prepared for the Iberia Airline attack.

In Delkamouni's car, police found one Toshiba Bombeat 453. The West Germans then made a major blunder. Within fifteen days of the arrests, they freed all but three of the seventeen men arrested. Khreesat and Ramzi Diab were among the first released; Khreesat to the safety of Jordan and Ramzi Diab to an uncertain fate, perhaps execution, in Syria. Only Delkamouni and Ghadanfar remained in jail and were convicted for their alleged role in bombing two U.S. military trains in West Germany. Careless handling of some of the confiscated bombs later killed two German ordnance officers.

As the ABC News investigation showed and U.S. federal investigators acknowledged, Marwan Khreesat did not make the Lockerbie bomb, as some have alleged. On the contrary, he saved many people's lives and warded off several major attacks planned by Jibril's men.

No one, however, found the fifth barometric trigger Khreesat made in Damascus. Was it never used? Used by someone else? And if so, did that someone wire it to the lump of plastic explosive inside a suitcase placed in the baggage hold of Pan Am Flight 103?

Warnings to Pan Am

On November 8, West German police began disseminating information and warnings about cassette/radio-recorder bombs to airlines and airport security personnel. They were followed by advisories from the U.S. Federal Aviation Agency (FAA) and the British. A mysterious but probably coincidental and irrelevant warning about a Frankfurt–New York Pan Am flight was telephoned by an Arab living in Finland to the U.S. Embassy in Helsinki on December 5, 1988. The FAA did issue a warning, and the U.S. Embassy in Moscow took the call seriously enough to post a travel warning.[14]

In early 1990 a Swedish court sentenced an Arab named Muhammad Abu Taleb to life in prison for terrorist bombings in Scandinavia. Lockerbie investigators, including FBI agents, discovered that a man fitting Abu Taleb's description had bought clothing at a shop in Malta in November 1988. The clothing matched fragments found near Lockerbie long after the explosion of Pan Am Flight 103. Forensic tests showed the clothing had been wrapped around the bomb. Abu Taleb apparently had contacts with Libya.

Later, Lockerbie investigators found that the bomb that brought down Pan Am Flight 103 had probably been put aboard an Air Malta feeder flight to Frankfurt and trans-loaded, in an unaccompanied suitcase, to the stricken jumbo jet. Pan Am's insurers in December 1990 began legal action against Air Malta and the Maltese government to recover $32 million in hull insurance they had paid out for the destroyed plane, alleging criminal negligence in allowing the suitcase aboard the Air Malta flight. But Abu Taleb in Sweden refused to answer any questions from the Lockerbie investigators.[15]

The Iran Connection

Most leaders are familiar with the tragic details of the explosion that turned Pan Am's "Maid of the Seas" jumbo jet into a fireball, which fell upon the peaceful village of Lockerbie, Scotland, the evening of December 21, 1988. The Bush administrations's reticence, especially during the UN-sponsored anti-Iraq military campaign of 1991, to implicate Syria (a coalition ally) and Iran (a neutral but anti-Saddam Hussein player) ruled out such disclosures. On three occasions, the first only hours after the Lockerbie incident on December 22, 1988, callers claimed Iranian responsibility. They warned the Bush administration to expel Prince Reza, son of the late Shah, from the United States unless it wished worse disasters to happen. Reza was never expelled.[16]

U.S. Agents Aboard Pan Am Flight 103

The Delkamouni cell of the PFLP-GC had already been smashed by the Germans when Pan Am Flight 103 went down. There is apparently no proof that would stand up in court, only raw intelligence, of an Iranian role in ordering a payback for the shootdown of the Iran airbus. But another enigma remains. It concerns Americans.

Four U.S. intelligence men were also aboard the doomed plane. They were Daniel O'Connor, a State Department regional security officer based in Cyprus; Matthew K. Gannon, allegedly a CIA officer assigned to Beirut; Ronald Lariviere, a regional security officer in Beirut; and Maj. Charles McKee, U.S. Army and perhaps in the ISA, also from Beirut. O'Connor is believed to have traveled from Larnaca to London on an unscheduled Cyprus Airways flight, set up that same day from Larnaca to accommodate heavy pre-Christmas traffic. Gannon, McKee, and Lariviere began their journeys in Beirut and then boarded a Larnaca-London flight. The baggage container that exploded in the Maid of the Seas carried their bags.

O'Connor's suitcase missed the flight on which its owner died. It surfaced two days later at New York's John F. Kennedy Airport, with a London Heathrow label. There was suspicion that O'Connor's bag could have been switched by terrorists for one carrying the bomb, but this will probably never be determined.[17]

A Hostage Rescue Operation?

There were circumstantial links between the destruction of Pan Am Flight 103 and the festering problem of the American hostages held in Lebanon. Maj. Charles McKee, the ISA man killed on Flight 103, had arrived in Lebanon in January 1987, a year before Lt. Col. Rich Higgins's kidnapping. Neither McKee nor the colleagues killed with him—Gannon, Lariviere, and O'Connor—had been able to do much about Higgins or the other hostages.

In January 1989, in Northumberland, Scotland, far north of Lockerbie, a search team of police, military men, and civilian volunteers collected the widely scattered wreckage of the crash. On the Otterburn firing range, used by the Royal Air Force for practice bombing, an army officer found a sheaf of papers including a rough sketch of a city, possibly Beirut. It had been widely speculated, but never confirmed, that there were marked locations on the sketch, indicating the real or presumed cells of American hostages, suggesting plans for a rescue mission.[18]

American inattention to the hostage issue ended abruptly with the kidnapping of Sheikh Abdel Karim Obeid by the Israelis on July 28, 1989. Obeid, as we have seen, had been linked to Rich Higgins's kidnapping. The crisis that ensued, and that brought Iran and the United States to the brink of open warfare once again, concerned another member of the staff of the much targeted AUB.

Joseph Ciccipio was an Italian-born naturalized American who, two years before his kidnapping in West Beirut on September 12, 1986, had converted to Islam and married a Lebanese woman, Elham Chandour. She worked at the U.S. Embassy in East Beirut, which was blown up a few days after Ciccipio's kidnapping. Ciccipio was no stranger to the Middle East. In the mid-1970s he had worked as a shipping manager in Saudi Arabia. In 1984, after a period of employment with an oil company in London, he accepted a job as an accountant at the American University Hospital in Beirut.

Ciccipio was grabbed and clubbed on the head as he emerged from the AUB building where he lived, then pushed into the trunk of a car under the eyes of a security guard held off at gunpoint. Over the next few days, various callers claimed to have him; the last, the Revolutionary Justice Organization (RJO), came to be held responsible. This appears to be another name used by pro-Iranian Hezbollah factions and perhaps by Palestinians as well.

Despite appeals from his family, there was almost no news of Ciccipio until January 17, 1987. On that day, the Beirut newspaper *Al Nahar* ran color photographs of Ciccipio and another American hostage, Edward Tracy, kidnapped October 19, 1986. The pictures were not authenticated. After French hostage Jean Louis Normandin was freed in November 1987, he contacted Ciccipio's family in the United States. He told of being kept with Ciccipio in chains for much of his, Normandin's, last year as a captive. Otherwise they had not been badly treated. On April 24, 1988, after the stinging defeat administered to Iran by the U.S. Navy, the RJO threatened to kill both Ciccipio and Tracy if there were further American assaults on Iranian interests in the Gulf. This statement was authenticated by a photocopy of Tracy's Lebanese residence permit.

On July 31, 1989, the RJO threatened to kill Ciccipio if the Israelis did not release Sheikh Obeid. Ciccipio's execution was set for August 1, 1989, and the kidnappers promised, it would be seen on worldwide television. Five hours before the deadline, his wife Elham pleaded for his life at an East Beirut news conference. In an act of "mercy" the RJO announced a forty-eight-hour reprieve for Ciccipio.

Rich Higgins's reported death and the new threat against Ciccipio touched off a mini-crisis in Washington. On August 2, the Pentagon confirmed a new naval buildup in the eastern Mediterranean.

Four hours before the final deadline for Ciccipio's death, another statement, accompanied by an audiotape of Ciccipio, said that in response to his own request the execution had been postponed for another seven hours. "I demand from the American people," said Ciccipio on the tape, "to oblige Israel to release Sheikh

Obeid immediately because his kidnapping is not human. We, the American people, are always the victim of Israel's politics and President Bush has not helped to free us." He bade his wife farewell.

With the world's news media and Washington officials hanging on every word and sign from Beirut, the cruel game reached a climax forty-five minutes before the new deadline. The execution of Joseph Ciccipio, said a communiqué from the RJO, had been "frozen." It announced "'the practical stages of the initiative for releasing Ciccipio immediately." In exchange for him, the RJO demanded a halt to Israeli deportation of Palestinians from the West Bank and Gaza, the return of those deported, and the release of Sheikh Obeid along with 150 Lebanese detainees and 300 prisoners taken by Israel during the *intifada*.[19]

The United States and Europe breathed more easily, as did Sixth Fleet commanders in the Mediterranean.

Meanwhile, French naval forces were deploying in the eastern Mediterranean, apparently on call to evacuate several hundred French citizens threatened by the destructive warfare in Lebanon. What the hostage-takers might not have known, but what Iranian intelligence surely had been told, was that during the previous February, off the French Mediterranean island of Corsica, French and American forces had tested their ability to liberate and evacuate hostages in a joint amphibious exercise called Phinia 89. It involved France's quick-reaction force, the U.S. Marine Corps Expeditionary Unit, the French carriers *Clemenceau* and *Foch*, the USS *Theodore Roosevelt*, the U.S. helicopter carrier *Guadalcanal*, and seventeen other warships from both navies. Although the last French hostages in Lebanon had been freed by 1988, the French wanted to show their continued support of U.S. and NATO goals by taking part. "Phinia 89 was a real success," a French Defense Ministry spokesman said.[20] Perhaps some future rescue mission—the thought of which most hostages themselves dreaded—would demonstrate whether Phinia 89 was a success. In any case, if French naval forces intervened in Lebanon, the RJO warned, it would make good its earlier threats to harm Ciccipio and Tracy. On October 23–24, 1989, to mark the sixth anniversary of the blasting of the U.S. Marine barracks at Beirut Airport and the French paratroop headquarters, Islamic Jihad renewed an offer to trade Western hostages it held for the al-Dawa prisoners in Kuwait. This statement was accompanied by pictures of Terry Anderson and photos of the stricken American and French bases.[21] Joseph Ciccipio remained in captivity.

After the allied liberation of Kuwait in 1991, there was also talk that if the Americans helped the anti-Saddam Shi'ite rebels in Iraq, the payback would be freedom for the hostages. But no help materialized by the summer of 1991.

Iran Celebrates the Khomeini Decade

In February 1989, as the health of the Ayatollah Khomeini declined, the Islamic republic celebrated its tenth anniversary. Though the war with Iraq had been over since August, the decade since the Shah's departure had seen no progress toward lasting peace. Because of the hostage crisis foreign investment was still withheld, and reconstruction of the shattered Iranian economy, totally dependent on oil, had barely begun. The cost of staple foods and other necessities remained close to wartime peaks, wartime rationing was still in effect, and the black market dollar hovered near its inflated wartime rates. As returning soldiers found little or no work, unemployment and poverty ravished families. Drug addiction and trafficking, the latter punishable by death, climbed. The dying Ayatollah exercised his fierce fanaticism once again by doling out jail terms and lashings to four male staffers of the state television network, the Voice and Vision of Iran. They had aired an interview with an Iranian woman who wanted to tell her side after the Ayatollah accused her of insulting the Prophet Muhammad's daughter. Muhammad's daughter, she suggested, might not be the ideal role model for the Muslim woman.

At about the same time, Khomeini wrote a candid letter to Soviet President Mikhail Gorbachev, who was shortly to face major upheavals among his own Muslim population in Soviet Azerbaijan, along the Iranian border. Khomeini recommended that Gorbachev abandon the bankrupt system of communism, something Gorbachev was already doing. Instead, wrote Khomeini, he should study Islam, which could solve basic human problems and "easily fill the ideological vacuum" of his system.[22]

All that remained, in this difficult year of 1989, to aggravate Iran's conflict with the West and increase its isolation was the affair of the Anglo-Indian author, Salman Rushdie.

14

The Khomeini Decade Ends

Enter Salman Rushdie

At the end of the 1980s, the strange affair of Anglo-Indian author Salman Rushdie and his novel *The Satanic Verses*, branded blasphemous by many Muslims, especially Iran's clergy, came to distort and dominate relations between the West and radical Muslims the world over.

The Rushdie episode amounted to what historians used to call a *Kulturkampf*, or a struggle between competing social and religious systems, indeed of rival conceptions of man in society. The bizarre case became an epilogue to the Khomeini decade.

Salman Rushdie, an Anglo-Indian and Muslim by birth, is a product of the two cultures that would often come to blows during the Khomeini decade: Islam and the West.

Rushdie's family joined the massive Muslim exodus from India to Pakistan, the new Islamic theocracy (Pakistan means "the State of the Pure"). Rushdie grew up in the same bicultural situation that is a constant theme of his books. He spoke both English and Urdu at home and studied in England. After graduating from King's College, Cambridge, in 1968, he followed his parents back to Pakistan.

One of Rushdie's first clashes with the Muslim religious establishment in Pakistan came when he tried to produce Edward Albee's play, *The Zoo Story*. The

172

script contained the word *pork* (a banned substance for Muslims), and the censor forbade it. Rushdie, disgusted, soon hurried back to England, where for ten years he earned a living writing advertising copy and started a family.

Rushdie's first novel, *Grimus* (1974), was not a success. His second, drawing on his Asian heritage, was *Midnight's Children*. A story of India's history and independence, it sold about a million copies around the world and won the Booker Prize, the most prestigious award for fiction in Britain. Next was *Shame* (1983), a fantasy set in a fictional version of contemporary Pakistan. The Pakistani Muslim authorities banned the book for its portrayal of the late authoritarian Gen. Zia al-Haq.

Critics began to call Rushdie's work "magical realism." He began to get involved in British politics in the 1980s, with heavy criticism of Prime Minister Margaret Thatcher and the Conservative government. His politics emerged strongly in *The Satanic Verses*. The Labour party, especially its leftists, and the disarmament movement, began to woo him and claim his views as their own. The book is an allegorical novel, the understanding of which requires not only a detailed grasp of the Koran and Islamic doctrine but also background in such (for Westerners) esoteric subjects as the workings of the Indian film industry. To Muslims, there are several highly offensive passages, including one in which prostitutes operating out of a brothel in a Muslim holy city bear the names of the prophet Muhammad's wives. Most offensive is the satirical allegory involving a scribe bearing the author's name Salman. He commits the supreme blasphemy of changing the word of God, which is recited to him by the fictional prophet Mahound. Salman's life—in the novel—is mercifully spared.

On September 26, 1988, Viking Penguin published *The Satanic Verses* in Britain.

The first signals of the cultural upheaval the novel would cause came in two Indian magazines that published interviews with Rushdie. An opposition Muslim member of the Indian parliament used the interviews to have the book banned in India. In October 1988, while the book was still unknown in Iran, Faiyazuddin Ahmad of the Islamic Foundation in Leicester, England, received copies of some pages. He flew to Saudi Arabia and got the attention of the Organization of the Islamic Conference (OIC), a pan-Islamic political and cultural group with considerable power and influence in Asia. During the weeks following India's banning of the book, the same action was taken in Pakistan, Saudi Arabia, Egypt, Somalia, Sudan, Malaysia, Qatar, Indonesia, and South Africa. Rushdie was forbidden to travel to these countries. In 1989, Jordan, Syria, Bangladesh, Kenya, Thailand, Kuwait, Turkey, and Nigeria also banned the book.

Meanwhile, the Rushdie affair heated up in Britain. Muslims in London and Bradford met to plan an anti-Rushdie strategy. Syed Pasha, Britain-based secretary of the Union of Muslim Organizations, wrote to Prime Minister Thatcher asking for the prosecution of Rushdie, a request that was refused. On January 14, 1989, the Muslims of Bradford staged a public book burning, but the broad public scarcely noticed it. W. H. Smith, Britain's largest bookseller, removed the book from its stock the next day. Muslims demonstrated in London on January 27, demanding that Viking Penguin withdraw the book from publication and sale.

Anticipation of the book's American release in February 1989 aroused new violence. On February 12 and 13, at least six people were killed and over 150 injured during demonstrations in Pakistan and Kashmir. In many places on the Indian subcontinent, the Rushdie affair became embroiled with local religious and political issues.[1]

Then the Ayatollah Khomeini exploded the issue into what was to become a worldwide confrontation between Islamic partisans and those who believed in the liberal Western concept of freedom of expression. At 2 P.M. (Tehran time) on February 14, 1989, three days after the Iranian revolution's tenth anniversary, the official state radio announced that "the Imam and Supreme Guide" had just issued a *fatwa*, or religious edict:

> The author of *The Satanic Verses* book, which opposes Islam, the Prophet, and the Koran, and all those involved in its publication who were aware of its content are sentenced to death. I call on faithful Muslims to promptly execute them wherever they find them, so that no one else will dare to blaspheme Muslim sanctities.[2]

Normally in the Islamic world, a *fatwa* is supposed to be "a formal legal opinion given by a *mufti* or canon lawyer of standing, in answer to a question submitted to him either by a judge or by a private individual."[3] It is not clear whether Khomeini's *fatwa* condemning Rushdie to death would fit that definition at all. By most accounts, he reached it on advice of certain radicals in his entourage, who brought the book to him and forced upon his attention the bloodshed and strife it was causing on the Indian subcontinent. They may have dwelt also on a rather unsavory character in the novel called "The Old Imam."

The Iranian leadership proceeded to show that it was in deadly earnest about the *fatwa*. On February 15, street mobs proclaimed a day of mourning and stoned the British Embassy. Iranian clerical officials announced a reward of $2.6 million to whomever executed Rushdie—with a million-dollar bonus if the executioner was an Iranian.

On February 18, Rushdie issued a statement through his literary agent. He regretted the violence and distress generated by the publication of *The Satanic Verses* but did not apologize for the contents of the book. The next day, Khomeini rejected his statement. Rushdie and his wife, the American author Marianne Wiggins, accepted the protective custody of Scotland Yard and the London Metropolitan Police and went into hiding, moving from one secret location to another. Iranians and others who showed interest in winning the death bounty were arrested and jailed; several were deported. In early 1990, Marianne Wiggins departed for the United States, finding it impossible to share her husband's underground existence.

In London and New York, the offices of Viking Penguin were disrupted by bomb threats. Major American booksellers—Waldenbooks, Barnes and Noble, and B. Dalton— removed *The Satanic Verses* from their shelves, then later restocked the book without displaying it prominently. Many Western literary groups, such as

PEN, the Author's Guild, and the Association of American Publishers, stoutly defended the book, the author, and the right to publish it. Three members of the Nobel Prize selection committee—Lars Gyllenstem, Werner Aspenstoem, and Kerstin Ekman—handed in their resignations because, they said, the academy had failed to condemn Khomeini's *fatwa*. (The academy refused the resignations because of its rule concerning lifelong tenure.)

In late March 1989, a Shi'ite spiritual leader of Muslims in Belgium, Imam Abdallah al-Ahdal, was murdered. He had condemned Rushdie's book as blasphemous but had also criticized the order to kill Rushdie. In London, the humanitarian organization, Amnesty International, urged Iran to withdraw the death threat against Rushdie.

Although there was pro- and anti-Rushdie agitation in America, diplomatic repercussions in the West centered mainly in Europe. Western European relations with revolutionary Iran sank to lower levels—far lower than European businessmen, anxious to restore their lucrative trade and contracts, would have liked.

On February 20, a week after the *fatwa*, the European Community agreed to withdraw its envoys from Iran for "consultation" in solidarity with Britain. This was something Thatcher had been reluctant to do, since full relations with Iran had only recently been restored, and Britain counted on Iran's help in getting British hostage Terry Waite and others out of Lebanon.

In 1990, the Rushdie affair proved a formidable roadblock to liberating British hostages in Lebanon. Even Rushdie's public repentance and announced conversion to Islam in December 1990 did not move Iran's hard-line religious authorities to lift his death sentence. In the United States, the sensational repercussions of the Rushdie affair died away more quickly than in Britain; it was just one more episode in the decade-long Western confrontation with Iran, soon to be eclipsed by Saddam Hussein's conquest of Kuwait.

For the Ayatollah Khomeini in the waning weeks of his life, *The Satanic Verses* proved to be a gift from Allah. His deadly *fatwa* against Rushdie allowed him to step once again onto the world stage to reclaim the spiritual leadership that had been eroding in the Muslim world. The crisis with the West gave his radicals an issue they could use to block the reforms and changes advocated by Rafsanjani and the liberals, especially reopening Iran to Western ideas and investments. It also gave the hostage-takers in Lebanon and Islamic activists everywhere a new cudgel with which to beat their local or Western opponents. According to Iranian spiritual leader Ali Khamenei's statement at Christmas 1990, the *fatwa* was still in effect.

Iran's Murder Machine

One of the last and critical events of Khomeini's life came amid the furor over Rushdie. In an exchange of letters on March 28, 1989, the Ayatollah dismissed his chosen successor, Muhammad Montazeri, accusing him of being unwilling and unprepared to assume the powers of Supreme Guide. What Montazeri had done, in response to letters from members of Amnesty International protesting mass killings of political prisoners, was criticize the revolution. He went so far as to complain that "people in the world got the idea that our business in Iran is just murdering people."[4]

For years Amnesty had been asking the Iranian government for information on political killings that started during the revolution in 1979 and accelerated near the end of the Iran-Iraq War in June and July 1988. The Iranian authorities finally answered: only a few people had actually been executed, they said. These people "had taken part in, or collaborated with, an armed incursion into Iran [the invasion of summer 1988] by the opposition national Liberation Army [the mujaheddin], and . . . the government had the right to punish those who took up arms against it."[5]

Despite the vague rebuttal, Amnesty and other investigators uncovered several cases where leading opponents of the Ayatollah were murdered in circumstances that "suggested the complicity of the Iranian authorities." These included Ayatollah Byahmadi, a former colonel in the Shah's intelligence service, shot dead in his Dubai hotel room in June 1989, and Abdel Rahman Ghassemlou, leader of the Kurdish Democratic Party of Iran, gunned down in a Vienna apartment with two companions while the three were negotiating with Iranian government emissaries. In August, 1989, Bahman Javadi, a veteran Iranian communist leader, was killed and a companion seriously injured when an unidentified gunman attacked them in Cyprus.[6] More Iranian exiles were murdered in Europe and the Middle East in 1990. Amid the clamor over Kuwait, these cases were scarcely noticed.

The Death of the Ayatollah

On June 3, 1989, tens of thousands of Tehran's faithful flocked to mosques and gathered in public places to pray for the life of Ayatollah Khomeini. Eleven days before, he had undergone intestinal surgery. Then he had suffered a heart attack. Was it possible? Would the Supreme Guide desert them at the age of 86? Then came an announcement on Tehran radio: "The exalted spirit of the leader of the Muslims and of the noble ones, His Eminence Imam Khomeini, has reached the highest status, and a heart filled with love of God and His true people, who have endured numerous hardships, has ceased to beat."[7]

In the days that followed, Khomeini's body appeared near the Behesht-e Zahra cemetery in a refrigerated glass box above a twenty-foot-high funeral bier in heat approaching 100°F.

The spasms of grief that swept over Iran surpassed in their violence and emotion even the joyous greetings Iranians had offered him on his return from France in 1979. Eight died and more than four hundred were injured in the crowds that surged toward the bier. Those present said it was a miracle that casualties were not higher; millions turned out to pay their respects. Many, including the Ayatollah's son Ahmed Khomeini, fainted in the heat. Emotions crested when zealots at the front of the crowd tried to wrest the body of Khomeini from its coffin. Later, when the coffin was lowered into a simple grave in Behesht-e Zahra, a cemetery outside Tehran named after the prophet Muhammad's daughter, an Iranian TV commentator lamented, "Oh stars, stop shining. Oh rivers, stop flowing."[8]

Over a year later, in July 1990, correspondents visited the gaudy mausoleum erected over the grave. Nearby lay row after row of martyrs killed in the war with Iraq that Khomeini had allowed to drag on for so long. Above the mausoleum, two high minarets ascending to a latticed platform showed steel girders that were supposed to be copper plated. The tomb glittered, shining heart of a revolutionary cult whose devotees would continue to project the Ayatollah's messianic message within and far beyond the frontiers of Iran. At least, they would try.

Amnesty International recorded in 1989, and knew of continuing incidents in 1990, nine cases where people convicted of repeated theft had four fingers of their right hands, or the whole hand, amputated. Hundreds of women and men had been flogged; a few women had even been stoned to death for adultery. Once again, in July 1990, the Revolutionary Guards tried to enforce "modest dress" on Iranian women, dragging them "off for lashings and humiliation at the hands of these thugs," as Michael Sheridan of the (London) *Independent* described it, for allowing too much hair to show under their *chadors*, wearing see-through silk stockings, or using too much lipstick or mascara.[9]

The Succession

Despite forecasts that Khomeini's passing meant the end of the Islamic republic as such—Prince Reza and Iran's first president, Abol Hassan Bani-Sadr, now in exile in the United States and France respectively, were among such pundits—nothing like that happened. Within twenty-four hours of Khomeini's death, the clerical oligarchy of the supreme Assembly of Experts chose his successor, as provided for in Iran's constitution. After rejecting Montazeri, Khomeini deemed no one fit to be his successor; therefore, the Assembly of Experts singled out one of its own number, President Ali Khamenei, to fill the position of Iran's spiritual leader. This was a temporary arrangement. Later, Khomeini yielded his post permanently to Muhammad Ali Araki, an obscure but well-liked cleric of Qom. When Khamenei's presidential term ended the strongest leader of the country, Ali-Akhbar Rafsanjani, came to power in an election that won him 94.5 percent of the votes cast. The 270-member *majlis*, or parliament, last elected in August 1988 as the Iran-Iraq War ended, and the twelve-man Assembly of Experts (six appointed Islamic jurists and six more elected by the parliament) became serious power centers in Iran.

In a simultaneous referendum, 97.4 percent of the votes cast approved Rafsanjani's constitutional reforms. These considerably strengthened the powers of the president, making him both chief of the government as well as head of state. The prime minister's office was abolished. Rafsanjani was able to install a working cabinet without having to include any of the most rabid radicals. He kept only ten ministers from the wartime government and eliminated opponents such as former

Interior Minister Ali-Akhbar Mohtashami from office, though they remained influential.

Iran in Dire Need

Rafsanjani's opponents resisted his attempt to lead Iran's ruined economy back to the market-friendly policies that would attract billions of dollars in Western investment the new Iran needed to survive. Recovery, most experts felt, depended on Iran's ultimate restoration of relations with the United States and its European allies. By 1991, Rafsanjani faced an economy ravaged by a war deficit of close to $200 billion and the disappearance of oil revenues and tourism. Arms purchases—from piecemeal deals with Israel and the White House basement enterprise of North and Poindexter to massive deals with Europe, North Korea, China, and the USSR—had cost the country far more than its oil revenues provided.

Bankers estimated in 1990 that Iran needed at least $80 billion, perhaps more, for repairing physical damage alone—ruined oil terminals, industrial plants, schools, houses, hospitals, roads, and bridges. But oil prices had dived in 1986, and by the end of the war, Iranian production was at scarcely half the level enjoyed under the Shah. The war left the country with a native arms industry but not much else. Since Iran lacked foreign currency, one answer seemed to be bartering. The government offered deals involving the exchange of carpets and pistachios—in which Rafsanjani had made a personal fortune—for machinery, medicine, arms, and anything else available.

The public misery Iran had known under the Ayatollah continues unabated. By 1989 the *Economist* estimated about 55 percent of the population lived in cities, including nearly six million (some observers believe as much as ten million) in the fastest growing city, Tehran. The housing shortage had grown steadily worse since the end of the war.[10] A great earthquake struck the northern parts of the country in June 1990; some thirty-six thousand people died, and entire towns were flattened. Iran produced only half the wheat it needed, and the 1989–90 harvest was poor. The earthquake ruined the production of rice, one of the country's leading staples. Subsidized food imports to feed hungry Iranians were costing $3 billion a year in 1990. Food riots, which had occurred during the late- and postwar years, threatened again. Khomeini's vague theories of self-sufficiency for Iran did not survive his death.

Inflation was rampant in 1990–91. A confidential report to the Iranian government from the International Monetary Fund (IMF) in the summer of 1990 said Iran should clean up its economic act by eliminating multiple exchange rates. A dollar-based black market—especially ironic in the land where the revolutionaries viewed the dollar as an instrument of the Great Satan—grew and flourished. In 1990, the U.S. embargo against Iraq provided opportunities for traders who wanted to smuggle food and other goods to Iran. In mid-1990, newsmen and other visitors found money changers in the streets offering 1,470 Iranian rials for one dollar.

Rafsanjani's personal crusade to inject sanity and rationalism into the economy and public life stood under constant threats of all sorts. Foreign newsmen in Tehran heard rumors that army officers were being executed from time to time for planning coups or assassinations. The mujaheddin committed various acts of violence against select targets. One of a series of rumored murder attempts against Rafsanjani himself was a mysterious explosion on a helicopter during rescue operations following the June 1990 earthquake. Rafsanjani, it was said, had traveled from Tehran to the ruined city of Rasht in that helicopter and he had planned to return in it. Shocked by the extent of the earthquake damage, he decided at the last minute to return by road and so better assess the situation. Rafsanjani had just accepted millions of dollars worth of foreign aid from Britain, France, and the Soviet Union, along with at least one planeload from the old enemy, Iraq, and a token offering of $295,000 in supplies from the United States.

The hard-liners, including Mohtashami, wanted to reject all Western aid, calling it a maneuver by the West to win back its old influence and get the remaining hostages and prisoners out of Lebanon and Iran.[11] Iraq's invasion of Kuwait seemed to offer Rafsanjani, who in July 1990 quickly reached a peace accord with Saddam, the opportunity to rebuild Iran's former position as a Persian Gulf power broker.

America's Financial Controversy with Iran

In seeking to end the long confrontation with revolutionary Iran, the Bush administration had one important and little-known means at its disposal: the Iran-U.S. Claims Tribunal, set up in The Hague under the 1981 agreement that freed American hostages in Tehran in January 1981.

When the hostages were seized in November 1979, the Carter administration froze Iranian assets in the United States. These included armaments and contracts for U.S. services, such as military training facilities, already paid for by the Shah. Many of the planes, warships, weapon systems, and spare parts were still stored in the United States. When President Rafsanjani asked for the "return of what is due us," an amount Iran evaluated at $12 billion, he was referring to these assets, known collectively in court documents as Claim B-1. The United States was unwilling to announce its own figure, but American diplomats said privately that the amount was more in the neighborhood of $1 billion.

The Iran-U.S. Claims Tribunal was the only public forum available to the two countries to iron out their differences after the break in diplomatic relations at the start of the Khomeini decade. The tribunal began work on January 19, 1982, after one year had been allowed for the filing of claims. Three judges each from Iran and the United States, and three each from the Netherlands (the host country), Sweden, and Switzerland presided. Of nearly four thousand claims presented to the tribunal by 1990, over fifteen hundred had been dealt with, either in or out of court, by the beginning of the summer of 1991.

On November 6, 1989, the Bush administration announced it was returning to

Iran $567 million of blocked assets totaling $810 million. The balance, $243 million, would be transferred to an escrow account with the Bank of England, as provided for in the original 1981 agreement, until remaining American claims for expropriated or nationalized assets were settled.

The release of this sum, Ali Nobari, one of the Iranian diplomats assigned to the tribunal, told me, "had eased the atmosphere and had speeded up all . . . procedures." The Bush action speeded up the process of settling claims, many out of court, and helped to reduce the personal recriminations that had earlier been known to interrupt the tribunal's work. (Tribunal judges consistently denied that politics, hostages, or other American-Iranian issues were discussed at working sessions in or out of court.)

Naturally, both Washington and Tehran looked to the lawyers and judges in The Hague for signs of a thaw that would mark the beginning of the end of their confrontation. On May 1, 1990, the day after American hostage Frank Reed was released in Lebanon, the tribunal began its eighth full meeting since June 1989. Under discussion was the settlement of about twenty-four hundred small claims (each under $250,000) by Americans, most related to private or commercial property they owned while living in Iran before the revolution. The claims were worth a total of $105 million; Iranian counterclaims of the same nature totaled $400,000. After the record time of one week, on May 9, 1990, agreement on all these claims was reached in an out-of-court settlement. On May 21, new talks began on the B-1 military claim.[12] Progress concerning that, however, was infinitely slow. Few observers in The Hague expected any breakthrough before the Gulf War between Iraq and Kuwait's allies was over; and indeed, there was none afterward either.

Perhaps such open, personal negotiations for a settlement would eventually prove to be the channel for mending the fractured links between Washington and Tehran. The nondiplomatic channel—covert operations—had been a miserable flop. The CIA's various efforts at secret warfare had led to nothing but trouble. And yet the temptation for fresh involvement was there: despite Rafsanjani's liberal policies and preoccupation with the Iranian economy, he was secretly rearming his country, playing catch up with Iraq in the fields of missiles and chemical weapons. In June 1989, for example, Iran purchased chemicals from a West German firm in Dusseldorf. The chemicals resembled precursors for a poison-gas factory like some of those in Iraq.[13]

The USSR's Exit from the Middle East

By the time the new crisis over Iraq's threats to Kuwait had begun to build in early 1990, communism was in collapse—first in the former Eastern European satellites of the Soviet Union, then in the Soviet Union itself. In a bitter speech in Damascus March 8, 1990, President Hafez Assad of Syria said these developments had helped only Israel, because they had removed the Soviet Union as a power factor in the Middle East. President Saddam Hussein of Iraq, who had begun to fulminate against the unwillingness of Kuwait and its Gulf neighbors to forgive his debts from the Iran-Iraq War era or to give him new cash advances, was saying similar things.

No longer could Arab states such as Syria, Iraq, or even South Yemen, where a violent civil war resulted in expulsion of communist influence and Soviet advisers, count on playing the Soviet Union off against the West for military or economic aid. Everywhere, Soviet aid began to phase out. The only superpower left in the Mideast arena was the United States. Doubly agonizing for Mikhail Gorbachev's regime in Moscow, as it progressively abandoned its political and military positions in Eastern Europe from East Germany to Bulgaria and faced burgeoning independence movements in the Baltic states, was the growing agitation in the Muslim republics of the southern Soviet Union. In a sense, the tables had been turned on Moscow. In the days when Joseph Stalin had threatened his southern neighbors Iran and Turkey, the United States had to come to their aid, with massive military assistance. And the aid continued to Turkey, now a NATO ally, and to the Shah of Iran, the self-appointed defender of Western interests in the Persian Gulf.

In the 1990s, the subject peoples in the southern Soviet Union looked to the West (as the Armenians looked to the huge Armenian-American community in the United States), or to countries like Turkey and Iran, for help in their own liberation (as for example the ethnic Turks in Soviet Central Asia, and the equally Turkic Azeri people in Soviet Azerbaijan, north of the border with Iran).

The effect of all this was to further question, but also to further increase American influence. This happened at a time when one regional leader—President Saddam Hussein of Iraq—began to raise his pretensions to dominate the Gulf and the Arabian Peninsula. Since he no longer enjoyed Soviet support or backing, his campaign was to collide with the might and power of the United States. The testing ground was to be Kuwait, and the opponent Saddam Hussein found himself facing was George Herbert Bush, president of the United States.

15

Desert Shield:
The Days of
Hesitation & Wrath

The "Godfather" Principle

"I am not going to be held a captive in the White House by Saddam Hussein of Iraq," said President George Bush in January 1991, shortly after the start of the war against Iraq.[1] The victory of America and its allies in that war would prove overwhelming, yet there were few early signs of hard resolve in the way the Bush administration behaved toward Iraq during that country's long dispute with Kuwait. The factors that were to turn President Bush around included oil, economics, the incredible miscalculations and arrogance of Saddam Hussein himself, and certainly the advice of friends.

From the end of the Iran-Iraq War until Saddam's invasion of Kuwait on August 1, 1990, the Bush administration seemed to be conducting a strange love affair with the Iraqi dictator. At no time during this two-year period did the Bush administration, at least those at the top of it, seem to perceive Saddam Hussein's ambitions, pretensions, and the seriousness of his determination to dominate the Middle East by whatever means necessary. Careful study of Saddam's modus operandi since his attack on Iran in 1980 shows that the dictator worked according to what might be

182

called the "Al Capone theory" of international relations.[2] Saddam conducted a sort of protection racket in the Gulf that degenerated into one of the major international conflicts of our time.

During the war with Iran, Saddam operated as a kind of godfather. He threatened smaller neighbors, crushed the Iraqi Kurds, and menaced Israel. At the same time, he offered protection to friends like Jordan and potential adversaries like Kuwait that felt the chill and spreading shadow of Khomeini's revolutionary Shi'ism in Iran.

For Saudi Arabia and the other petro-monarchies in the Gulf that usually relied on American rather than Iraqi protection, the menace of Iran was very real. They gave more and more money to Saddam's war chest. When the war ended with the cease-fire of August 1988, they hoped somehow to recover the billions of dollars they had forked over for protection, but mainly they wanted to distance themselves from him. Saddam, preferring the old system, began to threaten again, demanding forgiveness of his immense war debts and new cash injections to keep the derelict Iraqi economy afloat.

Like Al Capone, Saddam Hussein became more violent when someone crossed him or failed to pay. In the United States, except among specialists, this went almost unperceived. It was business as usual, and lobby groups and most congressmen preferred to ignore documented tales of prison abuse, torture, arbitrary executions, and other violations of human rights.

The Oil Factor

Some of the principal actors in the Middle East believe that the crisis of 1990–91 was the result of collusion between the United States and Kuwait. According to this theory, the two countries wanted to set a trap for Saddam Hussein. One leader ready to discuss this is Crown Prince Hassan of Jordan. In several conversations during the fall of 1990, he told me and other visitors that the rest of the Arab world had not been able to understand Kuwait's defiant attitude toward Iraq. The Kuwait-Iraq dispute over boundaries, money, and oil developed into an international crisis—in the eyes of the Arabs but not of the United States. The Arabs saw the crisis as arising partly because Kuwait, perhaps encouraged but certainly not discouraged by Washington, was overproducing oil and forcing the price well below OPEC's preferred levels. On August 8, 1988, one day after the Iran-Iraq cease-fire, Kuwait decided to boost its oil production in violation of OPEC agreements, One of the fields where pumping was stepped up was Rumaila, straddling the vaguely defined Iraq-Kuwait frontier and claimed entirely by Iraq.

Iraq, exhausted and financially drained by the eight-year war with Iran, was desperate at the time to get oil prices up and maximize its revenues. From the very beginning of his reign, Saddam Hussein had understood that oil was the critical factor in building power in a country like his. He had put his own men in key sectors of the oil industry and nationalized some, though not all, shares of the Western-owned Iraq Petroleum Company (IPC) and its subsidiaries to enhance his nationalist image.

Soon Iraq was maximizing its oil revenues by cutting prices and breaking accords with other members of OPEC. When oil demand slackened in the 1970s, Iraq's production rose while OPEC's total output declined. Even with the government's policies of keeping the shops full of goods and of giving away automobiles to family survivors of the dead in the Iran-Iraq War, Iraq's economy could hardly absorb even a fraction of its huge oil revenues. It could not even invest them wisely, since the war cut Iraq off from the mainstream of world business. With the aid of Western bankers and consultants, Iraq concentrated on building up its war machine instead.

It is not entirely true that Kuwait profited from the 1980–88 war, as Iraq and its partisans often charged. Kuwait took losses, too. The drop in world oil prices reduced the emirate's oil income from $18.4 billion in 1980 to $9 billion in 1984. During the same period, as we have seen, Shi'ite supporters of the Ayatollah Khomeini led terrorist attacks in Kuwait. The external Iranian threat pushed Kuwait to obtain U.S. naval protection for its tankers in 1987.

Kuwait was a country of only half a million or so fully enfranchised citizens enjoying cradle-to-grave benefits. It had enormous foreign investments, probably in excess of $100 billion. These generated more income than its oil sales did. Iraq had a population of 18 million, was deeply in debt from eight years of war with Iran, and had little or nothing left for rebuilding and development.

Kuwait and Saudi Arabia operated according to the strategic principle that world oil consumption could be pushed up, and they could get a larger market share of that consumption. A corollary of this strategy was to keep prices at a level that would discourage the development of alternative energy sources by industrialized countries. Kuwait has thus been more willing than other oil producers to tolerate lower prices. Iraq, by contrast, sought the instant gratification of cash up front.

Why then did Kuwait raise production after the Iran-Iraq War ended? During that war, both Kuwait and Saudi Arabia had pumped so much oil in excess of quotas that the price collapsed. This happened just as Iran, a competing member of OPEC, ran out of cash reserves, hastening that war-weary country's acceptance of the cease-fire. Jordan's Crown Prince Hassan believes that Kuwait, by raising its oil output, perhaps in accord with Saudi Arabia, hoped to repeat the same pattern with Iraq—and while Washington was aware of it.[3] In any case, Iraq knew that by overproducing and lowering the price Kuwait would cut Iraqi revenue by the amount of money it would cost to service Iraq's debt: $7 billion a year.[4]

As the dispute between Kuwait and Iraq began to heat up, Saddam had plenty of signs of encouragement from Washington. John Kelly, U.S. assistant secretary of state for Middle East affairs, visited Saddam in Baghdad on February 12, 1990. Iraqi and Jordanian sources said Kelly told Saddam that the U.S. government considered him a "force for moderation" and wanted better relations with Iraq. This was good news for Saddam, who immediately telephoned his friend King Hussein of Jordan with the news. Saddam's mood changed, however, when two contradictory signals went out from Washington. The Voice of America (VOA) broadcast a strong anti-Saddam editorial on February 15. Six days later, the U.S. State Department published its annual report on human rights; this included twelve pages detailing the abuses Iraq meted out to the Kurds.

The oil dispute figured prominently at the meeting of the Arab Cooperation Council in Amman, Jordan, on February 24, 1990. In an angry speech, Saddam spoke of the serious impact on the Arabs of the end of the cold war and the concomitant rise of American influence. Washington and Moscow were both supporting the immigration of Soviet Jews to Israel, to the detriment of the Palestinian Arabs, and Washington's continuing armament of Israel might lead the Jewish state to commit "new stupidities." If the United States would remove its war fleet from the Gulf, he continued, this would help break American control of the world oil market. Saddam called on fellow Arabs to set up an action plan that would create an Arab power base. In this way, the Arabs could deal with the big powers on an equal footing. He berated the "cowardly and timid" Arab leaders who recognized the United States as a superpower, indirectly referring to King Fahd of Saudi Arabia and President Mubarak of Egypt.

Washington heeded Saddam's next warning because it was a pointed threat to Israel. In a speech to the Iraqi armed forces on April 2, he vowed to "burn half of Israel" with his chemical weapons if that country attacked Iraq's "metallurgical plants." He also referred to Iraq's execution of Farzad Bazoft, an Anglo-Iranian journalist accused of spying for Israel, as "just punishment."

The powerful Israeli lobby in the United States added its voice to others urging caution in American "appeasement" of Iraq. John Kelly and Dennis Ross, of policy planning at the State Department, drafted proposals for economic sanctions against Iraq. These included cancellation of Commodity Credit Corporation financing of Iraq's large-scale purchases of American wheat and prohibition of military exports of technology and equipment useful in both civilian and military spheres (dual-use), such as the Bell helicopters already sold to that country. Both the Department of Commerce and the National Security Council objected, however, and the plan died. At that time, spring 1990, the top echelon of the Bush administration was distracted by the German unification process and preparations for a Bush-Gorbachev summit. On April 12, Senator Robert Dole (of Kansas) led a Senate delegation to Iraq to meet with Saddam. Dole expressed U.S. concern over Iraq's chemical and biological weapons programs and informed Saddam that the journalist who had written the offending VOA editorial in February had been fired. He added that President Bush wanted better relations with Iraq, a statement confirmed by April Glaspie, U.S. ambassador to Iraq.[5]

On May 3 Iraqi Foreign Minister Tariq Aziz announced that OPEC's overproduction was an increasing threat to his country. OPEC oil ministers had met in Vienna in March with the subject high on their agenda, but both Kuwait and the UAE refused to agree to production cuts. An emergency OPEC session, nearly coinciding with Aziz's announcement, did produce an agreement; however, according to the Paris-based International Energy Agency (IEA), OPEC output fell only 400,000 barrels per day (bpd)—a figure attributed to cuts only in Saudi production. It was far short of the 1.45 million bpd cut pledged at the OPEC emergency session. On June 5 oil prices fell to $15.60 a barrel, down from $19.50 on February 20.

Even the usually oil-conscious U.S. administration of former oilman George Bush seemed not to grasp the connection between Iraq's deportment and the security threat to Kuwait. In a closed session of an Arab summit on May 30, Saddam claimed that Iraq lost a billion dollars a year each time the oil price dropped by one dollar—"a kind of war against Iraq," he called it. In late June, OPEC president Saddek Boussena toured some OPEC member states to encourage production cuts before the next OPEC ministerial meeting set for Geneva in July. His trip coincided with visits by Sa'adoun Hammadi, Iraq's deputy prime minister, to Kuwait, Saudi Arabia, Qatar, and the UAE. In his persuasive style, far less confrontational than Saddam's, Hammadi pressed for cuts. Again, there was scarcely a ripple of this in the summer torpor of Washington.

In Jidda on July 10–11, oil ministers from Iraq, Saudi Arabia, Kuwait, Qatar, and the UAE held their last prewar meeting and managed to agree on curbing overproduction. Kuwait and the UAE were both supposed to reduce their output to 1.5 million bpd each until the OPEC reference price, $18 a barrel, was restored. This meant a cut of 300,000 bpd for Kuwait and 400,000 bpd for the UAE.

Less than a week after this accord, however, Saddam Hussein began beating the war drums. On July 17, in a speech marking the twenty-second anniversary of the Iraqi revolution, he threatened that "if words fail to protect Iraqis, something effective must be done to return things to their natural course and restore usurped rights to their owners." He warned Arab states serving American interests that Iraq would not forget the Arab proverb, Cutting necks is better than cutting the means of living.

In a memorandum to this speech, Tariq Aziz recited a litany of debts and accused Kuwait of "stealing oil" from Iraq through the Rumaila field as well as installing military posts inside Iraqi territory. Kuwait and the UAE were part of a "Zionist plot aided by imperialists against the Arab nation." As usual, only a few alarm bells rang in Washington, but this was sufficient for the Kuwaitis to place their army on alert and hold an emergency session of the recently elected Kuwait National Council to study the Iraqi charges.[6]

The Kuwaitis began to take other discreet measures to safeguard their financial empire. In July a representative in Kuwait's Investment Office in London quietly started selling off Kuwait's bank assets and property in Asia.[7] In a letter to the UN secretary general, Kuwait said the Iraqi charges "falsified reality" and asked that the Arab League sponsor a committee to address the disputed Iraq-Kuwait frontier. In Washington, State Department officials seemed to agree with a statement by President Mubarak of Egypt, who dismissed the crisis as a "summer cloud" that fairer winds would soon blow away. Spokesmen repeated the assurances every American administration had given since that of President Franklin D. Roosevelt: the United States was determined to assure free movement of oil and to "support our friends in the Gulf."

Intelligence Failures and Defense Technology Leaks

CIA and other agency reports backed by sat-int, detailing the deployment of about 100,000 Iraqi troops on the Kuwaiti border, must have reached the NSC and the White House. (It appears that incomplete Israeli intelligence reports were channeled to Defense Minister Moshe Arens.) Only after the actual movement of Iraqi troops into Kuwait on the night of August 1–2, however, did the Bush administration begin to draw certain conclusions about policy and act. One decision was to curb American sales to Iraq of strategic materials.

Immediately prior to this, on August 1 in fact, the administration approved the sale of advanced data-transmission devices to Iraq. Government records obtained by the *Washington Post* indicate that the Reagan and Bush administrations had permitted Iraq to buy $1.5 billion in high-tech military or dual-use items between 1985 and 1990. These items, many of which allied bombers would destroy during Desert Storm in February 1991, included advanced computers, radio equipment, graphics terminals useful for designing missiles and analyzing their flights, high-tech machine tools, computer mapping systems, and imaging devices for reading satellite pictures. Much of this technology, including some approved in the last days before the invasion of Kuwait, went to key Iraqi bodies such as the defense and interior departments and the nuclear energy commission. Iraqi universities and scientific institutions, which formed part of the poison gas and nuclear research institutes and other industrial networks, acquired some of the U.S. equipment; this was later to make them allied bombing targets.

Much of the other equipment sold was dual use, such as $45.4 million worth of personal VIP helicopters for President Saddam, dignitaries, and visitors. Other helicopters, worth $25 million, were to be used for dusting crops but, in fact, were used to spray poison gas on Kurdish civilians in 1988 and probably again in strikes against rebels after Saddam's defeat in February–March 1991. Sources told the *Washington Post* that the companies that sold U.S. technology to the Iraqis included big names like Hewlett-Packard, Scientific Atlanta, Tektronics, and Wiltron.[8]

The PLO and Last-Minute Peace Efforts

The PLO has been widely seen as a major loser in the allied war against Iraq. Because it supported Saddam, its participation in postwar Mideast peace talks was rejected by Israel. There is an important aspect to the PLO story never adequately understood by the Bush administration or the American public. For his own reasons, Chairman Yassir Arafat and several of his aides made efforts to resolve the Israeli-Palestinian crisis peacefully before the invasion of Kuwait. Afterward, Arafat, like King Hussein of Jordan, struggled to secure an Iraqi withdrawal and so avoid war. On July 28 Arafat was in Baghdad paying one of his many visits to Saddam, who asked him to go to Kuwait and meet with the emir. Saddam told Arafat he would cut down the forces deployed on the Iraq-Kuwait border provided Kuwait pay him $10 billion for the oil it was pumping from the disputed Rumaila oilfields.

The next day Arafat met with the emir in his palace in Kuwait City. The Kuwaiti ruler would not talk about oil or the border, saying he would be flying to Jidda in forty-eight hours for talks with Iraq. King Fahd had just convinced Iraq and Kuwait to meet there July 31.

Arafat then held a separate meeting with Crown Prince Sheikh Saad al-Sabah, Kuwait's prime minister and the emir's cousin. The Iraqis were a threat to Kuwait. "I counsel you," Arafat said, "to try to solve the problem." The crown prince threw out his hands, palms up in the Arab gesture of powerlessness. "The decision is not in my hands," he insisted. Arafat, a master of persuasive if elusive argument, tried again. "Don't go to Jidda empty-handed. Can you handle a military confrontation?" The crown prince shook his head. "No, we don't have the strength Iraq has. We don't intend to fight Iraq."[9]

Although he may not have told Arafat, the Kuwaitis also had reason to believe they would not have to fight because either America or Britain, or both, would hasten to their rescue if Saddam attacked. The memory lingered of Britain sending in troops to defend its newly gained independence when Kuwait was first threatened by Iraq in 1961. As for the United States, according to one of King Hussein's advisers the Kuwaitis officially informed the Jordanians that U.S. troops would fly to their rescue within twenty-four hours. This belief in intervention overrode America's noninterventionist position, spelled out by Assistant Secretary of State John Kelly, before a House subcommittee in Washington on July 31, the day of the futile Saudi-Iraqi-Kuwaiti summit in Jidda. Kelly confirmed that, despite the American reflagging of Kuwaiti tankers in 1987, the United States had no treaty with Gulf states. When Representative Lee Hamilton asked Kelly a direct question about a U.S.-Kuwait defense treaty, Kelly repeated that no formal agreement obliged the United States to use American forces to defend Kuwait.

Within minutes, Saddam Hussein heard Kelly's testimony. He listened to it in Arabic on the BBC World Service.[10]

The Saddam–April Glaspie Meeting

Saddam must have felt John Kelly's statements confirmed signals he had already received, or so he believed, from April Glaspie, the able career diplomat and Arab world specialist who was U.S. ambassador to Iraq. In a meeting with Glaspie and his foreign minister, Tariq Aziz, on July 25, Saddam gave Glaspie a message for President Bush. After U.S.-Iraqi diplomatic relations had been broken by Iraq in 1967 and reestablished in 1984, he recalled, there was the trouble caused by Irangate and the Iraqi occupation of the Fao Peninsula. "We accepted the apology . . . of the U.S. President regarding Irangate," Saddam said, "and we wiped the slate clean." Unfortunately, "certain parties" in the United States that had not appreciated his country's newfound strength after the Iran-Iraq War "began to contact Gulf states to make them fear Iraq, to persuade them not to give Iraq economic aid." Iraq emerged from the war over $40 billion in debt.

More serious, Saddam went on, "planned and deliberate policy" by Kuwait and the UAE had been forcing down the price of oil while "Kuwait began to expand at the expense of our territory." He reminded the ambassador that it had been Iraq, not the United States, that protected Americans during the war with Iran. If the Iranians had overrun the region, "American troops would not have stopped them except by the use of nuclear weapons. . . . Yours is a society which cannot accept 10,000 dead in one battle." He gave clear warning that Iraq would "take its rights . . . one by one," following with a clear threat to unleash terrorism if crossed by the United States: "We cannot come all the way to you in the United States but individual Arabs may reach you." He seemed to anticipate the high-tech war that would be launched against him barely six months later: "When we feel that you want to injure our pride and take [away our opportunity for] a high standard of living, then we will cease to care and death will be the choice for us. Then we would not care if you fired one hundred missiles for each missile we fired. Because without pride, life would have no value."

Glaspie was able to give Saddam what he might have regarded as encouragement. President Bush, she said, had "directed the U.S. administration to reject the suggestion of implementing trade sanctions." The U.S. media had certainly been unfair. Glaspie found the interview with Saddam by Diane Sawyer on ABC's "Prime Time Live" program "cheap and unjust. . . . Your appearance in the media, even for five minutes, would help us to make the American people understand Iraq."

President Bush, she went on, "is not going to declare an economic war on Iraq." She and the Iraqi president seemed to agree that neither Iraq nor the United States wanted to see oil prices go too high. To Saddam's statement that "$25 a barrel is not a high price," Glaspie replied, ". . . many Americans . . . would like to see the price go above $25 because they come from oil-producing states." Glaspie also expressed understanding Iraq's need to reconstruct.

Then Glaspie came to what Saddam must have felt was the most encouraging signal of all: "We have no opinion on the Arab-Arab conflicts, like your border disagreement with Kuwait." The issue, she continued, was independent of U.S. foreign policy. An Arab solution to the problem, using the Arab League for collective security or a solution proposed by President Mubarak of Egypt, would be preferable.

Saddam warned that the "aggressor," meaning Kuwait, should not "believe that he is getting support for his aggression." He informed Glaspie that he had agreed to the Saudi proposal to meet with King Fahd and the Kuwaitis in Jidda July 31. In response to President Mubarak's expressions of concern about Iraqi troop deployments against Kuwait, he had said, "Assure the Kuwaitis . . . that we are not going to do anything until we meet with them. When we meet and when we see that there is hope, then nothing will happen. But if we are unable to find a solution, then it will be natural that Iraq will not accept death. . . ." Saddam interrupted his talk with Glaspie for one telephone conversation with Mubarak. Later Mubarak was to claim Saddam had given a promise not to attack at all.

Glaspie told Saddam and Aziz that she would be traveling to the United States July 30 and that she would convey all of this news to President Bush. [11]

On March 20, 1991, the Department of State allowed Glaspie to break her long silence about the meeting. In testimony before the Senate Foreign Relations Committee, she claimed that the Iraqi transcript was edited to delete references to the warnings she had given Saddam against using violence to resolve his dispute with Kuwait. She insisted that she had warned Saddam against using force, but the Iraqi transcript omitted all mention of this. Glaspie also said the transcript fails to indicate that Saddam had interrupted their meeting to make a telephone call to President Mubarak. Saddam reassured him that Iraq did not have warlike intentions against Kuwait, according to Glaspie.

King Hussein's Final Efforts

On July 28, 1990, King Hussein of Jordan landed in Baghdad and was driven immediately to Saddam's well-fortified presidential palace. During their meeting, the king told me later, Saddam rehashed his oil, boundary, and financial grievances against Kuwait, stressing the need for access to sea frontage on the Gulf. Iraq had repeatedly asked Kuwait to lease the islands of Bubiyan and Warbeh so that Iraq could go through with its plans to expand the small Iraqi seaport of Umm Kasr. Saddam would do nothing against Kuwait until, or unless, the negotiations in Jidda on July 31 broke down.

The king emerged from the meeting with the feeling that everything now hinged on the Jidda summit. The crisis had reached a new height of tension. Troops were massed on the border. Saddam was infuriated. King Hussein resolved to fly directly to Kuwait City in an effort to encourage the Kuwaiti royals to go to Jidda with a positive attitude. On the way to Baghdad Airport, he sat in the car with Jordan's prime minister, Mudar Badran. Badran had been briefed on an Iraqi intelligence report that indicated that if the Iraqis invaded Kuwait, Kuwaiti forces would try to hold them at the border for twenty-four hours, after which U.S. forces would land. Some of the king's other advisers, who had been talking with Iraqi counterparts, had similar news.

In Kuwait, the emir and his family and aides told the king they couldn't "give up an inch of territory," which seemed to exclude any deal leaving Bubiyan and Warbeh, or for that matter the Rumaila oilfield, in Iraqi hands. The Kuwaiti foreign minister said, "We cannot bargain over an inch of territory. It's against our constitution. If he comes across, let him come. The Americans will get him out. They'll come under pressure from Israel, and it will be a big embarrassment for U.S.-Israeli relations."

The next morning, the king and his party returned to Amman. The following morning, he called both the American chargé d'affaires and a senior officer at the

British embassy to share with them his perceptions of the danger. Later the king reflected, "I was not at all comfortable about Jidda. I knew that if the meeting there didn't make real progress, a huge problem would arise. But I didn't imagine that it would turn out the way it did—with the Iraqis invading Kuwait."

The Jidda Fiasco

The final Arab attempt to solve the crisis was the weekend conference in Jidda. The emir of Kuwait refused to attend, sending in his place Crown Prince Sheikh Saad al-Sabah and the Kuwaiti ministers of foreign affairs and justice. This was thoroughly insulting to Saddam. He canceled his own trip and sent instead Izzat Ibrahim, vice chairman of the Revolution Command Council. With Izzat were Deputy Prime Minister Sa'adoun Hammadi and Ali Hassan al-Majid, Saddam's cousin and confidant who had directed the acquisition of Western defense technology and the building of Iraq's war industry. Al-Majid was destined to become governor of occupied Kuwait.

At the opening session, Ibrahim read out a long list of charges against Kuwait, then repeated Saddam's old request for $10 billion in cash from Kuwait. A loan would be fine if a gift were impossible. The Crown Prince offered $9 billion. Ibrahim refused, saying Saddam would not accept anything less than $10 billion.

Participants prayed in the conference mosque, then met Abdallah Bishara, a dynamic Kuwaiti diplomat who chaired the Gulf Cooperation Council. Bishara proposed a step-by-step plan for confidence-building measures, to be preceded by demobilization and an end to propaganda attacks by both sides.

During the state dinner given by King Fahd, he announced he would make up the extra billion demanded by Iraq. The Iraqis thanked him courteously, and Fahd retired, thinking matters were, on the mend. Crown Prince Saad turned to Izzat Ibrahim and told the Iraqi that before dealing with the $9 billion loan they should trace a final Kuwait-Iraq boundary, then and there, at the table. The Iraqis rejected this. "We know very well," retorted Ibrahim, "how to get the money we need from you and the Saudis."

"Don't make threats," answered Saad. "Kuwait has powerful friends. We have allies as well. You will be forced to pay us the money you owe us."

The next day the participants left without a communiqué. In Baghdad, Saddam convened the Revolution Command Council and made the decision to invade Kuwait.[12]

That night, interagency conferences in Washington began to deal with the crisis. Gen. Colin Powell, chairman of the Joint Chiefs of Staff, convened his key military leaders and staff. And in Amman, Prime Minister Mudar Badran prepared his government for news of the slide toward war. Israel learned of it, too, at an hour so late that it would later raise questions about an Israeli intelligence failure. Israel, in turn, informed the CIA.[13] The signals had been plentiful, but those in power hadn't until then seemed to see or hear them.

Invasion

The first Iraqi columns rolled into Kuwait at 1:30 A.M. Kuwait time on August 2. About thirty thousand Iraqi soldiers of the hundred thousand massed on the border, including elite Republican Guard units, took part in the assault, using tanks, helicopters, gunships, troop carriers, fighter jets, naval units, and truck-borne infantry.

There was scattered opposition from some Kuwaiti units, and fighter pilots made a few passes and attacks on the advancing Iraqis before flying some of their planes to safety in Saudi Arabia. But on the whole the Kuwaiti armed forces appear to have been taken almost completely by surprise, this despite intelligence reports sent by a Kuwaiti military attaché in Basra and U.S. sat-int and other reports. Either they had not shared with the Kuwaitis, or they had not been taken seriously. Awakened at 2:00 A.M. by a military post near the frontier, Crown Prince Saad is reported to have said that Iraq intended to take only the disputed islands of Warbeh and Bubiyan and the Rumaila oilfields.

By about 4 A.M. the emir and some of his family and entourage had been driven to the U.S. Embassy. Ambassador Nathaniel Howell sent the emir and a few family members by helicopter—the rest of the entourage and cabinet members by car—across the frontier to safety in Saudi Arabia. They were to wait out the crisis in Taif, Saudi Arabia's summer capital.

By 7 A.M. the Iraqis had entered Kuwait City. On the steps of the emir's splendid seafront palace his half-brother and a few members of the palace guard made a brave but foolhardy stand and were shot dead.

By mid-afternoon of August 2 Iraqi troops held most of Kuwait City's center while units of the Kuwait army held out at their barracks in Shuwaikh, north of the city. Iraqi forces landed and quickly consolidated control of Kuwait's main islands—Warbeh, Bubiyan, and Faylakah. Kuwait's elite Maghaweer Brigade fought bravely from their barracks at al-Jahrah, west of Kuwait City near Kuwait Bay, but were crushed by tank fire and aircraft strafing, reportedly losing one thousand dead.

As the Iraqis fanned out over the country, sending some units directly to the Saudi border and so ringing new alarm bells in Washington and Riyadh, Baghdad radio began broadcasting a series of claims and communiqués. One was that Iraqi troops had been invited into Kuwait by local "revolutionaries" who had staged a coup against the emir and then asked for Saddam's help. This reminded old-timers in the West of Hitler's claim in September 1939 that Free Germans in the port city of Danzig had seized control and appealed to German troops to free them from their Polish "oppressors," triggering the German invasion of Poland and World War II. The crucial difference was that while Hitler had an effective fifth column inside the mainly German city of Danzig, Saddam had none worth mentioning inside Kuwait apart from some operatives of the Iraqi *mukhabarat*, the secret intelligence service. The pro-Iraqi Provisional Free Kuwait Government began broadcasting as the troops drove in, announcing that it had replaced the "defunct and corrupt" al-Sabah regime, proclaiming closure of the borders, and imposing an indefinite curfew. A Revolution Command Council broadcast from Baghdad threatened to "turn Kuwait into a cemetery" if any country interfered. Iraq closed its airspace and land borders. Saddam ordered fifteen infantry and armored divisions, disbanded after the 1988 ceasefire with Iran, to mobilize. Volunteers were encouraged to join Iraq's popular militia, the People's Army.

In Baghdad there were mass demonstrations to celebrate the invasion. But on August 3 the Cairo newspaper, *Al-Ahram*, reported that 120 Iraqi officers had been executed by Saddam for opposing the invasion. The stunned population of Kuwait City for the most part stayed holed up in their homes. Some people tried to dash to shops and supermarkets, sensing the impending looting and pillaging by the occupiers. Others piled into their cars and headed for the Saudi border. Many of the one million foreigners—more than half of whom were Pakistanis and other Asians who did mainly menial tasks, along with an estimated 400,000 Palestinians, mostly educated people who performed managerial, technical, and professional jobs for Kuwaitis—tried to escape. A few thousand made it to Saudi Arabia before the border was sealed. Thousands of American, British, and European expatriates, many caught in luxury hotels and apartments, hesitated over what to do.

Soon, however, Iraqi patrols began to hunt the foreigners down and round them up. A few reached their embassies before a long siege of the embassies began. The U.S. Embassy took in and cared for as many Americans as it could, for the invasion of Kuwait soon became, among other things, the biggest hostage crisis since the Nazi and Stalinist occupations of World War II.[14]

Two Days of Decision

On the second and third of August the major players in the new Gulf crisis— Saddam, President Bush, Prime Minister Margaret Thatcher of Britain, King Hussein of Jordan, and President Hosni Mubarak of Egypt—made the decisions that would set the course for war.

On August 1, at 6:30 P.M. Washington time, National Security Council Director Brent Scowcroft and Richard Haass, his Middle East aide, left the State Department for the White House. The two of them discussed the Kuwait crisis for forty-five minutes with President Bush. Meanwhile, Assistant Secretary of State Robert Kimmit, in charge of State Department affairs while Secretary James Baker and his deputy, Lawrence Eagleburger, were meeting with Foreign Minister Eduard Shevardnadze in the Soviet Union, phoned them to report firing on the Kuwait-Iraq border. Shevardnadze, apprised of this by Baker, showed incredulity. "He's our client," the foreign minister said, referring to the Soviet military aid that had flowed to Saddam since 1972, when an Iraq-Soviet friendship and cooperation treaty had been signed. "I don't believe he has prepared an invasion plan." When the two held a joint news conference shortly afterward, they were still unaware of the full-scale Iraqi attack.[15]

In the early hours of August 2, coded video links were set up between the Situation Room in the White House basement and the Pentagon, State Department, CIA, and Office of the Joint Chiefs of Staff. CIA chief William Webster and his deputy, Robert Kerr, along with Robert Kimmet, Assistant Treasury Secretary John Robson, Deputy JCS Chairman Adm. David Jeremiah, and Paul Wolfowitz of the Defense Department took part in the early deliberations. Justice Department lawyers were summoned to the White House and told to draw up documents freezing Kuwaiti assets the world over and Iraqi assets in American banks. This would prevent Saddam's men, who would soon be robbing Kuwait's banks of their cash and gold reserves, from touching the vast overseas assets.

So far, the question of military action had been avoided.

A Secret U.S. Proposal to Saddam Hussein

Late on the night of August 1, about twenty hours before Prime Minister Thatcher discussed the situation with Bush, a hastily convoked UN Security Council debate began. At 4:30 A.M. New York time, Security Council Resolution 660 was voted unanimously. Yemen, whose representative said he had no instructions from his government and who later on would take strong positions in favor of Iraq, abstained from the vote. The Iraqi ambassador protested that his government had sent its troops into Kuwait in response to a call for help by "young, revolutionary Kuwaitis," probably one of the most nonsensical statements ever heard in the UN's chambers.

The council resolution condemned the Iraqi invasion, demanded immediate and unconditional withdrawal of Iraqi forces, and specified the need for a negotiated settlement between Kuwait and Iraq. (Countries like Yemen, Algeria, and Sudan, which wanted an Arab solution without Western intervention, would protest that this last clause of the resolution was neglected.) The resolution also referred to chapter 7 of the UN Charter providing for sanctions against an aggressor state, and if sanctions should fail, for "a blockade or other operations by air, sea or land on the part of member states. . . ." Thus was a legal, supranational basis laid for the dispatch of the allied expeditionary forces.

During these proceedings Thomas Pickering, U.S. ambassador to the UN and a skilled diplomat who knew both Israel and the Arab world, glanced across the room and saw the crestfallen face of Jordan's UN ambassador, Abdallah Salah. Aware of King Hussein's deep involvement in efforts to solve the crisis, Pickering walked over and sat down. "Buck up," he told Salah. "Get off a message to Amman and insist on a reply. It's not too late to save the situation."

Pickering listed for Salah the points to be covered. First, there should be a withdrawal by Saddam's forces with publicized details specifying the schedule. Second, the question of the return of the emir and his family to Kuwait could be put aside for the time being. Third, the United States believed there was some merit in Iraq's position in the disputes with Kuwait. While the United States would not take a stand one way or another, it would do whatever was necessary to develop the machinery for settling matters. Fourth, the United States acknowledged Iraq's need for a better opening to Gulf sea-lanes. The issue of access to Warbeh and Bubiyan islands was one on which the United States could look favorably. Fifth, Iraq should call publicly for a UN-sponsored plebiscite enabling Kuwait citizens to decide their future.

Ambassador Salah hurried to the office of Jordan's UN mission and sent off a coded message to Amman. He was awakened by the response, a telephone call from Zayed bin Shaker, chief of Jordan's royal court. King Hussein was overnighting in Baghdad, as we shall see, and it is doubtful whether bin Shaker had been able to reach him on a secure line. The five-point memorandum, said bin Shaker, was "fascinating. But is it off the top of Pickering's head, or is it a trial balloon from the Bush administration?"

Salah phoned Pickering and repeated the question to him. Pickering said he didn't know for sure but was pretty certain it was close to administration views. He then phoned Secretary of State Baker in the Soviet Union. Baker said he would get right back to Pickering. Five minutes later he did, almost certainly without speaking to President Bush, although theoretically he could have reached him on a fast, secure link. "We can live with this," Baker said.

The royal court in Amman was to have sent this crucial message to Saddam. As far as any of the principals know, it never reached the Iraqi dictator.[16] This was probably because of communications failures.

The next sign that President Bush might give Arab peace a chance came on August 2. Early that morning King Hussein was awakened by a telephone call from an angry King Fahd in Riyadh. The Iraqis were in Kuwait City. According to King Hussein, Fahd said, "Do whatever you can, and please do it fast, in God's name." All that morning Hussein tried to reach the Iraqi president, now in his war bunker and virtually cut off. Hussein did manage to reach Tariq Aziz, who confirmed the news. Then, at about 1 P.M. Amman time, Saddam called King Hussein. "We had to go in," the Iraqi said. "We were driven to it. I am now in full control." And, although Pickering's message had almost certainly not reached him, Saddam went on to say that he was "committed to withdrawal. It will start within days and will last several weeks. Please do whatever you can do with the Arabs to impress on them that condemnations and threats don't work with us. We might end up with Kuwait being part of Iraq." Saddam added that the other Arab rulers should not allow foreign troops into Saudi Arabia or the Gulf states.

King Hussein then placed a call to President Mubarak in Alexandria, Egypt. Repeating to Mubarak Saddam's assurances about withdrawal and his wish that the Arabs not unleash polemics against him during this period, Hussein proposed holding a mini-summit, in either Saudi Arabia or Cairo, on the morning of August 4. The king then flew to Alexandria to see Mubarak in person before going on to Baghdad to seek Saddam's consent to his peace plan. Mubarak, says King Hussein, agreed both on the telephone and face to face in Alexandria to suspend polemics for the time being, although he rejected Hussein's suggestion that Mubarak speak personally with Saddam. "Saddam deceived me," Mubarak reasoned.

From Alexandria, in Mubarak's presence, King Hussein placed a secure radio-telephone call to President Bush. By this time Bush was en route to a meeting with Prime Minister Thatcher in Aspen, where she was to receive the Aspen Institute's prestigious Statesman's Award. The White House switchboard put the call through to Bush aboard Air Force 1. The president spoke first with Mubarak, then with the king. He expressed concern about when Saddam would withdraw from Kuwait. Hussein replied, "This is what we are working on." The president asked for an estimate. "Give me . . . 48 hours," Hussein said.

"My impression," Hussein later told me, "was that he [Bush] would give me the time I needed."[17] Hussein then told Mubarak that the solution would be for Iraq to withdraw to the disputed area on the border. Iraq would probably keep the two islands and the oilfield, for which Saudi Arabia might put up the cash. Only hostile polemics before the August 4 summit could spoil the plan. Mubarak, says Hussein, agreed.

After arriving at Aspen and meeting with Mrs. Thatcher, President Bush told reporters he was "heartened" by "conversations with President Mubarak, King Hussein, and President Ali Abdallah Salih of Yemen, all of whom I consider friends of the United States, and all of whom are trying to engage in what they call an Arab answer to the question. . . . There are collective efforts beginning to be undertaken by these worthy countries, and let's hope that they result in a satisfactory resolution of this international crisis."

For some months the president's relations with Prime Minister Yitzhak Shamir's government in Israel had been cooler than usual. Bush acknowledged that contacts with that state had not been conducted by him personally. Interestingly enough, he told the news conference that Israel had "asked for restraint, . . . a short period of time in which to have this Arab solution evolve and be placed into effect. . . ."[18]

Many American observers later condemned King Hussein for "siding" with Saddam. In reality, the king condemned the attack on Kuwait from the first hours of the crisis and eventually subscribed to the UN embargo and boycott measures, even though it cost his already strained economy dearly from loss of trade and aid and support of war refugees. Careful reading of the president's words about Israel would have helped the king's critics to understand something otherwise incomprehensible to them: that Hussein was bent chiefly on political survival. Saddam's cause was popular with the Jordanian people. Israel certainly understood this. As one of the most senior Jordanians explained to me privately in March 1991, "Sometimes we think our supposed enemy, Israel, understands us better than the United States, or some of the American people, do."

After their Aspen talks, both Bush and Thatcher confirmed that they would seek collective action by the UN to secure Iraq's withdrawal from Kuwait. "There is no place," said President Bush, "for this sort of naked aggression in today's world, and I have taken a number of steps." At their joint news conference Thatcher had already suggested severing transportation and communications links with Iraq as well as enforcing an embargo. She expressed "deep concern . . . over the events that have taken place. . . . We're not ruling any options in, but we're not ruling any options out."[19]

Getting the Soviets Aboard

On August 2, 10:30 A.M. local Soviet time, Jim Baker and Eduard Shevardnadze left for the Irkutsk Airport. Shevardnadze returned to Moscow, accompanied by Dennis Ross of Policy Planning. Baker took off for Ulan Bator, the capital of Mongolia. En route, on secure telephone, the secretary was briefed by Bush and other officials about the Iraqi invasion. He passed some of the details on to newsmen aboard his plane. Shevardnadze meanwhile landed in Moscow. To his embarrassment, waiting reporters knew details about the invasion that he was unaware of. Dennis Ross drove to the Moscow embassy and phoned Baker, suggesting a joint U.S.-Soviet communiqué not only condemning the invasion but also calling for joint action against Iraq. Baker got an endorsement from President Bush and instructed Ross to prepare the text.

Baker cut short his trip to Mongolia and returned to Moscow to read the joint statement with Shevardnadze. The idea, Ross told Shevardnadze's aide, Sergei Tarasenko, was to convince other Arab states not to support Iraq and to prevent Saddam Hussein from playing on the rivalry between the superpowers, as he had tried so often to do in the past. The final Baker-Shevardnadze communiqué condemned the invasion of Kuwait, called for Iraqi withdrawal, and proposed a world ban on arms sales to Iraq.

Blocking an Arab Solution

"None of us can do it separately," said Prime Minister Thatcher after the Aspen meeting with President Bush. "We need a collective and effective will of the nations of the United Nations." Even as she spoke, a special session of the Arab League Council was meeting in Cairo to prove that the Arab states had a collective will too. The chairmanship of the council rotates, and at the time Foreign Minister Farouk Khaddoumi of the PLO held the chair. The Kuwaiti delegation requested that the council immediately invoke and apply the Arab League defense pact protecting members under attack. Only the UAE agreed. The session then adjourned to wait for Iraq's deputy prime minister, Sa'adoun Hammadi, who it was hoped would be bringing something constructive from Saddam in Baghdad. When he arrived that evening, instead of offering a peace plan, Hammadi reiterated Iraq's indictments of Kuwait. There was not a sign of concession.

In the meantime King Hussein had reached Baghdad. Saddam reminded him that if talks failed he would have to use other means of persuading the Kuwaitis. He said the major threat was foreign intervention—something the Arab League Council meeting in Cairo that evening also opposed, though this fact was buried by the media. Another threat was "American intransigence and ignorance of the Arab world."

Early the next day, August 3, Kuwait found its frantic calls for help from the Arab world unanswered. (The Kuwaiti ambassador in Washington had already formally asked the United States for military aid; President Bush and his advisers were considering the request.) At a crucial meeting in Baghdad, King Hussein got Saddam to consent to attend a mini-summit in Saudi Arabia and to repeat his assurance of the previous day that Iraq would withdraw, provided its differences with Kuwait were resolved. He agreed to negotiate with King Fahd, though not with members of Kuwait's royal family. According to one of King Hussein's advisers, Saddam threatened that if the Arab League condemned him he would announce Kuwait's formal annexation.[20]

Directly after this meeting King Hussein spoke with his foreign minister, Marwan al-Qassim. "I have good news," he told al-Qassim. "Saddam Hussein has told me he's going to withdraw from Kuwait."[21] The foreign minister's news was less good. "The Egyptians," he said, "have issued a statement attacking Saddam for invading Kuwait."

This threatened to destroy everything. Hussein phoned Mubarak in Egypt and asked him for an explanation. "I was under tremendous pressure from the media and my own people," Mubarak told him. "My mind is not functioning."

"Call me back when it's functioning," Hussein responded, and hung up.

Shortly after King Hussein left Baghdad, Saddam published a communiqué to announce that Iraq would begin withdrawing from Kuwait on Sunday, August 5. The al-Sabah family, however, would not be permitted to return to power in Kuwait. When Sunday came, Iraqi television news bulletins showed tanks being loaded on flatbed trucks and tank carriers moving, presumably homeward. Baghdad Radio said other units would be withdrawn on August 7.

In a series of telephone calls to King Fahd and others, President Bush began persuading his Arab friends and allies that Saddam's expansion into Saudi Arabia was inevitable. News came in that Iraqi troops had entered the Saudi-Kuwait Neutral Zone, a diamond-shaped piece of desert territory containing important oilfields. Saudi forces were placed on the alert. Fahd and other Arab leaders nonetheless still hoped that Saddam would begin a serious pullout from Kuwait. Foreign observers and intelligence agencies saw no sign of such a pullout. Several U.S. statements warned Iraq against invading the Saudi kingdom.[22]

For three days after the invasion President Bush and his advisers—among them, Secretary of Defense Richard Cheney, JCS Chairman Gen. Colin Powell, Secretary of State Baker, White House Chief of Staff John Sununu, National Security Adviser Brent Scowcroft, and Scowcroft's deputy Robert Gates, a career intelligence officer who had been deputy director of the CIA—conducted a series of crisis meetings. These were the men who, over the next five months, as Desert Shield gradually merged into Desert Storm, would make most of the decisions in Washington.[23]

Bush, who had announced before the session with Thatcher on August 2 that he did not intend to send troops to Saudi Arabia, now changed his course. The crisis-management team shifted into planning for an immense deployment to be commanded by the dynamic Gen. Norman Schwarzkopf. Bush said in Washington on August 7 that Saddam had lied about withdrawing. He denounced the provisional administration of Iraqi officers in Kuwait as a "puppet regime."[24]

General Powell had been an aide to Defense Secretary Caspar Weinberger during the Lebanon deployment in 1983–84. During that crisis Weinberger, remembering Vietnam, had issued the following rule of military engagement: "Before the U.S. commits combat forces abroad, there must be some reasonable assurance we will have the support of the American people and their representatives in Congress." If troops were to be committed, it should be done "wholeheartedly, and with the clear intention of winning"—not, alas, the case in Lebanon. Powell's staff, with the clear purpose of deterring and if necessary repelling an Iraqi invasion of Saudi Arabia, selected parts of the 82d Airborne Division, the 101st Airborne Division, the 24th Mechanized Infantry Division, and the 3rd Cavalry Division. There would have to be an ample naval force and combat air force, and, as in Lebanon, a marine amphibious unit. There would be more than 100,000 troops.[25]

Cheney flew to Saudi Arabia on August 5 to convince the Saudis that such a deployment was needed. Meanwhile, Saddam Hussein was angling for an American green light for his kind of Arab solution. He summoned the remaining senior U.S. diplomat in Baghdad, Chargé d'Affaires Joseph Wilson, and repeated his arguments about Kuwait. According to the Iraqi transcript of the meeting, to prove that he had no intention of attacking Saudi Arabia, Saddam reminded Wilson that he had signed a nonaggression treaty with the Saudis. He had offered one to Kuwait too, but Kuwait had rejected the idea. "Thank God," said Saddam, "because otherwise we could not have invaded." He assured Wilson that Saudi Arabia was safe from Iraq but warned the United States against stirring up Saudi fears. He also repeated that his promise not to move militarily against Kuwait applied only as long as talks continued. The United States could destroy Iraq's technology, economy, and oil industry; if it did, Iraq would attack U.S. interests in the region. As for withdrawal from Kuwait: "Our army took three days to enter Kuwait and withdrawal can't happen in one day. Withdrawal . . . should rest upon an international accord, and we won't quit Kuwait for it to fall into the hands of another power. If the threats against Kuwait increase, we'll send other troops. . . . When the threats cease, our forces will withdraw."[26]

Meanwhile, Cheney had arrived in Saudi Arabia. He signed a secret accord with King Fahd and the defense and aviation minister, Prince Sultan bin Abdul Aziz. An Arab source said later that it defined the powers of Saudi, American, and what would later be allied commanders, giving the Saudi commander in chief supremacy inside Saudi territory. The Saudis would provide aid and logistical support, and the Americans would be subject to a Saudi veto on offensive actions beyond Saudi territory.[27] Cheney returned and announced the U.S. decision to send ground and air combat units as part of a multinational force, which was being discussed with the British, Saudis, French, Egyptians, and other allies.

U.S. troops left the United States for Saudi Arabia and early on August 8 began arriving at Dhahran Airport, which became the central air base for Operations Desert Shield and Desert Storm. That day Turkey, the NATO ally to the north and west of Iraq, closed vital Iraqi oil pipelines and terminals in Turkish territory.

As soon as American troops appeared in the Saudi kingdom, Saddam Hussein withdrew his promise to attend a new Arab summit, and there was no more talk of withdrawal from Kuwait. At this point, President Bush began referring to the Iraqis as "international renegades and outlaws."

American pressure to avoid an "Arab solution" and to ensure Arab acceptance of coalition expeditionary forces was critical, according to observers at the Arab summit conference in Cairo on August 10. I had spent several days in Amman, where King Hussein and his government anxiously watched for signs that the Israelis might take advantage of the crisis, expel the West Bank and Gaza Palestinians, and move them into Jordan, thus implementing the "Sharon Plan" to convert Jordan into Palestine. Meanwhile, the Israelis watched, equally anxiously, to see whether Iraq would move military forces into Jordan.

The Cairo Summit

The Cairo summit was a meeting of twenty Arab heads of state called at the request of Syria. Saddam did not go. In Baghdad on August 9, Yassir Arafat and Abu Iyad (Salah Khalaf) of the PLO had tried in vain to convince Saddam to attend. Saddam threatened to draw Israel into the war and so split the Arab coalition. "From the moment I am attacked," he said, "I will attack Israel. . . . This aggression against Iraq will then be perceived as an American-Zionist plot." He outlined his plan for defense lines inside Kuwait and for terrorist attacks inside Saudi Arabia, backed in part by dissident Saudi tribesmen with East Bloc arms. By the time the session ended, Arafat was certain that the Cairo summit would only make matters worse for collective Arab security.[27]

The summit lasted only a few hours, but it was eventful. During the meeting Egypt regained its old primacy in the Arab League, Washington demonstrated that it could exercise remote-control influence of Arab allies, and Kuwait gathered broad support. For neutrals or admirers of Saddam Hussein—including Yemen, Sudan, and Algeria—and for Jordan's King Hussein, the summit was a disaster.

It opened in Cairo's new conference hall in suburban Nasser City with an informal foreign ministers' session. Only newsmen with special security passes or Egyptian presidential press passes were admitted, and we were all forced to watch the comings and goings of delegates from behind glass in a lounge. Occasionally one of the Arab delegates would wander out and brief special friends; the few official Egyptian briefings were almost worthless in their content. Later, we learned of the tension between the Iraqis and the Kuwaitis; the emir of Kuwait had come but only for a few hours, and Saddam of course had not. At lunch in the hall's restaurant, Vice Premier Taha Yassine Ramadan of Iraq threw a plate at Crown Prince Saad of Kuwait and almost hit him. Other delegates threw bread at one another. One Kuwaiti minister fainted with shock.

President Mubarak presided over a closed plenary session in the afternoon. Yassir Arafat claims that when he resumed his chair after a prayer break, he found before him the text of a final communiqué that, because of awkward phrasing, appeared to have been written in English and then translated into Arabic. (This was also the judgment of several other delegates and of newsmen who read Arabic.) He also insists that Mubarak did not allow him to get in a word about a PLO plan for Arab mediation. Several accounts agree that Mubarak prevented any real debate before the final vote.[28]

When that was taken, twelve out of twenty came out in favor of the resolution.[29] The old Arab League method of voting by consensus was put aside. The resolution supported sovereignty and independence for Kuwait, upheld the UN resolution demanding Iraqi withdrawal, and sustained Saudi Arabia's right to turn to foreign and Pan-Arab troops in self-defense.

During the summit Baghdad Radio broadcast a call from Saddam Hussein for a holy war to save "Mecca and the tomb of the Prophet from occupation by American troops." Within hours of the summit's conclusion, the Egyptian elements of the Pan-Arab force were en route to Saudi Arabia. Initially this was three thousand men; at least thirty-six thousand more were sent in over the following months. The Arab force also included thirteen hundred men from Morocco, in addition to the over five thousand Moroccan troops serving with UAE forces since the early 1980s; but they were never used directly in Desert Shield. The first eleven hundred Syrians grew to about fifteen thousand later on.[30]

The Link with Palestine

Two days after the Arab summit, Saddam Hussein tried to convince the Arabs and the rest of the world that he was linking Kuwait with the Arab-Israeli conflict, a point he continued to insist on during the countdown to war. In an August 12 statement, he said the occupation of Kuwait had to be solved in connection with other Mideast occupations: Syria in Lebanon, remaining Iraqi forces in Iran, and Israel in Palestine. All these issues should be negotiated. He went on to demand that the newly imposed UN sanctions and embargoes against Iraq be lifted first. Allied forces should pull out of Saudi Arabia and be replaced by Pan-Arab forces (excluding Egyptians). The United States and Israel immediately rejected the idea, as did the Iranians on August 13.

The first Arab troops had landed in Saudi Arabia on August 11. Pro-Saddam demonstrations began to sweep through the West Bank, Gaza, and East Jerusalem; there were fresh outbreaks of the *intifada*, now featuring Saddam's face on posters and banners. Although many Kuwaiti Palestinians were exporting alarming reports of the excesses of Saddam's forces, to most Palestinians under Israeli occupation occupied Kuwait was less real than their own daily misery.

Israeli government leaders were apprehensive. Prime Minister Yitzhak Shamir called Saddam's linkage declaration a "maneuver to weaken the international alliance forged against him [Saddam]."[31] There was fresh violence when Israeli police fired on Arabs at Jerusalem's Temple Mount in October. Charges and counter-charges raged over who was responsible for the violence and whether the police had fired in self-defense. Saddam tried to fit the situation to his propaganda campaign. In a broadcast, he said Iraq possessed a missile called *al-Hajira*, "the stone," a reference to the stones Palestinian demonstrators hurled against Israeli security forces. He repeated his threat to hit Israel if Iraq was attacked.

For some time Israel had considered Iraqi forces its biggest military threat. Israel, as we have seen, supported Iran during the 1980–88 war with Iraq. Its oil, its large army, its extensive water resources, and its fairly literate, technologically advanced population increased the threat posed by Iraq. That country, moreover, had played a part in most of the Arab-Israeli wars since 1948. Most of all, Iraq had put in place a growing number of missile-launching sites. It now sent warnings that if Israel tried to take them out, as it had Iraq's Osirak nuclear reactor in June 1981, such action would unleash hostilities.

The Israelis concluded an agreement with the United States to develop the Arrow antimissile missile. They were not counting on the acquisition of American Patriot missiles, which, with American crews, would later be hurriedly provided when Iraq's Scud missiles began hitting Israel.[32]

In September, before the Temple Mount riots, the Israeli government expressed a desire to take part in operational planning for the air war against Iraq by sharing targeting information with the allies. It was rebuffed. A British diplomat told John Newhouse of the *New Yorker* that the official Washington position on Israeli in-volvement was, "We'll take care of Iraq . . . [T]he biggest danger is that you might try to help us."[33] At the time, President Bush and Secretary Baker were scarcely on speaking terms with the Shamir government. Saddam Hussein's war would soon reverse this completely.

Representative Stephen Solarz, questioning Secretary of State Baker before the House Foreign Affairs Committee in September, asked if an unconditional with-drawal of Saddam from Kuwait would not be a "Pyrrhic victory for the international community, inasmuch as it would leave intact his nuclear, chemical, and biolog-ical weapons programs, not to mention his million-man army and the rest of his military infrastructure as a whole." Baker's reply was that Iraq's weapons could be eliminated only if they were destroyed. It would be possible, however, to work out a "security structure" that would protect Iraq's neighbors against their use. Dissat-isfied with this, Solarz—in conjunction with Saudi ambassador Prince Bandar bin Sultan, Egyptian and Kuwaiti diplomats, and several other congressmen—set up a bipartisan group to lobby for a tough policy against Iraq. Called the Committee for Peace and Security in the Gulf, it found advocates in Brent Scowcroft and his top Mideast aide, Richard Haass. Haass called for continued close U.S. support of Israel, especially in crises. Haass was also concerned about the security of Egypt and Saudi Arabia.[34] The influence of such men as Haass and Solarz helped the pres-ident not only to keep the determination encouraged by Thatcher and others but also to work for a close relationship with Israel.

The Failure of Diplomacy

On August 19 Saddam Hussein began to propose a deal: all foreigners would be released and allowed to leave Iraq and Kuwait in return for the evacuation of U.S. forces from the Gulf region. This was Iraq's response to UN Security Council Resolution 664 directing Iraq to let foreigners leave. On August 20 Deputy Prime Minister Hammadi of Iraq arrived in Moscow to seek Soviet support. He was told by Foreign Minister Shevardnadze that the foreigners must be freed and that Iraq must get out of Kuwait. Shevardnadze did phone Secretary Baker to ask for a new delay, until August 27, before voting tougher UN resolutions, this to see whether the latest Soviet message would induce Saddam to comply. Baker secured Shevardnadze's agreement to a new resolution voted on August 24. Apparently the Soviet foreign minister warned Baker that pressure on Bush to act fast in the Gulf had its equal and contrary pressure in the USSR, where the Soviet military was urging caution.

On August 24 Resolution 665 authorizing the use of force to support the UN embargo was approved thirteen to zero, with Cuba and Yemen abstaining.

Baker's tireless diplomacy and Shevardnadze's acquiescence to the allied effort was rewarded on September 9. In a summit meeting in Helsinki Presidents Bush and Gorbachev reached a kind of compromise. Soviet Mideast envoy Yevgeny Primakov would keep up contacts with Saddam Hussein. In return Gorbachev would support, or at least not obstruct, U.S. military preparations. A joint communiqué upheld a peaceful settlement but added that if diplomacy failed, both parties were prepared to envisage other initiatives "in accordance with the UN Charter."

Some of the diplomatic efforts of this period were aimed at freeing hundreds of thousands of foreigners trapped inside Iraq, the "human shields" being held at industrial and military installations to protect them against attack. Thousands of Asian workers fled Kuwait through Iraq, while thousands of others in Iraq fled to Jordan. During the autumn many refugees camped in tent cities inside the Jordanian border. Jordan and various international relief services tried to feed, shelter, and protect them, then speed them back home, but it was not an easy task. Its economy suffering from compliance with the embargo, Jordan couldn't adequately feed its own people, let alone the thousands of refugees.

Another testimony to the failure of diplomacy was the plight of Kuwait. According to an Amnesty International report of December 19, 1990, approximately 800,000 Arabs—300,000 Kuwaiti citizens and about half a million foreign residents—fled the country. Over one thousand Kuwaitis had been summarily executed by the Iraqis. Amnesty claims that Iraqi soldiers murdered hundreds of unarmed Kuwaitis and that hundreds more had disappeared in detention. Torture was widespread. Some Kuwaiti prisoners, Amnesty's witnesses reported, had been castrated or had their eyes gouged out. Victims suffering the most were members of the Kuwaiti army; they would later charge that Palestinians residing in Kuwait had colluded with the Iraqi occupiers. Others also suffered severely, including civilians who had simply painted slogans on walls or raised Kuwaiti flags.

Iraq also took extreme measures to extinguish traces of that country's independent existence: street names were changed, identification papers and license plates collected, and beards forbidden. Members of the Iraqi army were known to pluck out offending beards with pliers.[35]

Saddam Hussein rarely took a major political or military step without covering all fronts. Before the invasion his half brother, Iraqi UN envoy Barzan Takrit, led a series of high-level talks with Iran. His idea was to harden the August 1988 cease-fire into a permanent peace. This would allow Saddam to protect his eastern flank and free over 500,000 Iraqi troops to defend Kuwait and the southeast approaches to Iraq. Deputy Prime Minister Sa'adoun Hammadi, the only Shi'ite in a position of real leadership in Iraq, helped to finalize the arrangements.

On August 17 I was visiting the Associated Press office in Bahrain when monitors recorded a Baghdad broadcast of a letter from Saddam to President Hashemi Rafsanjani of Iran. It finally accepted most of Iran's long-standing conditions for a peace agreement, including the adoption of a median line in the Shatt al-Arab waterway to mark the Iran-Iraq boundary. Iraq also agreed to evacuate Iranian territory still occupied and to exchange prisoners, soon facilitated by the International Committee of the Red Cross in Geneva. On September 9 and 10 in Tehran, Tariq Aziz and the Iraqi oil minister visited and normalized diplomatic relations, although Iran refused to help Iraq to break the oil embargo the allies had by now imposed.[36]

Thus did Iraq neutralize its neighbor and the other regional Gulf power, Iran. Under the UN umbrella President Bush was leading a political coalition, backed by a huge military force, that had the diplomatic support of the Soviet Union. The way lay open to plan the details of the most ambitious military campaign undertaken by the United States for two generations. Its successful execution would alter the face of the Middle East for generations to come.

16

Desert Storm

Planning the War

Before the launching of Desert Storm, the top echelon of America's military, like so many of their predecessors throughout history, were more cautious about sending men to fight a war than were many senior civilian authorities. Take, for instance, Gen. Norman Schwarzkopf, the four-star field commander who was to prove the master strategist and military hero of Desert Storm. Economic sanctions alone, many Americans and Europeans believed, could force Iraq out of Kuwait. The UN Security Council resolutions crippled Iraq's oil exports and most of its other trade. On September 28, 1990, answering a stream of impatient calls from the public and Congress for early military action, General Schwarzkopf said, "It's premature to say that we need to have something happen in a few weeks. We all want to get this thing over with . . . but I think that it is unrealistic to expect that the sanctions would have an effect in a few weeks. . . . It's a longer-term thing."[1] That may well have been President Bush speaking through the lips of his senior commander in the field. It also expressed the views of many thoughtful observers.

Other civilians eyed the benefits Desert Shield might have for an American economy hit by recession and the continued backwash from massive savings and loan failures. L. William Seidman, chairman of the Federal Deposit Insurance Corporation (FDIC), remarked the day after Schwarzkopf's cautionary words that the crisis promised "to be one of the best things for the U.S. economy and the U.S. banking system that's happened in ten years . . . because our ability to go in and protect the world's largest oil supply at the invitation of Saudi Arabia . . . has put us in a much more stable energy position than we've been in years."[2]

The Pentagon had no deployment plan that precisely fitted the ejection of Iraqi armed forces from Kuwait, although it did have a holdover from the cold war, a scheme for a U.S. reaction to a Soviet invasion of Iran upon which various other plans and war games had been based. The emergency scheme Schwarzkopf worked out now set deployment levels for every job in the military, from gunners and tank drivers to cooks, medical technicians, and Arabic-language specialists. All their equipment had to go with them, for not enough had been pre-positioned in the Gulf–Indian Ocean area. The first phase of the deployment was to include about 200,000 men and women, which Gen. Colin Powell would later compare to "moving the entire city of Richmond, Virginia, 8,000 miles to the Saudi desert."

Once orders went out from the Pentagon, the U.S. Military Airlift Command (MAC) without the advance warning time usually available for mobilizations, staged the largest and one of the most successful airlifts in history. During the first three weeks of Desert Shield, MAC lifted more people and equipment to the Persian Gulf than were flown into Korea during the first three months of that war in 1950. Correspondents based near Dhahran Air Base reported aircraft landing almost every ten minutes. At the peak of the airlift, C-141 Starlifters flew from bases in the continental United States through European staging areas, then Hercules C-130 planes completed the missions. Chartered civilian planes supplemented the MAC flights in the first activation of the U.S. Civil Reserve Air Fleet.

Weary MAC aircrews, flying overtime, were aided by reservists even before reserve and Air National Guard units were called up. In early November President Bush announced deployment of more troops to the Gulf to provide an offensive option. MAC was called for a repeat performance. It had to airlift nearly 200,000 more troops and their equipment.[3]

Agonizing Appraisals and Reappraisals

The first phase of the deployment for Desert Shield touched off a great debate in America and among its allies over the wisdom and the purpose of such a huge deployment, bolstered by smaller numbers of European, Arab, and African allied troops. One former secretary of the navy, James Webb, felt that the United States "overreacted militarily . . . after we underreacted diplomatically for a number of years."[4] John B. Connally, navy secretary under President Kennedy, warned that armed conflict with Iraq would be "disastrous," costing U.S. casualties "probably in excess of 50,000." Connally thought that everything possible should be done to avoid war, but that if war did break out the United States should shorten it and save lives by using nuclear weapons.[5]

Many congressional leaders, including Chairman of the Senate Armed Services Committee Sam Nunn, were anxious for President Bush to wait for sanctions to work before going to war with Iraq. In late October and early November President Bush and Secretary Baker denounced Iraq's "barbaric" treatment of hostages and of officials in the besieged U.S. Embassy in occupied Kuwait. They began to talk specifically of taking military action if necessary. Until then, the administration had been playing down the hostage situation, hoping to avoid the error made by the Carter and Reagan administrations. During the Iranian hostage crisis and the affair of the American hostages in Lebanon, they had allowed the explosive human appeal of hostages to supersede larger strategic objectives.

The president and his secretary of state seemed to many to be sending mixed signals. Bush and White House spokesman Marlin Fitzwater endorsed congressional pleas for patience despite the increased stress on hostages. Fitzwater insisted that "sanctions have every chance of working," and he denied that there was already an administration timetable for military action or that war was considered inevitable. Meanwhile, Bush continued to lambast Saddam Hussein—trying, in Fitzwater's words, "to prepare the American people for any eventuality."[6]

As a result of considerable wrangling among the allies over the chain of command, U.S. and Saudi officials made public on November 5 the essence of the secret accord reached by Cheney with the Saudis in August. Any military initiative undertaken from Saudi soil would require the joint approval of both President Bush and King Fahd. Once such authorization was given, however, U.S. forces would be free to plan and execute an attack moving beyond the Saudi frontier without Saudi military involvement. As it turned out, the Saudis would be closely and massively involved in Desert Storm, further cementing the U.S.-Saudi military alliance.[7]

This difficulty cleared away, on November 8 President Bush felt free to announce an augmentation of forces in the Gulf—200,000 more troops. The offensive capability to wage a ground war would be increased by transferring mechanized and armored divisions from Germany. There would also be more air force units, three additional aircraft carrier battle groups (bringing the total in the Mideast region to six), and another battleship and amphibious group. The new deployment gave statesmen and diplomats who still hoped for a negotiated solution what they saw as a breathing space: the increased time needed to deploy this military force effectively made it highly unlikely speculation that the United States and its allies would attack as soon as December.

Many observers wondered at the time whether Gen. Colin Powell used disinformation when he refused to say whether the reinforcements would be adequate in wartime. "We're not planning to go to war with Saddam Hussein's army," he said.[8]

The Arab Solution

During the months between August 1990 and January 1991, PLO chairman Yassir Arafat and his deputy Abu Iyad (Salah Khalaf) continued their efforts to achieve an Arab solution. One crucial meeting took place in Baghdad on August 26. At the start of the crisis on August 2 Saddam had declared that his main objective was to resolve by force his problems with Kuwait. By the time of the August 26 meeting, that objective had increased considerably.

"Now that the Gulf crisis has expanded," Saddam, according to Abu Iyad, said, "how can I reduce the crisis to the islands and the oilfields, especially after I gave up the Shatt al-Arab? That's not enough. If I tell the Iraqi people I'll withdraw because I solved something like the Palestinian problem, they'll understand. But if I pull out only for the islands and the oilfields, the people will never accept it. It will be bigger than losing the war."

Saddam told his Palestinian visitors that he was not afraid of war. He understood the technological edge that could make American air strikes deadly. But he believed they could harm only part, not all, of the Iraqi forces. He was optimistic about being able to fight allied ground forces in Kuwait to a standstill. When Arafat said he had information that Saddam would be personally targeted by the Americans, the Iraqi smiled. "Are you trying to scare me, get me to surrender?" he scoffed. "That's a joke!"

Some individual PLO members passed such information quietly to the West, especially France. Arafat himself, however, still refused to condemn Saddam in public. He made the huge mistake of often being photographed embracing the Iraqi dictator, and he was frequently quoted as approving Saddam's supposed championing of the Palestine cause. This would cost Arafat dearly in terms of financial support from the Saudis and their Gulf allies. While Palestinians lost their jobs in several Gulf states, Arafat lost popularity, if not with the Jordanians and the residents of the occupied territories, then certainly with the Arab coalition and many thoughtful Palestinians.

On November 16, 1990, Saddam held another one of his meetings with Arafat and Abu Iyad in Baghdad. This one was to prove fateful for both Abu Iyad and the future of the PLO. Abu Iyad lost his temper and dared to criticize Saddam for his invasion of Kuwait.

Abu Iyad had once been a mastermind of terrorism. He helped to conceive and lead the Black September movement, which among other exploits carried out the abhorrent attack against Israeli athletes at the Munich Olympic Games in 1972. However, over the years, as I was able to observe myself during a number of meetings with him from 1972 to 1990, he became a firm opponent of terrorism and an enthusiastic advocate of a negotiated solution with Israel, writing articles to this effect in Western journals and communicating with Israeli leftists. Abu Iyad was criticized by some of his Palestinian colleagues for devoting too much time to tracking down and destroying key members of the anti-Arafat and antipeace terrorist movement of Abu Nidal (Sabry al-Banna). Abu Nidal and his Fatah Revolutionary Council had broken with Arafat in the early 1970s, when Arafat and al-Banna mutually condemned each other to death.

Though he lived in Tunis, Abu Iyad had family, including a wife and children, in Kuwait. He was enraged by Iraq's occupation. "You say you want to help the Palestinian movement in Kuwait," Abu Iyad told Saddam in the November meeting. "You are destroying my family in Kuwait. They have all lost their jobs. . . ." Saddam had Abu Iyad removed from his presence. Arafat had to convince Saddam not to arrest his deputy; that would be a serious political mistake. The two Palestinians left Baghdad together, Abu Iyad vowing never again to meet Saddam.

On November 29, 1990, UN Security Council foreign ministers approved U.S.-sponsored Resolution 668 authorizing the use of force if Iraq did not withdraw from Kuwait by January 15. The vote was twelve to two, with Cuba and Yemen voting against and China abstaining. This solid backing had been secured by Jim Baker's tireless diplomacy. The next day, November 30, President Bush invited Iraqi Foreign Minister Tariq Aziz to Washington the week of December 10. Aziz said he had asked Secretary Baker to visit Baghdad to meet Saddam "at a mutually convenient time" before January 15. There was an initially favorable reaction by Iraqi officials. Almost instantly, the price of oil dropped four dollars a barrel.

As soon as news of the projected Iraqi-American contacts reached the PLO in Tunis, Arafat called in his top deputies. They drafted a secret message to Saddam that was transmitted to him through the Iraqi embassy in Tunis. There were three main points: Saddam should accept President Bush's offer before any talks with the Americans; he should release all of the foreign hostages; and Iraq should pull out of Kuwait. King Fahd of Saudi Arabia would let Iraq keep the Rumaila oilfields and the islands. (It is not clear why Arafat thought Fahd had accepted, or would accept, this.) Arafat flew to Amman to enlist the aid of King Hussein in this initiative, while Abu Iyad flew to Yemen to get the support of the Yemeni government.

On December 4 Arafat, King Hussein, and the vice president of Yemen met with Saddam for five hours in Baghdad. Two days later Saddam announced he would release the foreign hostages.

On January 15, 1991, the day before the air phase of Desert Storm began, Abu Iyad was assassinated in Tunis along with another important PLO figure, Intelligence Chief Abu Hol, and a guard. The assassin was an ex-bodyguard of Abu Nidal, and the possibility has since emerged that Abu Nidal's movement was responsible. Many Palestinian insiders believe that Saddam ordered the attack as a payback for Abu Iyad's defiance on November 16. Whoever ordered it, the murder weakened the PLO at a time when the Kuwait crisis had already dealt the leadership several severe blows.[9]

Abu Iyad was in many ways a one-man brain trust and Arafat's steady hand. After his death Arafat made some foolish remarks—for example, the Pentagon was ready to use chemical weapons against Iraq—that only worsened his position. By March 1991 his fortunes in the PLO had sunk so low that a London meeting of ten Palestinian millionaires, including the entrepreneur Hassib Sabbagh, who had sometimes served as Arafat's secret emissary to the White House and other seats of power, decided by nine votes to one that Arafat should resign and be replaced.[10] This, however, could only be done by convening the PLO "parliament," the Palestine National Council. As of this writing, Arafat remains at the helm of the PLO.

The Syrian Dimension

Syria was one of the first governments to denounce the Iraqi invasion of Kuwait. Syrian President Hafez Assad sent Foreign Minister Farouk al-Sharraa to the Cairo summit. Al-Sharraa strongly supported President Mubarak and cast Syria's vote for the Egyptian-sponsored resolutions. Syrian troops were soon dispatched to Saudi Arabia; their mission was described as purely defensive. With this action, President Assad was able to kill several birds with one stone, one of which was Maronite Christian suzerainty in Lebanon.

In return for Assad's participation in the coalition the U.S. ambassador in Damascus, Edward Djeridjian, with the tacit approval of his close personal friend and the leading Soviet Mideast expert, Soviet Ambassador Alexander Zotov, permitted Assad a free hand to deal with General Michel Aoun. In November and December, Syrian and pro-Syrian Lebanese forces bombarded Aoun's fortified bunker headquarters in Baabda on the Beirut outskirts and forced its surrender, sending Aoun into political asylum in the French embassy in Beirut. President Mitterrand, who was swinging France squarely into the anti-Saddam Gulf coalition with the third largest military participation of the Western allies (behind the United States and Britain), decreed that Aoun should stay in his embassy refuge and did not grant him asylum in France. Israel did not intervene on the general's behalf.

Syria also sought the lifting of sanctions against it that Britain, the United States, and the EC maintained since Prime Minister Thatcher's rupture with Damascus over the Hindawi affair in 1986. After Margaret Thatcher resigned on November 28, 1990, having failed to win a leadership election in the Conservative party, John Major's new government immediately renewed diplomatic relations with Syria. Soon the other sanctions and restrictions imposed by Western governments and the EC were on the way out.

Syria's government, involved in joint oil ventures with several large American firms, forbade antiwar demonstrations of any kind. Syrian-based terrorist and guerrilla groups, notably Ahmed Jibril's PFLP-GC, were restricted and muzzled to prevent them from making comments to the Western media. The tightly controlled Syrian media even delayed reporting on skirmishes between Syrian and Iraqi forces on the Saudi-Iraqi frontier around February 10, 1991. Syria remained a steadfast member of the coalition, sending a battalion-size detachment to Kuwait with the Egyptian, Saudi, and other Arab coalition forces when the land war began February 24.[11]

The Maghreb in Ferment

The pro-Iraq and pro-Saddam sentiments of the four states of the Maghreb Union (Libya, Tunisia, Algeria, and Morocco) proved to be the despair of the American diplomats serving in the region. American influence in North Africa suffered from the military intervention in the Gulf.

Tunisia had stayed away from the Arab summit of August 10. Its government was strictly neutral in the Gulf crisis. The population, however, sympathized with Saddam. The legal opposition parties, the illegal Islamist En-Nahda (Rebirth) movement, and Tunisian intellectuals identified the American-led coalition as an attempt to reimpose old-style colonialism.

While Algeria had played a key role in settling the U.S.-Iran hostage crisis in 1979–81 and had helped the United States in subsequent terrorist incidents, Algerian sentiment was even more radically pro-Iraq than in Tunisia. Algerian Foreign Minister Ahmed al-Ghozali, a technocrat who had earlier helped to orient Algeria's booming oil and natural gas business toward Western Europe and the United States, made public statements extremely sympathetic to the Iraqi cause.

On December 22, 1990, Algerian President Chadli Bendjedid, after seeing President Mitterrand in Paris, suggested that a "concrete signal on the Palestinian question" by the United States and the West would be a "decisive step" in solving the Kuwait crisis. After seeing Saddam in Baghdad, he also suggested that Iraq would pay "a certain price" (never spelled out) to settle.[12] With his war plans so advanced by the end of December, Bush rebuffed Chadli's last-minute request to see him in Washington and apparently talked King Fahd, a special friend of Chadli, out of seeing him too.[13] Bush later tried to make up for this by referring warmly to Chadli in his 1991 State of the Union address.

Morocco's King Hassan, traditionally America's best ally in the region, took a more complicated position. Morocco was "neutral" in the Iraq-Kuwait conflict, but the king acknowledged Saddam's claims for economic justice. Hassan gave Saddam credit for "awakening international conscience about the Arab-Israel crisis" and called on Saddam to "exit through the great gateway of honor."

King Hassan disapproved using force against Iraq—a position he reaffirmed to Pierre Salinger and me during an audience in Rabat in February 1991. Following a huge pro-Iraqi demonstration in Rabat in early February, the royal family organized large shipments of food and medicine to relieve the sufferings of the Iraqis.

Morocco remained at odds with its former colonial power, France, which because of its cooperation with the United States in Desert Shield and Desert Storm, the publication of an anti-Hassan book in Paris, and growing demands for reform in Morocco, raised official as well as popular anti-Western feeling. However, wanting to benefit from coalition membership, in 1991 the king maintained his thirteen hundred-man force in Saudi Arabia (to guard the Safaniya oil refinery on the Gulf coast) and his five thousand troops in the UAE. At the same time, in his kingdom, he tried to ride the crest of the wave of anti-American and anti-Israeli feeling bred by the war.

All this caused the Americans in Morocco to question the future of agreements the Carter administration concluded in 1980 with King Hassan for possible future use of the big U.S.-built (but now Moroccan-flagged) bases of Sidi Slimane, Ben Guerir, and Kenitra. In early 1991 local Moroccans at Sidi Slimane reported the arrival of big tanker planes, bringing fuel to stockpile for some unidentified contingency. Also, the U.S. National Aeronautics and Space Administration (NASA) continued to use Ben Guerir as a space tracking station and a standby emergency landing base for space shuttles.[14]

The Europeans and Desert Storm

Britain more than lived up to its promise of support for Desert Shield and Desert Storm. The first British military deployments to the Gulf began almost as soon as the advance elements of the U.S. 2d Airborne Division had landed at Dhahran on August 7–8. To bases used by the Royal Air Force in Oman, Bahrain, and Saudi Arabia, the Thatcher government first sent combat and patrol aircraft and a number of helicopters, most of which were later to see action in Desert Storm. The initial British ground force sent to the Gulf was about sixteen thousand troops. British destroyers, frigates, fleet auxiliaries, and minehunters assisted the U.S. Navy in taking out the mines Iraq sowed off the Kuwaiti coast.

When John Major replaced Margaret Thatcher as prime minister, nothing changed the British effort. One of Thatcher's final actions was to commit fourteen thousand more British army personnel to Desert Shield, nearly doubling the British presence. This pushed the United Kingdom's operating costs in the Gulf to about £10 million (about $19.8 million) a week—no small burden for the British taxpayer in an economy already sliding fast into recession.[15]

Aside from the British effort, European waffling was soon to set in. Initially the NATO alliance, facing what its defense analysts like to call an "out of area" problem, looked firm. On August 10 an emergency meeting of NATO's sixteen foreign ministers endorsed the U.S. military deployment and called for reinforcement of UN sanctions against Iraq. The Council of the Western European Union (WEU), adding nonmembers Denmark, Greece, and Turkey as observers, agreed on August 21 to a coordinated military presence in the Gulf. It also urged the UN Security Council to put more teeth into enforcing its embargo against Iraq. The next day, on the basis of WEU Council decisions, Belgium, Spain, Greece, Italy, and the Netherlands decided to send naval units to the Gulf. President Mitterrand had already ordered independent French action, later coordinated with the U.S.-Saudi command.

On September 12 the European Parliament resolved that Iraq must restore Kuwait's independence and free all foreign hostages. It upheld the UN-imposed embargo and praised swift U.S. military intervention in the Gulf. On September 24, before the UN General Assembly, President Mitterrand expressed French resolve but added that "if Saddam Hussein will affirm his intention to withdraw his troops and liberate hostages, everything becomes possible." He hinted that France was less enthusiastic than the United States and Britain about restoring the unpopular al-Sabah family to power in Kuwait. Most appealing to the Arab states, Mitterrand envisaged extending the negotiating process to all important Mideast conflicts, including the Arab-Israeli one—the linkage so dreaded by Israel and rejected by the United States.[16]

During the countdown to war in January 1991, France was one of the most active participants in a veritable ballet of international diplomacy aimed at convincing Saddam to withdraw peacefully from Kuwait before the January 15 UN deadline. On January 2 Michel Vauzelle, a parliamentarian, saw Saddam and Tariq Aziz in Baghdad, then met Arafat in Tunis, but to no avail. At a meeting of the EEC foreign ministers on January 4, participants heard of the projected Aziz-Baker meeting in Geneva on January 9; they agreed on a communiqué vaguely promising collective action and invited Aziz to Luxembourg. Iraq rejected this as well as an offer made on January 9 for talks in Algiers.

The Europeans were ultimately disappointed: Baker never went to Baghdad; Aziz never went to Washington. On January 9 they met in Geneva for over six hours only to emerge and announce a stalemate. A diplomatic adviser to Arafat present in Geneva said Iraq was amenable to talks in Baghdad no earlier than January 17; this was two days after the January 15 deadline for withdrawal from Kuwait that looked to Iraq and its supporters like an ultimatum. Both Baker and Mitterrand consulted President Bush on the telephone during the Aziz-Baker meeting. Bush said no.

On January 14, after a futile last-minute visit by UN Secretary Perez de Cuellar to Baghdad, the EC foreign ministers met in Brussels and said they were abandoning the attempt to launch a new European initiative for peace. Then, without a word to the EC or to Britain, the French placed a set of eleventh-hour peace proposals before the UN Security Council. It called for a "chain" of events, beginning with Iraqi withdrawal from Kuwait and ending with a conference on the Middle East "at an appropriate time," a phrase used earlier in some tentative Bush administration statements about the possibility of an international conference. The proposal was dropped in the face of tough U.S. and British opposition, and Prime Minister Michel Rocard of France conceded that the idea had "not met with the least response from the Iraqi side."[17]

France began its military commitment by sending the aircraft carrier *Clemenceau* and its escorts to the Gulf. By August 13, as Mitterrand developed his two-track strategy of military deployment and negotiation, he sent another ship, a cruiser, and over three thousand men equipped with transport and attack helicopters. Plans to commit ground forces were announced on August 21 following Iraq's harassment of various embassies, including France's, in Kuwait. At the beginning of Desert Storm on January 17, Prime Minister Rocard announced that French forces in the Gulf were being placed under U.S. military command "for a strictly defined time and missions." Later, French Defense Minister Jean Pierre Chevenement resigned after announcing that French forces would fight only in Kuwait, not in Iraq. French Foreign Legion units, however, would eventually join the U.S. 101st Airborne in its triumphant sweep from Saudi territory into western Iraq. The French air contribution included deployment of new French C-160-G Gabriel aircraft, based at al-Hasa Air Base south of Dhahran. These planes performed electronic intelligence and jamming missions for the allied air forces, which included a number of French combat planes based at Qatar.

At the beginning of the war French forces, mostly deployed in northern Saudi Arabia, numbered about 13,500 (U.S. forces by then totaled 500,000 and British forces 35,000).[18]

Such European commitment notwithstanding, from mid-August 1990 on, frequent complaints were heard in the United States about lack of support abroad for the American position. When King Hussein of Jordan visited President Bush in Kennebunkport, Maine, on August 16, he drew widespread criticism in the American media because he needed U.S. help but would not join the Western coalition to get it.

On December 5 Secretary of State Baker warned a Senate Foreign Relations Committee hearing that economic strains created by the UN trade embargoes and sanctions would hit certain countries more than others. He named Poland, Egypt, and Turkey. This ignited Senator Paul S. Sarbanes of Maryland. He shouted at Baker: "The Saudis are making $50 billion a year in a financial windfall from this crisis," he said. "Why don't they cough up some of that $50 billion so that Eastern European countries . . . don't hurt economically?" Baker's response was that the Saudi estimate of its oil revenues came to far less than $50 billion. Moreover, the Saudis had eighty thousand troops of their own to support as well as an open-ended commitment to the United States to provide things like water, fuel, base facilities, and local transportation.

Certain congressional defense spokesmen had been underscoring the slowness of allies like Germany and Japan to make good on their pledges of financial support (in 1990 alone, $2 billion from Japan and $1.5 billion from Germany). In November chairman of the House Armed Services Committee, Les Aspin of Wisconsin, had rated the performance of the allies in support—military, financial, and otherwise—of Desert Shield. In his so-called Burdensharing Report Card, Aspin gave an A-plus to only two countries, Egypt and Turkey. During Desert Storm Turkey would allow U.S. F-111 fighter bombers based at Incirlik air base to fly attack missions inside Iraq, and it would close its oil pipelines to Iraq. Aspin issued C to both Japan and Germany. Germany later met some of his reproaches by shipping a squadron of its fighters to defend Turkey in case Saddam retaliated against Incirlik or other sites there. Chancellor Helmut Kohl justified this to a skeptical German public by pointing out that, as Germany, Turkey was a NATO member, and this was definitely a NATO defense commitment.

Senate Majority Leader George Mitchell of Maine summed up the sentiment of many Americans when he pointed out that opposing aggression was not solely a duty of the United States. Others besides Americans and their fighting allies should join whatever battle lay ahead instead of merely offering passive or token support.[19]

Huge quantities of pre-positioned U.S. equipment on Diego Garcia and closer locations, along with Saudi Arabia's superior roads, ports, and airfields facilitated the deployment of the huge U.S. force. Offshore, the U.S. Navy had a greater presence than during its escort duty for the reflagged Kuwaiti tankers in 1987–88.

The all-pervading desert sand—the enemy of all land armies in the Middle East since Greek and Roman times—and heat forced the coalition troops to improvise shade in daytime and fight many patrol actions at night. For any number of reasons, Saddam Hussein never carried out his threat to use chemical warfare. Gas masks and protective clothing, or "noddy suits" as the British called them, were donned but never needed.

Even though chemical warfare failed to materialize as predicted, the allied air warfare launched in January 1991 was accurately forecast by at least one highly placed American, former U.S. Air Force Chief of Staff Gen. Michael J. Dugan. In a September 1990 interview, Dugan outlined the swift, massive bombing and numerous cruise missile attacks from U.S. warships that would cripple Iraq's military and civilian infrastructure. Dugan also talked about what tactics would be used to dislodge the Iraqi forces from Kuwait: carpet bombing and destroying Iraqi tanks and men from A-10 "Warthog" attack planes and helicopters. Dugan even explicitly suggested that Saddam Hussein should be targeted and killed. Defense Secretary Dick Cheney immediately dismissed Dugan, citing that this measure would violate an executive order prohibiting the assassination of foreign leaders—an order aimed at halting CIA involvement in assassination plots in the 1970s.[20]

Dead End for Perez de Cuellar

As mentioned earlier, after the failure of the Baker-Aziz talks on January 9, almost at the time of the final French peace efforts, Secretary General Perez de Cuellar of the UN went on a personal visit to Baghdad. Perez de Cuellar, according to a transcript of his remarks leaked to newspapers in Jordan, emphasized to Saddam that he was speaking only for himself, not the UN as a whole and not the United States, and implored Saddam to withdraw. Apparently Saddam made a few contemptuous remarks but then settled down to listen.

The UN secretary general said he had "full support" from the Soviet Union, as expressed in a message from President Gorbachev on January 11. He had also met with President Mitterrand as well as the Yugoslavian foreign minister in Paris on January 11 and King Hussein in Amman that evening. Without authority from the Security Council, the coalition, or the United States, all that Perez de Cuellar could do was guarantee that Iraq would not be attacked if it complied with the UN resolutions; suggest vague plans for self-determination for the Kuwaitis, which might efface the al-Sabah regime (something the United States and Britain stoutly opposed); and promise that the Palestinian issue would be discussed later. On January 13, White House Chief of Staff Sununu insisted there could be no such linkage but conceded that there would be "opportunities after the Gulf crisis is resolved" for a conference on the Palestinian issue.

Perez de Cuellar returned to the Security Council empty-handed. On January

15, after the last-minute French demarche had failed, he made a futile appeal to Saddam Hussein to "turn the course of events away from catastrophe and toward a new era of justice and harmony. . . ."[21]

The Air War Begins

For the journalists and television teams hunkered down in the Al Rashid Hotel in Baghdad, there was plenty of warning for what was coming. On the night of January 15, after the failure of Perez de Cuellar's and Mitterrand's peace initiatives became known, the French government ordered French journalists out of Iraq. Most obediently left for Amman the next morning. The next evening, ABC News and most other networks—Cable News Network (CNN) excepted—told their staff people to get out. Freelancers could not be forced to leave. At least one of the other American networks received a coded message from its Pentagon correspondent that operations would start that night. Most of the correspondents and crews planned to leave in the morning.

They never got a chance. At about 2:04 A.M. Baghdad time, or 7:04 P.M. Washington time, ABC News cameraman Fabrice Moussus, who had filmed Sadat's assassination in October 1981, was awakened by the crackling of antiaircraft fire being unleashed against approaching allied bombers. There were no air raid sirens, no prior warning of any kind. American electronic intelligence and countermeasures planes flew ahead of the bombers, jamming Iraqi radar and scrambling air defense frequencies. Next came the bombs and cruise missiles booming and thudding over a city that hadn't had the time or foresight to order a blackout. A speckled nightscape of lighted windows lay beneath a network of tracer fire and red and purple flashes. Using his night lens, Moussus captured everything on tape.

With the networks still in Baghdad, Americans knew that Desert Storm had started even before President Bush in the White House told Marlin Fitzwater to announce it. At 7:06 P.M. Washington time Fitzwater walked into the White House briefing room and said, "The liberation of Kuwait has begun."

The next day those journalists privileged or condemned (depending on how you looked at it) to be in Baghdad as well as television viewers around the world watched an incredible spectacle. Wave upon wave of American planes—F-15Es, A-6E Intruders, F/A-18s, and F-17 Stealth fighters, which were invisible to Iraqi radar but some British warships in the Gulf, it later turned out, picked them up—pounded Baghdad. Outside the capital the Royal Air Force, assigned the mission of suppressing an Iraqi air opposition that never materialized, sent Tornado planes armed with special JP-233 runway denial bombs to put craters in airfields and destroy Iraqi planes inside and outside bunkers. JP-233s also scattered time-delayed mines to hamper repair work during those first few hours.

The targets Moussos filmed, though it was impossible to tell from the hotel window what they were, included Saddam Hussein's well-fortified presidential palace, apparently hit by Tomahawk cruise missiles roaring in flat trajectories across

Baghdad. The Ministry of Defense, Saddam International Airport, the Daoura oil refinery, and scores of other government buildings and public installations were also hit. Soon electric power plants, water reservoirs, pipes, and other targets vital to the support of civilian as well as military life would be struck as well. Chemical warfare plants and top-secret sites where nuclear work of one sort or another had been carried out were systematically targeted. B-52s unleashed laser-guided Smart bombs and standoff missiles on command and control and intelligence centers thought or known to be nerve centers for Iraqi forces in Kuwait.

The Scud Missile Attacks

Surprisingly few Iraqi planes took to the air to oppose these allied thunderbolts, but there was an immediate Iraqi response, if not precisely the one promised by Saddam Hussein: in the early hours of January 17, seven Scud missiles landed in Tel Aviv and Haifa, Israel, and one near Dhahran, Saudi Arabia. With sirens wailing in the background, the Voice of Israel urged families to put on gas masks and get into their prepared shelters, rooms sealed with plastic sheets to keep out poison gas. Saddam, it was feared, might keep his promise about chemical warfare.

While the world watched on television, Saddam's Scuds killed four people and injured more than 120 during the first week of the air war. The Scuds were aged Soviet missiles. A Soviet military adviser who made friends with a member of the ABC team in Baghdad later confided that "those are 1950s junk—the kind of stuff we used to throw away or sell to second- and third-rate clients in the Third World."

After the first Scud attacks, the United States was anxious that Israel not intervene directly in the war, fearing this would fulfill Saddam's goal of splitting the Arab coalition and make it impossible for states like Egypt, Saudi Arabia, and Syria to fight on the same side as Israel. So the Bush administration rushed some seventeen-foot-long Patriot missiles with their multibarreled launchers and U.S. crews to the Jewish state. This was the first time American soldiers had directly defended Israeli territory. The Patriots' performance would not prove perfect by any means: fragments of intercepted Scuds would cause ground casualties, and some Scud warheads would merely be detached from the missile, not destroyed in the air. Near Dhahran, Saudi Arabia, two Patriots launched themselves, damaging buildings; a third, in pursuit of a Scud, damaged an insurance agency in Riyadh.

On January 18 Israeli Defense Minister Moshe Arens had promised that "we will react, certainly." While both Egypt and Syria indicated they would not leave the alliance if Israel did react, Arens's promise was not kept. President Bush sent Deputy Secretary of State Lawrence Eagleburger to Israel for what State Department veterans like to call a "hand-holding" session. By January 21 he was able to confirm Israel's pledge to work with the United States and to consult it before taking any unilateral action. On January 22 Israeli Foreign Minister David Levy said the United States would give Israel battle reports, logistical information, and "real time" satellite reconnaissance data coordinated by a "joint apparatus." At the same time

Eagleburger was informed by Finance Minister Yitzhak Modai that Israel wanted no less than $13 billion more than the annual $3 billion it was already getting in U.S. military and economic aid to meet Gulf war losses up to mid-February and to absorb Jewish immigrants from the Soviet Union.

But Israeli's threats to retaliate, like the attacks, continued. Each Scud or bit of Scud debris that landed was checked carefully for chemicals. Meanwhile Israelis reconciled themselves to spending long hours in their sealed rooms.

The worst Scud attack came not in Israel but in Saudi Arabia, where an incredibly well-aimed or lucky (from the Iraqi viewpoint) hit took out a U.S. Marine barracks near Dhahran Air Base on the evening of February 25. The London bureau chief for ABC News Radio, Linda Albin, was working in the International Hotel close to the base when a loud boom shook the hotel and set off its internal warning siren. Albin assumed that the boom was a Patriot being launched. Many journalists began pulling on their "mop gear," protective antigas clothing and masks. No one seemed overly worried. Then someone brought in an amateur video of a burning building, and a marine recognized it. "It's the compound where we sleep," he said. When Albin and other reporters from the International Hotel arrived at the scene, many dead and injured had already been removed from the rubble. The barracks, which had taken a direct hit from a Scud warhead (though it could have been something else; this was never entirely clear), looked to Albin "like a burnt, twisted pretzel. . . . It was terrible, terrible."

After this, a sense of unreality about the war gave way to a far more somber mood for even the rather cynical crowd of newsmen and newswomen clustered in Dhahran. The attack had caused more allied casualties than any other single incident: twenty-eight Americans dead and over one hundred injured.

Prisoners and Progress

One sad development for the allies amid the progress of the air offensive was the display of seven captured airmen on Baghdad television on January 20. I watched the program in Cyprus. All seven gave their names. They sent greetings to their families and made statements, muffled and off-mike for the most part, critical of the allied war effort. Several showed signs of injury. Baghdad broadcasts answered allied charges that this was a clear violation of the Geneva Convention's rules of war and denounced the allied bombing of civilian targets. It added that since the allies were not providing information on the true extent of their air losses, Iraq would not treat all of the captured airmen as prisoners of war. Some might be used as human shields in target areas. After seeing the pictures of the captured men, President Bush condemned their "brutal treatment." The possibility of their acting as human shields, however, would not affect the bombing campaign. On January 21, both British Prime Minister John Major in London and President Bush promised that Saddam would be held accountable for the treatment of prisoners.

On January 23, with still a month to go before the land phase of Desert Storm,

Gen. Colin Powell announced that the allies had achieved general air superiority in the skies over Iraq and Kuwait. Enemy nuclear installations were "finished." Iraqi aircraft, he said, were now able to operate from only five of Iraq's sixty-six airfields. The effectiveness of Iraq's air defense radar had been cut by 95 percent. After more than ten thousand allied air sorties, however, only forty-one enemy aircraft had been destroyed. Over one hundred more had flown to safe havens in Iran. Saddam and his military staff still had effective control over their forces. Powell indicated that the air campaign would have to go on for some time before the ground attack could begin. Then Powell made the often-quoted prediction about the Iraqi army entrenched and buried underground in Kuwait: "First we are going to cut it off, then we are going to kill it."[22]

Environmental Warfare

For months Saddam had been warning in clear terms that once hit, he would unleash "terrible weapons." These threats went largely unheeded in the West— unheeded, that is, until Saddam's troops ignited hundreds of oil wells and other oil installations in Kuwait. His first act was to pump oil from storage tanks in Kuwait, some of which were set afire immediately, into the Gulf. Iraq claimed that the oil spilling into the Gulf had been released by allied attacks on two Iraqi tankers on January 22.

Within days, wind and currents had carried the spreading, burning oil slick south, where it began devastating Gulf marine life. Fears ignited about the northern Gulf, especially vulnerable because, being closed in, it lacked natural turbulence and tidal flushing. News personnel hurried northward from Dhahran to observe the protective measures being taken to defend desalination plants on the coasts of Saudi Arabia and Bahrain: huge orange booms were being placed in the sea to block the oil's flow. By January 27 the Iraqis had released between 5 million and 10 million barrels of oil in what was probably the worst spill ever and possibly the only deliberate one.

At allied headquarters in Riyadh Brig. Gen. Buster C. Glosson and his staff, who were directing the air war, decided on drastic measures to halt the oil spill. They dispatched U.S. F-111 jets equipped with laser-guided bombs. On January 26 and 27 these knocked out two oil-pressure controls, or manifolds, at the Mina al-Ahmadi port, which fed the offshore Sea Island terminal. Gradually the southward spread of the slick slowed. Some photographers and television teams, anxious for pictures, rushed to record images of smaller slicks caused when the Iraqis had shelled Saudi oil installations at Khafji and Al Mishab, near the Kuwait border.

Oil spill experts from many countries began to converge on the region. Initial cleanup operations were limited to protecting the intake at desalination plants with booms and skimmer boats. Chemical dispersants were not effective because the slick was too large. Later, international concern was almost overshadowed by another menace, that of oil fires. These began at the end of January and multiplied in

February and March as the Iraqis blew up carefully laid mines and charges. The fires were to darken the skies of the entire Gulf region, threatening the environment and the way of life of its inhabitants indefinitely.

On the Brink of Land War

On January 29 two battalion-sized Iraqi groups invaded Saudi Arabia, the first action of the ground war. Khafji is a border town that had been largely evacuated a few days before the air war began. There were few allied troops there. Saudi and Qatari troops saw a line of Iraqi tanks entering the town with their gun turrets reversed, a sign of surrender suggested by allied leaflets dropped by U.S. planes. But it was an Iraqi ruse; soon the tanks opened fire. The Saudi and Qatari troops, supported by U.S. Marine artillery, jets, and helicopter gunships, counterattacked in a house-to-house street battle lasting about thirty-six hours.

Despite intensive allied bombing of the Iraqi columns, now out in the open where they could be pummeled from the air, two other Iraqi units entered Saudi territory. During the fighting, an Associated Press reporter in Saudi Arabia phoned Khafji's seaside hotel. An Iraqi soldier answered the telephone, announcing proudly that he was an Iraqi. "See you in Jerusalem!" he shouted, before the connection was broken. Casualty figures included about twelve U.S. Marines and fifteen Saudi soldiers killed, thirty Iraqi soldiers killed, and several tanks destroyed. Nearly five hundred Iraqi troops were captured and taken to POW camps prepared for them in Saudi Arabia. Some thirty-one U.S. personnel were declared missing or captured, including the first of two women prisoners taken in the war.

General Schwarzkopf called the surprise Iraqi attacks no more harmful than "a mosquito to an elephant." President Bush said that if the Iraqis had been trying to precipitate the land war before the allies were ready, this was futile: it would begin "on our timetable, not on Saddam Hussein's timetable."[23]

Despite major antiwar demonstrations in the United States and continued congressional opposition to war, Bush's leadership drew him, in a poll published on January 29, an approval rating of 79 percent. In his annual State of the Union address, the president appealed to all Americans to stand by him, arguing that the cost in lives "is beyond our power to measure, but the cost of closing our eyes to aggression is beyond mankind's power to imagine." He contended that only the United States had "both the moral standing and the means to back it up" required for leadership. The president then reaffirmed U.S. war aims: "to drive Iraq out of Kuwait, to restore Kuwait's legitimate government, and to ensure the stability and security of this critical region. . . . We do not seek the destruction of Iraq, its culture or its people. Rather, we seek an Iraq which uses its great resources . . . to build a better life for itself and its neighbors."[24]

With the land war fast approaching, European states declared varying degrees of solidarity. Neutral Ireland, a member of the EC though not of NATO, continued, as it had from August 1990 on, to permit U.S. military planes to stage through

Shannon Airport. Czechoslovakia, freshly emerged from its long imprisonment in the communist bloc, sent military experts to Saudi Arabia, including a chemical weapons decontamination unit. Hungary sent military doctors; Poland, two hospital ships.

The Soviet Union, keeping a wary eye on Iran—a nation that remained neutral while calling for an end to both the Iraqi occupation of Kuwait and the American and allied military presence in the Gulf—tried to support continuing Arab diplomatic initiatives to stop the war, but without success.

After three days of talks in Washington Secretary Baker and Soviet Foreign Minister Alexander Bessmertnykh, less well disposed toward the U.S. action than his predecessor Eduard Shevardnadze, issued a joint statement on January 29. It suggested that fighting would end if Iraq made "an unequivocal commitment" to quit Kuwait and "take immediate, concrete steps" to comply with the UN resolutions passed since August 2.

Despite the reservations of Mikhail Gorbachev, the Soviet Union was still aboard.

The War of a Hundred Hours

On Saturday night, February 23, 1991, President Bush ordered the land war to begin. Lt. Gen. Charles Horner, the supreme allied air commander, and many other commanders and analysts wanted to wait and let the unremitting air offensive continue before risking land armies. Opponents argued that the devastating bombing of Baghdad had sown doubt in the public mind about how the war was being conducted; that, and a new flurry of shuttle diplomacy between Moscow and Baghdad via Tehran, might weaken the allied war effort in unforeseen ways. The devastating effects of constant bombing on the Iraqi units dug into Kuwait and the elite Republican Guard in the north had reduced the Pentagon's computer projections of American casualties from forty thousand to five thousand. Military arguments about the approach of hotter weather, among other factors, helped the president to decide to go ahead.

Just after 8 P.M. Washington time, or 3 A.M. in the war theater, the order was given for the first elements of the XVIII Corps to move from Saudi Arabia to the west of Kuwait. They were to go straight into Iraq.

General Schwarzkopf had already launched what he later called his "Hail Mary" play to outflank the Iraqis far in the west. The XVIII Corps and VII Corps, with vast quantities of supplies, had to be trucked westward over three hundred miles of desert along the Tapline road, following an old American-built oil pipeline from the Dhahran area. In charge were Army Commander Lt. Gen. John Yeosock; Army Operations Officer Brig. Gen. Steve Arnold; and Logistics Chief Lt. Gen. Gus Pagonis. They moved their men in forty-five hundred trucks down the road, starting out ten days before the assault. Neither Iraq nor its potential allies seem to have picked up what was going on. The columns kept radio silence.

One operation that in some ways was part of the gigantic feint of amphibious landings that General Schwarzkopf and British General de la Billiere worked out with their naval commanders and had great symbolic value at the time was recapturing the tiny Kuwaiti island of Qaruh, about 35 kilometers off the coast of Kuwait. An Iraqi antiaircraft crew had been firing from a rocky outcrop on which stood a navigational beacon. On January 24, an air strike was flown against Qaruh, and after suffering some casualties the twenty-nine remaining Iraqi soldiers surrendered.

While the U.S. and British fleets maneuvered offshore with ship-based marines and other troops, feigning preparations for a giant amphibious landing from the Gulf, Schwarzkopf made feints on land as well. He ordered the U.S. Army's 1st Cavalry Division to attack the most obvious route, the Wadi al Batin corridor in western Kuwait. This and the seaborne threat pinned down ten Iraqi divisions.[25]

Intelligence and Secret Warfare

Much of the credit for the allies' preparation during the war goes to their superb intelligence-gathering capabilities. These included a series of sensing and photographic satellites launched in 1990 and data from special forces like the Green Berets, U.S. Navy SEAL (sea-air-land) teams, and Britain's Special Air Services (SAS). Some satellite observation was provided by payloads carried aboard spacecraft, such as an improved KH-11 satellite ejected from the spaceship *Columbia*, launched barely a week after the invasion of Kuwait.[26] One reason the emir of Kuwait and his family had been able to escape the Iraqis before the invasion was data from a "tethered aerostat," a kind of balloon that resembles a blimp with tail fins. Moored to the ground at low altitude and used to warn of aircraft since the Iran-Iraq War, on August 2, 1990, it detected the Iraqi assault.[27] And after the Scud attacks against Israel and Saudi Arabia began on January 27, two U.S. Air Force Space Command missile-warning spacecraft were maneuvered into orbit over the equator to monitor further Scud launches. They flashed warnings to air-defense systems in Israel and the Gulf, allowing time for Patriot batteries to be activated and gas masks and suits to be donned.[28]

Not even the best technology can function without human intelligence (HUMINT) to serve it. Gen. Leonard Peroots, director of the Defense Intelligence Agency until 1989, acknowledged that in 1990 too many American eyes and ears in space were still directed at the USSR and not enough at the Gulf. While some overhead satellites were able to help bombers, "information provided by human sources, . . . a fellow with a trenchcoat" who had spied on the target, made the difference. For instance, one strategic building in Baghdad was destroyed because the British had the building's original construction plans.[29] Ground teams of the SAS infiltrated Iraq, hiding half a mile or so from various targets, and helped guide Smart bombs to them with hand-held laser-beam projectors that only the attacking pilot could see.

Tomahawk cruise missiles were guided by built-in electronic maps that told them when and where to strike. General Peroots admitted that the built-in images could mislead as well as lead. A factory hit hard by U.S. weapons, first branded by the military as a biological weapons mixing center, was apparently a baby milk plant, as the Iraqis claimed. As for the Amiriya air raid shelter in Baghdad, despite claims in official U.S. briefings that it was a command and control center, this, said General Peroots, was not true "at the time we struck."[30] Several camera crews in Baghdad inspected the site and found no evidence of its having been a command and control center.

According to the BBC, Lt. Col. William Cowan, formerly of the Army's Intelligence Support Activity (ISA), slipped secretly into Kuwait after Iraq's invasion "with a few old Army friends to rescue American businessmen being held as hostages." Using hand-held satellite transmitters, Cowan's group did burst transmissions to an overhead satellite that beamed the information straight to General Schwarzkopf's headquarters in Saudi Arabia.[31] Early in the war, a British SAS team operating inside Iraq on anti-Scud patrols—searching for Scud launching sites and either destroying them or guiding allied planes to destroy them—was able to "extract" a complete Iraqi antiaircraft system and take it out by helicopter to Saudi Arabia.

The favorite American "dirty trick" of the war probably was flying out four helicopters carrying U.S. Special Forces teams that had been operating far behind Iraqi lines. Disinformation was fed to correspondents in Saudi Arabia to the effect that the four helicopters, painted to look like Iraqi choppers, were bringing out Iraqi defectors. Some respected Western news organizations were taken in briefly by that story—long enough, at least, to safeguard the operation from Iraqi countermeasures.[32]

The Ground Attack

On the original D-day for the ground war, February 21, Tariq Aziz had managed to reach Moscow through a circuitous route, dodging allied air surveillance, to confer with Gorbachev about an Iraqi plan to withdraw, at last, from Kuwait. President Bush decided to give Saddam an ultimatum to begin withdrawing by noon, Washington time, February 23. When the deadline passed and nothing happened, the allies moved.

The 101st Airborne Division captured Objective Gold, a patch of southwestern Iraq suitable for helicopter and light-plane landings. Much further west, France's 6th Light Armored Division and one brigade of the U.S. 82d Airborne Division easily took the first Iraqi town of the campaign, Al-Salman. Iraqi troops began surrendering wholesale, anxious to end the prolonged agony of battering from the air and being without vital supplies. In Kuwait, Iraq's III Corps tried to counterattack but was routed by the U.S. Marines. The Republican Guard's Tawakalna Division tried to move to southern Iraq, but all the Republican Guards inside Kuwait were trapped by destroyed bridges and highways to Basra. Allied forces had advanced into western Iraq by a series of leapfrogging airborne and overland movements, part of Schwarzkopf's Hail Mary scheme.

On the first night of the drive two Saudi forces punched through Iraqi defenses and moved up the Kuwaiti coast road toward Kuwait City. Egyptian and Syrian forces then moved in. At a point just south of where the main Iraqi defense was concentrated, the 1st and 2d Marine divisions easily overwhelmed the border defenses and moved into the Kuwaiti desert. By now the 101st Airborne had set up a logistics base deep inside Iraq. The 24th Mechanized Division and the 101st, many wearing gas-protection outfits, rolled into the Iraqi hinterland and the Tigris-Euphrates Valley. A prevailing south wind slowed the allied advance, as did the twenty-five thousand or so Iraqi prisoners of war choking the roads leading back into Kuwait.

On Tuesday, February 26, Defense Secretary Cheney and General Powell were able to tell President Bush that victory was about twenty-four hours away. The 24th Mechanized Infantry Division camped south of the Euphrates River, blocking escape routes from Kuwait and the highways toward Baghdad. The slaughter of the retreating Iraqi army, which a Baghdad Radio broadcast had announced would pull out of Kuwait, now began in earnest.

B-52 bombers continued carpet bombing Kuwait and southern Iraq, laying sticks of bombs across the ragged columns of fleeing Iraqi troops north of Kuwait City, especially in the area known as the Mutlah Ridge. AH-64 attack helicopters hit the remnants of Iraq's Hammurabi Division, named after one of the illustrious ancient kings of Mesopotamia whom Saddam professed to admire. Fuel-air bombs caused widespread burning. Mud choked the roads as rain poured down, limiting carnage because it created bad flying conditions. On the ground, the 1st and 3d Armored Divisions and the 1st Mechanized Division took out large groups of the Tawakalna and Medina divisions of the Republican Guard.

On Wednesday night, February 27, President Bush held a final meeting with his advisers. General Powell, according to Newsweek, told the president: "By tonight, there really won't be an enemy there. If you go another day, you're basically just fighting stragglers." The advisers suggested that President Bush should announce a cease-fire at midnight, February 27.[33]

In a television interview with British commentator David Frost, General Schwarzkopf said later that he felt the allies should have gone after Iraq's bedraggled army the way Hannibal, one of Schwarzkopf's heroes, had crushed the Romans at Cannae in 216 B.C. Hannibal encircled the entire Roman army and hacked it to pieces. "Frankly," said Schwarzkopf, "my recommendation had been . . . [to] continue the march. . . . We could have completely closed the door and made it a battle of annihilation. [But] the President made the decision that we should stop at a given time, at a given place, that did leave some escape routes open for them to get back out, and I think it was a very humane decision and a very courageous decision on his part."[34] After the war Shi'ite rebels in southern Iraq, Kurds who had liberated large portions of the north, as well as people stubbornly trying to resist the firepower of the remaining Republican Guards shielding Saddam in Baghdad would disagree.

Whatever his earlier thoughts, General Schwarzkopf followed the president's orders when General Powell spoke with him on the direct line from the White House. At midnight February 27, allied guns fell silent, and the air armada ceased bombing, flying only surveillance missions. By the following Sunday Iraqi officers had met Schwarzkopf, General de la Billiere, and their staffs and agreed to a provisional cease-fire, leaving Kuwait free, shattered, and burning, covered by the billowing smoke of hundreds of oil wells. Allied troops now occupied nearly 30 percent of southern Iraq.

The ground war had lasted exactly one hundred hours. According to provisional official estimates, Desert Storm had cost less than 150 allied dead and several hundred wounded. Many thousands of Iraqis, mainly soldiers but also several hundred civilians, had died. The most violent and historically significant phase of America's long war in the Middle East, which had raged in one form or another since the Shah's fall in 1979, had ended. But no one knew who would win the peace, or how, or when.

17

Ending America's Long War in the Middle East

A Decade of Payback

If all men did not make hasty judgments, says a proverb from Lebanon, all men would go to heaven. During the long history of U.S. dealings with the Middle East, especially the decade that is the focus of this book, many Americans in positions of power made fast and faulty judgments about the region. This has given rise to a great number of political problems from the fall of the Shah of Iran to one of the costliest wars since Vietnam, costly not only in financial terms but also in human loss and suffering.

To a reporter like myself, on a journey through the last bewildering generation in the Middle East, it has often seemed as though each well-meaning attempt by Americans to bring to that region ideas of peace, freedom, and happiness, essential ingredients of the American dream, has collided with the ghosts of the region's past: Arab wars against the Persians, colonial and postcolonial struggles, and conflicting promises made to Arabs, Jews, Iranians, Kurds, and other minorities by Western statesmen. These ghosts hover alongside concrete reminders of past good works such as the American-style schools, colleges, and universities that have brought some measure of enlightenment to the region.

Many Americans, for example, those who first supported, then questioned, the authority of the Shah of Iran, tried to make new and better policies only to encounter older conflicts that they often did not understand and with which they could not cope. I cannot resist quoting the remark of the Lebanese-American Shi'ite Muslim scholar Fouad Ajami, made to Thomas Friedman of the *New York Times*: "Men thought they were turning a corner, and guess what they met when they did? The past."[1]

The string of paybacks for America's bad judgment or misunderstanding began with the Shah. A generation of American statesmen, soldiers, academics, businessmen, and others built the self-styled King of Kings into a pillar to defend American interests. From Franklin Roosevelt to Jimmy Carter, American presidents habitually identified the interests of the Shah's imperial Iran with those of the United States. Most U.S. diplomats and journalists, myself included, either ignored or paid too little attention to Iran's swelling popular resentment of the man, the tyranny of SAVAK, and the corruption and abuses of his court, which unfortunately accompanied the considerable good he did for his people and for some of his neighbors. He was a benevolent despot. His sudden fall to religious zealots that came out of the world of Iranian Shi'ite Islam, a world of which we know little, and to the revolutionaries until then ignored by us, spread consternation among Americans who had relied on his power, trusted his judgment, and given him virtually everything he wanted, except nuclear weapons, to keep him protecting Western and Israeli interests.

The payback for America's overreliance on this single man was shattering. With his fall, the seeming impregnable position of America in Iran—until then, in many ways, its most important cold war base on the Soviet southern flank—was lost. So was the confidence and trust in America on the part of people in Iran and of neighboring rulers, who feared for their own survival.

Since the British military had formally quit the Persian Gulf region in 1971, the Shah's departure left America's other two major Mideast allies—Israel and Saudi Arabia—the standard-bearers for American interests in the region, despite their often differing agendas. The American commitment to Israel, dating back before the Jewish state's creation, was above all an emotional and ideological one. Vast financial resources, mainly from American Jews, Christian well-wishers, and later the economic and military power of the U.S. government, supported Israel. The drawback to that support was Arab hostility. Until the Israeli-Egyptian peace treaty of 1979 provided hope, it complicated the lives and tasks of Americans dealing with the region.

The result of such hostility was that the Jewish state sought non-Arab allies on the edges of the Arab world. In Iran it found Muslim Persians. The Shah's secret dealings with Israel, and Israel's wish to safeguard Iranian Jews, would ultimately draw the Reagan administration into its own secret deals involving international arms dealers and wildcat operators like Col. Oliver North. At the time of the early Israeli deals to supply Iran with arms, Iran was holding U.S. hostages in Tehran. Later, despite the success of North and company in freeing a few hostages in return for arms, Iran continued at least to condone the imprisonment of other Americans in Lebanon. Some of these are still being held. Meanwhile, Iranian military and financial assets held in the United States at the time of the Shah's demise remain frozen.

One payback for this murky triangle of arms deals with Iran, Israel, and the United States was a legacy of mistrust of the United States in the Middle East. In the wake of Irangate, for example, Iraq's leadership mistrusted American intelligence reports given to Iraq during its war with Iran. And the Iranian "moderates" whom North, McFarlane, and other American envoys visited in Tehran in May 1986 mistrusted (not without reason) the quality of the clandestine arms shipments they sought and were already receiving. Neither Iraq nor Iran had total faith in American pronouncements or offers after that. This proved a handicap in many official and unofficial dealings Americans subsequently had with those two countries.

In 1984 the United States resumed diplomatic relations with Iraq broken during the Arab-Israeli War of 1967. Washington began to tilt toward Iraq, selling or turning a blind eye to others' sales of strategic and dual-use technology that eventually reached Iraq's defense establishment and that the allied air forces devastated during Desert Storm in 1991. Hoping Iraq would stem the tide of the militant Iranian revolution, the Reagan and Bush administrations ignored the multiple human rights violations suffered by Iraq's Kurds and other dissidents, some of whom were perceived in Washington, London, and Paris, as they were in Baghdad, to be tools of the Ayatollah Khomeini and his successors in Iran.

In 1982, when Israel invaded Lebanon hoping to shatter the PLO's base and to install a Christian regime friendly to Israel, Israel's adversary, Syria, allowed Iran to send its Revolutionary Guards into Lebanon. Ostensibly they were sent to help fight the Israelis. Instead, they helped the Lebanese Shi'ites, an underprivileged segment of the fractured republic's sectarian society, to organize cells of the militant Hezbollah. In this way they planned to turn the war-torn little country into an Islamic satellite of Iran.

Although few Americans understood this at the time, Hezbollah and its Iranian mentors became advance guards for a campaign of terror and kidnapping aimed at eradicating 150 years of American cultural influence in the region. Among their targets were the American marines and soldiers that the Reagan administration naively believed could sort out the domestic battles of the Lebanese and at the same time protect the sovereignty of a Maronite Christian government. The kidnappings began in July 1982 while Israeli troops lay siege to Muslim West Beirut, where AUB was located. The first American taken was David Dodge, then acting president of AUB and a direct descendant of one of the patrician families that had worked diligently in the service of higher education for the Middle East. The abductions culminated in February 1988 when U.S. Marine Lt. Col. William Higgins, assigned to UN troops in southern Lebanon, was taken. He died later at the hands of his kidnappers. This was the bitter payback to America for the brains, talents, and careers it had invested in the Middle East.

Serving the same aim, expelling American influence from the region, was the suicide truck bombing of the U.S. Embassy in West Beirut in 1983; the bombing of marine headquarters in Beirut; another suicide attack on the new embassy building in East Beirut in 1984; and the 1985 hijacking of a TWA airliner to Beirut during which Shi'ite terrorists murdered an American seaman. Other outrages came later: the 1985 murder of a Jewish passenger on the hijacked cruise liner *Achille Lauro* and the bombing of U.S. servicemen in a Berlin discotheque in 1986, among others. America paid back one of the sponsors of both attacks, Colonel Qaddafi's Libya, by bombing Tripoli and Benghazi in mid-April 1986.

The United States was then drawn into limited but active participation in the Iran-Iraq War after an Iraqi attack on the U.S. destroyer *Stark* in the Gulf in 1987. Partly to reassure its important and now panicked Gulf ally, Saudi Arabia, the United States began the reflagging and escort of Kuwaiti oil tankers in 1988. U.S. warships and aircraft chased and sank a number of Iranian warships, including the gnatlike speedboats of the naval branch of Iran's Revolutionary Guard. The successful operation reassured Kuwaitis that the United States would come to their aid in the future.

The final and devastating phase of American involvement in the Iran-Iraq War came near its end, when in July 1988 the USS *Vincennes* accidentally shot down an Iran Air plane, killing all of its passengers and crew. The United States stumbled in its response, first blaming the Iranians themselves for the error and then making what seemed to many only halfhearted apologies and much-delayed offers of compensation for the victims' families.

When, at the urging of Ali-Akhbar Hashemi Rafsanjani, the Ayatollah Khomeini effectively ended the Iran-Iraq War in August 1988, the Iranian radicals opposed to the move engineered—or so it appears—one of the worst terrorist acts of our time: the bombing over Lockerbie, Scotland, of Pan Am Flight 103 on December 21, 1988, killing 270 people, most of them American. As of this writing no one has been brought to justice for the act, although investigators have found strong evidence for the involvement of a coalition of Iranians, Palestinians, and others, including members of Arab intelligence services.

The *realpolitik* of fashioning a transnational coalition to expel Saddam Hussein's forces from Kuwait in 1990–91 seemed to decree that Syrian and Iranian involvement in past terrorism should be overlooked by the Bush administration. This broke with tradition: the United States, for its own good reasons, had chosen long before Desert Storm to support Israel, Egypt, Saudi Arabia, Kuwait, and other regional Gulf powers against adversaries like Iran and Syria, allied with radical Palestinian forces not beholden to mainstream PLO leader Yassir Arafat. Until Desert Storm the price the United States had to pay was subversive warfare by Iran and Syria, a new demonstration of the Arab adage, The enemy of my enemy is my friend, and its converse, The friend of my enemy is my enemy.

By summer 1990, it had become clear to Americans that whatever clout they had in the Middle East was not sufficient to liberate Kuwait. That did not mean that war was inevitable; the right combination of Arab diplomacy and sanctions might have obliged Saddam to terminate his occupation peacefully. Had certain regional powers acted differently between August 2, the day of the invasion, and August 12, when Saddam Hussein announced Kuwait's annexation by Iraq, such an end could have been realized.

In any case, with the end of Desert Storm came yet another payback for America: the terrible responsibility, freely assumed by the Bush administration, for the millions of Kurds fleeing massacres by Saddam's forces. U.S. policymakers, absorbed in the military planning of Desert Storm, apparently failed to do any long-range *political* planning for the war's aftermath. In retrospect, President Bush's proclaimed "new world order" sounds like so many empty words. The United States thus inherits another Mideast problem with which it will most likely have to wrestle for generations. The long, tired history of paybacks has not yet come to an end.

Looking to the Future

Americans at home began to realize what those who had fought in Desert Storm already knew: that many, many thousands of Iraqi soldiers and civilians had been killed. Making matters worse, Iraq's electricity, water, and transport systems were in shambles, and the millions of Iraqis who rose against Saddam with President Bush's blessing—Kurds in the north and Arabs in the south—had been routed. Saddam's authority, though battered, remained intact.

In Kuwait, its skies and soil blackened by the oil fires set by Saddam's retreating forces, the al-Sabah rulers showed no willingness to restore even the modest beginnings of democracy. Nor, in Saudi Arabia, was the house of Saud in any hurry to allow its people, especially women, more participation in their government. Indeed, there seemed no more immediate chance for democracy in the Gulf and Arabian states than there was in theocratic Iran.

As of mid-1991, the central question of the Arab-Israeli conflict and the Palestinians remained unanswered. Nearly all the regional powers, including Israel, realized that only a strong American hand could clear away obstacles. But they did little to strengthen that hand. When Iraq's Scud missiles rained on Tel Aviv, Israeli government spokesmen had argued that the Arabs, in gratitude for the American defeat of their deadly enemy Iraq, would finally have to agree to peace with Israel. Meanwhile, Israel felt its abstention from war and reprisals against Saddam entitled Israel to much more American aid than it was already getting.

Arab spokesmen for the allied coalition were saying the exact opposite. Not only did the Saudi government initially resist the idea of attending a Mideast peace conference where the Palestinian issue was discussed, other Arab governments argued that, rather than the Arabs owing the Americans anything, the Americans should be rewarding them for the support that had made Desert Storm possible. The Arabs wanted America to use its leverage to get Israel to trade back Arab land in exchange for peace. Israel's Likkud government refused. The grudging community of interest developed between Israel and the Arab coalition during the war seemed to erode, until Syria in July agreed to peace talks with Israel.

What was more, the Palestinians themselves had lost the degree of international respect the *intifada* had given them before the war. This and the postwar persecution of Palestinians in Kuwait could be attributed to Yassir Arafat's ostentatious support for Saddam. Amid calls by Israel, the Saudis, and others for its exclusion from the peace process, Arafat's PLO had begun to waver and lose ground to fundamentalist and far more fanatically anti-Israeli and anti-American elements.

Thus the old issues, many explosive and likely to cause war, continue to face Americans in the Middle East. One of the most fundamental is the issue of boundaries, drawn around many of the Mideast states by former colonial powers while the superpowers looked on with indifference or approval. Not all those boundaries are recognized today by the states they supposedly demarcate. Iraq, a remnant of the Ottoman Empire that Britain conquered in World War I, has never agreed to the boundary Britain drew with its neighbor Kuwait at the end of that war. Nor have its Arab neighbors ever been willing to recognize Israel's frontiers. The Arabs often reply that no Israeli government has been willing to put down on paper exactly what it considers its final boundaries to be, except those with Lebanon and, since the 1979 peace treaty, with Egypt.

Most glaring of the conflicts reaching us from the Woodrow Wilson era is the Kurdish problem. It seems certain to generate more violence in the future, violence likely to compel American attention. Kurds were promised a national state in the 1920 Treaty of Sevres; for various reasons this promise could not be kept. The Kurdish state was stillborn; few Kurdish leaders today demand independence, though most seek autonomy within Iraq, Turkey, and Iran. In so doing, as the United States recently discovered after years of neglect, the 30 million Kurds threaten to destabilize the region's fragile political environment.

The politics of oil will also continue to dog the United States. Unable to keep or exploit Kuwait's oil, Saddam Hussein brought on ecological disaster by setting it afire. This removed as much as 3 million barrels per day or more from world markets. As of this writing, Iraq's oil remains off the worldwide market until UN sanctions against its sale abroad are lifted. The UN-decreed embargoes and boycotts crippled the already debt-laden Iraqi economy, and Saddam was obliged under UN resolutions to make restitution for his plundering of Kuwait.

Water is another regional problem facing policymakers in the Middle East. Turkey, Syria, and Iraq all depend on water from the Euphrates River, which starts in Turkey. Completion of its huge Atatürk Dam in 1990 means that Turkey can cut off water to both its neighbors if it so chooses. Water was being rationed in Jordan and Syria in 1989. Israel, which consumes far more water than those two countries, drastically cut drilling of water wells by Arab inhabitants of the occupied territories, leaving more water for Jewish settlements. Although Syria and Jordan had U.S. backing for an American-designed dam on the Yarmuk River, they could not move ahead with construction because of disagreements between themselves and with Israel about water quotas. Egypt, as one of its most senior diplomats once told me, fears that its next war might be fought over life-giving Nile River water if Ethiopia blocks the flow into that country.[2]

Population explosion continues in the Middle East no matter how poor the various states may be. Egypt and Iran will have to import more and more food each year to feed the burgeoning number of hungry mouths, spending a growing amount of scarce hard currency. Even Syria, a granary for the Roman Empire of old, has to buy many millions of dollars' worth of food abroad for its small but expanding population of thirteen million. Like most other Mideast states, however, the lion's share of its budget goes for arms.

In the past the United States had ambitious aid programs, especially agricultural, for many Mideast countries. By the end of the last decade such aid, however, was concentrated on Egypt and Israel, leaving emergency aid to drought- or war-stricken areas like Ethiopia, the Sudan, or indeed Iraq to private initiatives or the discretion of oil-rich states like Saudi Arabia. Today the Saudis do not show much interest in helping countries like the Sudan, Yemen, or Jordan, which they feel sided against them during Desert Storm. The U.S. Congress, in a similar mood, cut aid to Jordan.

The 1990–91 Gulf conflict proved again how many forces work against central decision-making on the Middle East by any American administration. Not only is policymaking in the United States decentralized itself, being shared among the president, the National Security Council, and Congress, but in the case of the Middle East, powerful lobbies and private interest groups have clout. The best known and one of the most effective lobbies in Washington is the American Israel Public Affairs Committee. It organizes telephone and letter campaigns and within legal limits manipulates campaign funds to persuade congressmen and their constituents to vote the way the Israeli government wants. Arab lobby groups such as the National Association of Arab-Americans and the Association of Arab-American University Graduates try to apply counterpressure. They are often hampered by differences among the Arab governments, less than effective public relations, and embarrassment and confusion about how to present the Palestinian problem to the American people.

Multinational oil companies with a major American component—Exxon, Texaco, Occidental Petroleum, and others—are not as active as they once were in efforts to make American opinion more sympathetic to Arab views. The same is true of corporations like Bechtel, heavily involved in Mideast construction and reconstruction. They do not need much domestic lobbying or public relations work to get overseas contracts like the reconstruction of Kuwait, for example. Their concern is business abroad, not American opinion at home, except when opinion works against their interests.

One need only remember how the armed attack by North Korea on South Korea aroused a complacent Truman administration in 1950 and sent the United States to war, or how Iraq's attack on Kuwait aroused the Bush administration, to understand how an action by one of the Mideast states to capture territory, oil, or water resources, or to come to the rescue of an oppressed people like the Kurds, could compel some future U.S. government to act.

The problems of trying to break down the barriers of misunderstanding and ignorance separating many Americans from the 6 billion or 7 billion other people of the earth will apply especially to the U.S. role in the Middle East. Protecting American interests there can only be achieved by greater knowledge, empathy, acceptance, and an attempt to understand the region's peoples rather than improvising and depending on regional policemen like the Shah, Israel, or the kings of Saudi Arabia.

Improvisation, as we have seen, breeds fear, contempt, and mistrust. If in the postcommunist era it is to prove to people abroad that democracy can be made to work for them, America cannot afford the policymaking of error, miscalculation, and terrible payback. For every terrorist I would venture that there are thousands of people of good will who still look hopefully to the United States for inspiration and the means to a better, peaceful life. Americans need to learn what is really happening in distant regions like Kurdistan and Saudi Arabia so that foreign policy can be made accountable to a large and informed public, and not just generated by specialists or special interest groups whose judgments are colored by their needs or biases.

The United States is engaged in the Middle East as never before. If Americans are to continue to promote, in the best sense, democracy and its associated ideals in that region, they must better understand the peoples and societies there. This is the only way to the sort of enlightened, longer-range policy that holds promise finally of bringing to an end America's long war in the Middle East.

Notes

1. King of Kings, Light of the Aryans

1. Later, as prime minister of Khomeini's first provisional revolutionary government, Bazargan promptly sent security forces to end the first, brief occupation of the U.S. Embassy in February 1979 by revolutionary militants. This led some Americans to wager that he could do the same for them in November 1979, when the diplomats were taken hostage. When Bazargan tried, the Americans lost their bet, and Bazargan lost his position as head of government and favored associate of the Ayatollah.
2. Although Shariat-Madary was a grand ayatollah of great prestige, especially in his native Azerbaijan, his mention as a friendly contact of the Americans in the documents the militants seized in the U.S. Embassy in 1979–80 ensured that he would spend his days in disgrace.

2. Eyes on the Ground, Spies in the Sky

1. Pierre Salinger, *America Held Hostage: The Secret Negotiations* (London: Andre Deutsch, 1981), p. 23.
2. Edward Jay Epstein, *Deception: The Invisible War Between the KGB and the CIA* (London: W. H. Allen, 1989), pp. 52–54 and 311–19.
3. "Documents from the Den of Spies," cited in James A. Bill, *The Eagle and the Lion: The Tragedy of American-Iranian Relations* (New Haven and London: Yale University Press, 1988), pp. 287–88.
4. *Time*, February 9, 1981, p. 19.
5. Personal interview, January 10, 1980. The article summarized a series of hostile assaults on or penetrations of U.S. communications security, starting with Israel's "accidental" attack on the U.S. spy ship *Liberty* off Sinai in 1967 and the North Koreans' seizure of the *Pueblo*, a similar but smaller ship, in 1968 (*Christian Science Monitor* [January 8, 1980], pp. 1, 9–10).
6. Col. Charles A. Beckwith (Ret.) and Donald Knox, *Delta Force: The U.S. Counter-Terrorist Unit and the Iranian Hostage Rescue Mission* (London: Arms and Armour Press, 1984), pp. 282–83.
7. *Time*, February 9, 1981, p. 19.
8. Kevin W. Kelly, ed., *The Home Planet: Images and Reflections of Earth from Space Explorers* (Moscow: Addison Wesley Publishing Company and U.S. and Mir Publishers, 1988), p. 54.

9. Personal experience of the author. See also John K. Cooley, "The Water War," *Foreign Policy* (Spring 1984): 3–26.

10. Reginald Turnill, ed., *Jane's Spaceflight Directory, 1989–90* (London: Jane's Publishing, 1989), p. 419.

11. Ibid., pp. 419–20.

12. William Arkin, ed., *Nuclear Battlefields* (Washington: Institute for Policy Studies Press, 1986), p. 19.

13. James Bamford, *The Puzzle Palace* (London: Sidgewick and Jackson, 1982), p. 198.

14. Nigel West, *The Secret Wireless War, 1900–68* (London: Coronet Books, Hodder and Staughton, 1986), pp. 345–46.

15. Bamford, *Puzzle Palace*, p. 199.

16. John K. Cooley, "U.S. Secret Code Network: A History of Costly Slipups," *Christian Science Monitor* (January 8, 1980), p. 3.

17. Gen. Robert E. Huyser, *Mission to Tehran* (London: Andre Deutsch, 1986), p. 180.

18. Ibid., pp. 181–85.

19. Ibid., p. 64.

20. Private communication, Washington D.C., June 3, 1981.

21. Bill, *The Eagle and the Lion*, p. 401.

22. Ibid., pp. 401–2.

23. *New York Times*, May 15 and May 29, 1979.

3. From Babylon to Moshe Dayan

1. ABC Radio News "Perspective" by Christine Powell, broadcast on ABC Radio Networks, November 11, 1989.

2. Private communication from the relative of a prisoner, February 1990.

3. Ibid.

4. Salinger, *America Held Hostage*, p. 268. The irony in this was that Gerhardt Ritzel himself was an anti-Nazi emigrant. From his ambassadorship in Tehran, he went on to become an intelligence adviser to West Germany's president.

5. Ibid., p. 24.

6. Ayatollah Ruhollah Khomeini, *Islamic Government*, translated by Joint Publications Research Service (New York: Manor Books, 1979), pp. 88–91.

7. Ibid., p. 66.

8. Ibid., p. 95.

9. Ibid., p. 96.

10. Gerhard Konzelman, *Allahs Schwert* (Munich and Berlin: Herbig, 1989), p. 247, my translation.

11. *The New Oxford Annotated Bible, with the Apocrypha*, revised standard ed. (New York: Oxford University Press, 1973), pp. 86–87.

12. A. J. Arberry, ed., *Religion in the Middle East* (Cambridge: Cambridge University Press, 1969), vol. 1, p. 126.

13. Konzelman, *Allahs Schwert*, p. 19.

14. Ibid., p. 85.

15. Ibid., p. 86.

16. Arberry, *Religion*, vol. 1, pp. 144 and 158.

17. Ibid., pp. 194–95.

18. Ibid., p. 190.

19. Bill, *The Eagle and the Lion*, p. 430.

20. Yossi Melman and Dan Raviv, *The Imperfect Spies: The History of Israeli Intelligence* (London: Sidgewick and Jackson, 1989), pp. 59–62.

21. Ibid., p. 89–90.

22. Ibid., p. 91.

23. Ibid., p. 92.

4. The Roots of Irangate

1. Bill, *The Eagle and the Lion*, p. 204.
2. Melman and Raviv, *Imperfect Spies*, p. 89.
3. Bill, *The Eagle and the Lion*, p. 205.
4. Ibid., p. 365.
5. Ibid., p. 366.
6. Stephen Green, *Living by the Sword: American and Israeli in the Middle East, 1967–1987* (London: Faber and Faber, 1988), p. 199.
7. Michael Ledeen and William Lewis, *Debacle: The American Failure in Iran* (New York: Knopf, 1981), p. 126.
8. *Facts on File* (New York: Facts on File, 1979), 126.
9. John K. Cooley, "Iran, the Palestinians and the Gulf," *Foreign Affairs Quarterly* (Summer 1979): 1017–22.
10. Ibid., p. 1022.
11. Ibid., pp. 1023–24.
12. Green, *Living by the Sword*, p. 200.
13. Ibid., p. 19.
14. Warren Christopher et al., eds., *American Hostages in Iran: The Conduct of a Crisis* (New York: Council on Foreign Relations, with Yale University Press, 1985), pp. 55–56.
15. Ibid., p. 201n.
16. Ibid., p. 164.
17. Ibid., p. 303.
18. Ibid., pp. 303–5.
19. Ibid., p. 166.
20. Photocopies of documents made available to author.
21. Jacques Dergoy and Hesi Carmel, *Israel Ultra-Secret* (Paris: Robert Laffont, 1989), p. 152.
22. Wilhelm Dietl, *Waffen für die Welt: Die Milliardengeschäfte der Rüstungsindustrie* (Munich: Knauer, 1986), pp. 144–45.
23. The National Security Archive, *The Chronology: The Documented Day-by-Day Account of the Secret Military Assistance to Iran and the Contras* (New York: Warner Books, 1987), p. 3.
24. John Bulloch and Harvey Morris, *The Gulf War: Its Origins, History and Consequences* (London: Methuen, 1989) p. 17.
25. The National Security Archive, *Chronology*, p. 6.
26. Ibid., p. 8; *Washington Post*, July 27, 1981, p. 1, and private communications in London.
27. The National Security Archive, *Chronology*, pp. 11–12.
28. Conversation at the International Institute for Strategic Studies annual conference in Barcelona, Spain, September 1988.

5. The Road to Mecca: Saudi Oil, American Defense

1. Zbigniew Brzezinski, *Power and Principle: Memoirs of the National Security Adviser, 1978–81* (London: Weidenfeld and Nicholson, 1983), p. 452.
2. Ibid., p. 452.
3. Ibid., p. 552, and annex 2, p. 568. Emphasis mine.
4. Ibid., p. 453.
5. Ibid., p. 454.
6. Ismail I. Nawab, Peter C. Speers, and Paul F. Hoye, eds., *ARAMCO and Its World: Arabia and the Middle East* (Dhahran and Washington, D.C.: Arabian-American Oil Company), pp. 184–202.
7. Forrestal letter to Secretary of State James F. Byrnes, August 1, 1945, in Aaron David Miller, *Search for Security* (Chapel Hill: University of North Carolina Press, 1980), p. 145, cited in William B.

Quandt, *Saudi Arabia in the 1980s: Foreign Policy, Security and Oil* (Washington, D.C.: The Brookings Institution, 1981), pp. 47–48.

8. Nawab et al, *ARAMCO and Its World*, p. 164.

9. Miller, *Search for Security*, p. 130, quoted in Quandt, *Saudi Arabia*.

10. The interviews with Faisal were published on July 6, 1973, in both the *Washington Post* and the *Christian Science Monitor*. This account of Yamani's firing by royal order is from Jeffrey Robinson, *Yamani: The Inside Story* (London: Simon and Schuster, 1988), p. 279. I have not been able to verify it with Yamani himself but heard it repeated by others who had not seen Robinson's book.

11. In January 1967, a group of newsmen and I were on the receiving end of an Egyptian air attack on the Saudi border village of Najran. We had trekked over rugged country in northern Yemen to see the miserable "royalist" village of Ketaf, where at least twenty citizens had died from an Egyptian poison-gas attack.

12. Quandt, *Saudi Arabia*, *passim*, and conversations with Kennedy advisers and Kennedy-era American and Arab diplomats. Dr. William Polk shared with me many of his experiences as a special Kennedy emissary in Egypt, Saudi Arabia, Yemen, and Israel.

13. Quandt, *Saudi Arabia*, p. 52.

14. Anthony H. Cordesman, *The Gulf and the Search for Strategic Security* (Boulder, Colo.: Westview Press, 1984), pp. 313–34 and *passim*. This is the best available account of all the military and technical aspects of the deal. It mentions some of the political ones as well.

15. There are many accounts of the Mecca revolt. I have followed most closely that of Wilhelm Dietl, *Holy War*, trans. Martha Humphries (New York: Macmillan, 1984), pp. 211–27. See also Amir Taheri, *Holy Terror* (London: Sphere Books, 1987), pp. 158–64.

16. Tony Geraghty, *The Bullet Catchers: Bodyguards and the World of Close Protection* (London: Grafton Books, 1988), pp. 405–6.

17. Taheri, *Holy Terror*, p. 160.

18. Dietl, *Holy War*, pp. 211–27 and *passim*.

6.   Islamic Revolution in Lebanon

1. Juliana S. Peck, *The Reagan Administration and the Palestinian Question* (Washington, D.C.: Institute for Palestine Studies, 1984), pp. 67–68. The Israelis rejected the idea, holding out for what they eventually got: total evacuation of all fulltime PLO fighters from Lebanon.

2. Robin Wright, *In the Name of God: The Khomeiny Decades* (New York, London: Simon and Schuster, 1989), p. 115 and *passim*. Another excellent reference for the Dodge-Motavasselian episode is David C. Martin and John Walcott, *Best Laid Plans: The Inside Story of America's War Against Terrorism* (New York: Harper and Row, 1988), p. 100 ff. Much of my own material comes from my notes on the Dodge investigation, which ABC News generously allowed me to pursue as part of my correspondent duties until his release in 1983.

3. Robert Brenton Betts, *Christians in the Arab East* (Athens: Lycabettus Press, 1978), p. 163.

4. Trevor Mosty, ed., *The Cambridge Encyclopedia of the Middle East and North Africa* (Cambridge: Cambridge University Press, 1988), p. 141.

5. Ibid., p. 147.

6. Ibid., p. 155.

7. Larry Pintak, *Beirut Outtakes: A TV Correspondent's Portrait of America's Encounter with Terror* (Lexington, Mass.: Lexington Books, 1988), p. 77.

8. Ibid., p. 82, and Kenneth Anderson, *U.S. Military Operations, 1945–1984* (London: Hamlyn, 1984), p. 184.

9. Ze'ev Schiff and Ehud Ya'ari, *Israel's Lebanon War* (New York: Simon and Schuster, 1984), p. 286.

10. Pintak, *Beirut Outtakes*, p. 83.

11. Private communication, Tripoli, January 8, 1982.

12. Martin and Walcott, *Best Laid Plans*, pp. 86–87.

7. America Versus Iran—in Lebanon

1. Pintak, *Beirut Outtakes*, p. 103, and Jane Mayer and Doyle McManus, *Landslide: The Unmaking of President Reagan* (London: Fontana/Collins, 1989), p. 142.
2. *Al-Liwa* (newspaper), April 19, 1983, Beirut, p. 1.
3. Among the many published sources for this are Pintak, *Beirut Outtakes*, p. 104, and Martin and Walcott, *Best Laid Plans*, p. 105.
4. Private communication from Corbett, January 1990.
5. Martin and Walcott, *Best Laid Plans*, p. 107.
6. Corbett, private communication, January 1990.
7. Ibid.
8. Amir Taheri, *The Iranian Triangle: The Untold Story of Israel's Role* (London: Hutchinson, 1985), p. 224.
9. Samuel Segev, *The Iranian Triangle: The Untold Story of Israel's Role in the Iran-Contra Affair* (New York: The Free Press), pp. 124–25.
10. One who did was David Ignatius, then with the *Wall Street Journal*. See his article in that newspaper, February 10, 1983, and the coverage in Melman and Raviv, *Imperfect Spies*, pp. 210–12.
11. Melman and Raviv, *Imperfect Spies*, pp. 289–90.
12. Martin and Walcott, *Best Laid Plans*, p. 109.
13. Ibid., pp. 109–10.

8. *"New Jersey! New Jersey!"*

1. Martin and Walcott, *Best Laid Plans*, pp. 119–20.
2. Ibid., p. 124.
3. Most of the facts here and in the following page come from Paul Stillwell, *Battleship* New Jersey (London: Arms and Armour Press, 1986), pp. 260–61.
4. Corbett, private communication, January 1990.
5. Martin and Walcott, *Best Laid Plans*, pp. 125–26.
6. Ibid., pp. 128–29.
7. Ibid., p. 131.
8. Corbett, private communication, January 1990.
9. Stillwell, *Battleship*, p. 263.
10. Martin and Walcott, *Best Laid Plans*, p. 133.
11. George C. Wilson, *Supercarrier: An Inside Account of Life Aboard the World's Most Powerful Ship, the USS* John F. Kennedy (New York: Berkeley Books, 1986), p. 120.
12. Ibid., pp. 121–22.
13. Wilson, *Supercarrier*, pp. 125–30.
14. Pintak, *Beirut Outtakes*, pp. 204–5.
15. Wilson, *Supercarrier*, p. 136.
16. Ibid., pp. 137–60.
17. Stillwell, *Battleship*, p. 264.
18. Robert Fisk, *Pity the Nation: Lebanon at War* (London: Andre Deutsch, 1990), pp. 527–28.
19. Martin and Walcott, *Best Laid Plans*, p. 145.

9. Beirut Addio

1. Fisk, *Pity the Nation*, pp. 532–33.
2. Ibid., p. 534.
3. Ibid., p. 534.
4. Stillwell, *Battleship*, pp. 268–72.
5. Corbett, private communication, January 1990.

6. Tony Geraghty, *The Bullet Catchers*, p. 240–44.
7. Corbett, private communication, January 1990.

10. Hostages to Misfortune

1. Taheri, *Holy Terror*, p. 154.
2. Ibid., p. 155.
3. Sis Levin, *Beirut Diary: A Husband Held Hostage and a Wife Determined to Set Him Free* (Downers Grove, Ill.: Intervarsity Press, 1988), *passim*.
4. Gordon Thomas, *Journey into Madness: Medical Torture and the Mind Controllers* (London: Bantam Press, 1988), p. 358.
5. Ibid., pp. 352–55, and Amnesty International informants.
6. Martin and Walcott, *Best Laid Plans*, p. 154, and Antoine Jalkh, "Le Hezbollah sous pression," *Arabiees* (Paris, November 1989): 21.
7. Documents in author's possession.
8. Private communications from PLO officials and confidential Iranian source.
9. Jeffrey Richardson, *The U.S. Intelligence Community*, 2d ed. (Cambridge, Mass.: Ballinger, 1989), p. 64.
10. Ibid., p. 65–66.
11. Thomas, *Journey into Madness*, p. 69.
12. Ibid., pp. 77–78.
13. Ibid., p. 79.
14. Ibid., p. 90.
15. Ibid., p. 91.
16. Segev, *The Iranian Triangle*, p. 269.
17. Richelson, *Intelligence Community*, p. 345.
18. Ibid., p. 346.
19. Thomas, *Journey into Madness*, p. 328, and Segev, *The Iranian Triangle*, p. 129.
20. Segev, *The Iranian Triangle*, p. 129.
21. Ibid., p. 165.
22. Martin and Walcott, *Best Laid Plans*, pp. 217 and 325.
23. James Adams, *Secret Armies: The Explosive Inside Story of the World's Most Elite Warriors* (New York: Bantam Books, 1989), pp. 360–61.
24. Mayer and McManus, *Landslide*, p. 204, and tape of Jacobsen news conference at St. Brides' Church, London, November 11, 1986.
25. Mayer and McManus, *Landslide*, pp. 204–5.
26. Ibid., p. 203.
27. Information on Anderson summarized in briefing notes by Hacheld (a private consultant in Nicosia, Cyprus), "The Foreign Hostage Crisis in Lebanon," updated February 15, 1990. Anderson's letter is quoted on p. 10.
28. Segev, *The Iranian Triangle*, p. 178.
29. Personal communication from Don Mell, 1986.
30. Ibid.

11. Mass Destruction for Sale

1. Author's notes and broadcasts from the *Chandler*. See also John K. Cooley, "In the Gulf: One Close Encounter," *International Herald Tribune*, February 19, 1988, op-ed page.
2. Edgar O'Ballance, *The Gulf War* (London: Brassey's Defence Publishers, 1988), p. 88.
3. Ibid., pp. 96–97.
4. Ibid., p. 122.
5. Ibid., p. 142.
6. Ibid., p. 146.

7. Ibid., pp. 146–47.
8. *Maghreb-Machrek*, La Documentation Française, Paris, no. 106, 1984, pp. 78–82.
9. Private communications from a U.S. diplomat and several Gulf ministers, 1987–90.
10. O'Ballance, *Gulf War*, p. 156.
11. Ibid., p. 157.
12. Thomas, *Journey into Madness*, p. 359.
13. Ibid., p. 186.
14. Ibid., p. 191.
15. Ibid., p. 196, and personal communications in Baghdad.
16. Ibid., p. 196.
17. John K. Cooley, "Poison Gas: No Place to Hide in the Middle East," *International Herald Tribune*, October 13, 1988, op-ed page.
18. O'Ballance, *Gulf War*, p. 140.
19. Bulloch and Morris, *The Gulf War*, p. 261.
20. O'Ballance, *Gulf War*, pp. 149–150.
21. Holder Koppe and Egmont R. Koch, *Bomben-Geschäfte: Tödliche Waffen für die Dritte Welt* (Munich: Knesebeck and Schuler, 1990), pp. 228–29 (author's translation).
22. Ibid., p. 224.
23. Bulloch and Morris, *The Gulf War*, p. 262.
24. Ibid., pp. 263–64. See also Michael Barone and Grant Ujisufa, *The Almanac of American Politics, 1990* (Washington: The National Journal, 1990), *passim*.
25. Adel Darwish and Gregory Alexander, *Unholy Babylon: The Secret History of Saddam's War* (London: Victor Gollancz Ltd., 1991), pp. 79–81.

12.   America Enters the Iran-Iraq War

1. Testimony of Richard Secord under crossexamination, in Senator William S. Cohen and George J. Mitchell, *Men of Zeal: A Candid Inside Story of the Iran-Contra Hearings* (New York: Penguin Books, 1989), p. 73.
2. O'Ballance, *Gulf War*, pp. 173–79.
3. Interview with Iraqi Vice President Taha Yassine Ramadan, Baghdad, April 11, 1990.
4. Interview with Gary Sick, June 18, 1987.
5. House of Commons Foreign Affairs Committee, session 1987–88, second report, "Current U.K. Policy Toward the Iran-Iraq Conflict," London, Her Majesty's Stationary Office, June 1988, p. xii.
6. Interview with Gary Sick, New York, June 23, 1987.
7. Caspar Weinberger, *Fighting for Peace: Seven Critical Years at the Pentagon* (London: Michael Joseph, 1990), pp. 274–75.
8. International Institute for Strategic Studies (IISS), *Strategic Survey, 1987–88* (London: IISS, 1988), pp. 75–76.
9. Weinberger, *Fighting for Peace*, p. 277.
10. Bulloch and Morris, *Gulf War*, pp. 226–27.
11. Weinberger, *Fighting for Peace*, p. 287.
12. Maghreb-Machrek, no. 118, pp. 106–7.
13. Bulloch and Morris, *Gulf War*, pp. 224–25.
14. James Adams, *Trading in Death: Weapons, Warfare and the New Arms Race* (London: Hutchinson, 1990), p. 123.
15. Ibid., pp. 71–72.
16. Maghreb-Machrek, no. 119, p. 98.
17. Vahe Petrossian, "Iran's Tactical Shift Heralds Gulf War Escalation," *Middle East Digest* (October 17, 1987): p. 20.
18. Weinberger, *Fighting for Peace*, p. 297.
19. Maghreb-Machrek, no. 120, pp. 89–90.
20. Maghreb-Machrek, no. 121, p. 84.

21. Ibid., pp. 85–86.
22. Private communication from Syrian government official, Damascus, January 1988.
23. Agence-France Presse dispatch, Beirut, July 31, 1989.

13. Swords Sheathed, Daggers Drawn

1. Maghreb-Machrek, no. 122, pp. 95–96.
2. Robin Wright, *In the Name of God: The Khomeiny Decade* (New York: Simon and Schuster, 1989), p. 186.
3. Weinberger, *Fighting for Peace*, p. 301. My account is based on a number of different press, radio, and television reports. See also summaries in *Keesings' Contemporary Archives: Record of World Events*, vol. 4 (Harlow, U.K.: Longman, October 1988), pp. 36169–71.
4. Capt. M. Eckhart, Jr., USN (Ret.), "The Vincennes Incident," *Proceedings of the U.S. Naval Institute* (March 1990): 32.
5. Wright, *In the Name of God*, p. 187.
6. Bulloch and Morris, *Gulf War*, p. 246.
7. Ibid., pp. 247–48.
8. IRNA (Islamic Republic News Agency), dispatch, July 20, 1988, London.
9. Maghreb-Machrek, no. 122, pp. 78–79.
10. Ibid., p. 80.
11. John K. Cooley, *Green March, Black September: The Story of the Palestinian Arabs* (London: Frank Cass, 1973), p. 140.
12. Ibid., p. 153, and Steven Emerson and Brian Duffy, *The Fall of Pan Am 103: Inside the Lockerbie Investigation* (New York: G.P. Putnam), pp. 114–15.
13. Segment broadcast by ABC News "Prime Time Live," June 28, 1990, from "Trial of Destruction," a one-hour television documentary broadcast in London by Thames Television on June 28, 1990, producer Michael Christman, correspondent Julian Manyon.
14. These documents are all in ABC News investigative files.
15. Most of these details, except for later information about Malta, are found in the ABC News "Prime Time Live" transcript of the broadcast of November 30, 1988.
16. Private communications in London from Iranian individuals, January 1989 to June 1990.
17. ABC investigative files.
18. Ibid.
19. "The Foreign Hostage Crisis in Lebanon," BBC Newspack, pp. 15–20.
20. Alexandra Schwartzbrod, "French, U.S. Forces Practice for Hostage Rescue in Mediterranean," *Armed Forces International* (April 1989): p. 23.
21. Agence-France Presse dispatch, October 24, 1989.
22. Wright, *In the Name of God*, pp. 197–98.

14. The Khomeini Decade Ends

1. *1990 Britannica Book of the Year* (Chicago: Encyclopedia Britannica, 1990); Newspack, compiled and produced by Memo (Nicosia, Cyprus, 1990), pp. 15–18.
2. IRNA dispatch, February 14, 1989.
3. H. A. R. Gibb and J. H. Kramers, eds., *Shorter Encyclopedia of Islam* (Leiden: A. H. Bull, 1964), p. 102.
4. *Amnesty International Report, 1990* (London: Amnesty International Publications, 1990), p. 125.
5. Ibid., p. 125.
6. Ibid., pp. 101–2.
7. IRNA dispatch, June 4, 1989.
8. Wright, *In the Name of God*, p. 204.
9. Michael Sheridan, "Iran Limps into the 'New Era,'" *The Independent*, July 6, 1990, p. 10. Other

similar accounts were sent by David Hirst of *The Guardian* and correspondents of news agencies.

10. *The Shape of the World Today* (London: Economist Books, Hutchinson, 1989), p. 261.
11. Michael Sheridan, "Iran Limps into the 'New Era,' " and "At the Heart of the Hostage Diplomacy," *The Independent on Sunday,* July 8, 1990, p. 12.
12. Personal interviews in The Hague, February 1988, October 1989, and April 1990; Associated Press dispatch from Amsterdam, May 9, 1990; Reuters from The Hague, May 21, 1990.
13. Segev, *The Iranian Triangle,* pp. 8–9.

15. Desert Shield: The Days of Hesitation & Wrath

1. Quoted in *Arms Control Today* (March, 1991): 30.
2. I owe much in this section to an article by Ghassan Salameh, "Les Enjeux d'une crise," in *Maghreb-Machrek,* no. 130 (October–December 1990): 5–13, cited in my article, "Pre-war Gulf Diplomacy," *Survival* 33, no. 2 (March–April 1991): 125–29.
3. Private communication from an international banker, May 1990; conversations with Prince Hassan, Amman, August 1990.
4. Pierre Salinger and Eric Laurent, *La Guerre de Golfe* (Paris: Olivier Orban, 1990), pp. 8–9.
5. Ibid., pp. 39–40. Full text in Foreign Broadcast Information Service (FBIS), *Daily Report,* "Near East and South Asia," 90–074 (April 17, 1990): 5–9.
6. Text of a memorandum submitted to the Arab League, obtained by the author in Tunis in October 1990; *Keesings Contemporary Archives: Record of World Events* (Harlow, U.K.: Longman, August 1990), p. 3763.
7. Private communications from a London banker, October 1990.
8. Stuart Auerbach, "U.S. Sold Hi-Tech Devices to Saddam Day Before Invasion," *Washington Post,* reprinted in *The Guardian* (London), March 12, 1991, p. 5.
9. Conversation with Abu Iyad (Salah Khalaf), Tunis, October 1990. See also Pierre Salinger's "PLO Peace Efforts," *The Guardian,* February 5, 1991, p. 19.
10. Salinger and Laurent, *La Guerre,* pp. 94–95; information confirmed by an adviser of King Hussein, Amman, October 1990.
11. Transcript of Glaspie–Saddam meeting, translated by Aolel Darwish, obtained by ABC News in Baghdad, August 1990.
12. Private communications from King Hussein and then–Jordanian Foreign Minister Marwan al-Qassim, Amman, October 1990 and March 6, 1991.
13. Salinger and Laurent, *La Guerre,* pp. 108–9.
14. Major newspaper and BBC broadcasts, August 2–3, 1990.
15. Salinger and Laurent, *La Guerre,* p. 11.
16. Private communications from several advisers of King Hussein, Amman, March 6, 1991.
17. Conversation with King Hussein, Amman, March 6, 1991.
18. The Associated Press, dispatch from Aspen, Colorado, August 2, 1990.
19. Quoted in *The Washington Report on Middle East Affairs* 9, no. 4 (Washington: The American Educational Trust, Inc., April 1990), p. 10.
20. Private communications from King Hussein, Amman, October 1990, and an Iraqi businessman, London, December 1990.
21. Confirmed by King Hassan of Morocco in a private audience, Rabat, February 1991.
22. *New York Times,* August 9, 1990, p. 1; *Keesings Contemporary Archives,* August 1990, p. 37633.
23. Michael Massing, "The Way to War," *New York Review of Books* 38, no. 6 (March 28, 1991): 16.
24. Transcript obtained by ABC News in Baghdad, September 1990.
25. Michael Massing, "The Way to War," p. 16.
26. Transcript supplied by Iraqi government, Baghdad, September 1990.
27. Private communication, London, December 1990.
28. Conversation with Abu Iyad, Tunis, October 1990.
29. Author's reports to ABC News, August 10, 1990; Abu Iyad, October 1990.
30. *Golfe: La Guerre,* special supplement of *Le Monde* (Paris), December 1990, chronology, p. 35.

31. Ibid., p. 35.
32. Stephen C. Pelletiere, Douglas V. Johnson, and Leif R. Rosenberger, *Iraqi Power and U.S. Security in the Middle East* (Carlisle Barracks, Penn.: U.S. Army War College: 1990), pp. 45–46.
33. John Newhouse, "The Diplomatic Round," *The New Yorker*, February 18, 1991, p. 77.
34. Michael Massing, "The Way to War," pp. 18–19.
35. Amnesty International Report, summarized in *The Economist* (London) December 22, 1990–January 4, 1991, p. 80.
36. Salinger and Laurent, *La Guerre*, pp. 227–29.

16. Desert Storm

1. Quoted in *The Washington Report on Middle East Affairs* (November 1990): 26.
2. Ibid., 26.
3. Gen. Hansord T. Johnson, "Operations," *Aviation Week and Space Technology* (January 7, 1991): 14–15.
4. Quoted in "The Talk of the Town," *The New Yorker* (January 21, 1991): 24.
5. Quoted in "Washington Roundup," *Aviation Week and Space Technology* (November 5, 1990): 19.
6. Ibid., 19.
7. *The Washington Report on Middle East Affairs* (January 1991): 47.
8. *Aviation Week* (November 15, 1990): 19.
9. Information received in personal communications from Abu Iyad, October and November 1990. Quotes may be found in Pierre Salinger's article "The PLO Tries for Peace," in *The Guardian* (London), February 5, 1991, p. 19.
10. Private communication from a Palestinian in London, March 1991.
11. Salinger and Laurent, *La Guerre de Golfe*, pp. 266–71, and conversations with Syrian, Soviet, and U.S. diplomats, Damascus, March 1991.
12. Conversations in Damascus, March 1991.
13. *Golfe: La Guerre*, p. 35.
14. Interviews with Moroccan officials and Western diplomats in Rabat, February 1991.
15. *Aviation Week* (December 3, 1990): 26.
16. *Maghreb-Machrek*, 130 (October–December 1990): 35.
17. Ibid.
18. *Keesings Contemporary Archives*, January 1991, p. 37935; conversations with Nabil al-Shaath, Arafat's diplomatic adviser, London, February 1991.
19. *Aviation Week* (January 21, 1991): 62; *Keesings Contemporary Archives*, January 1991, p. 37936.
20. *Aviation Week* (September 24, 1990): 16–18; *Washington Post*, September 15, 1990, p. 1.
21. Conversations in Amman with Jordanian officials, March 1991, and *Keesings Contemporary Archives*, January 1991, p. 37935.
22. This section was compiled from the international media, my own monitoring reports in Nicosia, Cyprus, and personal accounts of ABC News personnel in Baghdad, Saudi Arabia, and Israel.
23. *Newsweek*, international edition (February 11, 1991): 10.
24. *Keesings Contemporary Archives*, January 1991, p. 37942.
25. International press, February 24–28, 1991; *Time* and *Newsweek* (March 18, 1991); BBC and ITN television broadcasts.
26. *Aviation Week* (August 14, 1990): 26–27.
27. *Aviation Week* (September 24, 1990): 21–22.
28. *Aviation Week* (January 28, 1991): 24.
29. "America's Secret War," a BBC "Panorama" television documentary, London, March 25, 1991, BBC transcript.
30. Ibid., p. 4.
31. Ibid., p. 5.
32. Ibid., p. 5.

33. Information about the battle's chronology may be found in *Newsweek* (March 18, 1991): 32.
34. Quoted in *The Guardian* (London), March 27, 1991, p. 24.

17.   Ending America's Long War in the Middle East

1. Thomas Friedman, *From Beirut to Jerusalem* (New York: Farrar, Straus & Giroux, 1987), p. 493.
2. See John K. Cooley, "The Water War," *Foreign Policy* no. 54 (Spring 1984): 3–26; and Joyce P. Starr, "Water Wars," *Foreign Policy* no. 82 (Spring 1991): 17–36.

Index

About the Author

John K. Cooley is an ABC news correspondent based in London. He has covered the Middle East and North Africa since 1957, for 13 years for the *Christian Science Monitor*. He has been a foreign correspondent fellow at the Council on Foreign Relations and a senior associate of the Carnegie Endowment for International Peace. He has received Overseas Press Club citations for his reporting of the Arab-Israeli war of 1967, the Turkish invasion of Cyprus in 1974, the Lebanese civil war in 1976, and the Falklands War in 1982. He was also a member of an ABC news team that received the annual Emmy Award in 1990 for the ABC News "Prime Time Live" documentary on the downing of Pan Am Flight 103.

John Cooley's books include *Baal, Christ and Mohammad*; *East Wind Over Africa*; *Green March, Black September: The Story of the Palestinian Arabs*; and *Libyan Sandstorm: The Complete Account of Qaddafi's Revolution*.

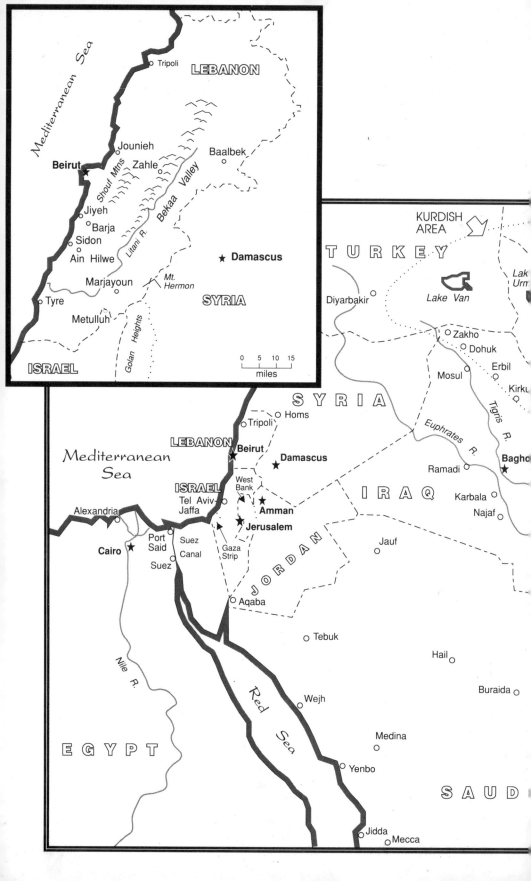